PONS

Traveller's Language Guide
GERMAN

PONS GmbH, Stuttgart

PONS Traveller's Language Guide
German

by Gordon Walker

Picture sources
The references for the individual images are given from top left to bottom right, or from top to bottom.
1: Shutterstock, Philip Lange; fotolia, Hans Ott; Shutterstock, Ints Vikmanis. **9:** H. Geißel, Stuttgart. **17:**Fotosearch, Photo Disk; Stock disc; Fotosearch, Photo Disk. **21:** Ifa, Stuttgart. **31:** HB-Verlag, Sabine Lubenow; HB-Verlag, Michael Campo. **41:** Wolpert Fotodesign, Stuttgart. **49:** HB-Verlag, Mike Schröder; GettyImages, PhotoDisc; HB-Verlag, Marin Specht. **58:** Fordwerke AG. **61:** Cycleurope Industries S.A., Romilly sur Seine. **75:** Avenue Images, image 100; iStockphoto, Uli Hamacher; Avenue Images, image 100. **79:** Bundesverband Selbsthilfe Körperbehinderter, Krautheim; Hotel Weisseespitze, Kaunertal; Wendt-Wolter (BSK). **85:** Picturemaxx. **97:** fotolia, Hans Ott; HB-Verlag, Rainer Hackenberg; HB-Verlag, Rainer Kiedrowski; **108-114:** Wolpert Fotodesign, Stuttgart. **125:** H. Geißel, Stuttgart. **133:** Shutterstock, Ints Vikmanis; Ifa Stuttgart. **145:** Creativ Collection; iStock, Bernd Klumpp; MEV. **151:** HB-Verlag, Rainer Kiedrowski. **172:** Wolpert Fotodesign, Stuttgart. **175:** Creativ Collection Verlag. **189**: MEV; Stock disc; Corel-Corporation.
Umschlag: Shutterstock, Ints Vikmanis; Fotosearch, Food Collection; fotolia, Hans Ott; Shutterstock, Philip Lange.

1. edition 2009 (1,01 - 2009)

Onlinedictionary: www.pons.eu
Shop: www.pons.de
E-Mail: info@pons.de

Project manager: Christiane Mackenzie, Stuttgart
Editor: Barbara Pflüger, Stuttgart
Cover design: Schmidt & Dupont, Stuttgart
Logo design: Erwin Poell, Heidelberg
Logo adaptation: Sabine Redlin, Ludwigsburg
Layout and composition: Fotosatz Kaufmann, Stuttgart
Printed in Italy at L.E.G.O. S.p.A., in Lavis (TN)

ISBN: 978-3-12-518653-8

Vowels		
phonetic	**sound in English**	**in German**
[a]	short 'a' – somewhere between 'fan' and 'fun'	danke, Land
[aː]	'ar'/'ah' - as in 'hard', 'calm'	Abend
[ɐ]	somewhere between 'er' and 'air'	Vater
[ɛ]	'e' – as in 'net'	wenn
[ɛː]	somewhere between the vowel sound in 'fay' and 'fair'	fährt, spät
[eː]	close to the long 'a' in 'bathe'	geht
[ə]	like first syllable of 'alive'	bitte, viele
[ɪ]	'i' – as in 'fit'	mit
[iː]	'ee' – as in 'seen', 'deal'	Ziel
[ɔ]	short 'o' – as in 'hot'	Gott
[oː]	somewhere between 'loan' and 'lawn'	Lohn
[ʊ]	as in 'put', 'look'	Mutter
[uː]	as in 'fool', 'rule'	Stuhl, Fuß
Special German vowels		
[ø]	as in 'Kent', but with rounded "kissing" lips	könnte
[øː]	almost as in 'bird', 'learn'	schön
[ʏ]	as in 'fill', with "kissing" lips	füllen
[yː]	as in 'feel', with "kissing" lips	fühlen
Diphthongs		
[aɪ]	as in 'by'	bei
[aʊ]	as in 'house'	Haus
[ɔɪ]	as in 'boy'	neu
Consonants		
[b]	as in 'ball'	Ball
[ç]	the 'h' sound at the beginning of 'hymn' or 'humour'	mich, zwanzig, Honig
[d]	as in 'down'	danke
[f]	as in 'fine'	fein
[g]	as in 'give' (never as in 'George')	geben
[h]	as in 'house'	Haus
[j]	the 'y' sound at the beginning of 'yes'	ja
[k]	as in 'kindly'	Kind

[l]	as in 'love'	Liebe
[m]	as in 'mister'	Mädchen
[n]	as in 'no'	nein
[ŋ]	the 'ng' sound as in 'longing'	lang
[p]	as in 'pair'	Paar
[ʀ]	as in French or Scottish English	warum
[s]	as in 'missing'	missen, Maß
[ʃ]	'sh' - as in 'show'	schon, Stein
[t]	as in 'table'	Tisch
[v]	as in 'very'	wo
[x]	as in 'Loch (Ness)'	Loch
[z]	as in 'zero'	sehr
[ʒ]	'zh' - as in 'massage', 'treasure', 'Zhivago'	Massage
[ts]	as in 'cats', 'its'	Zeit, Blitz
[tʃ]	'ch' – as in 'check'	deutsch
Other symbols		
[ˈ]	main stress	
[ˌ]	secondary stress	
[:]	long vowel	
[ˀ]	glottal stop	

More detailed information about German pronunciation may be found at "A short guide to German pronunciation" on page 211.

The alphabet

A	a	[a:]	J	j	[jot]	S	s	[ɛs]
B	b	[be:]	K	k	[ka:]	T	t	[te:]
C	c	[tse:]	L	l	[ɛl]	U	u	[u:]
D	d	[de:]	M	m	[ɛm]	V	v	[fau]
E	e	[e:]	N	n	[ɛn]	W	w	[ve:]
F	f	[ɛf]	O	o	[o:]	X	x	[iks]
G	g	[ge:]	P	p	[pe:]	Y	y	[ˀˈʏpzilɔn]
H	h	[ha:]	Q	q	[ku:]	Z	z	[tsɛt]
I	i	[i:]	R	r	[ɛr]			

Abbreviations

adj	Adjektiv, Eigenschaftswort	adjective
adv	Adverb, Umstandswort	adverb
conj	Konjunktion, Bindewort	conjunction
el	Elektrotechnik, Elektrizität	electricity

f	Femininum, weiblich	feminine gender
fam	Umgangssprache, familiär	familiar, colloquial
fig	bildlich, übertragen	figurative
m	Maskulinum, männlich	masculine gender
n	Neutrum, sächlich	neuter gender
pl	Plural, Mehrzahl	plural
poss prn	Possessivpronomen, besitzanzeigendes Fürwort	possessive pronoun
prp	Präposition, Verhältniswort	preposition
rel	kirchlich, geistlich	religious
sing	Singular, Einzahl	singular
s.o.	jemand	someone
s.th.	etwas	something
tele	Telekommunikation	telecommunications
vb	Verb, Zeitwort	verb

Common abbreviations

A	Österreich	Austria
ADAC	Allgemeiner deutscher Automobilclub	German motoring association
BRD	Bundesrepublik Deutschland	Federal Republic of Germany
bzw.	beziehungsweise	or, respectively
°C	(Grad) Celsius	(degrees) Celsius/Centigrade
CH	Schweiz (Helvetia)	Switzerland
CHF	Schweizer Franken	Swiss francs
D	Deutschland	Germany
DB	Deutsche Bahn	German railways
etw.	etwas	something
EU	Europäische Union	European Union
H	Haltestelle	bus or tram stop
jdm.	jemandem	for, to someone
jdn.	jemand	someone
Jh.	Jahrhundert	century
JH	Jugendherberge	youth hostel
n. Chr.	nach Christus	AD
ÖBB	Österreichische Bundesbahnen	Austrian railways
PKW	Personenkraftwagen	car/auto
PS	Pferdestärke	horsepower
s.	siehe	see
SB	Selbstbedienung	self-service
SBB	Schweizerische Bundesbahnen	Swiss railways
Std.	Stunde	hour
Str.	Straße	street
StVO	Straßenverkehrsordnung	traffic regulations
tgl.	täglich	daily
v. Chr.	vor Christus	BC
z. B.	zum Beispiel	e.g.

Different countries, different customs

Intercultural Tips

General

German is spoken not only in Germany but also in Austria and Switzerland. There are, however, numerous differences. In general, people in Austria and Switzerland speak more slowly than they do in Germany; their intonation is softer, so that it is sometimes difficult to differentiate between a **b** and a **p**. Only the context would show whether an Austrian was talking about a cake or a case when (s)he said **Gepäck**.
In contrast to German and Austrian regional dialects, Swiss German is treated as a separate language and is spoken on TV and radio, and at school. Some words are derived from French, although stress is often placed on the first syllable of a word. Like the Germans, the Swiss also use a lot of English words, especially those for sport, e.g. **goal** instead of **Tor**, or **corner** instead of **Eckball**.
There is no **ß** in Swiss German; all words that are written with **ß** in German - even after the recent spelling reforms - are written with **ss** in Swiss German: e.g. **Grüsse** instead of **Grüße**, or **Füsse** instead of **Füße**. Some nouns in Swiss German are also a different gender to their counterparts in German: thus the Swiss say **der Butter** and **das Tram**.

Forms of address

Until you become closely acquainted, you should use the formal **Sie** when speaking to an adult. On meeting someone for the first time, it is usual to shake hands and say your surname; only when you have got to know each other well and have exchanged first names, should you use the informal **du**. Between children and young people it is normal to use **du**. A short handshake is also common when meeting up with someone, and young people often give each other a kiss on the cheek.
In Austria it is normal for work colleagues and people of the same age to use **du** to each other and, especially in country areas, **du** is sometimes even used between strangers.
Although **Fräulein** (*'Miss'*) is no longer used as a form of address in Germany, it is still fairly common in Austria. In Vienna, women can expect to be addressed as **Gnädige Frau**, usually shortened to **Gnä Frau**, meaning *'madam'*.
Titles are important in Germany and Austria. For example, someone with a doctorate (PhD) would be addressed as **Frau/Herr Doktor**. Titles are less important in Switzerland.

Greetings

The most general form of greeting in German-speaking countries is **Guten Tag** or the more informal **Hallo**; in the morning you could say **Guten Morgen**, in the afternoon **Guten Tag** (**not** *'Guten Nachmittag'*) and in the evening **Guten Abend**. In southern Germany and Austria it is common to hear **Grüß Gott**, and in northern Germany **Moin, Moin!**, both of which just mean *'Hello!'*
If you know someone well, you could say **Grüß dich!** and then **Wie geht's?**, meaning *'How are things?'* or *'How are you doing?'*; more formally, you would use **Wie geht es Ihnen/dir?**, meaning *'How are you?'* In reply, you could say **Danke, gut. Und Ihnen/dir?** = *'Fine, thanks. And you?'*
The Swiss greet each other with **Grüezi**, or more informally **Hoi** or **Sali**. In Austria they say **Servus** or more rarely **Habe die Ehre**.

Farewells

The most common way of saying goodbye is **Auf Wiedersehen!** or informally **Tschüs(s)** or **Mach's gut!** = *'See you!'*, or **Bis morgen** = *'See you tomorrow'*. Among friends you could hear the Italian **Ciao**, and on parting late at night, you might also say **Gute Nacht!**
In Austria and parts of Bavaria, rather than **Tschüs(s)**, you are likely to hear **Pfiat' di** (which roughly means *'May God be with you'*). In Switzerland they say **Auf Wiederluege** or **Adieu**.

Please and Thank You

In Germany it is not nearly as common as in the UK and the US to use *'please'* and *'thank you'*, so do not take it as a sign of impoliteness or curtness if you do not hear a **bitte** or **danke** where you might expect to hear one in English. It is common in Germany, however, to reply to someone who says *'thank you'* to you. So if someone says **Vielen Dank** or **Danke schön**, you could reply **Bitte schön** or **Bitte sehr** or **Gern geschehen** = *'Not at all'* or *'You're welcome'* or *'It's a pleasure/My pleasure'*. In Austria you reply **Gerne**. A Swiss person is more likely to say **Merci** or **Merci vielmals** rather than **Danke**.

Mealtimes

At mealtimes it is common to say **Guten Appetit!** or **Mahlzeit!** and to reply **Danke, gleichfalls!** = *'Thank you, and the same to you!'* As in the UK, there are numerous expressions for *'Cheers!'* when having a drink with someone, but the most common is **Prost!** or more formally **Zum Wohl!**
In Switzerland, you wish each other **Guten Appetit!** or **En Guete**. Breakfast is called **Morgenessen** or **Zmorge**, lunch is **Zmittag** and dinner/supper is **Nachtessen** or **Znacht**.

Telephone

When answering the telephone in Germany it is usual to give your surname or to say **Hallo** or **Ja, bitte?** if you prefer to stay anonymous - rather than to state your phone number. When saying goodbye on the phone, you say **(Auf) Wiederhören** rather than **(Auf) Wiedersehen**.

Numbers

To make a clear distinction between 1 and 7, Germans put a short horizontal line through the stem of the seven. One billion (1.000.000.000: a thousand million) = **eine Milliarde** in German; **eine Billion** in German = '*one trillion*' in English (= a million million). Decimal points are written with a comma in German: **3,14** and you should say: **drei Komma eins vier** although it is also common to hear **drei Komma vierzehn**.

Time

Use of the 24-hour clock is widespread, but beware! - **halb zwei** does NOT mean '*half two*' but '*half past one*'. In southern Germany you could also hear **viertel zwei** = '*(a) quarter past one*' or **drei viertel zwei** = '*(a) quarter to two*'.

Speed limits

The speed limit on motorways (**Autobahnen**) in Switzerland is 120 km/h (75 mph) and in Austria 130 km/h. Although there is no official speed limit on German motorways, there are numerous places (such as exits and interchanges) where speed is restricted and these are often quite strictly controlled. In built-up areas the speed limit is 50 km/h (c. 30 mph) and in residential 'housing zones' actual walking speed. Interspersed with the motorway service stations (**Raststätte**), you will also find numerous places to pull off and take a break (**Rastplatz**).

Stamps

In Germany, the basic price of a stamp for a letter or postcard to anywhere in the EU is the same as the price within Germany.

School

Most schoolchildren wear a satchel or rucksack (for older children) to school; pupils do not wear a school uniform and there are usually no lessons in the afternoons. Those pupils who perform extremely poorly and do not achieve the required marks at the end of the year have to stay down a year.

Military Service

A system of compulsory military service operates in Germany. Every young man must do either 9 months' military service or, if they object on conscientious grounds, 10 months' community service, **der Zivildienst**.

Bars/Restaurants

Buying a round of drinks is not common practice in Germany. Drinks are brought directly to your table and a mark made on your coaster or beer mat. At the end of the evening these marks are counted up and you are asked if you want to pay **zusammen** (all together) or **getrennt** (individually). Tipping is normal, but in smaller amounts than in the UK; more than 10% of the bill would be considered excessive unless the service had been absolutely wonderful.

In the wine-growing regions of Austria you are likely to find a **Heurige**, an inn selling new local wine, accompanied by a **Jause** (snack) or **Hausmannskost** (pub grub). In Switzerland, a pub is called a **Beiz**; the waitress is called a **Serviertochter** and you can order such things as a **Panaschee** (shandy), a **Stange** (small beer) or a **Jus** (fruit juice). The phrase **à discrétion** on a menu means that you can help yourself to as much as you like for a set price.

Tea

Tea in Germany is invariably made with a teabag and is very weak for most English tastes. It is also served without milk but occasionally with lemon. It is far more common to have **Kaffee und Kuchen** (*coffee and cake*) at teatime rather than tea.

Domestic Matters

Expect to pay for plastic bags in supermarkets and in Germany to pay a refundable deposit (**Pfand**) on all bottles and cans of mineral water, soft drinks and beer. Household rubbish is sorted into sometimes 5 different containers: one for glass, one for paper, one for plastic, foil, cartons and tins, one for organic waste, and one for everything else.

There is a collection for bulky household waste on demand, called **Sperrmüll**, which is simply placed in piles by the roadside. It is quite acceptable to take anything from these piles that takes your fancy - thus are many items recycled rather than just thrown away.

Christmas, New Year & Easter

In German-speaking countries the most important day over Christmas is Christmas Eve (**Heiliger Abend**), during the evening of which most children are allowed to unwrap their presents.

The biggest excuse for a big fireworks party is New Year's Eve (**Silvester[abend]**).
The Easter bunny (**Osterhase**) comes at Easter and hides brightly decorated hard-boiled eggs (in their shells), chocolate Easter eggs and chocolate bunnies, and other presents round the house and garden for the children to find.

And Finally ...

There are many more dedicated bicycle lanes than in the UK, and some are integrated into the normal pavement - so watch out where you walk, and remember to drive on the right!

Do's and Don't's for German-speaking countries

Eating and drinking

"*Warum rülpset und furzet ihr nicht, hat es euch denn nicht geschmecket?*"
[ˈvaʁʊm ˈʁʏlpsət ˀʊnt ˈfʊɐtsət ˀiɐ nɪçt – hat əs ˀɔɪç dɛn nɪçt gəˈʃmɛkət]
("Why don't you belch and fart - did you not enjoy the meal?") - attributed to Martin Luther.
In general, the image of raucous, belching Germans at the dinner table is just another unfortunate cliché, but, as with everything else, the table manners expected of you and the table manners you will experience in Germany will greatly depend on the circumstances and occasion. Obviously no one is too concerned about table manners at informal events such as beer and wine festivals or in 'hands-on' snack bars and fast-food restaurants or beer gardens. On more formal occasions, however, at dinner parties or in 'higher class' restaurants for example, acceptable table manners are very similar to those elsewhere in the Western World - with a few minor exceptions.

- You may, if you wish, tilt your soup plate towards you
- It is not generally regarded as bad form to eat mainly with your fork, 'American-style'
- On finishing your main course, lay your cutlery to the side, i.e. not at 6.30 on a clockface but more at 4.20
- Do not leave tips in cash on your table. It is customary to round up the price of your meal or drinks when paying.

A tip for those who enjoy a tipple:
Germans (along with Austrians and Swiss) love to propose toasts in a group and then clink glasses with everyone else present. Important here is to *look into the eyes of the person whose glass you are currently striking*. If you do not, the offence caused will only be slight, but you are likely to hear - with great amusement on the part of whoever is informing you - that you are now condemned to seven years of bad sex!

On the street

Discipline, order and tidiness are legendary in German-speaking regions. No one likes to see litter, cigarette ends and old chewing gum in public places, but in Germany, Austria and Switzerland, those who do not use the bins and ashtrays provided will incur the wrath not only of any passers-by, but also of the authorities. Fines for litter-related violations can be extremely high, and are often to be paid on the spot. The same applies if you are travelling with a dog: make sure that you 'clean up' after it.
Do not use mobile phones while driving a car or riding a bicycle. The penalties for offences of this nature are, again, extremely high.
On the subject of mobile phones, the reactions to loud ringtones in public places will almost always be negative, especially in restaurants and cafés, where people are trying to relax. There is no problem with actually using your mobile to a moderate extent, but it is advisable, if you wish to avoid looks that could kill, to switch your phone to the 'silent mode'.
Some may find it strange, but openly drinking alcohol in public is *not* prohibited in German-speaking countries.

Smoking

In Germany, smoking is now prohibited in all restaurants and pubs that serve food. In all other pubs, the regulations vary from one region to the next. You might find, for example, designated or enclosed smoking areas in some pubs (**Raucherzone** [ˈʁaʊxɐˌtsoːnə]). Recently (2008), legal proceedings have forced the German government to review the legislation introduced in 2007, so changes can be expected, although these might not be to the advantage of smokers.
In German-speaking Switzerland, which is not bound by European Union Directives, smoking is still permitted in pubs and restaurants, but usually only in separate areas. In the Italian-speaking region (Ticino), the Swiss have adopted the strict rules from neighbouring Italy, and it is likely that this policy will soon spread to the entire country.
In Austria, new legislation (2008) is likely to be similar to that in Spain, i.e. smoking zones will be established in larger bars and restaurants and the owners of smaller pubs will be allowed to decide for themselves whether or not to permit smoking.

Dealing with officials

It is compulsory for Germans, Swiss and Austrians to carry identification (**ein Ausweis** [ˀaɪn ˈˀaʊsvaɪs]) at all times. The police and other officials are more likely to take a tolerant approach to travellers who are unused to carrying ID, the British for example, but it is a good idea to carry your passport, ID card or driving licence anyway.
Bear in mind when travelling from Switzerland into Germany, France,

Italy or Austria or vice versa that Switzerland is not a member of the European Union. You must be carrying your passport (with visa if you are from outside Europe), and there are tight restrictions on the value of goods and amount of cash that you may take across the border. Regular random checks are commonplace.
Should you be suspected of having committed a criminal offence, whether in a motor vehicle, at a border crossing, or otherwise, the best policy is to remain as respectful and polite as possible - and to say as little as necessary. Contact your Consulate (**Konsulat** [kɔnzuˈlaːt]) or Embassy (**Botschaft** [ˈboːtʃaft]) as quickly as possible.
It goes without saying that you should *never* attempt to bribe a police or customs officer in Germany, Switzerland or Austria. The chances of success are virtually non-existent.

Travel preparations

Booking a Hotel by Email

Dear Sir or Madam,
I would like to book a single/double/twin-bedded room for 2 nights on the 24 and 25 June. Please let me know if you have any vacancies and the total cost per night (plus dinner).

Yours faithfully,

Sehr geehrte Damen und Herren,

am 24. und 25. Juni benötige ich für zwei Nächte ein Einzel-/ Doppel-/ Zweibettzimmer. Bitte teilen mir mit, ob Sie ein Zimmer frei haben und was es pro Nacht (einschließlich Abendessen) kostet.

Mit freundlichen Grüßen

Hiring a Car by Email

Dear Sir/Madam,

I would like to hire a small/mid-range/7-seater people carrier from July 20–25 from Munich Airport.
I depart from Frankfurt Airport so wish to leave the car there. Please inform me of your rates and what documents I shall require.

Yours faithfully,

Sehr geehrte Damen und Herren,

für den Zeitraum vom 20.–25. Juli möchte ich am Flughafen München einen Kleinwagen/Mittelklassewagen/eine 7-sitzige Großraumlimousine mieten. Ich fliege von Frankfurt ab und möchte deshalb dort den Leihwagen abgeben. Bitte teilen Sie mir Ihre Tarife mit und welche Unterlagen ich benötige.

Mit freundlichen Grüßen

General enquiries

I am planning to spend my holiday in … . Can you give me details of accommodation in the area?
Ich habe vor, meinen Urlaub in … zu verbringen. Können Sie mir bitte Informationen über Unterkünfte in der Gegend geben? [ˀɪç haːbə ˈfoɐ maɪnn ˈˀuɐlaʊp ˀɪn … tsʊ fɐˈbʀɪŋŋ kønn zi miɐ ˈbɪtə ˀɪnfɔɐmaˈtsjoːnn ˀˌyːbɐ ˈˀʊntɐkʏnftə ˀɪn dɐ geːgŋt geːbm]

Where is the best place to go on a boating holiday?
Welche Gegend empfiehlt sich für Ferien auf einem Boot?
[ˈvɛlçə geːgŋt ˀɛmpˈfiːlt zɪç fyɐ ˈfeːʀɪən ˀaʊf ˌˀaɪnəm ˈboːt]

What sort of accommodation are you looking for?
An welche Art von Unterkunft haben Sie gedacht?
[ˀan ˈvɛlçə ˀaːt fɔn ˈˀʊntɐkʊnft haːbm zi gəˈdaxt]

a hotel
ein Hotel [ˀaɪn hoˈtɛl]
guest house
eine Pension [ˌˀaɪnə paŋˈzjoːn]
bed and breakfast
ein Fremdenzimmer [ˀaɪn ˈfʀɛmdntsɪmɐ]
self-catering accommodation
eine Ferienwohnung [ˌˀaɪnə ˈfeːʀɪənˌvoːnʊŋ]

Accommodation enquiries

Hotel - Guest house - Bed & Breakfast

I'd like to stay in a hotel, but nothing too expensive - something in the mid-price range.
Ich suche ein Hotel, jedoch nicht zu teuer - etwas in der mittleren Preislage. [ˀɪç ˈzuːxə ˀaɪn hoˈtɛl jeˈdɔx nɪçt tsʊ ˈtɔjɐ ˈˀɛtvas ˀɪn dɐ ˈmɪtləʀən ˈpʀaɪslaːgə]

I'd like to stay in a hotel with a swimming pool/a golf course/tennis courts.
Ich suche ein Hotel mit Hallenbad/Golfplatz/Tennisplätzen.
[ˀɪç ˈzuːxə ˀaɪn hoˈtɛl mɪt ˈhalnbaːt/ˈgɔlfplats/ˈtɛnɪsplɛtsn]

Can you recommend a good bed-and-breakfast?
Können Sie mir ein schönes Fremdenzimmer mit Frühstück empfehlen?
[kønn zi miɐ ˀaɪn ˈʃøːnəs ˈfʀɛmdntsɪmɐ mɪt ˈfʀyːʃtʏk ˀɛmpˈfeːln]

How many people does it sleep?
Für wie viele Leute soll es sein? [fyɐ ˈviː fiːlə ˈlɔɪtə zɔl əs ˈzaɪn]

Are dogs allowed?
Sind dort Hunde erlaubt? [zɪnt dɔɐt ˈhʊndə ˀɐˈlaʊpt]

Self-catering accommodation

I'm looking for a self-catering flat or bungalow.
Ich suche eine Ferienwohnung oder einen Bungalow.
[ˀɪç ˈzuːxə ˌˀaɪnə ˈfeːʀɪənˌvoːnʊŋ ˌˀoːdɐ ˌˀaɪnn ˈbʊŋgalo]

Can you recommend a farmhouse, suitable for children?
Können Sie mir einen kinderfreundlichen Ferienbauernhof empfehlen?
[kønn zi miɐ ˌˀaɪnn ˈkɪndɐˌfʀɔɪntlɪçn ˈfeːʀɪənˌbaʊɐnhoːf ˀɛmpˈfeːln]

Is there ...?
Gibt es ...? [gɪpt əs]
a baby's cot
ein Kinderbett [ˀaɪn ˈkɪndɐbɛt]
high chair
einen Hochstuhl [ˀaɪnn ˈhoːxʃtuːl]
TV
einen Fernseher [ˀaɪnn ˈfɛɐnze.ɐ]
telephone
ein Telefon [ˀaɪn ˈteːləfoːn]
washing machine
eine Waschmaschine [ˌˀaɪnə ˈvaʃmaˌʃiːnə]
dishwasher
eine Spülmaschine [ˌˀaɪnə ˈʃpyːlmaˌʃiːnə]
microwave
eine Mikrowelle [ˌˀaɪnə ˈmɪkʀoˌvɛlə]

Is electricity included in the price?
Sind die Stromkosten im Preis eingeschlossen?
[zɪnt di ˈʃtʀoːmkɔstn ˀɪm pʀaɪs ˈˀaɪngəʃlɔsn]

Are bed linen and towels provided?
Werden Bettwäsche und Handtücher gestellt?
[veɐdn ˈbɛtvɛʃə ˀʊnt ˈhantyːçɐ gəˈʃɛlt]

How much deposit do you require and how long in advance?
Wie viel muss ich anzahlen und wann ist die Anzahlung fällig?
[ˈviː fiːl mʊs ɪç ˈˀantsaːln ˀʊnt ˈvan ˀɪst di ˈˀantsaːlʊŋ ˈfɛlɪç]

Where and when should I pick up the keys?
Wo und wann kann ich die Schlüssel abholen?
[ˈvoː ˀʊnt ˈvan kan ɪç di ʃlʏsl ˈˀaphoːln]

Camping

I'm looking for a smallish camping site in .... Do you have anywhere you can recommend?
Ich suche einen kleinen Campingplatz in ... Können Sie mir irgend etwas empfehlen? [ˀɪç ˈzuːxə ˀaɪnn ˈklaɪnn ˈkɛmpɪŋplats ˀɪn ... kønn zi miɐ ˈˀɪɐgŋt ˌˀɛtvas ˀɛmpˈfeːln]

General

A regular language

For the most part German is very regular in pronunciation. Most words are spoken with stress on the first syllable: *danke, Deutschland.* Important exceptions are words beginning with *ge-, ver-, ent-* (*gegessen, verboten, Entschuldigung* – these are stressed on the second syllable) – and words borrowed from other languages. In general, words borrowed from French and English retain their original pronunciation – to the extent that German speakers can imitate this. Borrowings from English have been increasing explosively for the last half century, particularly in "modern" areas such as computer technology, high-tech, business and entertainment. You will run into countless English words in German; your best bet is simply to rely on your own familiar way of saying these.

Like most other languages, however, German has many regional dialects and accents. Even if your German is proficient, you are likely to find it difficult to understand exactly what is being said in some areas such as South Germany, Austria and Switzerland. For example, the Swiss pronounce a great many words in a completely different way to standard German: the German 'ei' is pronounced as if it were 'ie' [iː], 'au' as if it were simply 'u' [uː]. *Ausweis* [ˈʔaʊsvaɪs], for example, becomes *Uswies* [ˈʔuːsviːs], *Feuerzeug* [ˈfɔɪɐtsɔɪk] becomes *Fürzüg* [ˈfyːrtsyːk], or *Zeit* [tsaɪt] becomes *Ziet* [tsiːt]. In North Germany, a great many words will sound even closer to English pronounciation. In Bavaria and Austria, you will encounter a very hard roll to the letter 'r', similar to that found in Scotland!

Basic phrases

➢ **also front inside cover**

Yes.
Ja. [jaː]

No.
Nein. [naɪn]

Please.
Bitte. [ˈbɪtə]

Thank you.
Danke! [ˈdaŋkə]

Many thanks!/Thanks a lot!
Vielen Dank! [fiːln daŋk]

Thanks, (and) the same to you!
Danke, gleichfalls! [ˈdaŋkə ˈglaɪçfals]

You're welcome!/Not at all!
Bitte!/Gern geschehen! [ˈbɪtə/ˈgɛɐn gəˈʃeːn]

Not at all!/Don't mention it!
Nichts zu danken! [ˈnɪçts tsʊ ˈdaŋkŋ]

Pardon?/Excuse me?
Wie bitte? [ˈviː bɪtə]

Of course.
Selbstverständlich! [zɛlpstfɐˈʃtɛntliç]

Agreed!
Einverstanden! [ˈʔaɪnfɐʃtandn]

OK!
Okay! [ʔoˈke], In Ordnung! [ʔɪn ˈʔɔɐtnʊŋ]

Excuse me.
Verzeihung! [fɐˈtsaɪʊŋ]

Just a minute, please.
Einen Augenblick, bitte. [ˈʔaɪnn ʔaʊgŋˈblɪk ˈbɪtə]

Right, that's enough!
Das reicht jetzt! [das ˈʁaɪçt jɛtst]

Help!
Hilfe! [ˈhɪlfə]

Who?
Wer? [veɐ]

What?
Was? [vas]

Which?
Welcher?/Welche?/Welches? [ˈvɛlçɐ/ˈvɛlçə/ˈvɛlçəs]

Where?
Wo? [voː]

Where is ...?/Where are ...?
Wo ist ...?/Wo sind ...? [voː ʔɪst .../voː zɪnt ...]

Why?
Warum? [vaˈʁʊm]/Weshalb? [vɛsˈhalp]/Wozu? [voˈtsuː]

How much?/How many?
Wie viel?/Wie viele?
[vi ˈfiːl/vi ˈfiːlə]

How long?
Wie lange? [vi ˈlaŋə]

When?
Wann? [van]

When?/(At) what time?
Um wie viel Uhr? [ˀʊm ˈviː fiːl ˈˀuɐ]

I'd like ...
Ich möchte ... [ˀɪç ˈmøçtə ...]

Is there ...?/Are there ...?
Gibt es ...? [gɪpt əs]

Numbers - Measures - Weights

➢ **See back inside cover and dictionary.**

Telling the time

Time

What time is it, please?
Wie viel Uhr ist es bitte? [ˈviː fil ˈˀuɐ ˈˀɪst əs ˈbɪtə]

It's (exactly/about) ...
Es ist (genau/ungefähr) ... [ˀəs ɪst gəˈnaʊ/ˀʊngəˈfeɐ]
three o'clock.
drei Uhr. [dʀaɪ ˀuɐ]
five past three.
fünf nach drei. [fʏnf nax ˈdʀaɪ]
ten past three.
drei Uhr zehn. [dʀaɪ ˀuɐ tseːn]
quarter past three.
Viertel nach drei. [ˈfɪɐtl nax dʀaɪ]
half past three.
halb vier. [halp fiɐ]
quarter to four.
Viertel vor vier. [ˈfɪɐtl fɔɐ fiɐ]
five to four.
fünf vor Vier. [fʏnf fɔɐ fiɐ]
twelve noon.
zwölf Uhr Mittag. [tsvølf ˀuɐ ˈmɪtaːk]
midnight.
Mitternacht. [ˈmɪtɐnaxt]

What time?/When?
Um wie viel Uhr?/Wann? [ˈˀʊm ˈviː fiːl ˈˀuɐ/van]

At one o'clock.
Um ein Uhr. [ˀʊm ˀaɪn ˀuɐ]

At two o'clock.
Um zwei Uhr. [ˀʊm tsvaɪ ˀuɐ]

At about four o'clock.
Gegen vier Uhr. [ˈgeːgŋ fiɐ ˀuɐ]

In an hour's time
In einer Stunde. [ˀɪn ˈˀaɪnɐ ˈʃtʊndə]

In two hours' time.
In zwei Stunden. [ˀɪn tsvaɪ ʃtʊndn]

Not before nine a.m.
Nicht vor neun Uhr morgens. [nɪçt foɐ ˈnɔɪn uɐ ˈmɔɐgŋs]

Between three and four.
Zwischen drei und vier. [ˈtsvɪʃn dʀaɪ ˀʊnt fiɐ]

After eight p.m.
Nach acht Uhr abends/zwanzig Uhr.
[nax ˈˀaxt uɐ ˈˀaːbms/ˈtsvantsɪç ˈˀuɐ]

Germans like to use the 24 hour time system. 10 a.m. is *zehn Uhr* and 10 p.m. is *zweiundzwanzig Uhr*.

How long?
Wie lange? [vi ˈlaŋə]

For two hours.
Zwei Stunden (lang). [tsvaɪ ʃtʊndn laŋ]

From ten to eleven.
Von zehn bis elf. [fɔn tseːn bɪs ˀɛlf]

Till five o'clock.
Bis fünf/siebzehn Uhr. [bɪs fʏnf/ˈziːptseːn ˀuɐ]

Since when?
Seit wann? [zaɪt ˈvan]

Since eight a.m.
Seit acht Uhr morgens. [zaɪt ˈˀaxt uɐ ˈmɔɐgŋs]

For half an hour.
Seit einer halben Stunde. [zaɪt ˈˀaɪnɐ ˈhalbm ˈʃtʊndə]

For a week.
Seit acht Tagen. [zaɪt ˀaxt taːgŋ]

about noon	gegen Mittag [ˈgeːgŋ ˈmɪtaːk]
in the afternoon	nachmittags [ˈnaxmɪtaːks]
daily	täglich [tɛːklɪç]
during the day	tagsüber [ˈtaːksˀyːbɐ]

during the morning	vormittags [ˈfɔɐmɪtaːks]
in the evening	abends [ˈʔaːbms]
every day	jeden Tag [jeːdn taːk]
every hour, hourly	stündlich [ˈʃtʏntlɪç]
now and then	ab und zu [ʔap ʊn ˈtsuː]
in a fortnight	in 14 (vierzehn) Tagen [ʔɪn ˈfɪɐtseːn ˈtaːgŋ]
at lunch time	mittags [ˈmɪtaːks]
last Monday morning	letzten Montagmorgen [lɛtstn moːntaːkˈmɔɐgŋ]
ten minutes ago	vor zehn Minuten [fɔɐ tseːn mɪˈnuːtn]
in the morning	morgens [ˈmɔɐgŋs]
never	nie [niː]
next year	nächstes Jahr [ˈnɛːçstəs ˈjaː]
at night	nachts [naxts]
now	jetzt [jɛtst]
on Sunday	am Sonntag [ʔam ˈzɔntaːk]
recently	kürzlich [ˈkʏɐtslɪç]
sometimes	manchmal [ˈmançmaːl]
soon	bald [balt]
the day before yesterday	vorgestern [ˈfɔagɛstɐn]
the day after tomorrow	übermorgen [ˈʔyːbɐmɔɐgŋ]
this morning/this evening	heute Morgen/heute Abend [hɔɪtə ˈmɔɐgŋ/hɔɪtə ˈʔaːbmt]
this week	diese Woche [ˈdiːzə ˈvɔxə]
today	heute [ˈhɔɪtə]
tomorrow	morgen [ˈmɔɐgŋ]
tomorrow morning/ tomorrow evening	morgen früh/morgen Abend [mɔɐgŋ ˈfʀyː/mɔɐgŋ ˈʔaːbmt]
at the weekend	am Wochenende [ʔam ˈvɔxnʔɛndə]
yesterday	gestern [ˈgɛstɐn]

The Days of the Week

Monday	Montag [ˈmoːntaːk]
Tuesday	Dienstag [ˈdiːnstaːk]
Wednesday	Mittwoch [ˈmɪtvɔx]
Thursday	Donnerstag [ˈdɔnɐstaːk]
Friday	Freitag [ˈfʀaɪtaːk]
Saturday	*(southern Germany)* Samstag [ˈzamstaːk] *(northern Germany)* Sonnabend [ˈzɔnaːbmt]
Sunday	Sonntag [ˈzɔntaːk]

The Months of the Year

January	Januar [ˈjanʊaː], *(Austria)* Jänner [ˈjɛnɐ]

February	Februar [ˈfeːbʀuaː]
March	März [mɛɐ̯ts]
April	April [ˀaˈpʀɪl]
May	Mai [maɪ]
June	Juni [ˈjuːni]
July	Juli [ˈjuːli]
August	August [ˀaʊˈgʊst]
September	September [zɛpˈtɛmbɐ]
October	Oktober [ˀɔkˈtoːbɐ]
November	November [noˈvɛmbɐ]
December	Dezember [deˈtsɛmbɐ]

The Seasons

spring	der Frühling [dɐ ˈfʀyːlɪŋ]
summer	der Sommer [dɐ ˈzɔmɐ]
autumn (*Am* fall)	der Herbst [dɐ ˈhɛɐ̯pst]
winter	der Winter [dɐ ˈvɪntɐ]

Holidays

In addition to the holidays mentioned below there are various local religious holidays.

New Year's Day	Neujahr [nɔɪˈjaː]
Swiss Holiday (2.1.)	Berchtoldstag [ˈbɛɐ̯çtɔldstaːk]
Epiphany (6.1.)	Erscheinungsfest [ˀɐˈʃaɪnʊŋsfɛst]
Monday before Shrove Tuesday	Rosenmontag [ʀoːznˈmoːntaːk], *(Switzerland)* Fastnachtmontag [ˌfasnaxtˈmoːntaːk]
Shrove Tuesday	Faschingsdienstag [ˌfaʃɪŋsˈdiːns taːk], Fas(t)nachtdienstag [ˌfasnaxtˈdiːns taːk]
Good Friday	Karfreitag [kaːˈfʀaɪtaːk]
Easter Sunday	Ostersonntag [ˌˀoːstɐˈzɔntaːk]
Easter Monday	Ostermontag [ˌˀoːstɐˈmoːntaːk]
Labour Day (*GB*)	Tag der Arbeit (Erster Mai) [taːk dɐ ˈˀaʀbaɪt (ˈˀeɐ̯stɐ ˈmaɪ)]
Whit Sunday/Pentecost	Pfingstsonntag [ˌpfɪŋstˈzɔntaːk]
Whit Monday	Pfingstmontag [ˌpfɪŋstˈmoːntaːk]
Ascension Day	Christi Himmelfahrt [ˌkʀɪsti ˈhɪmlˌfaːt]
Corpus Christi	Fronleichnam [fʀoːnˈlaɪçnaːm]
German Unification Day (October 3rd)	Tag der deutschen Einheit [taːk dɐ dɔɪtʃn ˈaɪnhaɪt]
Austrian National Day	26. (Sechsundzwanzigster) Oktober [ˈzɛksʊnˌtsvantsɪçstɐ ˀɔkˈtoːbɐ]
Swiss National Day	Erster August [ˈˀeɐ̯stɐ ˀaʊˈgʊst]
All Saints (Nov. 1st)	Allerheiligen [ˀalɐˈhaɪlɪgŋ]

General

Christmas Eve	Heiliger Abend [ˈhaılıgɐ ˈʔa:bmt], Heiligabend [ˌhaılıç ˈʔa:bmt]
Christmas	Weihnachten [ˈvaınaxtn]
Christmas Day	Erster Weihnachts(feier)tag [ˈʔeɐstɐ ˈvaınaxtsˌ(faıɐ)ta:k]
Boxing Day	Zweiter Weihnachts(feier)tag [ˈtsvaıtɐ ˈvaınaxtsˌ(faıɐ)ta:k]
New Year's Eve	Silvester [sılˈvɛstɐ]

The date

Can you tell me what the date today is, please?
Können Sie mir bitte sagen, den Wievielten wir heute haben? [kønn zi miɐ ˈbıtə za:gŋ den ˈvi:fi:ltn viɐ ˌhɔıtə ˈha:bm]

Today's the fourth of August.
Heute ist der vierte August. [ˈhɔıtə ʔıst dɐ ˈfıɐtə ʔaʊˈgʊst]

The weather

What wonderful/dreadful weather!
Was für ein herrliches/schreckliches Wetter!
[ˈvas fyɐ ʔaın ˈhɛɐlıçəs/ˈʃʀɛklıçəs vɛtɐ]

It's very cold/hot/humid.
Es ist sehr kalt/heiß/schwül. [ʔəs ıst zeɐ kalt/haıs/ʃvy:l]

It's foggy/windy..
Es ist neblig/windig. [ʔəs ıst ˈne:blıç/ˈvındıç]

It's going to stay fine.
Es bleibt schön. [ʔəs blaıpt ʃø:n]

It's going to get warmer/colder.
Es wird wärmer/kälter. [ʔəs vıɐt ˈvɛɐmɐ/ˈkɛltɐ]

It's going to rain/snow.
Es wird regnen/schneien. [ʔəs vıɐt ˈʀe:knən/ˈʃnaıən]

It's blowing a gale.
Ein Sturm tobt. [ʔaın ʃtʊɐm to:pt]

The roads are icy.
Die Straßen sind glatt. [di ˈʃtʀa:sn zınt ˈglat]

Visibility is only 20 metres.
Die Sicht beträgt nur zwanzig Meter.
[di ˈzıçt bəˈtʀɛkt nuɐ ˈtsvantsıç ˈme:tɐ]

You need snow chains.
Schneeketten sind erforderlich. [ˈʃne:kɛtn zınt ʔɐˈfɔɐdɐlıç]

air	die Luft [di lʊft]
black ice	das Glatteis [das ˈglataɪs]
changeable	wechselhaft [ˈvɛkslhaft]
cloud	die Wolke [di ˈvɔlkə]
cloudy	bewölkt [bəˈvølkt]
cold	kalt [kalt]
fog	der Nebel [dɐ ˈne:bl]
frost	der Frost [dɐ fʀɔst]
gale	der Sturm [dɐ ʃtʊɐm]
gust of wind	die Bö [di bø:]
hail(stones)	der Hagel [dɐ ˈha:gl]
heat	die Hitze [di ˈhɪtsə]
high tide	die Flut [di flu:t]
hot	heiß [haɪs]
humid	schwül [ʃvy:l]
ice	das Eis [das ˀaɪs]
lightning	der Blitz [dɐ blɪts]
low tide	die Ebbe [di ˀɛbə]
rain	der Regen [dɐ ˈʀe:gŋ]
rainy	regnerisch [ˈʀe:knəʀɪʃ]
shower	der Regenschauer [dɐ ˈʀe:gŋʃaʊɐ]
snow	der Schnee [dɐ ʃne:]
storm	der Sturm [dɐ ʃtʊɐm]
sun	die Sonne [di ˈzɔnə]
sunny	sonnig [ˈzɔnɪç]
temperature	die Temperatur [di ˌtɛmpəʀaˈtuɐ]
thunder	der Donner [dɐ ˈdɔnɐ]
warm	warm [va:m]
weather forecast	die Wettervorhersage [di ˈvɛtɐfoˌheɐza:gə]
weather report	der Wetterbericht [dɐ ˈvɛtɐbəʀɪçt]
wet	nass [nas]
wind	der Wind [dɐ vɪnt]
wind-force	die Windstärke [di ˈvɪntʃtɛɐkə]

Colours

beige	beige [be:ʃ]
black	schwarz [ʃva:ts]
blue	blau [blaʊ]
brown	braun [bʀaʊn]
coloured	farbig [ˈfaʀbɪç]
green	grün [gʀy:n]
grey	grau [gʀaʊ]
pink	rosa [ˈʀo:za]
plain	einfarbig [ˀaɪnfaʀbɪç]
purple	lila [ˈli:la]

red	rot [ʀoːt]
turquoise	türkisfarben [tʏɐˈkiːsfaːbm]
white	weiß [vaɪs]
yellow	gelb [gɛlp]
dark blue/dark green	dunkelblau [dʊŋklˈblaʊ]/ dunkelgrün [dʊŋklˈgʀyːn]
light blue/light green	hellblau [hɛlˈblaʊ]/hellgrün [hɛlˈgʀyːn]

Personal contact

Two "yous"
Germans have two ways of saying "you", depending on their relationship to the person they are talking to. With some people - members of the family, children and good friends - they are on familiar terms, use first names and the word *du* [du:]. Other people they address using last names (surnames); with these people they have a formal relationship and use the word Sie [zi:].

Greetings and farewells

Saying hello

Good morning!
Guten Morgen! [ˈgu:tn ˈmɔɐgŋ]

Good afternoon!
Guten Tag! [ˈgu:tn ta:k]

Good evening!
Guten Abend! [ˈgu:tn ˈa:bmt]

Hello!/Hi!
Hallo!/Grüß dich! [ˈhalo:/ˈgʀy:s dɪç]

What's your name? *(formal)*/*(familiar)*
Wie ist Ihr Name? [vi: ˀɪst ˀiɐ ˈna:mə]/Wie heißt du? [vi ˈhaist du]

My name's ...
Mein Name ist ... [maɪn ˈna:mə ˀɪst]

I'm called ...
Ich heiße ... [ˀɪç ˈhaɪsə]

How are you? *(formal)*/*(familiar)*
Wie geht es Ihnen? [vi ˈge:t əs ˀi:nn]/Wie geht's? [vi ˈge:ts]

Fine thanks. And you? *(formal)*/*(familiar)*
Danke. Und Ihnen/dir? [ˈdaŋkə. ˀʊnt ˈdiɐ]

Introductions

May I introduce you?
Darf ich bekannt machen? [ˈda:f ɪç bəˈkant maxn]

This is ...
Das ist ... [das ˀɪst]
  Mrs/Ms ...
  Frau ... [fʀaʊ ...]

Mr ...
Herr ... [hɛɐ ...]
my husband.
mein Mann. [maɪn 'man]
my wife.
meine Frau. [ˌmaɪnə 'fʀaʊ]
my son.
mein Sohn. [maɪn 'zo:n]
my daughter.
meine Tochter. [ˌmaɪnə 'tɔxtɐ]
my girlfriend.
meine Freundin. [maɪnə 'fʀɔɪndɪn]
my boyfriend.
mein Freund. [maɪn 'fʀɔɪnt]

Nice to meet you.
Es freut mich, Sie kennen zu lernen.
[ˀəs 'fʀɔɪt mɪç zi 'kɛnn tsʊ lɛɐnn]

May I give you my calling card/business card?
Darf ich Ihnen meine Visitenkarte geben? ['da:f ɪç ˀi:nn 'maɪnə vi'zi:tnka:tə ge:bm]

Saying goodbye

Auf Wiedersehen is the German way of saying "goodbye". But you will often hear it shortened to *Wiederseh'n* ['vi:dɐze:n]. Less formal variations are Ciao [tʃaʊ] *(from Italian)* or Tschüs [tʃy(:)s]. Use *bis dann* [bɪs 'dan] to say "see you later".

Goodbye!
Auf Wiedersehen! [ˀaʊf 'vi:dɐze:n]

See you soon!
Bis bald! [bɪs 'balt]

See you later!
Bis später! [bɪ 'ʃpɛ:tɐ]

See you tomorrow!
Bis morgen! [bɪs 'mɔɐgŋ]

All the best!
Mach's gut! [maxs 'gu:t]

See you soon!
Bis bald! [bɪs 'balt]

Good night!
Gute Nacht! [ˌgu:tə 'naxt]

Cheerio! Bye-bye!
Tschüs! [tʃy:s]

Have a good trip!
Gute Reise! [ˌgu:tə ˈʀaɪzə]

Politeness

Requesting and thanking

Please.
Bitte. [ˈbɪtə]

Yes, please.
Ja, bitte. [ja: ˈbɪtə]

Thank you.
Danke. [ˈdaŋkə]

Thank you very much.
Vielen Dank. [fi:ln ˈdaŋk]

You're welcome.
Bitte sehr. [ˈbɪtə zeɐ]

No, thank you.
Nein, danke. [naɪn ˈdaŋkə]

Yes, thank you.
Danke, sehr gern. [ˈdaŋkə zeɐ ˈgɛɐn]

That's very kind, thank you.
Das ist nett, danke. [das ɪst ˈnɛt ˈdaŋkə]

Don't mention it.
Gern geschehen. [ˈgɛɐn gəˈʃe:n]

Do you mind?
Gestatten Sie? [gəˈʃtatn zi]

Please forgive the interruption.
Entschuldigen Sie bitte die Störung.
[ˀɛntˈʃʊldɪgŋ zi ˈbɪtə di ˈʃtø:ʀʊŋ]

Excuse me, may I ask you something?
Entschuldigen Sie bitte, dürfte ich Sie etwas fragen?
[ˀɛntˈʃʊldɪgŋ zi ˈbɪtə ˈdʏɐftə ˀɪç zi ˌˀɛtvas ˈfʀa:gŋ]

Can/Could I ask you a favour?
Darf/Dürfte ich Sie um einen Gefallen bitten?
[da:f/ˈdʏɐftə ˀɪç zi ʊm ˀaɪnn gəˈfaln bɪtn]

Would you be so kind as to ...?
Würden Sie bitte so freundlich sein und ...?
[ˈvʏɐdn zi ˈbɪtə zo ˈfʀɔɪntlɪç zaɪn ˀʊnt ...]

Thank you very much/Thanks a million, you've been a great help.
Vielen/Tausend Dank, Sie haben mir sehr geholfen. [fi:ln/ˈtaʊznt ˈdaŋk zi ha:bm miɐ ˈzeɐ gəˈhɔlfn]

That was very kind of you.
Das war sehr lieb von Ihnen. [das va: zeɐ li:p fɔn ˀi:nn]

Can you tell me..., please?
Können Sie mir bitte sagen, ...? [kønn zi miɐ ˈbɪtə za:gŋ]

Can you recommend ...?
Können Sie mir bitte ... empfehlen?
[kønn zi miɐ ˈbɪtə ... ˀɛmpˈfe:ln]

Could you help me, please?
Können Sie mir bitte helfen? [ˈkønn zi miɐ ˈbɪtə ˈhɛlfn]

Every *danke* should be followed up by the response *bitte* or *gerne* in Austria. This may seem almost like a ritual, but it's a sign of elementary politeness. *Bitte* has basically two meanings: (1) "You're welcome" when used after *danke*; (2) "please" when added to requests such as above, *Können Sie mir bitte helfen?* But be careful: if someone offers you something and you reply with *danke*, this will be interpreted as meaning "no, thank you". If you want to accept something, say *ja, bitte.*

Apologies

I'm sorry!
Entschuldigung! [ˀɛntˈʃʊldɪgʊŋ]

I'm very sorry!
Das tut mir sehr leid! [das tu:t miɐ zeɐ ˈlaɪt]

I didn't mean it.
Es war nicht so gemeint. [ˀəs va: nɪçt zo gəˈmaɪnt]

That's all right!/It doesn't matter!
Keine Ursache!/Macht nichts! [ˈkaɪnə ˈˀuɐzaxə/maxt nɪçts]

Congratulations/Best wishes

Congratulations!
Herzlichen Glückwunsch! [ˌhɛɐtslɪçn ˈglʏkvʊnʃ]

All the best!
Alles Gute! [ˌˀaləs ˈgu:tə]

Good luck!
Viel Glück! [fi:l glʏk]/Viel Erfolg! [fi:l ˀɐˈfɔlk]

I'll keep my fingers crossed for you.
Ich drück' Ihnen die Daumen. [ˀɪç ˈdʀʏk ˀi:nn di ˈdaʊmm]

Bless you! *(after sneezing)*
Gesundheit! [gəˈzʊnthaɪt]

Get well soon!
Gute Besserung! [ˌgu:tə ˈbɛsəʀʊŋ]

Opinions and feelings

Agreement

Good.
Gut. [gu:t]

Right.
Richtig. [ˈʀɪçtɪç]

Agreed!/It's a deal!
Einverstanden!/Abgemacht! [ˈˀaɪnfɐʃtandn/ˈˀapgəmaxt]

That's all right!
Geht in Ordnung! [ge:t ɪŋ ˈˀɔɐtnʊŋ]

Okay!/O.K.!/OK!
Okay!/o.k.!/O.K.! [ˀoˈke:]

Exactly!
Genau! [gəˈnaʊ]

Oh!
Ach! [ˀax]

Oh, I see!
Ach, so! [ˀax ˈzo:]

Really?
Wirklich? [ˈvɪɐklɪç]

How interesting!
Interessant! [ˀɪntʀəˈsant]

How nice!
Wie schön! [vi ˈʃø:n]

I understand.
Ich verstehe. [ˀɪç fɐˈʃte:(ə)]

That's how it is.
So ist es eben. [zo: ˀɪst əs ˀe:bm]

I entirely agree with you.
Ganz Ihrer Meinung. [ˈgants ˌʔiːʀɐ ˈmaɪnʊŋ]

That's right.
Das stimmt. [das ʃtɪmt]

I think that's a good idea.
Das finde ich gut. [das fɪndə ʔɪç guːt]

With pleasure.
Mit Vergnügen! [mɪt fɐˈgnyːgŋ]

That sounds good to me.
Das hört sich gut an. [das høɐt zɪç ˈguːt an]

Refusal

I don't want to.
Ich will nicht. [ʔɪç ˈvɪl nɪçt]

I don't feel like it.
Dazu habe ich keine Lust. [ˈdaːtsu habə ɪç ˈkaɪnə lʊst]

I can't agree to that.
Damit bin ich nicht einverstanden.
[ˈdaːmɪt bɪn ɪç nɪçt ˈʔaɪnfɐʃtandn]

That's out of the question.
Das kommt nicht in Frage. [das kɔmt ˈnɪçt ʔɪn ˈfʀaːgə]

Certainly not!/No way!
Auf gar keinen Fall! [ʔaʊf ˈgaː kaɪnn fal]

Count me out!
Ohne mich! [ˌʔoːnə ˈmɪç]

I don't like this at all.
Das gefällt mir gar nicht. [das gəˈfɛlt miɐ ˈgaː nɪçt]

Preferences

I like it.
Das gefällt mir. [das gəˈfɛlt miɐ]

I don't like it.
Das gefällt mir nicht. [das gəˈfɛlt miɐ nɪçt]

I'd rather ...
Ich möchte lieber ... [ʔɪç ˈmøçtə ˈliːbɐ]

I'd really like ...
Am liebsten wäre mir ... [ʔam ˈliːpstn ˈvɛːʀə miɐ]

I'd like to find out more about it.
Darüber würde ich gerne mehr erfahren.
[ˈdaːʀyːbɐ ˈvʏɐdə ʔɪç ˌgɛɐnə ˈmeɐ ʔɐˈfaːʀən]

Ignorance

I don't know (that).
Das weiß ich nicht. [das ˈvaɪs ɪç nɪçt]

No idea!
Keine Ahnung! [ˈkaɪnə ˈʔa:nʊŋ]

Indecision

I don't care.
Das ist mir egal. [das ɪst mɪɐ eˈgal]

I don't know yet.
Ich weiß noch nicht. [ʔɪç ˈvaɪs nɔx nɪçt]

Perhaps./Maybe.
Vielleicht. [fɪˈlaɪçt]

Probably.
Wahrscheinlich. [vaˈʃaɪnlɪç]

Delight

Great!
Großartig! [ˈgʀo:sa:tɪç]

Fine!
Prima! [ˈpʀi:ma]

Fantastic!
Toll! [tɔl]

Contentment

I am completely satisfied.
Ich bin voll und ganz zufrieden. [ʔɪç bɪn ˈfɔl ʊnt gants tsʊˈfʀi:dn]

I can't complain.
Ich kann mich nicht beklagen. [ʔɪç kan mɪç nɪçt bəˈkla:gŋ]

That worked out extremely well.
Das hat hervorragend geklappt. [das hat hɐˈfoɐʀa:gŋt gəˈklapt]

Boredom

How boring!/What a bore!
Wie langweilig!/So was von langweilig!
[vi ˈlaŋvaɪlɪç/ˈzo:vas fɔn ˈlaŋvaɪlɪç]

... is dead boring.
... ist total öde. [ʔɪst toˈta:l ˈʔø:də]

Astonishment – Surprise

Oh, I see!
Ach so! [ˀax ˈzoː]

You don't say!
Ach nein! [ˀax ˈnaɪn]

Really?
Wirklich? [ˈvɪɐklɪç]

Incredible!
Unglaublich! [ˀʊnˈglaʊplɪç]

Relief

It's lucky ...!
Ein Glück, dass ...! [ˈˀaɪn ˈglʏk das]

Thank God!
Gott sei Dank! [ˌgɔt zaɪ ˈdaŋk]

At last!
Endlich! [ˈˀɛntlɪç]

Composure

Don't panic!
Nur keine Panik! [ˈnuɐ ˌkaɪnə ˈpaːnɪk]

Don't get excited!
Nur keine Aufregung! [ˈnuɐ ˌkaɪnə ˈˀaʊfʀeːgʊŋ]

Don't you worry about a thing.
Machen Sie sich keine Sorgen. [maxn zi zɪç ˈkaɪnə ˈzɔɐgŋ]

Annoyance

How annoying!
Das ist aber ärgerlich! [das ˀɪst ˈˀaːbɐ ˈˀɛɐgɐlɪç]

Blast!
Verflixt! [fɐˈflɪkst]

What a nuisance!
So ein Mist! [zo ˀaɪn mɪst]

Enough of this!
Jetzt reicht's! [jɛtst ˈraɪçts]

... is getting on my nerves/wick.
... geht mir auf den Geist/Wecker/Keks.
[geːt miɐ ˀaʊf den ˈgaɪst/ˈvɛkɐ/ˈkeːks]

That's outrageous!/What a cheek!
Eine Unverschämtheit ist das!/So eine Frechheit!
[ˌʔaɪnə ˈʔʊnfɐʃɛːmthaɪt ʔɪst das/ˈzoː ˌʔaɪnə ˈfrɛçhaɪt]

That can't be true!
Das darf doch wohl nicht wahr sein!
[das daːf dɔx voːl nɪct ˈvaː zaɪn]

Rebuking

What do you think you're doing!
Was fällt Ihnen ein! [vas ˈfɛlt ʔiːnn ˈʔaɪn]

Don't come anywhere near me!
Kommen Sie mir bloß nicht zu nahe!
[kɔmm zi miɐ ˈbloːs nɪçt tsʊ ˈnaː]

That's completely out of the question.
Das kommt gar nicht in Frage. [das kɔmt ˈgaː nɪçt ɪn ˈfʀaːgə]

Apologies - Disappointment

I'm (so) sorry!
Es tut mir leid! [ʔɛs tuːt miɐ laɪt]

I feel really sorry for ...
Es tut mir richtig leid für ... [ʔɛs tuːt miɐ ˈʀɪçtɪç ˈlaɪt fyɐ]

Oh dear!
Oh je! [ʔoˈjeː]

What a pity!
Schade! [ˈʃaːdə]

German gestures

Most German gestures can be easily understood by English-speaking people as they differ only marginally from ones we use ourselves. There are however, one or two that may need further explanation.

- The German expression for good luck is not "I'll keep my fingers crossed", but "I'll press my thumbs for you – Ich drück' dir die Daumen", thus the corresponding gesture involves wrapping the four fingers of one hand around the thumb of the same hand and pressing firmly.
- Tapping one's index finger against one's temple does **not** indicate that you think someone has been rather clever - on the contrary, in Germany it indicates that you think they're mad.
- If people start rapping loudly on the table with their knuckles in Germany it means that they either agree with what you have said or are expressing their thanks. If this happens in a pub, it's a form of welcome.

Good luck!

Excellent!

Maybe?

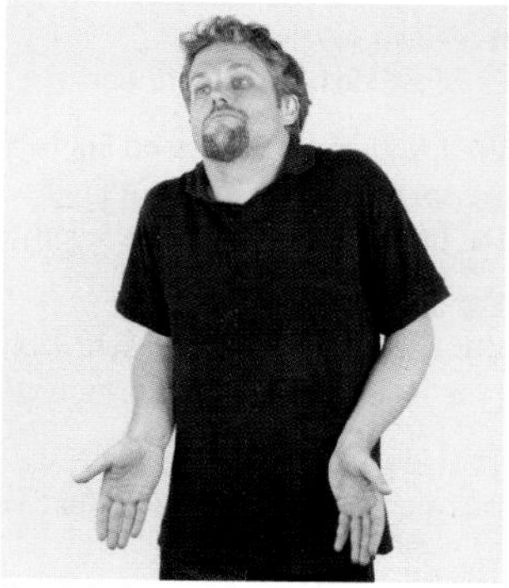
Can't help it!

Idiot!

No idea!/Don't know!

Compliments

How nice!/That's lovely!
Wie schön! [viː 'ʃøːn]

That is very kind/nice of you.
Das ist sehr nett von Ihnen/dir. [das ˀɪst zeɐ 'nɛt fɔn 'ˀiːnn/diɐ]

I think you're very nice.
Ich finde Sie sehr sympathisch/nett.
[ˀɪç 'fɪndə zi zeɐ zɪm'paːtɪʃ/nɛt]

That meal was really excellent!
Das Essen war ausgezeichnet! [das 'ˀɛsn va ˀaʊsgə'tsaɪçnət]

We've seldom had such a good meal.
Wir haben selten so gut gegessen wie bei Ihnen.
[viɐ 'haːbm 'zɛltn soː guːt gə'gɛsn viː baɪ 'ˀiːnn]

It really is lovely here!
Es ist wirklich traumhaft hier! [ˀəs ɪst 'vɪɐklɪç 'tʀaʊmhaft hiɐ]

Well, you speak very good English.
Sie sprechen aber sehr gut Englisch.
[zi 'ʃpʀɛçn ˌˀaːbɐ 'zeɐ guːt 'ˀɛŋglɪʃ]

We felt very welcome here.
Wir haben uns bei Ihnen sehr wohl gefühlt.
[viɐ 'haːbm ʊns baɪ 'ˀiːnn zeɐ voːl gə'fyːlt]

That looks good!
Das sieht gut aus! [das ziːt 'guːt ˀaʊs]

The dress suits you.
Das Kleid steht Ihnen/dir gut. [das klaɪt ʃteːt ˀiːnn/diɐ 'guːt]

cosy	gemütlich [gə'myːtlɪç]
delicious	köstlich ['køstlɪç]
friendly	freundlich ['fʀɔɪntlɪç]
gorgeous	hinreißend ['hɪnʀaɪsnt]
impressive	beeindruckend [bə'ˀaɪndʀʊkŋt]
kind	liebenswürdig ['liːbmsvʏɐdɪç]
lovely	schön [ʃøːn]
pleasant	angenehm ['ˀangəneːm]
pretty	hübsch [hʏpʃ]
tasty	lecker ['lɛkɐ]
excellent	ausgezeichnet [ˀaʊsgə'tsaɪçnət]
glorious, splendid	herrlich ['hɛɐlɪç]

Conversation

Personal information

Where are you from?
Woher kommen Sie? [ˌvoheɐ ˈkɔmm ziː]

I'm from ...
Ich bin aus ... [ˀɪç bɪn aʊs …]

Have you been here long?
Sind Sie schon lange hier? [ˈzɪnt zi ʃon ˈlaŋə hiɐ]

I've been here since ...
Ich bin seit ... hier. [ˀɪç bɪn zaɪt … hiɐ]

How long are you staying?
Wie lange bleiben Sie? [vi ˈlaŋə ˈblaɪbm ziː]

Is this your first time here?
Sind Sie zum ersten Mal hier? [ˈzɪnt zi tsʊm ˈɛɐstn maːl hiɐ]

Do you like it here?
Gefällt es Ihnen hier? [gəˈfɛlt əs ˀiːnn hiɐ]

How old are you?
Wie alt sind Sie? [vi ˈˀalt zɪnt ziː]

I'm thirty-nine.
Ich bin neununddreißig. [ˀɪç bɪn ˌnɔɪnʊnˈdʀaɪsɪç]

What do you do for a living?
Was machen Sie beruflich? [vas maxn zi bəˈʀuːflɪç]

I'm ...
Ich bin ... [ˀɪç bɪn]
  unemployed
  arbeitslos. [ˈˀaːbaɪtsloːs]
  a freelancer/self-employed
  Freiberufler. [ˈfʁaɪbəʁuːflɐ]

I work for ...
Ich arbeite bei ... [ˀɪç ˈˀaːbaɪtə baɪ]

I'm retired.
Ich bin Rentner/Rentnerin. [ˀɪç bɪn ˈʀɛntnɐ/ ˈʀɛntnəʀɪn]

I'm still at school.
Ich gehe noch zur Schule. [ˀɪç geː nɔx tsʊɐ ˈʃuːlə]

I'm a student.
Ich bin Student/Studentin. [ˀɪç bɪn ʃtʊˈdɛnt/ ʃtʊˈdɛntɪn]

Family

Are you married?
Sind Sie verheiratet? [ˈzɪnt zi fɐˈhaɪʀa:tət]

Do you have any children?
Haben Sie Kinder? [ˈha:bm zi ˈkɪndɐ]

Yes, but they're all grown up.
Ja, aber sie sind schon erwachsen. [ja: ˈʔabɐ zi zɪnt ʃo:n ʔɐˈvaksn]

How old are your children?
Wie alt sind Ihre Kinder? [vi: ʔalt zɪnt ˈʔi:ʀə ˈkɪndɐ]

My daughter is 8 (years old) and my son is 5.
Meine Tochter ist acht (Jahre alt) und mein Sohn ist fünf.
[maɪnə ˈtɔxtɐ ʔɪst ʔaxt (ˈja:ʀə ʔalt) ʔʊnt maɪn ˈzo:n fʏnf]

Hobbies

➢ **also "Other sporting activities" and "Creative holidays"**

Do you have a hobby?
Haben Sie/Hast du ein Hobby? [ha:bm zi/hast du ʔaɪn ˈhɔbi]

I spend a lot of time with my children.
Ich verbringe viel Zeit mit meinen Kindern.
[ʔɪç fɐˈbʀɪŋə fi:l tsaɪt mɪt maɪnn ˈkɪndɐn]

I surf the Internet a lot.
Ich surfe viel im Internet. [ˈʔɪç ˈsə:fə fi:l ɪm ˈʔɪntɐnɛt]

I do a little painting.
Ich male ein wenig. [ʔɪç ˈma:lə ʔaɪn ˈve:nɪç]

I collect antiques/stamps.
Ich sammle Antiquitäten/Briefmarken.
[ʔɪç ˈzamlə ʔantɪkvi:ˈtɛ:tn/ˈbʀi:fma:kŋ]

What are you interested in?
Wofür interessieren Sie sich so? [ˈvo:fyɐ ʔɪntʀəˈsi:ʀən zi zɪç zo:]

I'm interested in ...
Ich interessiere mich für ... [ʔɪç ʔɪntʀəˈsi:ʀə mɪç fyɐ ...]

I'm active in ...
Ich bin bei ... aktiv. [ʔɪç bɪn baɪ ... akˈti:f]

... is one of my favourite pastimes.
... ist eine meiner Lieblingsbeschäftigungen.
[ʔɪst ˈʔaɪnə ˌmaɪnɐ ˈli:plɪŋsbəˌʃɛftɪgʊŋŋ]

cooking	kochen [ˈkɔxn]
drawing	zeichnen [ˈtsaɪçnn]
handicrafts	basteln [bastln]
learning languages	Sprachen lernen [ˈʃpʀa:xn lɛɐnn]
listening to music	Musik hören [mʊˈzi:k ˈhø:ʀən]
making music	musizieren [mʊzɪˈtsi:ʀən]
playing cards/chess	Karten/Schach spielen [ˈka:tn/ʃax ʃpi:ln]
pottery	töpfern [ˈtøpfɐn]
reading	lesen [le:zn]
surfing the Internet	im Internet surfen [ˈʔɪntɐnɛt sə:fn]
travelling	reisen [ʀaɪn]
watching television	fernsehen [ˈfɛɐnze:n]
writing	schreiben [ʃʀaɪbm]

You can also say, *ich koche gern* - *I like cooking* (literally: "I cook gladly") or *ich arbeite gern im Garten – I like gardening* etc.

Fitness

➢ **also Other sporting activities**

How do you keep fit?
Wie halten Sie sich fit? [vi: haltn zi zɪç fɪt]

I go jogging/swimming/cycling.
Ich jogge/schwimme/fahre Rad. [ʔɪç ˈdʒɔgə/ˈʃvɪmə/ˈfa:ʀə ʀa:t]

I play squash/tennis/golf once a week.
Ich spiele einmal die Woche Squash/Tennis/Golf.
[ʔɪç ˈʃpi:lə ˈʔaɪnma:l di ˈvɔxə skvɔʃ/ˈtɛnɪs/gɔlf]

I go to a fitness centre regularly.
Ich gehe regelmäßig ins Fitnesscenter.
[ʔɪç ge:ə ˈʀe:glmɛ:sɪç ʔɪns ˈfɪtnəsˌtsɛntɐ]

I work out twice a week.
Ich trainiere zweimal die Woche. [ʔɪç treˈni:ʀə ˈtsvaɪma:l di: ˈvɔxə]

I live a healthy life.
Ich lebe gesund. [ʔɪç le:bə gəˈzʊnt]

What sport do you go in for?
Welchen Sport treiben Sie? [vɛlçn ʃpɔɐt tʀaɪbm zi:]

I play ...
Ich spiele ... [ʔɪç ˈʃpi:lə]

I'm a ... fan.
Ich bin ein Fan von ... [ʔɪç bɪn ʔaɪn fɛ:n fɔn …]

I like to go to ...
Ich gehe gern ... [ˀɪç ˈgeː gɛɐn]

Can I play too?
Kann ich mitspielen? [kan ɪç ˈmɪtʃpiːln]

Making a date

Have you got any plans for tomorrow evening?
Haben Sie/Hast du morgen Abend schon etwas vor?
[ˈhaːbm zi/hast dʊ ˈmɔɐgŋ ˈˀaːbmt ʃon ˌˀɛtvas ˈfoɐ]

Shall we go together?
Wollen wir zusammen hingehen? [ˈvɔln viɐ tsʊˈzamm ˈhɪngeːn]

Shall we go out together this evening?
Wollen wir heute Abend miteinander ausgehen?
[ˈvɔlən viɐ ˈhɔɪtə ˈabɛnt ˈmɪtaɪnˈandɐ ˈaʊsgeːn]

Can I take you out for dinner tomorrow evening?
Darf ich Sie/dich morgen Abend zum Essen einladen?
[ˈdaːf ɪç zi/dɪç mɔɐgŋ ˈˀaːbmt tsʊm ˈˀɛsn ˈˀaɪnlaːdn]

When shall we meet?
Wann treffen wir uns? [van ˈtʀɛfn viɐ ˀʊns]

Let's meet at 9 o'clock in front of ...
Treffen wir uns um neun Uhr vor ...
[ˈtʀɛfn viɐ ˀʊns ˀʊm nɔɪn uɐ foɐ ...]

I'll pick you up.
Ich hole Sie/dich ab. [ˀɪç hoːlə zi/dɪç ˈˀap]

Can I see you again?
Kann ich dich wieder sehen? [ˈkan ɪç dɪç ˈviːdɐzeːn]

That was a really nice evening!
Das war wirklich ein netter Abend! [das va ˈvɪɐklɪç ˀaɪn ˈnɛtɐ ˈˀaːbmt]

Flirting

You have lovely eyes.
Du hast wunderschöne Augen. [du hast ˈvʊndɐʃøːnə ˈˀaʊgŋ]

I like the way you laugh.
Mir gefällt, wie du lachst. [mɪɐ gəˈfɛlt vi du laxst]

I like you.
Du gefällst mir. [du gəˈfɛlst mɪɐ]

I like you a lot.
Ich mag dich. [ˀɪç maːk dɪç]

I think you're great.
Ich finde dich ganz toll! [ˀɪç ˈfɪndə dɪç gants tɔl]

I'm crazy about you.
Ich bin verrückt nach dir. [ˀɪç bɪn fɐˈʀʏkt nax diɐ]

I'm in love with you.
Ich bin in dich verliebt. [ˀɪç bɪn ɪn dɪç fɐˈli:pt]

I love you.
Ich liebe dich. [ˀɪç ˈli:bə dɪç]

Do you have a steady boyfriend/a steady girlfriend?
Hast du einen festen Freund/eine feste Freundin?
[hast du: ˀaɪnn ˈfɛstn fʀɔɪnt/ˈˀaɪnə ˈfɛstə ˈfʀɔɪndɪn]

Do you live with someone?
Lebst du mit jemandem zusammen?
[ˈle:pst du mɪt ˈje:mandəm tsʊˈzamm]

I'm divorced.
Ich bin geschieden. [ˀɪç bɪn gəˈʃi:dn]

We're separated.
Wir leben getrennt. [viɐ le:bm gəˈtʀɛnt]

I would like to sleep with you.
Ich möchte mit dir schlafen.
[ˀɪç ˈmøçtə mit diɐ ˈʃla:fn]

But only with a condom!
Aber nur mit Kondom!
[ˈˀa:bɐ nuɐ mɪt kɔnˈdo:m]

Do you have any?
Hast du welche? [ˈhastʊ ˈvɛlçə]

Where can I buy some?
Wo kann ich welche kaufen? [vo: kan ɪç ˌvɛlçə ˈkaʊfn]

Let's have a cuddle.
Wir können kuscheln. [viɐ kønn ˈkʊʃln]

Please go now.
Bitte geh jetzt! [ˈbɪtə ge: jɛtst]

Please leave me alone.
Lassen Sie mich bitte in Ruhe! [lasn zi mɪç ɪn ˈʀuə]

Stop that right now!
Hören Sie sofort damit auf! [høɐn zi zoˈfɔɐt ˌdamɪt ˈˀaʊf]

Pardon?/Excuse me?
Wie bitte? [ˈviː bɪtə]

I don't understand.
Ich verstehe Sie nicht. [ˀɪç fɐˈʃteː zi nɪçt]

Would you repeat that, please?
Könnten Sie das bitte wiederholen? [køntn zi das ˈbɪtə viːdɐˈhoːln]

Would you speak more slowly, please?
Könnten Sie bitte etwas langsamer sprechen?
[køntn zi ˈbɪtə ˌˀɛtvas ˈlaŋzamɐ ʃpʀɛçn]

Yes, I understand/see.
Ja, ich verstehe. [jaː ˀɪç fɐˈʃteː]

Do you speak ...
Sprechen Sie ... [ˈʃpʀɛçn zi]
German?
Deutsch? [ˈdɔɪtʃ]
English?
Englisch? [ˈˀɛŋlɪʃ]
French?
Französisch? [fʀanˈtsøːzɪʃ]

I only speak a little German.
Ich spreche nur wenig Deutsch. [ˀɪç ˈʃpʀɛçə nuɐ ˈveːnɪç ˈdɔɪtʃ]

Getting around

First-class roads and public transportation

Travellers in the German-speaking countries profit from excellent road systems and reliable public transportation. IC and ICE trains provide the fastest and most convenient connections between city centres. Reservations on trains are easy to make and will make your trip more pleasant. If you prefer to go by car, you will have the advantage of flexibility in getting to destinations outside city centres. Be ready, however, for rather aggressive driving behaviour by Anglo-Saxon standards. Tailgating is a national sport, and many drivers seem oblivious to speed limits. These are well-posted on freeways/motorways and highways. Be advised that there are radar checks and police who may stop speeders. This can be quite expensive.

Asking for directions

Useful words

left	links [lɪŋks]
right	rechts [ʀɛçts]
straight on/straight ahead	geradeaus [gʀa:də'ʔaʊs]
in front of	vor [foɐ]
behind	hinter ['hɪntɐ]
next to	neben ['ne:bm]
in the vicinity (of)	in der Nähe (von) [ɪn dɐ 'nɛ:ə fɔn]
opposite	gegenüber [ge:gŋ'ʔy:bɐ]
here	hier [hiɐ]
there	dort [dɔɐt]
near	nah [na:]
far	weit [vaɪt]
after	nach [na:x]
street/road	die Straße [di 'ʃtʀa:sə]
curve/bend	die Kurve [di 'kʊɐvə]
intersection/junction	die Kreuzung [di 'kʀɔɪtsʊŋ]
traffic light	die Ampel [di 'ʔampl]
the street corner	die Straßenecke [di 'ʃtʀa:snʔɛkə]

Directions

Excuse me, how do you get to ...?
Entschuldigen Sie bitte, wie komme ich nach ...?
[ʔɛnt'ʃʊldɪgŋ zi 'bɪtə vi: kɔmə ɪç nax]

Straight on until you get to ...
Immer geradeaus bis ... ['ʔɪmɐ gʀa:də'ʔaʊs bɪs ...]

Then turn left/right at the traffic lights.
Dann bei der Ampel links/rechts abbiegen.
[dan baɪ dɐ ʔampl lɪŋks/ʀɛçts ˈapbiːgŋ]

Follow the signs.
Folgen Sie den Schildern. [ˈfɔlgŋ zɪ den ˈʃɪldɐn]

How far is it?
Wie weit ist das? [viː vaɪt ʔɪst das]

It's very near here.
Es ist ganz in der Nähe. [ʔəs ʔɪst gants ɪn dɐ ˈnɛːə]

Excuse me, is this the road to ...?
Bitte, ist das die Straße nach ...? [ˈbɪtə ʔɪst ˈdas di ˈʃtʀaːsə nax]

Excuse me, where's ..., please?
Bitte, wo ist ...? [bɪtə voː ʔɪst …]

I'm sorry, I don't know.
Tut mir leid, das weiß ich nicht. [tut miɐ laɪt das ˈvaɪs ɪç nɪçt]

I'm not from round here.
Ich bin nicht von hier. [ʔɪç ˈbɪn nɪçt fɔn hiɐ]

Go straight on.
Gehen Sie geradeaus. [geːn zi graːdəˈʔaʊs]

Turn left/right.
Gehen Sie nach links/nach rechts. [geːn zi nax lɪŋks/nax ʀɛçts]

The first street on the left.
Erste Straße links. [ˈʔeɐstə ˈʃtʀaːsə lɪŋks]

The second street on the right.
Zweite Straße rechts. [ˈtsvaɪtə ˈʃtʀaːsə ʀɛçts]

Cross ...
Überqueren Sie ... [ʔyːbɐˈkveɐn zi …]
  the bridge.
  die Brücke. [di ˈbʀʏke]
  the square.
  den Platz. [den ˈplats]
  the street.
  die Straße. [di ˈʃtʀaːsə]

The best thing would be to take the number ... bus.
Sie nehmen am besten den Bus Nummer ...
[zi ˈneːmm am ˈbɛstn den bʊs ˈnʊmɐ …]

Passport control

Your passport, please.
Ihren Pass, bitte! [ˀiɐn pas ˈbɪtə]

Have you got a visa?
Haben Sie ein Visum? [ha:bm zi ˀaɪn ˈvi:zʊm]

Can I get a visa here?
Kann ich das Visum hier bekommen?
[ˈkan ɪç das ˈvi:zʊm ˈhiɐ bəˈkɔmm]

Customs

Have you got anything to declare?
Haben Sie etwas zu verzollen? [ˈha:bm zi ˈˀɛtvas tsʊ fɐˈtsɔln]

Pull over to the right/the left, please.
Fahren Sie bitte rechts/links heran!
[ˈfa:ʀən zi ˈbɪtə ʀɛçts/lɪŋks həˈʀan]

Open the boot/trunk, please.
Öffnen Sie bitte den Kofferraum! [ˈˀøfnən zi ˈbɪtə den ˈkɔfɐʀaʊm]

Open this case, please.
Öffnen Sie bitte diesen Koffer! [ˈˀøfnən zi ˈbɪtə di:zn ˈkɔfɐ]

Do I have to pay duty on this?
Muss ich das verzollen? [ˈmʊs ɪç das fɐˈtsɔln]

Particulars/Personal statistics

Christian name/first name	der Vorname [dɐ ˈfoɐna:mə]
date of birth	das Geburtsdatum [das gəˈbʊɐtsda:tʊm]
maiden name	der Geburtsname [dɐ gəˈbʊɐtsna:mə]
marital status	der Familienstand [dɐ faˈmi:ljənʃtant]
married	verheiratet [fɐˈhaɪʀa:tət]
single	ledig [ˈle:dɪç]
widow, widower	verwitwet [fɐˈvɪtvət]
nationality	die Staatsangehörigkeit [di ˈʃta:tsˌˀangehø:ʀɪçkaɪt]
place of birth	der Geburtsort [dɐ gəˈbʊɐtsˀɔɐt]
place of residence	der Wohnort [dɐ ˈvo:nˀɔɐt]
surname/last name	der Familienname [dɐ faˈmi:ljənna:mə]

At the border

border crossing	der Grenzübergang [dɐ ˈgʀɛnts?yːbɐgaŋ]
customs	der Zoll [dɐ ˈtsɔl]
driving licence	der Führerschein [dɐ ˈfyːʀɐʃaɪn]
duties	die Zollgebühren *f pl* [di ˈtsɔlgəbyːʀən]
duty-free	zollfrei [ˈtsɔlfʀaɪ]
entering (a country)	die Einreise [di ˈʔaɪnʀaɪzə]
EU citizen	EU-Bürger/EU-Bürgerin [ʔeˈʔuː bʏʀgɐ/ʔeˈʔuː bʏʀgəʀɪn]
green card	die grüne Versicherungskarte [di ˈgryːnə fɐˈzɪçəʀʊŋskaːtə]
identity card	der Personalausweis [dɐ p(ɛ)ɐzoˈnaːlˌʔaʊsvaɪs]
international car index mark	das Nationalitätskennzeichen [das natsjonalɪˈtɛːtskɛntsaɪçn]
international vaccination certificate	der internationale Impfpass [dɐ ˈʔɪntɐnatsjonaːlə ˈʔɪmpfpas]
leaving (a country)	die Ausreise [di ˈaʊsraɪzə]
liable to duty	zollpflichtig [ˈtsɔl(p)flɪçtɪç]
number plate/license plate	das Nummernschild [das ˈnʊmɐnʃɪlt]
passport	der Reisepass [dɐ ˈʀaɪzəpas]
passport check	die Passkontrolle [di ˈpaskɔntʀɔlə]
valid	gültig [ˈgʏltɪç]
visa	das Visum [das ˈviːzʊm]

Cars and motorcycles

In German-speaking countries people drive on the right side of the road and overtake on the left. There are three main categories of roads: *Landstraßen* (ordinary roads), *Bundesstraßen* (highways) and *Autobahnen* (motorways/freeways).
On Swiss and Austrian motorways motorists have to pay a toll. Safety belts (*Sicherheitsgurte*) and special child seats for small children are mandatory.

country road	die Landstraße [di ˈlantʃtʀaːsə]
dual carriageway/divided highway	die Schnellstraße [di ˈʃnɛlʃtʀaːsə]
fine	das Bußgeld [das ˈbuːsgɛlt]
to hitchhike	trampen [tʀɛmpm]
hitchhiker	der Anhalter [der ˈʔanhaltɐ]
legal alcohol limit	die Promillegrenze [di pʀoˈmɪləˌgʀɛntsə]
main street	die Hauptstraße [di ˈhaʊptʃtʀaːsə]
motorway/freeway	die Autobahn [di ˈʔaʊtobaːn]

motorway toll	die Autobahngebühren [di ˈˀaʊtoba:ngəˌby:ʀən]
radar check	die Radarkontrolle [di ʀaˈda:kɔnˌtʀɔlə]
(motorway) service area	die Raststätte [di ˈʀastʃtɛtə]
side-street	die Nebenstraße [di ˈne:bmʃtʀa:sə]
sign *(directions)*	der Wegweiser [dɐ ˈve:kvaɪzɐ]
street/road	die Straße [di ˈʃtʀa:sə]
traffic jam	der Stau [dɐ ʃtaʊ]

Road traffic regulations and common practices on the road are similar to those in the rest of Europe, but there are a few notable exceptions:

- At roundabouts (Kreisverkehr [ˈkʁaɪsfɐkeɐ]), only indicate when you are already on the roundabout, just before you wish to turn off, but make sure that you do indicate, as otherwise you will annoy drivers wishing to join the traffic flow.
- On motorways, especially if there is no speed limit, only pull out into the overtaking lane if you are prepared (and able) to drive at a relatively high speed. Not doing so will simply provoke tailgaters and annoy everyone involved, including yourself.
- On a motorcycle, it is customary to acknowledge other (oncoming) motorcyclists with a brief hand signal.
- Take care at pedestrian crossings (Fußgängerübergang [ˈfu:sgɛŋɐˌˀy:bɐgaŋ]) when you are turning right or left! You will have a green light, *but pedestrians (and cyclists) on your right and left will also have a green light!* You must stop and wait until the crossing is clear before proceeding. In most cases, a flashing amber light beside your own green light acts as a warning.
- If your journey is interrupted, e.g. traffic gridlock, tram or railway crossings etc., it is expected that you switch off your engine to save energy. As a matter of fact, many modern German cars do this automatically.
- Many traffic lights are switched off at night. At more dangerous junctions or intersections, the lights may be switched to flashing amber, indicating you should exercise caution and approach more slowly.
- Especially in South Germany, Austria and Switzerland, it is becoming increasingly more common to switch on your low-beam headlights during the daytime to enhance safety, and it is of course compulsory to do so in poor visibility conditions.

At the gas/petrol station

➣ **also At the garage**

Where's the nearest gas/petrol station, please?
Wo ist bitte die nächste Tankstelle?
[voː ˀɪst ˈbɪtə di ˈnɛːçstə ˈtaŋkʃtɛlə]

I'd like ... litres of ...
Ich möchte ... Liter ... [ˀɪç ˈmøçtə ... ˈlɪtɐ]
regular (petrol)/normal gasoline.
Normalbenzin. [nɔˈmaːlbɛntsiːn]
super/premium.
Super. [ˈzuːpɐ]
diesel.
Diesel. [ˈdiːzl]
leaded.
verbleit. [fɐˈblaɪt]
unleaded.
bleifrei. [ˈblaɪfʀaɪ]

Super/premium, please. For 50 euros.
Super bitte, für fünfzig Euro. [ˈzuːpɐ ˈbɪtə fyɐ ˈfʏnftsɪç ˈˀɔɪro]

Fill her up, please.
Volltanken, bitte. [ˈfɔltaŋkŋ ˈbɪtə]

Would you mind checking the oil?
Würden Sie bitte den Ölstand prüfen?
[vʏɐdn zi ˈbɪtə den ˈˀøːlʃtant pʀyːfn]

I'd like a road map of this area, please.
Ich hätte gern eine Straßenkarte dieser Gegend.
[ˀɪç ˈhɛtə gɛɐn ˀaɪnə ˈʃtʀaːsnkaːtə dizɐ ˈgeːgŋt]

Parking

Parking can be a problem in inner cities. As elsewhere, you'll have to live with parking meters (*Parkuhren*), or you'll need a parking disc (*Parkscheibe*) for restricted zones. Find a car park/garage (*Parkhaus* – look for a sign with a large "P" on it), or park on the outskirts of town and take the bus. In either case, make sure you have enough small change.

Excuse me, is there a place to park near here?
Entschuldigen Sie bitte, gibt es hier in der Nähe eine Parkmöglichkeit?
[ˀɛntˈʃʊldɪgŋ zi ˈbɪtə gɪpt əs hiɐ ˀɪn dɐ ˈnɛːə ˈˀaɪnə ˈpaːkmøːklɪçkaɪt]

Can I park my car here?
Kann ich den Wagen hier abstellen? [ˈkan ɪç den ˈvaːgŋ hiɐ ˈˀapʃtɛln]

Is there an attendant?
Ist der Parkplatz bewacht? [ˀɪst dɐ ˈpa:kplats bəˈvaxt]

How much is it by the hour?
Wie hoch ist die Parkgebühr pro Stunde?
[vi: ho:x ˀɪst di ˈpa:kgəbyɐ pʀo ˈʃtʊndə]

Is the car park/garage open all night?
Ist das Parkhaus die ganze Nacht geöffnet?
[ˀɪst das ˈpa:khaʊs di ˈgantsə naxt gəˈˀœfnət]

A breakdown

My car's broken down.
Ich habe eine Panne. [ˀɪç ˈha:bə ˈˀaɪnə ˈpanə]

Is there a garage near here?
Ist hier in der Nähe eine Werkstatt?
[ˀɪst hiɐ ˀɪn dɐ ˈnɛ:ə ˈˀaɪnə ˈvɛɐkʃtat]

Would you call the breakdown service, please?
Würden Sie bitte den Pannendienst anrufen?
[vʏɐdn zi ˈbɪtə den ˈpanndi:nst ˈˀanʀu:fn]

Could you help me out with some petrol?
Könnten Sie mir mit Benzin aushelfen?
[ˈkøntn zi miɐ mɪt bɛnˈtsi:n ˈˀaʊshɛlfn]

Could you help me change the tyre?
Könnten Sie mir beim Reifenwechsel helfen?
[ˈkøntn zi miɐ baɪm ˈʀaɪfnvɛksl ˈhɛlfn]

Could you help me jump-start my car?
Könnten Sie mir Starthilfe geben? [ˈkøntn zi miɐ ˈʃta:thɪlfə ge:bm]

Could you give me a lift to the nearest garage?
Würden Sie mich bis zur nächsten Werkstatt mitnehmen?
[ˈvʏɐdn zi mɪç bɪs tsʊɐ nɛ:çstn ˈvɛɐkʃtat ˈmɪtne:mm]

Three main motoring associations, the *ADAC* in Germany, the *ÖAMTC* in Austria and the *TCS* in Switzerland will assist you if your car breaks down. You can call from emergency telephones on all motorways and on many main roads. Simple repair jobs are free, but you'll have to pay for towing service. There may also be reciprocal agreements if you're a member of an automobile association in your own country.

breakdown	die Panne [di ˈpanə]
breakdown service	der Pannendienst [dɐ ˈpanndi:nst]
breakdown vehicle	der Abschleppwagen [dɐ ˈˀapʃlɛpva:gŋ]
emergency telephone	die Notrufsäule [di ˈno:tʀufzɔɪlə]
flat (tyre)	die (Reifen)Panne [di ˈ(ʀaɪfn)panə]
gasoline can	der Benzinkanister [dɐ bɛnˈtsi:nkaˌnɪstɐ]

hazard warning lights	die Warnblinkanlage [di ˈvaːnblɪŋkˀanlaːgə]
jack	der Wagenheber [dɐ ˈvaːgŋheːbɐ]
jump leads	das Starthilfekabel [das ˈʃtaːthɪlfəkaːbl]
petrol can	der Benzinkanister [dɐ bɛnˈtsiːnkaˌnɪstɐ]
puncture	die Panne [di ˈpanə]
spare tyre	der Ersatzreifen [dɐ ˀɐˈzatsʀaɪfn]
to tow (away)	abschleppen [ˈˀapʃlɛpm]
tools	das Werkzeug [das ˈvɛɐktsɔɪk]
tow truck	der Abschleppwagen [dɐ ˈˀapʃlɛpvaːgŋ]
towing service	der Abschleppdienst [dɐ ˈˀapʃlɛpdiːnst]
towrope	das Abschleppseil [das ˈˀapʃlɛpzaɪl]
warning triangle	das Warndreieck [das ˈvaːndʀaɪɛk]

At the garage

The car won't start.
Der Motor springt nicht an. [dɐ ˈmoːtoɐ ʃpʀɪŋt nɪçt ˈˀan]

There's something wrong with the engine.
Mit dem Motor stimmt was nicht. [mɪt dem ˈmoːtoɐ ʃtɪmt vas nɪçt]

The brakes don't work.
Die Bremsen funktionieren nicht. [di ˈbʀɛmzn fʊŋktsjoˈniɐn nɪçt]

I'm losing oil.
Der Wagen verliert Öl. [dɐ ˈvaːgŋ fɐˈliɐt ˀøːl]

When will the car be ready?
Wann ist der Wagen fertig? [ˈvan ˀɪst dɐ ˈvaːgŋ ˈfɛɐtɪç]

Roughly how much will it cost?
Was wird es ungefähr kosten? [vas vɪɐt əs ˈˀʊngəfɛɐ ˈkɔstn]

alarm system	die Alarmanlage [di ˀaˈlaːmanlaːgə]
anti-freeze	das Frostschutzmittel [das ˈfʀɔstʃʊtsmɪtl]
accelerator/gas pedal	das Gaspedal [das ˈgaːspedaːl]
air filter	der Luftfilter [dɐ ˈlʊftfɪltɐ]
automatic (transmission)	das Automatikgetriebe [das ˀaʊtoˈmaːtɪkgəˌtʀiːbə]
bonnet/hood	die Motorhaube [di ˈmoːtɔˌhaʊbə]
brake fluid	die Bremsflüssigkeit [di ˈbʀɛmsflʏsɪçkaɪt]
brake lights	die Bremslichter [di ˈbʀɛmslɪçtɐ]
clutch	die Kupplung [di ˈkʊplʊŋ]
cooling water	das Kühlwasser [das ˈkyːlvasɐ]
dent	die Delle [di ˈdɛlə]
dipped/dimmed headlights	das Abblendlicht [das ˈˀapblɛntlɪçt]
dynamo/generator	die Lichtmaschine [di ˈlɪçtmaʃiːnə]

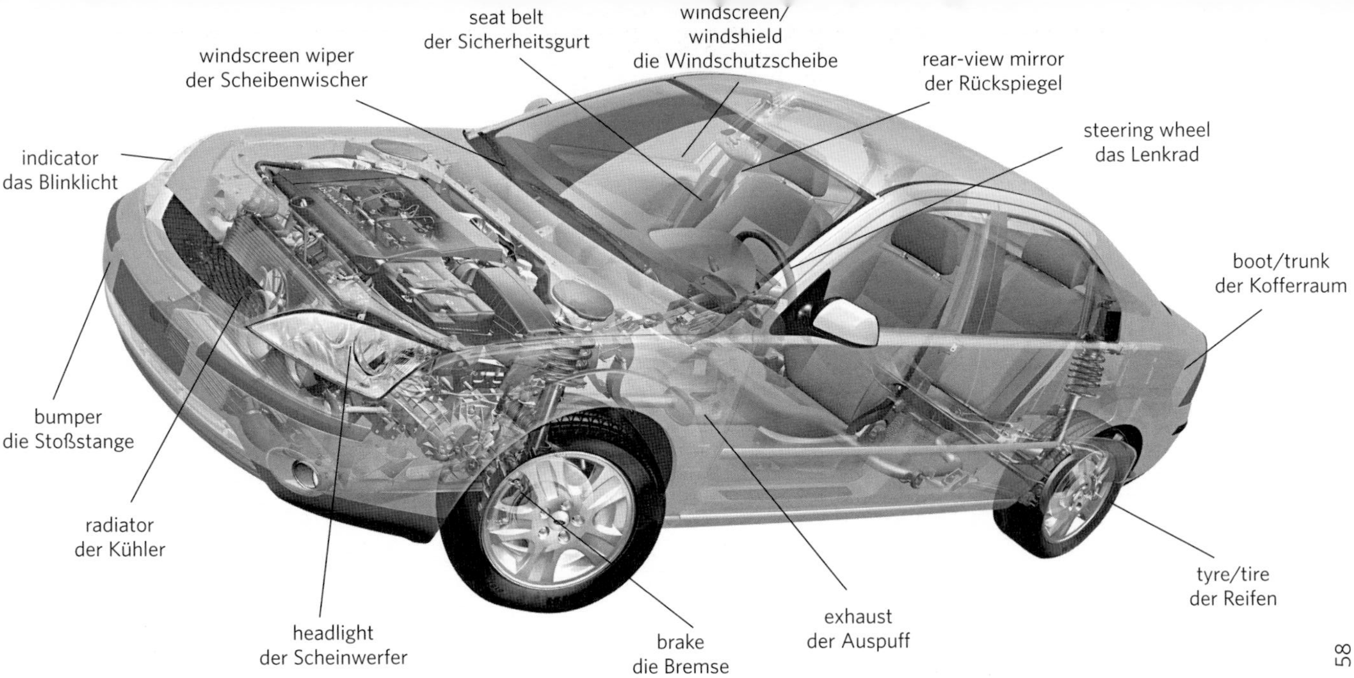
windscreen wiper
der Scheibenwischer
seat belt
der Sicherheitsgurt
windscreen/
windshield
die Windschutzscheibe
rear-view mirror
der Rückspiegel
steering wheel
das Lenkrad
indicator
das Blinklicht
boot/trunk
der Kofferraum
bumper
die Stoßstange
radiator
der Kühler
headlight
der Scheinwerfer
brake
die Bremse
exhaust
der Auspuff
tyre/tire
der Reifen

engine/motor	der Motor [dɐ ˈmoːtoɐ]
fault	der Defekt [dɐ deˈfɛkt]
first-aid kit	der Verbandskasten [dɐ fɐˈbantskastn]
full beam/high beams	das Fernlicht [das ˈfɛɐnlɪçt]
garage	die Werkstatt [di ˈvɛɐkʃtat]
gear	der Gang [dɐ gaŋ]
first/bottom/low gear	erster Gang [ˈʔeɐstɐ gaŋ]
neutral	der Leerlauf [dɐ ˈleɐlaʊf]
reverse gear	der Rückwärtsgang [dɐ ˈʀʏkvɛɐtsgaŋ]
gearbox/transmission	das Getriebe [das gəˈtʀiːbə]
hand brake/emergency brake	die Handbremse [di ˈhantbʀɛmzə]
horn	die Hupe [di ˈhuːpə]
ignition	die Zündung [di ˈtsʏndʊŋ]
left-hand-drive car	der Linkslenker [dɐ ˈlɪŋkslɛŋkɐ]
motorbike/motorcycle	das Motorrad [das moˈtoːʀat]
natural gas/fuel station for electric cars	die Erdgas-/die Elektrotankstelle [di ˈʔeɐtgaːs-/di ʔeˈlɛkʁto-ˌtaŋkʃtɛlə]
oil	das Öl [das ʔøːl]
oil change	der Ölwechsel [dɐ ˈʔøːlvɛksl]
petrol/gas pump	die Benzinpumpe [di bɛnˈtsiːnpʊmpə]
petrol/gas tank	der Tank [dɐ taŋk]
rear/tail light	das Rücklicht [das ˈʀʏklɪçt]
right-hand-drive car	der Rechtslenker [dɐ ˈʀɛçtslɛŋkɐ]
scratch	der Kratzer [dɐ ˈkʁatsɐ]
screw	die Schraube [di ˈʃʀaʊbə]
short-circuit	der Kurzschluss [dɐ ˈkʊɐtʃlʊs]
sidelights	das Standlicht [das ˈʃtantlɪçt]
spark plug	die Zündkerze [di ˈtsʏntkɛɐtsə]
speedometer	der Tacho(meter) [dɐ ˌtaxo(ˈmeːtɐ)]
starter	der Anlasser [dɐ ˈʔanlasɐ]
transmission/ gearbox	das Getriebe [das gəˈtʀiːbə]
warning triangle	das Warndreieck [das ˈvaːndʁaɪ(ɛ)k]
wheel	das Rad [das ʀaːt]
winter tyre	der Winterreifen [dɐ ˈvɪntɐʀaɪfn]

Accident

There's been an accident.
Es ist ein Unfall passiert. [ʔɛs ʔɪst aɪn ˈʔʊnfal paˈsiɐt]

Quick! Please call ...
Rufen Sie bitte schnell ... [ˈʀuːfn zi ˈbɪtə ʃnɛl ...]
an ambulance.
einen Krankenwagen. [ʔaɪnn ˈkʀaŋkŋvaːgŋ]
the police.
die Polizei. [di pɔlɪˈtsaɪ]
the fire brigade/department.
die Feuerwehr. [di ˈfɔjɐveɐ]

Have you got a first-aid kit?
Haben Sie Verbandszeug? [ha:bm zi fɐˈbantstsɔɪk]

It is mandatory in Germany, Austria and Switzerland to carry a first-aid kit and a warning triangle in your vehicle. If you're involved in an accident, do not move your car nor allow the other party to leave until the police come.

You ...
Sie haben ... [zi ˈha:bm]
didn't yield (observe the right of way).
die Vorfahrt nicht beachtet. [di ˈfoɐfa:t nɪçt bəˈʔaxtət]
didn't signal/indicate.
nicht geblinkt. [nɪçt gəˈblɪŋkt]

You ...
Sie sind ... [zi zɪnt]
were speeding (driving too fast).
zu schnell gefahren. [tsʊ ˈʃnɛl gəˈfa:ʀən]
were too close behind/tailgating.
zu dicht aufgefahren. [tsʊ dɪçt ˈʔaʊfgəfa:ʀən]
went through a red light.
bei Rot über die Kreuzung gefahren.
[baɪ ʀo:t ʔy:bɐ di ˈkʀɔɪtsʊŋ gəˈfa:ʀən]

Can you testify as a witness?
Können Sie als Zeuge aussagen? [ˈkœnn zi ʔals ˈtsɔɪgə ˈʔaʊssa:gŋ]

Please give me your name and address.
Geben Sie mir bitte Ihren Namen und Ihre Anschrift.
[ge:bm zɪ miɐ ˈbɪtə ʔiɐn ˈna:mm ʊnt ˌiʀə ˈʔanʃʀɪft]

We should call the police.
Wir sollten die Polizei holen. [viɐ zɔltn di pɔlɪˈtsaɪ ho:ln]

Can we settle this ourselves, without the police?
Können wir uns so einigen, ohne die Polizei?
[kønn viɐ ʔʊns ˈzo: ˈʔaɪnɪgŋ o:nə di: pɔlɪˈtsaɪ]

Thank you very much for your help.
Vielen Dank für Ihre Hilfe! [fi:ln ˈdaŋk fyɐ ˈʔi:ʀə ˈhɪlfə]

I'd like to hire/rent ... for two days/for a week.
Ich möchte für zwei Tage/für eine Woche ... mieten.
[ˀɪç ˈmøçtə fʏɐ tsvaɪ ˈtaːgə/fyɐ ˈˀaɪnə ˈvɔxə … miːtn]

a car
einen Wagen/ein Auto [ˀaɪnn ˈvaːgŋ/ˀaɪn ˈˀaʊto]
a jeep
einen Geländewagen [ˀaɪnn gəˈlɛndəvaːgŋ]
a motorbike/motorcycle
ein Motorrad [ˀaɪn moˈtoːʀat]
a scooter
einen Roller [ˀaɪnn ˈʀɔlɐ]
a bike/bicycle
ein Fahrrad [ˀaɪn ˈfaːʀat]

How much does it cost per week?
Wie hoch ist die Wochenpauschale? [vi hoːx ˀɪst di ˈvɔxnpaʊʃaːlə]

Does that include unlimited mileage?
Ist das einschließlich unbegrenzter Kilometerzahl?
[ˀɪst das ˈˀaɪnʃliːslɪç ˈˀʊnbəgrɛntstɐ kɪloˈmeːtɐtsaːl]

What do you charge per kilometre?
Wie viel verlangen Sie pro gefahrenen Kilometer?
[ˈviː fiːl fɐˈlaŋŋ zi pʀo gəˈfaː(ʀə)nn kɪloˈmeːtɐ]

Conversion factor for kilometres: 1 mile = 1.6 km; 1 km = 0.6 mile. Cut the kilometres in half, add 10 percent of the original, and you'll have it in miles. 40 km = 20 + 4 = 24 miles.

How much is the deposit?
Wie hoch ist die Kaution? [vi ˈhoːx ˀɪst di kaʊˈtsjoːn]

Does the vehicle have comprehensive insurance/full coverage?
Ist das Fahrzeug vollkaskoversichert?
[ˀɪst das ˈfaːtsɔɪk ˈfɔlkaskofɐˌzɪçɐt]

Is it possible to leave the car in ...?
Ist es möglich, das Fahrzeug in ... abzugeben?
[ˀɪst əs ˈmøːklɪç das ˈfaːtsɔɪk ˀɪn ... ˈˀaptsʊgeːbm]

I'd like to rent a crash helmet.
Ich möchte einen Schutzhelm leihen.
[ˀɪç ˈmœçtə ˀaʊx aɪnn ˈʃʊtshɛlm laɪn]

child seat	der Kindersitz [dɐ ˈkɪndɐzɪts]
crash helmet	der Sturzhelm [dɐ ˈʃtʊɐtshɛlm]
to deposit *(money)*	Geld hinterlegen [gɛlt hɪntɐˈleːgŋ]
deposit	die Kaution [di kaʊˈtsjoːn]
driving licence	der Führerschein [dɐ ˈfyːʀɐʃaɪn]
fully comprehensive insurance	die Vollkasko [di ˈfɔlkasko]
green card	die grüne Versicherungskarte [di ˈgʀyːnə fɐˈzɪçəʀʊŋskaːtə]
ignition key	der Zündschlüssel [dɐ ˈtsʏntʃlʏsl]
safety belt	der Sicherheitsgurt [dɐ ˈzɪçɐhaɪtsgurt]
papers	die Papiere *n pl* [di paˈpiːʀə]
sunroof	das Schiebedach [das ˈʃiːbədax]
third party, fire and theft	die Teilkasko [di ˈtaɪlkasko]
weekend rate	die Wochenendpauschale [di ˈvɔxnˀɛntpaʊʃaːlə]

Signs and Notices

Achtung	look out, danger
Anlieger frei	residents only
Anfänger	learner, beginner
Ausfahrt	exit
Ausfahrt freihalten	keep exit clear
... ausgenommen	except for ...
Autofähre	car-ferry
Behelfsausfahrt	temporary exit
Bis zur Haltelinie vorfahren	drive up to line
Bitte einordnen	get in lane
Bushaltestelle	bus stop
Einbahnstraße	one-way street
Einfahrt	entrance
Fahrbahn wechseln	change lane
Fahrbahnverengung	road narrows
Feuerwehrzufahrt	fire brigade/department access

Frauenparkplätze	parking spaces for women only
Fußgängerzone	pedestrian precinct/zone
Gefahr	danger
Gefährliche Kurve	dangerous bend/curve
Gegenverkehr	two-way traffic
Geschwindigkeitsbegrenzung	speed limit
Gesperrt (für Fahrzeuge aller Art)	closed (to all vehicles)
Gewichtsgrenze	weight limit
Glatteis	black ice
Haarnadelkurve	hairpin bend/curve
Hochwasser	flooding
Industriegebiet	industrial area
Innenstadt	city centre, downtown
Keine Einfahrt	no entry
Krankenhaus	hospital
Kreisverkehr	roundabout/traffic circle
Kreuzung	cross-road/intersection
Kurzparkzone	limited parking zone
Ladezone	loading zone
Langsam fahren	reduce speed
Licht	headlights
Nebel	fog
Notruf	emergency phone
Ölspur	oil slick
Parken verboten	no parking
Parkhaus	parking building/garage
Parkplatz	parking lot, car park
Parkscheinautomat	ticket machine
Rechts (Links) fahren	keep right (left)
Rechtsabbiegen verboten	no right turn
Rutschgefahr	slippery road
Sackgasse	dead end
Schritt fahren	drive at walking speed
Schule	school
Schulkinder überqueren	children crossing
Seitenwind	side-wind
Spielstraße	children playing
Starkes Gefälle	steep hill
Stau	traffic jam
Steinschlag	falling rocks
Straßenarbeiten	construction, road works
Tunnel	tunnel
Überholverbot	no overtaking/passing
Umleitung	detour/diversion
Unbeschrankter Bahnübergang	crossing – no gates/unprotected crossing
Unfall	accident
Verschmutzte Fahrbahn	muddy road surface
Vorfahrt beachten	give way/yield
Vorsicht	caution
Wenden verboten	no U-turn

Wildwechsel	deer crossing
Zebrastreifen	zebra crossing
Zentrum	city centre, downtown

Plane

Booking a flight

Can you tell me when the next flight to ... is, please?
Können Sie mir bitte sagen, wann die nächste Maschine nach ... fliegt?
[kˈønn zi miɐ ˈbɪtə za:gŋ van di ˈnɛ:çstə maˈʃi:nə nax … fli:kt]

Are there any seats left?
Sind noch Plätze frei? [zɪnt nɔx ˈplɛtsə fʀaɪ]

I'd like to book a single/one-way flight to ...
Ich möchte einen einfachen Flug nach ... buchen.
[ˀɪç ˈmøçtə ˀaɪnn ˈˀaɪnfaxn flu:k nax … bu:xn]

I'd like to book a return flight to ...
Ich möchte einen Hin- und Rückflug nach ... buchen.
[ˀɪç ˈmøçtə ˀaɪnn hɪn ʊnt ˈʀʏkflu:k nax … bu:xn]

How much is an economy class/a first class ticket?
Was kostet bitte der Flug Touristenklasse/ erste Klasse?
[vas ˈkɔstət bɪtə dɐ ˈflu:k tʊˈʀɪstnklasə/ˈˀeɐstɐ ˈklasə]

Smoking or non-smoking?
Raucher oder Nichtraucher? [ˈʀaʊxɐ ˈˀo:dɐ ˈnɪçtʀaʊxɐ]

I'd like ...
Ich möchte ... [ˀɪç ˈmøçtə …]
a window seat.
einen Fensterplatz. [ˀaɪnn ˈfɛnstɐplats]
an aisle seat.
einen Platz am Gang. [ˀaɪnn plats am gaŋ]

I'd like to cancel my flight.
Ich möchte diesen Flug stornieren. [ˀɪç ˈmøçtə ˈdi:zn flu:k ʃtɔˈniɐn]

I'd like to change the booking.
Ich möchte diesen Flug umbuchen.
[ˀɪç ˈmøçtə ˈdi:zn flu:k ˈˀʊmbu:xn]

At the airport

Where is terminal ...?
Wo ist Terminal...? [vo: ˀɪst ˈtœɐmɪnəl]

Where's the ... counter, please?
Wo ist bitte der Schalter der ...-Fluggesellschaft?
[vo: ˀɪst bɪtə dɐ ˈʃaltɐ dɐ …ˈflu:kgəˌzɛlʃaft]

Is it possible to check in for the flight the evening before/by telephone/ on the Internet?
Gibt es für den Flug einen Vorabend-/Telefon-/Internet-Checkin?
[ˈgɪpt əs fyɐ den ˈflu:k ˀaɪnn ˈfoɐˀa:bmt-/ˈte:ləfo:n-/ˈˀɪntɐnɛt-tʃɛkˈˀɪn]

Could I see your ticket, please?
Könnte ich bitte Ihren Flugschein sehen?
[ˈkøntə ɪç ˈbɪtə ˈˀi:ʀən ˈflu:kʃaɪn ze:n]

Can I take this as hand luggage?
Kann ich das als Handgepäck mitnehmen?
[kan ɪç das ˀals ˈhantgəpɛk ˈmɪtne:mm]

Can I take this onto the plane?
Darf ich das in die Maschine mitnehmen?
[ˈda:f ɪç das ɪn di maˈʃi:nə ˈmɪtne:mm]

When does the flight from ... land?
Wann landet die Maschine aus ...? [van ˈlandət di maˈʃi:nə ˀaʊs]

On board

Could you bring me a glass of water, please?
Könnten Sie mir bitte ein Glas Wasser bringen?
[ˈkøntn zi miɐ ˈbɪtə ˀaɪn gla:s ˈvasɐ brɪŋŋ]

Could I have another cushion/blanket, please?
Könnte ich bitte noch ein Kissen/ eine Decke haben?
[ˈkøntə ɪç ˈbɪtə nɔx ˀaɪn kɪsn/ˀaɪnə ˈdɛkə ha:bm]

Would it be possible for us to change seats?
Wäre es möglich, dass wir den Platz tauschen?
[vɛ:ʀə ˀəs ˈmø:klɪç das viɐ den plats taʊʃn]

Arrival ➢ **also Lost-property office**

My luggage is missing.
Mein Gepäck ist verloren gegangen.
[maɪn gəˈpɛk ˀɪst fɐˈloɐn gəˈgaŋŋ]

My suitcase has been damaged.
Mein Koffer ist beschädigt worden. [maɪn ˈkɔfɐ ˀɪst bəˈʃɛ:dɪkt vɔɐdn]

Where does the bus to ... leave from?
Wo fährt der Bus in Richtung ... ab?
[vo: feɐt dɐ bʊs ˀɪn ˈʀɪçtʊŋ … ˀap]

➣ **also Train**

accompanying adult	die Begleitperson [di bəˈglaɪtp(ɛ)ɐzoːn]
airline	die Fluggesellschaft [di ˈfluːkgəˌzɛlʃaft]
airport	der Flughafen [dɐ ˈfluːkhaːfn]
airport bus	der Flughafenbus [dɐ ˈfluːkhaːfnˌbʊs]
airport tax	die Flughafengebühr [di ˈfluːkhaːfngəˌbyɐ]
arrival	die Ankunft [di ˈʔankʊnft]
baggage	das Gepäck [das gəˈpɛk]
boarding card	die Bordkarte [di ˈbɔɐtkaːtə]
to cancel	stornieren [ʃtɔˈniɐn]
to change the booking	umbuchen [ˈʔʊmbuːxn]
to check in	einchecken [ˈʔaɪntʃɛkŋ]
connection	der Anschluss [dɐ ˈʔanʃlʊs]
delay	die Verspätung [di fɐˈʃpɛːtʊŋ]
departure	der Abflug [dɐ ˈʔapfluːk]
scheduled time of departure	planmäßiger Abflug [ˈplaːnmɛːsɪgɐ ˈʔapfluːk]
domestic flight	der Inlandsflug [dɐ ˈʔɪnlantsfluːk]
duty-free shop	zollfreier Laden [ˈtsɔlfʀaɪɐ laːdn]
emergency chute	die Notrutsche [di ˈnoːtʀʊtʃə]
emergency exit	der Notausgang [dɐ ˈnoːtʔaʊsgaŋ]
emergency landing	die Notlandung [di ˈnoːtlandʊŋ]
excess baggage	das Übergepäck [das ˈʔyːbɐgəpɛk]
flight	der Flug [dɐ fluːk]
gate	der Flugsteig [dɐ ˈfluːkʃtaɪg]
international flight	der Auslandsflug [dɐ ˈʔaʊslantsfluːk]
landing	die Landung [di ˈlandʊŋ]
life jacket	die Schwimmweste [di ˈʃvɪmvɛstə]
luggage	das Gepäck [das geˈpɛk]
luggage van/baggage car	der Gepäckwagen [dɐ gəˈpɛkvaːgŋ]
luggage/baggage reclaim	die Gepäckausgabe [di gəˈpɛkʔaʊsgaːbə]
passenger	der Passagier [dɐ pasaˈʒiɐ]
pilot	der Pilot [dɐ piˈloːt]
security charge	die Sicherheitsgebühr [di ˈzɪçɐhaɪtsgəˌbyɐ]
security control	die Sicherheitskontrolle [di ˈzɪçɐhaɪtskɔnˌtʀɔlə]
steward/stewardess	der Steward/die Stewardess [dɐ ˈstjuaːt/diː ˈstjuadɛs]
stopover	die Zwischenlandung [di ˈtsvɪʃnˌlandʊŋ]
take-off	der Abflug [dɐ ˈʔapfluːk]
terminal	das Terminal [das ˈtəːmɪnəl]
time of arrival	die Ankunftszeit [di ˀankʊnfˌtsaɪt]

Train

Intercity trains (IC) connect most cities on an hourly basis. *EuroCity* (EC) trains connect European cities. The fastest trains are the *InterCity Express* (ICE), but they connect fewer places. In addition, there are *InterRegio* (IR) trains and *D-Zug/Schnellzug* (express) trains. For a small fee it is possible to reserve seats in advance. If you travel less than 50 km, you have to pay an extra fee for express trains.

Buying tickets

Single/One-way to Frankfurt, please.
Eine einfache Fahrt nach Frankfurt, bitte.
[ˈʔaɪnə ˈʔaɪnfaxə faːt nax ˈfʀankfʊɐt ˈbɪtə]

Two returns to Stuttgart, please.
Zweimal Stuttgart hin und zurück, bitte.
[ˈtsvaɪmal ˈʃtʊtgaːt hɪn ʊnt tsʊˈʀʏk ˈbɪtə]

first-class
erster Klasse [ˈʔeɐstɐ ˈklasə]

Is there a reduction for children/students/senior citizens?
Gibt es eine Ermäßigung für Kinder/ Studenten/Senioren?
[gɪpt əs ʔaɪnə ʔɐˈmɛːsɪgʊŋ fyɐ ˈkɪndɐ/ ʃtʊˈdɛntn/zenˈjoːʀən]

I'd like to book two non-smoking seats, please,
Ich möchte gern zwei Nichtraucherplätze reservieren:
[ʔɪç ˈmøçtə gɛɐn tsvaɪ ˈnɪçtʀaʊxɐˌplɛtsə ʀezɐˈviːʀən]
for the EC to ...
für den EC nach ... [fyɐ den ʔeˈtseː nax]
on ... at ... (o'clock)
am ... um ...Uhr [ʔam … ʔʊm … ˈʔuɐ]
in the couchette car
im Liegewagen [ʔɪm ˈliːgəvaːgŋ]
in the sleeping car
im Schlafwagen [ʔɪm ˈʃlaːfvaːgŋ]
in the restaurant car
im Speisewagen [ʔɪm ˈʃpaɪzəvaːgŋ]

Is there a motorail train to ...?
Gibt es einen Autoreisezug nach ...?
[gɪpt əs ʔaɪnn ˈʔaʊtoˌʀaɪzetsuːk nax]

Is there a connection to Leipzig at Fulda?
Habe ich in Fulda Anschluss nach Leipzig?
[haːb ɪç ʔɪn ˈfʊlda ˈʔanʃlʊs nax ˈlaɪptsɪç]

How many times do I have to change?
Wie oft muss ich da umsteigen? [viː ʔɔft mʊs ɪç da ˈʔʊmʃtaɪgŋ]

At the station

I'd like to register/check this suitcase.
Ich möchte diesen Koffer als Reisegepäck aufgeben.
[ˀɪç ˈmøçtə di:zn ˈkɔfɐ ˀals ˈʀaɪzəgəpɛk ˈˀaʊfge:bm]

Where can I check in my bicycle?
Wo kann ich mein Fahrrad aufgeben?
[ˈvo: kan ɪç maɪn ˈfa:ʀa:t ˈˀaʊfge:bm]

Excuse me, which platform does the train to Heidelberg leave from?
Entschuldigen Sie bitte, von welchem Gleis fährt der Zug nach Heidelberg ab?
[ˀɛntˈʃʊldɪgŋ zi ˈbɪtə fɔn vɛlçm glaɪs fɛɐt dɐ tsu:k nax ˈhaɪdlbɛɐk ˀap]

The intercity ... from Hamburg is running 10 minutes late.
Der Intercity ... aus Hamburg hat voraussichtlich zehn Minuten Verspätung.
[dɐ ˀɪntɐˈsɪti ˀaʊs ˈhambʊɐk hat foˈʀaʊsɪçtlɪç ˈtse:n mɪˈnu:tn fɐˈʃpɛ:tʊŋ]

On the train

All aboard, please!
Bitte einsteigen! [ˈbɪtə ˈˀaɪnʃtaɪgŋ]

Is this seat taken/free?
Ist dieser Platz noch frei? [ˀɪst ˈdi:zɐ plats nɔx fʀaɪ]

Excuse me, I think that's my seat.
Entschuldigen Sie, ich glaube das ist mein Platz.
[ˀɛntˈʃʊldɪgŋ zi ˀɪç ˈglaʊbə das ɪst ˈmaɪn plats]

Here is my seat reservation.
Hier ist meine Platzreservierung. [hiɐ ˀɪst ˌmaɪnə ˈplatsʀezɐvi:ʀʊŋ]

May I open/shut the window?
Darf ich bitte das Fenster aufmachen/schließen?
[daf: ɪç ˈbɪtə das ˈfɛnstɐ ˈˀøfnən/ʃli:sn]

Tickets, please.
Die Fahrkarten, bitte. [di ˈfa:ka:tn ˈbɪtə]

➢ **also Plane**

arrival	die Ankunft [di ˈˀankʊnft]
baggage	das Gepäck [das geˈpɛk]
children's ticket	die Kinderfahrkarte [di ˈkɪndɐˈfa:ka:tə]
coach number	die Wagennummer [di ˈva:gŋnʊmɐ]
compartment	das Abteil [das ˀapˈtaɪl]
corridor	der Gang [dɐ gaŋ]
departure	die Abfahrt [di ˈˀapfa:t]

to get on	einsteigen [ˈˀaɪnʃtaɪgŋ]
to get off	aussteigen [ˈˀaʊʃtaɪgŋ]
guard/conductor	der Zugbegleiter/die Zugbegleiterin [dɐ ˈtsu:kbəˌglaɪtɐ/di ˈtsu:kbəˌglaɪtəʀɪn]
(left-luggage) locker	das Schließfach [das ˈʃli:sfax]
left-luggage office/ baggage deposit	die Gepäckaufbewahrung [di gəˈpɛkˌˀaʊfbəva:ʀʊŋ]
luggage	das Gepäck [das geˈpɛk]
luggage counter	der Gepäckschalter [dɐ gəˈpɛkʃaltɐ]
main station	der Hauptbahnhof [dɐ ˈhaʊptba:nho:f/ ˈhaʊpba:nof]
motorail train	der Autoreisezug [dɐ ˈˀaʊtoˌʀaɪzətsu:k]
no-smoking compartment	das Nichtraucherabteil [das ˈnɪçtʀaʊxɐˀapˌtaɪl]
open-plan carriage/ open seating area car	der Großraumwagen [dɐ ˈgʀo:sʀaʊmva:gŋ]
platform	das Gleis [das glaɪs]
railcard	die Bahncard [di ˈba:nka:t]
reduction	die Ermäßigung [di ɐˈmɛ:sɪgʊŋ]
reservation	die Reservierung [di ʀezɐˈvi:ʀʊŋ]
restaurant car	der Speisewagen [dɐ ˈʃpaɪzəva:gŋ]
return ticket/round-trip	die Rückfahrkarte [di ˈʀʏkfa:ˌka:tə]
seat reservation	die Platzreservierung [di ˈplatsʀezɐˌvi:ʀʊŋ]
severely handicapped person	der/die Schwerbehinderte [dɐ/di ˈʃveɐbəhɪndɐtə]
smoking compartment	das Raucherabteil [das ˈʀaʊxɐˀapˌtaɪl]
station	der Bahnhof [dɐ ˈba:nho:f]
stop	der Aufenthalt [dɐ ˈˀaʊfntalt]
supplementary charge	der Zuschlag [dɐ ˈtsu:ʃla:k]
ticket collector/conductor	der Schaffner/die Schaffnerin [dɐ ˈʃafnɐ/di ˈʃafnəʀɪn]
track	das Gleis [das glaɪs]
train fare	der Fahrpreis [dɐ ˈfa:pʀaɪs]
ticket	die Fahrkarte [di ˈfa:ka:tə]
ticket check/inspection	die Fahrkartenkontrolle [di ˈfa:ka:tnkɔnˌtʀɔlə]
ticket office	der Fahrkartenschalter [dɐ ˈfa:ka:tnˌʃaltɐ]
timetable	der Fahrplan [dɐ ˈfa:pla:n]
train	der Zug [dɐ tsu:k]
waiting room	der Wartesaal [dɐ ˈva:təza:l]
wheelchair user	der Rollstuhlfahrer/die Rollstuhlfahrerin [dɐ ˈʀɔlʃtu:lˌfa:ʀɐ/di ˈʀɔlʃtu:lˌfa:ʀəʀɪn]
window seat	der Fensterplatz [dɐ ˈfɛnstɐplats]

Ship

Information

Can you tell me when the next ship/ the next ferry leaves for ..., please?
Können Sie mir bitte sagen, wann das nächste Schiff/die nächste Fähre nach ... abfährt?
[kønn zi miɐ ˈbɪtə zaːgŋ van das ˈnɛːçstə ʃɪf/diː ˈnɛːçstə ˈfeːʀə … ˀapfeɐt]

How long does the crossing take?
Wie lange dauert die Überfahrt? [vi ˈlaŋə ˈdauɐt di ˈˀyːbɐfaːt]

When do we land at ...?
Wann legen wir in ... an? [van ˈlegŋ viɐ ˀɪn … an]

How long are we stopping at ...?
Wie lange haben wir in ... Aufenthalt?
[vi laŋə haːbm viɐ ˀɪn … ˈˀaʊfntalt]

I'd like ..., please.
Ich möchte bitte ... [ˀɪç ˈmøçtə ˈbɪtə]
a ticket to ...
eine Schiffskarte nach ... [ˈˀaɪnə ˈʃɪfskaːtə nax]
first class
erste Klasse [ˈˀeɐstə ˈklasə]
tourist class
Touristenklasse [tʊˈʀɪstnklasə]
a single cabin
eine Einzelkabine [ˈˀaɪntslkabiːnə]
a double cabin
eine Zweibettkabine [ˈtsvaɪbɛtkabiːnə]

I'd like a ticket for the round trip at ... o'clock.
Ich möchte eine Karte für die Rundfahrt um ... Uhr.
[ˀɪç ˈmøçtə ˈˀaɪnə ˈkaːtə fyɐ diː ˈʀʊntfaːt ˀʊm … ˀuɐ]

On board

I'm looking for cabin number ...
Ich suche Kabine Nr. ... [ˈˀɪç ˈzuːxə kaˈbiːnə ˈnʊmɐ]

Where's the restaurant/lounge, please?
Wo ist bitte der Speisesaal/der Aufenthaltsraum?
[voː ˀɪst ˈbɪtə dɐ ˈʃpaɪzəzaːl/dɐ ˈˀaʊfntaltsˌʀaʊm]

I don't feel well.
Ich fühle mich nicht wohl. [ˀɪç ˈfyːlə mɪç nɪçt voːl]

Could you call the ship's doctor, please.
Könnten Sie bitte den Schiffsarzt rufen?
[køntn zɪ bɪtə den ˈʃɪfsˀaːtst ʀuːfn]

Could you give me something for seasickness, please?
Könnten Sie mir bitte ein Mittel gegen Seekrankheit geben? [køntn zi miɐ ˈbɪtə ˀaɪn ˈmɪtl ge:gŋ ˈze:kʀaŋkaɪt ge:bm]

booking	die Buchung [di ˈbu:xʊŋ]
cabin	die Kabine [di kaˈbi:nə]
captain	der Kapitän [dɐ kapiˈtɛ:n]
car ferry	die Autofähre [di ˈˀaʊtofɛ:ʀə]
coast	die Küste [di ˈkʏstə]
deck	das Deck [das dɛk]
to dock at	anlegen in [ˈˀanle:gŋ ˀɪn]
excursion	der Landausflug [dɐ ˈlantˀaʊsflu:k]
ferry	die Fähre [di ˈfɛ:ʀə]
harbo(u)r	der Hafen [dɐ ˈha:fn]
hovercraft	das Luftkissenboot [das ˈlʊftkɪsnbo:t]
to land at	anlegen in [ˈˀanle:gŋ ˀɪn]
life jacket	die Schwimmweste [di ˈʃvɪmvɛstə]
life belt/life preserver	der Rettungsring [dɐ ˈʀɛtʊŋsʀɪŋ]
lifeboat	das Rettungsboot [das ˈʀɛtʊŋsbo:t]
port	der Hafen [dɐ ˈha:fn]
quay	der Kai [dɐ kaɪ]
round trip	die Rundfahrt [di ˈʀʊntfa:t]
seasick	seekrank [ˈze:kʀaŋk]
ticket	die Fahrkarte [di ˈfa:ka:tə]

Local transportation

Take advantage of the excellent public transportation found in Germany. There will often be different providers, one for say the city area, another for the surrounding area. These providers are usually integrated into a network, and you will be able to buy tickets valid for all vehicles. Ask for help if you're not sure. A good place to start is the local tourist office. Within a municipal area, you will find buses, trams/streetcars, and even a *U-Bahn* (underground/subway). Rural areas are almost always served by buses.

Normally, you can buy a ticket from the driver, but it may be cheaper to buy one from a vending machine. Multiple tickets, family tickets (*Familienkarte*) and day passes for all routes (*Netzkarte*) are usually available. Make sure the ticket has a date and time stamped on it, otherwise you will be expected to have it stamped by a separate machine, labelled *entwerten*. There are no longer conductors on German buses or trams, but you may run into a *Kontrolleur* (inspector) who fines people without valid stamped tickets.

Excuse me, where's the next ...
Bitte, wo ist die nächste ... ['bɪtə vo: ˀɪst di nəçstə ...]
bus stop?
Bushaltestelle? ['bʊshaltəʃtɛlə]
tram/streetcar stop?
Straßenbahnhaltestelle? ['ʃtʀa:snba:nˌhaltəʃtɛlə]
underground station?
U-Bahnstation? ['ˀu:ba:nʃtaˌtsjo:n]

Which line goes to ... ?
Welche Linie fährt nach ...? ['vɛlçə 'li:njə feɐt nax ...]

When's the last (underground/tube) train to ...?
Wann fährt die letzte U-Bahn nach ...?
['van feɐt di 'lɛtstə 'ˀu:ba:n nax]

Excuse me, does this bus go to ...?
Entschuldigen Sie, ist das der Bus nach ...?
[ˀɛnt'ʃʊldɪgŋ zi ˀɪst das dɐ bʊs nax]

How many stops is it?
Wie viele Haltestellen sind es? ['vi: fi:lə 'haltəʃtɛln ˌzɪnt əs]

Excuse me, where do I have to get out?
Entschuldigen Sie, wo muss ich aussteigen?
[ˀɛnt'ʃʊldɪgŋ zi vo: mʊs ɪç 'ˀaʊʃtaɪgŋ]

Excuse me, will I have to change?
Entschuldigen Sie, muss ich umsteigen?
[ˀɛnt'ʃʊldɪgŋ zi mʊs ɪç 'ˀʊmʃtaɪgŋ]

Could you let me know when I have to get off, please?
Könnten Sie mir bitte Bescheid geben, wann ich aussteigen muss?
[køntn zi miɐ 'bɪtə bə'ʃaɪt ge:bm vɛn ɪç 'ˀaʊʃtaɪgŋ mʊs]

A ticket to ..., please.
Bitte, einen Fahrschein nach ... ['bɪtə ˀaɪnn 'fa:ʃaɪn nax]

The ticket machine is bust/broken.
Der Fahrkartenautomat ist kaputt/defekt.
[dɐ 'fa:ka:tnˀaʊtoˌma:t ˀɪst ka'pʊt/de'fɛkt]

The machine doesn't accept notes.
Der Automat nimmt keine Geldscheine an.
[dɐ ˀaʊto'ma:t nɪmt 'kaɪnə 'gɛltʃaɪnə ˀan]

bus	der Bus [dɐ bʊs]
bus station	der Busbahnhof [dɐ 'bʊsˌba:nho:f]
departure	die Abfahrt [di 'ˀapfa:t]
direction	die Richtung [di 'ʀɪçtʊŋ]
fare	der Fahrpreis [dɐ 'fa:pʀaɪs]
to get on	einsteigen ['ˀaɪnʃtaɪgŋ]

inspector	der Kontrolleur [dɐ kɔntʀoˈløɐ]
local train	der Nahverkehrszug [dɐ ˈnaːfɐˌkeɐstsuːk]
day ticket (pass)	die Tageskarte [di ˈtaːgəskaːtə]
rack-railway/cable car	die Zahnradbahn [di ˈtsaːnʀatˌbaːn]
stop	die Haltestelle [di ˈhaltəʃtɛlə]
suburban train	die S-Bahn [di ˈɛsbaːn]
terminus	die Endstation [di ˈʔɛntʃtatsjoːn]
ticket	der Fahrschein [dɐ ˈfaːʃaɪn]
conductor/ ticket collector	der Schaffner [dɐ ˈʃafnɐ]
ticket machine	der Fahrkartenautomat [dɐ ˈfaːkaːtnʔaʊtoˌmaːt]
timetable	der Fahrplan [dɐ ˈfaːplaːn]
tram/streetcar	die Straßenbahn [di ˈʃtʀaːsnbaːn]
underground/subway *(US)*	die U-Bahn [di ˈʔuːbaːn]
weekly season ticket/ one-week pass	die Wochenkarte [di ˈvɔxnkaːtə]

Taxi

Hello. Could you please send a taxi/cab to the following address ... as soon as possible/tomorrow at ... o'clock?
Hallo! Bitte ein Taxi an die Adresse ... für jetzt gleich/für (morgen) ... Uhr. [ˈhaloː – ˈbɪtə ʔaɪn ˈtaksi ʔan di ʔaˈdʁɛsə … fyɐ ˈjɛtst/ˈglaɪç/fyɐ (ˈmɔɐgŋ) … ˈʔuɐ]

Excuse me, where's the nearest taxi rank/stand?
Entschuldigen Sie bitte, wo ist der nächste Taxistand?
[ʔɛntˈʃʊldɪgŋ zi ˈbɪtə ˈvoː ʔɪst dɐ ˈnɛːçstə ˈtaksiʃtant]

To the station, please.
Zum Bahnhof, bitte. [tsʊm ˈbaːnhoːf ˈbɪtə]

To the ... Hotel, please.
Zum ... Hotel, bitte. [tsʊm … hoˈtɛl ˈbɪtə]

To ... Street, please.
In die ...-Straße, bitte. [ʔɪn di … ˌʃtʀaːsə ˈbɪtə]

To *(name of a town)*..., please.
Nach ..., bitte. [nax … ˈbɪtə]

How much will it cost to ...?
Wie viel kostet es nach ...? [ˈviː fil ˈkɔstət əs nax]

That's too much.
Das ist zu viel. [das ɪst tsʊ ˈfiːl]

Could you stop here, please?
Halten Sie bitte hier. [ˈhaltn zi ˈbɪtə hiɐ]

Could you write me a receipt?
Könnten Sie mir bitte eine Quittung ausstellen?
[ˈkœntn zi miɐ ˈbɪtə ˀaɪnə ˈkvɪtʊŋ ˈˀaʊʃtɛln]

That's for you.
Das ist für Sie. [das ˀɪst fyɐ ˈzi:]

Keep the change.
Behalten Sie das Restgeld. [bəˈhaltn zi das ˈʀɛstgɛlt]

fasten one's seat belt	anschnallen [ˈˀanʃnaln]
flat rate	der Pauschalpreis [dɐ paʊˈʃa:lpʀaɪs]
house number	die Hausnummer [di ˈhaʊsnʊmɐ]
price per kilometre	der Kilometerpreis [dɐ kiloˈme:tɐpʀaɪs]
receipt	die Quittung [di ˈkvɪtʊŋ]
seat belt	der Sicherheitsgurt [dɐ ˈzɪçɐhaɪtsˌgʊɐt]
to stop	anhalten [ˈˀanhaltn]
taxi rank/stand	der Taxistand [dɐ ˈtaksiˈʃtant]
taxi driver	der Taxifahrer/die Taxifahrerin [dɐ ˈtaksifa:ʀɐ/di ˈtaksifa:ʀəʀɪn]
tip	das Trinkgeld [das ˈtʀɪŋk(g)ɛlt]

Travelling with children

Adequate facilities
If you are travelling with small children, you will find adequate facilities almost everywhere. Playgrounds are easy to find, the larger department stores usually have baby-care rooms, and almost all restaurants have highchairs for the asking. If you are driving, you will find resting areas at regular intervals along the autobahn with play areas and child-friendly restaurants.

Useful phrases

Could you tell me if there is a children's playground here, please?
Könnten Sie mir bitte sagen, ob es hier einen Kinderspielplatz gibt?
[kønn zi miɐ ˈbɪtə zaːgŋ ˀɔp əs hiɐ ˀaɪnn ˈkɪndɐʃpiːlplats gɪpt]

Is there a baby-sitting service here?
Gibt es hier eine Kinderbetreuung?
[gɪpt əs hiɐ ˌˀaɪnə ˈkɪndɐbətʀɔɪʊŋ]

From what age onward?
Ab welchem Alter? [ab ˈvɛlçm ˈˀaltɐ]

Do you know anyone who could baby-sit for us?
Kennen Sie jemanden, der bei uns babysitten kann?
[ˈkɛnn zi ˈjeːmandn dɐ baɪ ˀʊns ˈbeːbisɪtn kan]

Do you have a baby intercom?
Haben Sie ein Babyfon? [ˈhaːbm zi ˀaɪn ˈbeːbifoːn]

Is there a reduction for children?
Gibt es eine Ermäßigung für Kinder?
[gɪpt əs ˌˀaɪnə ˀɐˈmɛːsɪgʊŋ fyɐ ˈkɪndɐ]

On the road

We're travelling with a young child.
Wir reisen mit einem Kleinkind. [viɐ ˈʀaɪzn mɪt ˌˀaɪnəm ˈklaɪnkɪnt]

Can we get seats right at the front?
Können wir Plätze ganz vorn bekommen?
[kønn viɐ ˈplɛtsə gants ˈfɔɐn bəˈkɔmm]

Do you rent out child seats for the car?
Verleihen Sie Kinderautositze? [fɐˈlaɪn zi ˈkɪndɐˌˀaʊtozɪtsə]

Do you possibly have any crayons and a colouring book for our child?
Haben Sie vielleicht Stifte und ein Malbuch für unser Kind? [ˈhaːbm zi fɪˈlaɪçt ʃtɪftə ˀʊnt aɪn ˈmaːlbuːx fyɐ ˀʊnsɐ ˈkɪnt]

At the restaurant

Could you bring us a highchair, please?
Könnten Sie bitte noch einen Kinderstuhl bringen?
[køntn zi ˈbɪtə nɔx ʔaɪnn ˈkɪndɐʃtuːl bʀɪŋŋ]

Do you also have children's portions?
Gibt es auch Kinderportionen? [gɪpt əs aʊx ˈkɪndɐpɔˈtsjoːnn]

Could you warm up the baby bottle, please?
Könnten Sie mir bitte das Fläschchen warm machen?
[ˈkøntn zi miɐ ˈbɪtə das ˈflɛʃçn vaːm maxn]

Could you tell me where I can breast-feed my baby?
Könnten Sie mir bitte sagen, wo ich hier stillen kann?
[køntn zi miɐ ˈbɪtə zaːgŋ voː ɪç hiɐ ˈʃtɪln kan]

adventure playground	der Abenteuerspielplatz [dɐ ˈaːbmtɔɪɐˌʃpiːlplats]
baby food	die Kindernahrung [di ˈkɪndɐnaːʀʊŋ]
baby intercom	das Babyfon [das ˈbeːbifoːn]
baby seat	die Babyschale [di ˈbeːbiʃaːlə]
baby's bottle	die Trinkflasche [di ˈtʀɪŋkflaʃə]
baby's changing table	der Wickeltisch [dɐ ˈvɪkltɪʃ]
baby-sitter	der Babysitter [dɐ ˈbeːbisɪtɐ]
baby-sitting service	die Kinderbetreuung [di ˈkɪndɐbətʀɔjʊŋ]
baby bonnet	die Schildmütze [di ˈʃɪltmʏtsə]
baby carriage *(US)*	der Kinderwagen [dɐ ˈkɪndɐvaːgŋ]
child reduction	die Kinderermäßigung [di ˈkɪndɐʔɐˈmɛːsɪgʊŋ]
child seat	der Kindersitz [dɐ ˈkɪndɐzɪts]
child seat cushion	das Kindersitzkissen [das ˈkɪndɐzɪtskɪsn]
children's bed	das Kinderbett [das ˈkɪndɐbɛt]
children's clothing	die Kinderkleidung [di ˈkɪndɐklaɪdʊŋ]
children's club	der Miniclub [dɐ ˈmɪniklʊp]
children's playground	der Kinderspielplatz [dɐ ˈkɪndɐʃpiːlplats]
children's pool	das Kinderbecken [das ˈkɪndɐbɛkŋ]
colouring book	das Malbuch [das ˈmaːlbuːx]
cot	das Kinderbett [das ˈkɪndɐbɛt]
diapers *(US)*	die Windeln *f pl* [di vɪndln]
dummy	der Schnuller [dɐ ˈʃnʊlɐ]
feeding bottle	die Saugflasche [di ˈzaʊkflaʃə]
highchair	der Kinderstuhl [dɐ ˈkɪndɐʃtuːl]
insect repellant	der Mückenschutz [dɐ ˈmʏkŋʃʊts]
nappies	die Windeln *f pl* [di vɪndln]
pacifier *(US)*	der Schnuller [dɐ ˈʃnʊlɐ]
paddling pool	das Planschbecken [das ˈplanʃbɛkn]

protection against sun	der Sonnenschutz [dɐ ˈzɔnnʃʊts]
rubber ring	der Schwimmring [dɐ ˈʃvɪmʀɪŋ]
sand-castle	die Sandburg [di ˈzantbuɐk]
swimming lessons	der Schwimmkurs [dɐ ˈʃvɪmkuɐs]
teat	der Sauger [dɐ ˈzaʊgɐ]
toys	die Spielsachen *f pl* [di ˈʃpi:l za:xn]
water wings	die Schwimmflügel *m pl* [di ˈʃvɪmfly:gl]

Health

Could you tell me if there's a pediatrician here?
Könnten Sie mir bitte sagen, ob es hier einen Kinderarzt gibt? [køntn zi miɐ ˈbɪtə za:gŋ ˈɔp əs hiɐ ˀaɪnn ˈkɪndɐˀa:tst gɪpt]

My child has ...
Mein Kind hat ... [maɪn ˈkɪnt hat]

My child is allergic to ...
Mein Kind ist allergisch gegen ... [maɪn ˈkɪnt ɪst ˀaˈlɛɐgɪʃ ge:gŋ ...]

He/She has been sick.
Er/Sie hat erbrochen. [ˀeɐ/zi hat ˀɐˈbʀɔxn]

He/She has (got) diarrhoea.
Er/Sie hat Durchfall. [ˀeɐ/zi hat ˈdʊɐçfal]

He/She has been stung.
Er/Sie ist gestochen worden. [ˀeɐ/zi ɪst gəˈʃtɔxn vɔɐdn]

allergy	die Allergie [di ˀal(ɛ)ɐˈgi:]
chickenpox	die Windpocken *f pl* [di ˈvɪntpɔkŋ]
children's illness	die Kinderkrankheit [di ˈkɪndɐˌkʀaŋkhaɪt]
cold	die Erkältung [di ˀɐˈkɛltʊŋ] , der Schnupfen [dɐ ʃnʊpfn]
fever	das Fieber [das ˈfi:bɐ]
fungal infection	der Pilz [dɐ pɪlts]
German measles	die Röteln *f pl* [di ʀø:tln]
inflammation of the middle ear	die Mittelohrentzündung [di ˈmɪtlˀoɐˀɛnˌtsʏndʊŋ]
insect bite	der Insektenstich [dɐ ˀɪnˈzɛktnʃtɪç]
measles	die Masern *f pl* [ˈma:zɐn]
medicinal food	die Heilnahrung [di ˈhaɪlna:ʀʊŋ]
mumps	der Mumps [dɐ mʊmps]
pediatric clinic	das Kinderkrankenhaus [das ˈkɪndɐˌkʀaŋknhaʊs]
rash	der Ausschlag [dɐ ˈˀaʊʃla:k]
scarlet fever	der Scharlach [dɐ ˈʃa:lax]
temperature	das Fieber [das ˈfi:bɐ]
vaccination card	der Impfpass [dɐ ˈˀɪm(p)fpas]
wind	die Blähungen *f pl* [di ˈblɛ:ʊŋŋ]

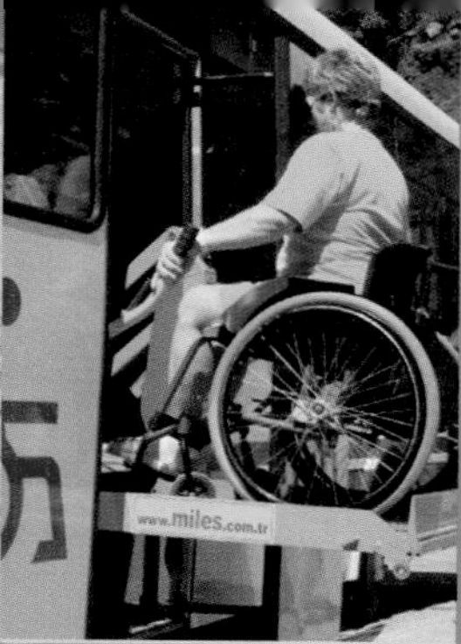

Disabled travellers

Problematical buildings, helpful people
Although most German cities are trying very hard to improve conditions, disabled people will encounter a number of problems. Historical sections of towns present obvious problems such as narrow streets with cobblestones. Older buildings usually have steps, and even if you get in, there may not be a lift for going up inside. Much work has been done in larger cities to level curbs and make public transportation accessible. Large department stores are almost always accessible and have suitable toilet facilities. It is possible to travel by train, but wheelchair users should try to travel by *IC* or *ICE* (express) trains and avoid older passenger trains marked *E-Zug* or those printed in black on schedules. Larger hotels and modern restaurants are usually fully prepared for the disabled. Information will be essential, so the tourist information office should be one of your first stops. Ask if there is a *Stadtführer für Behinderte*, a guide to the city for the disabled. Most people are very willing to help if you run into trouble.
Expert information on how to travel without barriers is also available free of charge from the German Self-help for the Disabled Association. (E-mail: **Reiseservice@bsk-ev.org**; Internet: **www.bsk-ev.org**).

I have a disability.
Ich habe eine Behinderung. [ˀɪç ˈhaːbə ˀaɪnə bəˈhɪndəʀʊŋ]

I'm ...
Ich bin ... [ˀɪç bɪn ...]
a paraplegic.
querschnittsgelähmt. [ˈkveɐʃnɪtsgəlɛːmt]
partially sighted/visually impaired.
sehbehindert. [ˈzeːbəhɪndɐt]

I have ...
Ich habe ... [ˀɪç ˈhaːbə]
a physical handicap.
eine körperliche Behinderung. [ˀaɪnə ˈkøɐpɐlɪçə bəˈhɪndəʀʊŋ]
multiple sclerosis.
Multiple Sklerose. [mʊlˈtiːplə skleˈʀoːzə]

Can you help me ...
Können Sie mir helfen, ... [ˈkønn zi mɪɐ hɛlfn]
to cross this street.
die Straße zu überqueren. [di ˈʃtʀaːsə tsʊ ˀybɐˈkveɐn]
to get into the bus.
in den Bus zu kommen. [ɪn den bʊs tsʊ kɔmm]

Can you help me up these steps?
Können Sie mir helfen, die Treppen hinaufzukommen?
[ˈkønn zi mɪr hɛlfn di tʀɛpm hɪnˈaʊftsʊkɔmm]

We have to go up backwards.
Wir müssen rückwärts hinauf. [viɐ mʏsn ˈʀʏkvɛɐts hɪnˈaʊf]

We'll need one more person to help.
Wir brauchen noch jemanden, der hilft.
[viɐ bʀaʊxn nɔx ˈjeːmandn deɐ hɪlft]

Tilt the wheelchair back first.
Zuerst den Rollstuhl kippen. [tsuˈʔeɐst den ˈʀɔlʃtuːl kɪpm]

Could you put the wheelchair in the back of the car?
Könnten Sie den Rollstuhl hinten ins Auto stellen?
[ˈkøntn zi den ˈʀɔlʃtuːl ˈhɪntn ɪns ˈʔaʊto ˈʃtɛln]

Do you have a bathroom/a toilet for disabled people?
Haben Sie ein Bad/eine Toilette für Behinderte?
[ˈhaːbm zi ʔaɪn baːt/ʔaɪnə toˈlɛtə fyɐ bəˈhɪndɐtə]

Getting around

Can I take a folding wheelchair with me on the plane?
Kann ich einen faltbaren Rollstuhl im Flugzeug mitnehmen?
[kan ɪç ʔaɪnn ˈfaltbaʀən ˈʀɔlʃtuːl ɪm ˈfluːktsɔɪk ˈmɪtneːmm]

Will a wheelchair be provided at the airport?
Wird ein Rollstuhl am Flughafen bereitgestellt?
[vɪɐd ʔaɪn ˈʀɔlʃtuːl am ˈfluːkhaːfn bəˈʀaɪtgəʃtɛlt]

I'd like an aisle seat.
Ich möchte einen Sitz am Gang. [ʔɪç ˈmøçtə ʔaɪnn zɪts am ˈgaŋ]

Is there a toilet for the disabled?
Gibt es eine Behindertentoilette? [gɪpt əs ʔaɪnə bəˈhɪndɐtntoˈlɛtə]

Is there a washroom for the disabled?
Gibt es einen Behindertenwaschraum?
[gɪpt əs ʔaɪnn bəˈhɪndɐtnˌvaʃʀaʊm]

Could someone help me change trains?
Könnte mir jemand beim Umsteigen behilflich sein?
[ˈkøntə miɐ ˈjeːmant baɪm ˈʔʊmʃtaɪgŋ bəˈhɪlflɪç zaɪn]

Is the entrance to the carriage at ground level?
Ist der Einstieg in den Wagen ebenerdig?
[ʔɪst dɐ ˈʔaɪnʃtiːk ɪn den vaːgŋ ˈʔeːbmʔɛɐdɪç]

Are there low-floor buses?
Gibt es Niederflurbusse? [gɪpt əs ˈniːdɐfluɐˌbʊsə]

Are there ramps to the platforms for wheelchair users?
Gibt es Rampen zu den Bahnsteigen für Rollstuhlfahrer?
[gɪpt əs ˈʀampm tsʊ den ˈbaːnʃtaɪgŋ fyɐ ˈʀɔlʃtuːlˌfaːʀɐ]

Are there rental cars with hand controls for the disabled?
Gibt es für Körperbehinderte Leihwagen mit Handbetrieb?
[gɪpt əs fyɐ ˈkøɐpɐbəˌhɪndɐtə ˈlaɪvaːgŋ mɪt ˈhantbətʀiːb]

Do you rent camper vans suitable for wheelchair users?
Vermieten Sie rollstuhlgerechte Wohnmobile?
[fɐˈmiːtn zi ˈʀɔlʃtuːlgəˌʀɛçtə ˈvoːnmobiːlə]

Is it possible to rent handbikes here?
Kann man hier Handbikes leihen? [kan man hiɐ ˈhɛntbaɪks laɪn]

Accommodation

Do you have information about hotels suitable for wheelchair users?
Haben Sie Informationen über Hotels, die für Rollstuhlfahrer geeignet sind? [ˈhaːbm zi ɪnfɔmaˈtsjoːnn ˀybɐ hoˈtɛls di fyɐ ˈʀɔlʃtuːlˌfaːʀɐ gəˈˀaɪknət zɪnt]

What hotels can you recommend for disabled people?
Welche Hotels können Sie Behinderten empfehlen?
[ˈvɛlçə hoˈtɛls ˈkønn zi bəˈhɪndɐtn ˀɛmˈpfeːln]

Could you tell me which hotels and camping sites have special facilities for the disabled?
Könnten Sie mir bitte sagen, welche Hotels und Campingplätze behindertengerechte Einrichtungen haben?
[køntn zi miɐ ˈbɪtə zaːgŋ ˈvɛlçə hoˈtɛls ʊnt ˈkɛmpɪŋplɛtsə bəˈhɪndɐtngəˌʀɛçtə ˈˀaɪnʀɪçtʊŋŋ haːbm]

Museums, sights, theatre ...

Is there a lift to the exhibition?
Gibt es einen Aufzug zu der Ausstellung?
[gɪpt əs ˀaɪnn ˈˀaʊftsuːk tsʊ dɐ ˈˀaʊʃtɛlʊŋ]

I'm a wheelchair user. How do I get up there?
Ich bin Rollstuhlfahrer. Wie komme ich da hoch?
[ˀɪç bɪn ˈʀɔlʃtuːlˌfaːʀɐ viː ˈkɔmə ˀɪç da ˈhoːx]

Are there guided tours (of the city) for the disabled?
Gibt es (Stadt)führungen für Behinderte?
[gɪpt əs (ˈʃtat)ˌfyːʀʊŋŋ fyɐ bəˈhɪndɐtə]

Do you have an induction loop?
Haben Sie eine Induktionsschleife?
[ˈhaːbn zi ˀaɪnə ˀɪndʊkˈtsjoːnsˌʃlaɪfə]

Are there museum tours for the blind?
Gibt es Museumsführungen für Blinde?
[gɪpt əs muˈzeʊmsˌfyːʀʊŋŋ fyɐ ˈblɪndə]

access	der Zugang [dɐ ˈtsu:gaŋ]
accessible	zugänglich [ˈtsu:gɛŋlɪç]
accompanying person	die Begleitperson [di bəˈglaɪtp(ɛ)ɐˌzo:n]
aid to walking	die Gehhilfe [di ˈge:hɪlfə]
amputated	amputiert [ampuˈtiɐt]
at ground level	ebenerdig [ˈˀe:bmˀeɐdɪç]
blind	blind [blɪnt]
blind person	der Blinde [dɐ ˈblɪnde]
braille	die Blindenschrift [di ˈblɪndnʃʀɪft]
cane	der Taststock [dɐ ˈtastʃtɔk]
care	die Betreuung [di bəˈtʀɔɪʊŋ]
crutch	die Krücke [di ˈkrʏkə]
deaf	gehörlos [gəˈhøɐlo:s]/taub [taʊp]
deaf person	der/die Gehörlose [dɐ/dɪ gəˈhøɐlo:zə]
deaf-mute	taubstumm [ˈtaʊpʃtʊm]
deaf-mute (person)	der/die Taubstumme [dɐ/dɪ ˈtaʊpʃtʊmə]
disability	die Behinderung [di bəˈhɪndəʀʊŋ]
disabled	behindert [bəˈhɪndɐt]
disabled person	der/die Behinderte [dɐ/dɪ bəˈhɪndɐtə]
disability identification	der Behindertenausweis [dɐ bəˈhɪndɐtnˈˀaʊsvaɪs]
door opener	der Türöffner [dɐ ˈtyɐˀøfnɐ]
door width	die Türbreite [di ˈtyɐbʀaɪtə]
doorstep	die Türschwelle [di ˈtyɐʃvɛlə]
elevator	der Lift [dɐ lɪft]
epilepsy	die Epilepsie [di epilɛpˈsi]
good clearance	unterfahrbar [ˈʊntɐfa:ba:]
gradient	die Steigung [di ˈʃtaɪgʊŋ]
guide dog	der Blindenhund [dɐ ˈblɪndnhʊnt]
hall width	die Flurbreite [di ˈfluɐbʀaitə]
hand throttle (*car*)	das Handgas [das ˈhantga:s]
hand-operated bike	das Handbike [das ˈhɛntbaɪk]
handicap	die Behinderung [di bəˈhɪndəʀʊŋ]
handle	der Haltegriff [dɐ ˈhaltəgʀɪf]
handrail	der Handlauf [dɐ ˈhantlaʊf]
hard of hearing	schwerhörig [ˈʃveɐhø:ʀɪç]
headphones	der Kopfhörer [dɐ ˈkɔpfhø:ʀɐ]
height	die Höhe [di hø:ə]
hydraulic ramp	die Hebebühne [di ˈhe:bəby:nə]
induction loop	die Induktionsschleife [di ɪndʊkˈtsjo:nˌʃlaɪfə]
in need of care	pflegebedürftig [ˈpfle:gəbədʏɐftɪç]
keyboard telephone	das Schreibtelefon [das ˈʃʀaɪpteləfo:n]
lift	der Lift [dɐ lɪft]
mentally handicapped	geistig behindert [ˈgaɪstɪç bəˈhɪndɐt]
mute	stumm [ʃtʊm]
out-patient	ambulant [ambʊˈlant]

paraplegic, quadriplegic	querschnittsgelähmt [ˈkveɐʃnɪtsgəˌlɛːmt]
parking space for disabled	der Behindertenparkplatz [der bəˈhɪndɐtnpaːkplats]
partially sighted	sehbehindert [ˈseːbəhɪndɐt]
passable	befahrbar [bəˈfaːbaː]
ramp	die Rampe [di ˈʀampə]
seeing-eye dog *(US)*	der Blindenhund [dɐ ˈblɪndnhʊnt]
self-opening door	die automatische Tür [di ˀaʊtoˈmaːtɪʃə tyɐ]
steering knob	der Lenkrad-Drehknopf [dɐ ˈlɛŋkʀatˌdʀeːknɔpf]
shower seat	der Duschsitz [dɐ ˈduːʃzɪts]
sign language	die Zeichensprache [di ˈtsaɪçnʃpʀaːxə]
step	die Stufe [di ˈʃtuːfə]
stairs	die Treppen *f pl* [di tʀɛpm]
suitable for the disabled	behindertengerecht [bəˈhɪndɐtngəˌʀɛçt]
suitable for wheelchair users	rollstuhlgerecht [ˈʀɔlʃtuːlgəˌʀɛçt]
toilet for the disabled	die Behindertentoilette [di bəˈhɪndɐtntoˌlɛtə]
transport service	das Fahrdienst [das ˈfaːdiːnst]
visually impaired	sehbehindert [ˈseːbəhɪndɐt]
wheelchair	der Rollstuhl [dɐ ˈʀɔlʃtuːl]
battery-driven	batteriebetrieben [batəˈʀiː bəˈtʀiːbm]
electric wheelchair	der E-Rollstuhl [dɐ ˈˀeːˌʀɔlʃtuːl]
folding wheelchair	der Faltrollstuhl [dɐ ˈfaltˌʀɔlʃtuːl]
wheelchair cabin *(ship)*	die Rollstuhlkabine [di ˈʀɔlʃtuːlkaˌbiːnə]
wheelchair hiking	das Rollstuhlwandern [das ˈʀɔlʃtuːlˌvandɐn]
wheelchair user *(man)*	der Rollstuhlfahrer [dɐ ˈʀɔlʃtuːlˌfaːʀɐ]
wheelchair user *(woman)*	die Rollstuhlfahrerin [di ˈʀɔlʃtuːlˌfaːʀəʀɪn]
width	die Breite [di ˈbʀaɪtə]

Accommodation

A good night's sleep
Finding a place to stay is easy enough in Germany. If you want to save money or get more of a "German feel" to your stay, time your overnight stops so you'll be in smaller towns or even rural areas. Hotels, especially in cities, are international in character. *Gasthaus* means basically a small hotel and will be more local in character. *Gasthof* is about the same thing, but in a rural area. A *Pension* is a bed-and-breakfast place, often your best value, and usually the most personal in character. *Hotel Garni* means they only serve breakfast. *Fremdenzimmer* means accommodation in a private house. Look for the sign *Zimmer frei* (vacancies).

Information

Can you recommend ..., please?
Können Sie mir bitte ... empfehlen?
[ˈkønn zi miɐ ˈbɪtə … ʔɛmˈpfeːln]
a good hotel
ein gutes Hotel [ʔaɪn ˈguːtəs hoˈtɛl]
a simple hotel
ein einfaches Hotel [ʔaɪn ˈʔaɪnfaxəs hoˈtɛl]
a bed-and-breakfast
eine Pension [ˈʔaɪnə paŋˈzjoːn]

Is it central/quiet/near the beach?
Ist es zentral/ruhig/in Strandnähe gelegen?
[ʔɪst əs tsɛnˈtʀaːl/ʀʊɪç/ʔɪn ˈʃtʀantnɛːə gəˈleːgŋ]

Is there ... here too?
Gibt es hier auch ... [gɪpt əs hiɐ ʔaʊx]
a youth hostel
eine Jugendherberge? [ˈʔaɪnə ˈjuːgŋthɛɐˌbɛɐgə]
a camping site
einen Campingplatz? [ʔaɪnn ˈkɛmpɪŋplats]

At the hotel

At the reception desk

I've reserved a room. My name's ...
Ich habe ein Zimmer reserviert. Mein Name ist ...
[ʔɪç ˈhaːbə aɪn ˈtsɪmɐ ʀezɐˈviɐt maɪn ˈnaːmə ʔɪst …]

We have a reservation.
Wir haben reserviert. [viɐ ˈhaːbm ʁezɐˈviɐt]

Have you got any vacancies?
Haben Sie noch Zimmer frei? [ˈha:bm zi nɔx ˈtsɪmɐ fʀaɪ]
... for one night
... für eine Nacht [... fyɐ ˈʔaɪnə naxt]
... for two days
... für zwei Tage [... fyɐ tsvaɪ ˈta:gə]
... for a week
... für eine Woche [... fyɐ ˈʔaɪnə ˈvɔxə]

Do you have family rooms?
Haben Sie Familienzimmer? [ˈha:bm zi: faˈmi:ljənˌtsɪmɐ]

No, I'm afraid not.
Nein, leider nicht. [naɪn ˈlaɪdɐ ˈnɪçt]

Yes, what sort of room would you like?
Ja, was für ein Zimmer wünschen Sie?
[ja: vas fyɐ ʔaɪn ˈtsɪmɐ ˈvʏnʃn zi:]

I'd like ...
Ich hätte gern ... [ʔɪç ˈhɛtə gɛɐn]
a single room
ein Einzelzimmer [ʔaɪn ˈʔaɪntsltsɪmɐ]
a double room
ein Doppelzimmer [ʔaɪn ˈdɔpltsɪmɐ]
a quiet room
ein ruhiges Zimmer [ʔaɪn ˈʀʊɪgəs ˈtsɪmɐ]
with a shower
mit Dusche [mɪt ˈdu:ʃə]
with a bath
mit Bad [mɪt ba:t]
with a balcony/terrace
mit Balkon/Terrasse [mɪt balˈkɔŋ/teˈʀasə]
with a view of the mountains
mit Blick auf die Berge [mɪt blɪk aʊf di ˈbɛɐgə]

Can I see the room?
Kann ich das Zimmer ansehen? [kan ɪç das ˈtsɪmɐ ˈʔanze:n]

Can I see a different one, please.
Kann ich bitte noch ein anderes sehen?
[kan ɪç ˈbɪtə nɔx aɪn ˈʔandəʀəs ze:n]

I'll take this room.
Dieses Zimmer nehme ich. [ˈdi:zəs ˈtsɪmɐ ˈne:mə ɪç]

Can you put a third bed/a cot in the room?
Können Sie noch ein drittes Bett/ein Kinderbett dazustellen?
[ˈkønn zi nɔx aɪn bɛt/aɪn ˈkɪndɐbɛt daˈtsu:ʃtɛln]

Beds usually have a duvet/comforter instead of a top sheet and blankets. There will be an extra blanket in the wardrobe/cabinet. In most hotels in Germany, Austria and Switzerland, a double room will have one large bed - but with two single mattresses! If you and your partner wish to avoid having a 'canyon' between the mattresses, ask specifically for a room with a king-size bed (*ein französchisches Bett* [ˀaɪn fʁanˈtsøːzɪʃəs bɛt]) when making your reservation or when checking in. Don't expect to find tea or coffee-making facilities in the room.

How much is the room with ...
Was kostet das Zimmer mit ..., bitte?
[vas ˈkɔstət das ˈtsɪmɐ mɪt ... bɪtə]

breakfast?
Frühstück [ˈfʀyːʃtʏk]
half-board (breakfast and dinner)?
Halbpension [ˈhalpaŋzjoːn]
full board (all meals)?
Vollpension [ˈfɔlpaŋzjoːn]

Could you fill out the registration form, please?
Wollen Sie bitte den Anmeldeschein ausfüllen?
[vɔln zi ˈbɪtə den ˈˀanmɛldəʃaɪn ˈˀaʊsfʏln]

May I see your passport?
Darf ich Ihren Ausweis sehen? [daːf ɪç ˈiːʀən/ˀiɐn ˈˀaʊsvaɪs zeːn]

Where can I park the car?
Wo kann ich den Wagen abstellen? [voː kan ɪç den ˈvaːgŋ ˈˀapʃtɛln]

In our garage.
In unserer Garage. [ˀɪn ˌʊnzəʀɐ gaˈʀaːʒə]
In our car park.
Auf unserem Parkplatz. [ˀaʊf ˌʊnzɐm ˈpaːkplats]

Asking for service

➣ **also Breakfast**

When is breakfast served?
Ab wann gibt es Frühstück? [ˀap ˈvan gɪpt əs ˈfʀyːʃtʏk]

When are the meals served?
Wann sind die Essenszeiten? [van zɪnt die ˈˀɛsnstsaɪtn]

Where's the restaurant?
Wo ist der Speisesaal? [voː ˀɪst dɐ ˈʃpaɪzəzaːl]

Where's the breakfast room?
Wo ist der Frühstücksraum? [voː ˀɪst dɐ ˈfʀyːʃtʏksʀaʊm]

Could you wake me at seven o'clock tomorrow morning, please.
Könnten Sie mich bitte morgen früh um sieben Uhr wecken? [køntn zi mɪç ˈbɪtə ˈmɔɐgŋ fʀʏ: ʊm ˈzi:bm ˀuɐ ˈvɛkŋ]

How does ... work?
Wie funktioniert ...? [vi: fʊŋktsjoˈniɐt]

Room 24 please!
Zimmernummer vierundzwanzig, bitte!
[ˈtsɪmɐnʊmɐ ˈfiɐ(ʊ)nˈtsvantsɪç ˈbɪtə]

Is there any post/mail for me?
Ist Post für mich da? [ˀɪst pɔst fyɐ mɪç da:]

Where can I ...
Wo kann ich ... [vo: kan ɪç]
get something to drink?
hier etwas trinken? [hiɐ ˌˀɛtvas ˈtʀɪŋkŋ]
hire a car?
ein Auto mieten? [ˀaɪn ˈˀaʊto mi:tn]
telephone from (here)?
hier telefonieren? [hiɐ teləfoˈni:ʀən/-ˈniɐn]

Can I leave my valuables in your safe?
Kann ich meine Wertsachen bei Ihnen in den Safe geben?
[kan ɪç ˌmaɪnə ˈveɐtzaxn baɪ ˀi:nn ˀɪn den ˈsɛɪf/se:f ge:bm]

Can I leave my luggage here?
Kann ich mein Gepäck hier lassen? [kan ɪç maɪn gəˈpɛk ˈhiɐ lasn]

Complaints

The room hasn't been cleaned today.
Das Zimmer ist heute nicht geputzt worden.
[das ˈtsɪmɐ ˀɪst ˈhɔɪtə nɪçt gəˈpʊtst vɔɐdn]

The air-conditioning doesn't work.
Die Klimaanlage funktioniert nicht.
[di ˈkli:maˀanˌla:gə fʊŋktsjoˈniɐt nɪçt]

The tap/faucet drips.
Der Wasserhahn tropft. [dɐ ˈvasɐha:n tʀɔpft]

There's no (hot) water.
Es kommt kein (warmes) Wasser. [ˀəs kɔmt kaɪn (va:məs) ˈvasɐ]

The toilet/washbasin is blocked up.
Die Toilette/Das Waschbecken ist verstopft.
[di tɔ(ɪ)ˈlɛtə/das ˈvaʃbɛkŋ ˀɪst fɐˈʃtɔpft]

I'd like to have a different room.
Ich hätte gern ein anderes Zimmer.
[ˀɪç ˈhɛtə gɛɐn ˀaɪn ˈˀandəʀəs ˈtsɪmɐ]

Departure

I'm leaving tomorrow at ... o'clock.
Ich reise morgen um ... Uhr ab. [ˀɪç ˈʀaɪzə mɔɐgŋ ʊm ... ˀuɐ ˈˀap]

I'd like my bill, please.
Könnten Sie bitte die Rechnung fertig machen?
[køntn zi ˈbɪtə di ˈʀɛçnʊŋ ˈfɛɐtiç maxn]

Can I pay by credit card?
Kann ich mit Kreditkarte bezahlen?
[ˈkan ɪç mɪt kʀeˈdiːtˌkaːtə bəˈtsaːln]

Would you call a taxi for me, please.
Könnten Sie mir bitte ein Taxi rufen?
[køntn zi miɐ ˈbɪtə ˀaɪn ˈtaksi ʀuːfn]

Thank you very much for everything. Goodbye!
Vielen Dank für alles! Auf Wiedersehen!
[ˈfiːln daŋk fyɐ ˈˀaləs ˀaʊf ˈviːdɐzeːn]

adapter	der Zwischenstecker [dɐ ˈtsvɪʃnʃtɛkɐ]
air-conditioning	die Klimaanlage [di ˈkliːmɐˀanˌlaːgə]
ashtray	der Aschenbecher [dɐ ˈˀaʃnbɛçɐ]
balcony	der Balkon [dɐ balˈkɔŋ]
bath	die Badewanne [di ˈbaːdəvanə]
bathroom	das Badezimmer [das ˈbaːdətsɪmɐ]
bath towel	das Badetuch [das ˈbaːdətuːx]
bed	das Bett [das bɛt]
bed linen	die Bettwäsche [di ˈbɛtvɛʃə]
bedside table	der Nachttisch [dɐ ˈnaxttɪʃ]
bidet	das Bidet [das biˈdeː]
bin	der Abfalleimer [dɐ ˈˀapfalˌˀaɪmɐ]
blanket	die Bettdecke [di ˈbɛtdɛkə]
breakfast	das Frühstück [das ˈfʀyːʃtʏk]
breakfast room	der Frühstücksraum [dɐ ˈfʀyːʃtʏksʀaʊm]
buffet breakfast	das Frühstücksbüfett [das ˈfʀyːʃtʏksbʏˌfeː]
chair	der Stuhl [dɐ ˈʃtuːl]
to clean	reinigen [ˈʀaɪnɪgŋ]
clothes closet/cabinet	der Kleiderschrank [dɐ ˈklaɪdɐʃʀaŋk]
coat hanger	der Kleiderbügel [dɐ ˈklaɪdɐbyːgl]

cover/place (for breakfast)	das Gedeck (für das Frühstück) [das gəˈdɛk fyɐ (da)s ˈfʀyːʃtʏk]
dining room	der Speisesaal [dɐ ˈʃpaɪzəzaːl]
dinner	das Abendessen [das ˈˀaːbmtˀɛsn]
door	die Tür [di tyɐ]
door code	der Türcode [dɐ ˈtyɐkoːt]
elevator	der Aufzug [dɐ ˈˀaʊftsuːk]
extra week	die Verlängerungswoche [di fɐˈlɛŋəʀʊŋsˌvɔxə]
fan	der Ventilator [dɐ vɛntiˈlaːtoɐ]
faucet	der Wasserhahn [dɐ ˈvasɐhaːn]
floor (= storey)	die Etage [di ˀeˈtaːʒə]
garage	die Garage [di gaˈʀaːʒə]
glass	das Wasserglas [das ˈvasɐglaːs], das Glas [das glaːs]
handheld shower	die Handbrause [di ˈhantbʀaʊzə]
heating	die Heizung [di ˈhaɪtsʊŋ]
high season	die Hauptsaison [di ˈhaʊptzɛˌzɔŋ]
in-room telephone	das Zimmertelefon [das ˈtsɪmɐteləˌfoːn]
key	der Schlüssel [dɐ ˈʃlʏsl]
lamp	die Lampe [di ˈlampə]
lavatory	die Toilette [di toˈlɛtə]
lift	der Aufzug [dɐ ˈˀaʊftsuːk]
light	das Licht [das lɪçt]
light bulb	die Glühbirne [di ˈglyːbɪɐnə]
lounge	der Aufenthaltsraum [dɐ ˈˀaʊfntaltsˌʀaʊm]
low season/off-season	die Vorsaison [di ˈfoɐzeˌzɔŋ]; die Nachsaison [di ˈnaːxzeˌzɔŋ]
lunch	das Mittagessen [das ˈmɪtakˌˀɛsn]
maid	das Zimmermädchen [das ˈtsɪmɐmɛːtçn]
mattress	die Matratze [di maˈtʀatsə]
motel	das Motel [das moˈtɛl]
mug	der Becher [dɐ ˈbɛçɐ]
notepad	der Notizblock [dɐ noˈtiːtsblɔk]
overnight stay	die Übernachtung [di ˀybɐˈnaxtʊŋ]
pillow	das Kopfkissen [das ˈkɔpfkɪsn]
plug	der Stecker [dɐ ˈʃtɛkɐ]
porter	der Portier [dɐ pɔɐˈtjeː]
price list	die Preisliste [di ˈpʀaɪslɪstə]
radio	das Radio [das ˈʀaːdjo]
reception	die Rezeption [di ʀetsɛpˈtsjoːn]
registration	die Anmeldung [di ˈˀanmɛldʊŋ]
to repair	reparieren [ʀɛpaˈʀiːʀən/-ˈʀiɐn]

reservation	die Reservierung [di ʀezɐˈvi:ʀʊŋ]
restaurant	das Restaurant [das ʁɛstoˈʁɑ̃/ʁɛstoˈʁaŋ]
restroom	die Toilette [di toˈlɛtə]
room	das Zimmer [das ˈtsɪmɐ]
room service	der Zimmerservice [dɐ ˈtsɪmɐøsə:vɪs]
safe	der Safe [dɐ sɛɪf/se:f]
shoe cleaning kit	das Schuhputzzeug [das ˈʃu:pʊtsˌtsɔɪk]
shower	die Dusche [di ˈdu:ʃə]
shower curtain	der Duschvorhang [dɐ ˈdu:ʃfoɐhaŋ]
showerhead	der Brausekopf [dɐ ˈbʀaʊzəkɔpf]
sliding door	die Schiebetür [di ˈʃi:bətyɐ]
socket	die Steckdose [di ˈʃtɛkdo:zə]
table	der Tisch [dɐ tɪʃ]
tap	der Wasserhahn [dɐ ˈvasɐha:n]
television, TV	der Fernseher [dɐ ˈfɛɐnzeɐ]
television lounge	der Fernsehraum [dɐ ˈfɛɐnze:ˌʀaʊm]
terrace	die Terrasse [di teˈʀasə]
toilet	die Toilette [di toˈlɛtə]
toilet paper	das Toilettenpapier [das toˈlɛtnpaˌpiɐ]
towel	das Handtuch [das ˈhantu:x]
tumbler	das Wasserglas [das ˈvasɐgla:s]
wardrobe	der Kleiderschrank [dɐ ˈklaɪdɐʃʀaŋk]
washbasin	das Waschbecken [das ˈvaʃbɛkŋ]
water	das Wasser [das ˈvasɐ]
cold water	kaltes Wasser [ˈva:məs ˈvasɐ]
hot water	warmes Wasser [ˈkaltəs ˈvasɐ]
water glass	das Wasserglas [das ˈvasɐgla:s]
window	das Fenster [das ˈfɛnstɐ]
writing paper	das Briefpapier [das ˈbʀi:fpapiɐ]

Holiday cottages and flats

Is electricity/water included in the price?
Ist der Stromverbrauch/Wasserverbrauch im Mietpreis enthalten?
[ˀɪst dɐ ˈʃtʀo:mfɐbʀaʊx/ˈvasɐfɐbʀaʊx ˀɪm ˈmi:tpʀaɪs ˀɛntˈhaltn]

Are pets allowed?
Sind Haustiere erlaubt? [zɪnt ˈhaʊsti:ʀə ˀɐˈlaʊpt]

Clean up thoroughly before you leave.
Machen Sie gründlich sauber, bevor Sie abreisen.
[maxn zi ˈgʀʏntlɪç ˈzaʊbɐ bəˈfoɐ zi ˈˀapʀaɪzn]

Do we have to clean the place ourselves before we leave?
Müssen wir die Endreinigung selbst übernehmen?
[mʏsn viɐ di ˈˀɛntʀaɪnɪgʊŋ ˈzɛlpst ˀybɐˈne:mm]

Hikers and mountaineers have a large choice of mountain huts, usually run by the national alpine clubs. Many serve meals, but otherwise you can bring your own food.

General

➢ **also At the hotel**

additional costs	die Nebenkosten [di ˈneːbmkɔstn]
apartment	die Wohnung [di ˈvoːnʊŋ]
bedroom	das Schlafzimmer [das ˈʃlaːftsɪmɐ]
bungalow	der Bungalow [dɐ ˈbʊŋgaloː]
day of arrival	der Anreisetag [dɐ ˈʔanʀaɪzəˌtaːk]
day of departure	der Abreisetag [dɐ ˈʔapʀaɪzəˌtaːk]
electricity	der Strom [dɐ ʃtʀoːm]
farm	der Bauernhof [dɐ ˈbaʊɐnhoːf]
flat	die Wohnung [di ˈvoːnʊŋ]
flat rate for electricity	die Strompauschale [di ˈʃtʀoːmpaʊˌʃaːlə]
fridge/refrigerator	der Kühlschrank [dɐ ˈkyːlʃʀaŋk]
garbage	der Müll [dɐ mʏl]
holiday camp	die Ferienanlage [di ˈfeːʀiənʔanlaːgə]
holiday home	das Ferienhaus [das ˈfeːʀiənhaʊs]
kitchenette	die Kochnische [di ˈkɔxniːʃə]
landlord/landlady	der Hausbesitzer/die Hausbesitzerin [dɐ ˈhaʊsbəzɪtsɐ/di ˈhaʊsbəzɪtsəʀɪn]
to let	vermieten [fɐˈmiːtn]
living room	das Wohnzimmer [das ˈvoːntsɪmɐ]
pets	die Haustiere *n pl* [di ˈhaʊstiːʀə]
to rent	vermieten [fɐˈmiːtn]
rent	die Miete [di ˈmiːtə]
rubbish	der Müll [dɐ mʏl]
separation of rubbish	die Mülltrennung [di ˈmʏltʀɛnʊŋ]
studio apartment	das Apartment [das ʔaˈpaːtmənt]
voltage	die Stromspannung [di ˈʃtʀoːmˌʃpanʊŋ]
water consumption	der Wasserverbrauch [dɐ ˈvasɐfɐbʀaʊx]

blender	der Mixer [dɐ ˈmɪksɐ]
broom	der Besen [dɐ beːzn]
bucket	der Eimer [dɐ ˈʔaɪmɐ]
bunk bed	das Etagenbett [das ʔeˈtaːʒnbɛt]
chopping board	das Schneidebrett [das ˈʃnaɪdəbʁɛt]
cleaning agent	das Putzmittel [das ˈpʊtsmɪtl]
coffee filter	der Kaffeefilter [dɐ ˈkafefɪltɐ/dɐ kaˈfeːfɪltɐ)]
coffee machine	die Kaffeemaschine [di ˈkafemaʃiːnə]
coffee spoon	der Kaffeelöffel [dɐ ˈkafelœfl/dɐ kaˈfeːlœfl]
cooker	der Herd [dɐ heɐt]
crockery	das Geschirr [das gəˈʃɪɐ]
cup/cups	die Tasse/Tassen [di ˈtasə/tasn]
dishes	das Geschirr [das gəˈʃɪɐ̯]
dishwasher	die Geschirrspülmaschine [di gəˈʃɪɐʃpyːlmaˌʃɪnə]
drier	der Trockner [dɐ ˈtʁɔknɐ]
dustpan	die Kehrschaufel [di ˈkeɐʃaʊfl]
egg cup	der Eierbecher [dɐ ˈʔaɪɐˌbɛçɐ]
gas cooker	der Gasherd [dɐ ˈgaːsheɐt]
glass/glasses	das Glas/die Gläser [das glaːs/di ˈglɛːzɐ]
grater	die Reibe [di ˈʁaɪbə]
iron	das Bügeleisen [das ˈbyːglʔaɪzn]
kettle	der Wasserkocher [dɐ ˈvasɐˌkɔxɐ]
key/keys	die Schüssel/n [di ʃʏsl(n)]
ladle *(GB)*/dipper *(US)*	die Schöpfkelle [di ˈʃœpfkɛlə]
microwave	die Mikrowelle [di ˈmiːkʀovɛlə]
mop	der Wischmopp [dɐ ˈvɪʃmɔp]
oven	der Backofen [dɐ ˈbakʔoːfn]
pan	die Pfanne [di ˈ(p)fanə]
pot	der Topf [dɐ tɔpf]
range	der Herd [dɐ heɐt]
roasting tray	der Bräter [dɐ ˈbʁɛːtɐ]
sieve	das Küchensieb [das ˈkʏçnziːp]
stir spoon	der Rührlöffel [dɐ ˈʁyɐlœfl]
stove	der Herd [dɐ heɐt]
studio couch	die Schlafcouch [di ˈʃlaːfkaʊtʃ]
tea towel	das Geschirrtuch [das gəˈʃɪɐtuːx]
toaster	der Toaster [dɐ ˈtoːstɐ]
vacuum cleaner	der Staubsauger [dɐ ˈʃtaʊpzaʊgɐ]
whisk	der Schneebesen [dɐ ˈʃneːbeːzn]

Camping

Could you tell me if there's a camping site nearby?
Könnten Sie mir bitte sagen, ob es in der Nähe einen Campingplatz gibt?
[køntn zi miɐ ˈbɪtə zaːgŋ ˀɔp əs ɪn dɐ ˈnɛːə ˀaɪnn ˈkɛmpɪŋplats gɪpt]

Have you got room for another caravan/tent?
Haben Sie noch Platz für einen Wohnwagen/ein Zelt?
[ˈhaːbm zi nɔx plats fyɐ ˀaɪnn ˈvoːnvaːgŋ/ˀaɪn ˈtsɛlt]

How much does it cost per day and person?
Wie hoch ist die Gebühr pro Tag und Person?
[viː hoːx ˀɪst di gəˈbyɐ pʀo taːk ʊnt pɐˈzoːn]

What's the charge for ...
Wie hoch ist die Gebühr für ... [viː hoːx ɪst di gəˈbyɐ fyɐ …]
the car?
das Auto? [das ˈˀaʊto]
the camper van/motor home/RV?
das Wohnmobil? [das ˈvoːnmoˌbiːl]
the caravan/trailer?
den Wohnwagen? [den ˈvoːnvaːgŋ]
the tent?
das Zelt? [das ˈtsɛlt]

We'll be staying for ... days/weeks.
Wir bleiben ... Tage/Wochen. [viɐ blaɪbm … ˈtaːgə/ˈvɔxn]

Where are ...
Wo sind ...? [voː zɪnt]
the toilets?
die Toiletten? [di toˈlɛtn]
the washrooms?
die Waschräume? [di ˈvaʃʀɔɪmə]
the showers?
die Duschen? [di ˈduːʃn]

Are there power points/outlets here?
Gibt es hier Stromanschluss? [gɪpt əs hiɐ ˈʃtʀoːmanʃlʊs]

Is the camping site guarded at night?
Ist der Campingplatz bei Nacht bewacht?
[ˀɪst dɐ ˈkɛmpɪŋplats baɪ ˈnaxt bəˈvaxt]

booking	die Voranmeldung [di ˈfoɐˀanmɛldʊŋ]
to camp	zelten [ˈtsɛltn]
camping	das Camping [das ˈkɛmpɪŋ]
camping guide	der Campingführer [dɐ ˈkɛmpɪŋfyːʀɐ]
camping site	der Campingplatz [dɐ ˈkɛmpɪŋplats]

cooker	der Kocher [dɐ ˈkɔxɐ]
dryer	der Wäschetrockner [dɐ ˈvɛʃətʀɔknɐ]
drinking water	das Trinkwasser [das ˈtʀɪŋkvasɐ]
electricity	der Strom [dɐ ʃtʀoːm]
gas canister	die Gasflasche [di gaːsflaʃə]
gas cartridge	die Gaskartusche [di ˈgaːskaˌtʊʃə]
lavatory	der Waschraum [dɐ ˈvaʃʀaʊm]
paraffin lamp	die Petroleumlampe [di peˈtʀoːleʊmˌlampə]
plug	der Stecker [dɐ ˈʃtɛkɐ]
power point/outlet	die Steckdose [di ˈʃtɛkdoːzə]
propane (gas)	das Propangas [das pʀoˈpaːngaːs]
sink	das Geschirrspülbecken [das gəˈʃɪɐspyːlbɛkŋ]
tent	das Zelt [das tsɛlt]
tent peg	der Hering [dɐ ˈheːʀɪŋ]
washroom	der Waschraum [dɐ ˈvaʃʀaʊm]
water	das Wasser [das ˈvasɐ]
water canister	der Wasserkanister [dɐ ˈvasɐkanˌɪstɐ]

Eating and drinking

Good eating and drinking
In Austria, Germany and Switzerland you have a number of different kinds of eating and drinking establishments to choose from:

- **Restaurant** - as elsewhere
- **Café** - a coffee house
- **Gasthaus** - a small hotel with a restaurant
- **Gasthof** - a *Gasthaus* in a rural area
- **Biergarten** - outdoor pub/tavern
- **Gartenwirtschaft** - an outdoor restaurant, usually with a limited menu
- **Ratskeller** - a restaurant in the cellar of the *Rathaus* (town hall)
- **Bistro** - a trendy pub or small restaurant, usually with a bar
- **Kneipe** - pub
- **Imbissstube** - fast-food place
- **Konditorei** - pastry shop usually with a café

In Austria you also encounter simple restaurants called **Beisl**.

Eating out

Is there ... here?
Gibt es hier ... ? [gɪpt əs hiɐ]

a good restaurant
ein gutes Restaurant [ˀaɪn ˈguːtəs ʀɛstoˈʀaŋ]

an inexpensive restaurant
ein preiswertes Restaurant [ˀaɪn ˈpʀaɪsveɐtəs ʀɛstoˈʀaŋ]

a gourmet restaurant
ein Feinschmeckerlokal [ˀaɪn ˈfaɪnʃmɛkɐloˌkaːl]

a fast-food place
einen Schnellimbiss [ˀaɪnn ˈʃnɛlɪmbɪs]

The restaurant business in Germany is rapidly falling into "exotic" hands. In cities and larger towns you'll easily find Italian, Greek, Chinese and even Indian restaurants. The Italians and Greeks are often your best bet for tasty, inexpensive food. There are numerous Turkish fast-food places as a good alternative to the international fast-food chains. If you insist on getting "typical German food", find a *Gasthof* outside town or go to a fancy hotel.

Where's a good place to eat near here?
Wo kann man hier in der Nähe gut essen?
[voː kan man hiɐ ˀɪn dɐ ˈnɛːə guːt ˀɛsn]

Is there a good, inexpensive restaurant here?
Gibt es hier ein preiswertes Restaurant? [gɪpt əs hiɐ ˀaɪn ˈpraɪsveɐtəs ʀɛstoˈʀaŋ]

At the restaurant

Would you reserve us a table for a party of four for this evening, please?
Reservieren Sie uns bitte für heute Abend einen Tisch für vier Personen.
[ʀɛzɐˈviːʀən zi ˀʊns ˈbɪtə fyɐ ˈhɔɪtə ˀaːbmt ˀaɪnn tɪʃ fyɐ fiɐ pɐˈzoːnn]

Is this table free?
Ist dieser Tisch noch frei? [ˀɪst ˈdiːzɐ tɪʃ nɔx ˈfʀaɪ]

In most restaurants you simply pick out your own table. It is also quite common, if the restaurant is crowded, to sit down with people who are strangers to you. You ask if there are seats "free" (not taken).

Are these seats taken?
Sind hier noch Plätze frei? [zɪnt hiɐ ˈplɛtsə nɔx ˈfʀaɪ]

A table for three, please.
Einen Tisch für drei Personen, bitte.
[ˀaɪnn tɪʃ fyɐ dʀaɪ pɐˈzoːnn ˈbɪtə]

Where are the toilets?
Wo sind die Toiletten? [voː zɪnt di toˈlɛtn]

Ordering

Can we have the menu/drinks list, please?
Können wir bitte die Speisekarte/Getränkekarte haben?
[kønn viɐ ˈbɪtə di ˈʃpaɪzəkaːtə/gəˈtʀɛŋkəkaːtə haːbm]

Traditionally, you address a waiter with *Herr Ober*, a waitress with *Fräulein.* This is going out of fashion, and most people simply say *hallo!* in a clear and resonant voice, depending how classy the restaurant is. If it's a high-class eating establishment, a discrete raising of hand and arm should do.

Are you ready to order?
Haben Sie schon gewählt? [ˈhaːbm zi ʃon gəˈvɛːlt]

What can you recommend?
Was können Sie mir empfehlen? [vas kønn zi miɐ ˀɛmˈfeːln]

I'll have ... to start off with.
Als Vorspeise nehme ich ... [ˀals ˈfoɐʃpaɪzə ˈneːmə ˀɪç]

I'll have ... for the main course.
Als Hauptgericht nehme ich ... [ˀals ˈhaʊptgəʀɪçt ˈneːmə ˀɪç]

I don't want any dessert, thank you.
Ich möchte keinen Nachtisch, danke.
[ˀɪç ˈmœçtə ˌkaɪnn ˈnaːxtɪʃ ˈdaŋkə]

I'm afraid we've run out of ...
Wir haben leider kein ... mehr. [viɐ ha:bm ˈlaɪdɐ ˈkaɪn … meɐ]

We only serve this dish if it's been pre-ordered.
Dieses Gericht servieren wir nur auf Bestellung.
[ˈdi:zəs gəˈʀɪçt zɐˈvi:ʀən viɐ nuɐ ˀaʊf bəˈʃtɛlʊŋ]

Could I have chicken instead of fish?
Könnte ich statt Fisch Huhn haben? [ˈkøntə ˀɪç ʃtat fɪʃ hu:n ha:bm]

I'm allergic to ...
Ich vertrage kein ... [ˀɪç fɐˈtʀa:gə kaɪn …]

Could you make this dish without ...?
Könnten Sie das Gericht ohne ... zubereiten?
[ˈkøntn zi das gəˈʀɪçt o:nə … ˈtsu:bəʀaɪtn]

Do you have children's portions?
Gibt es auch Kinderportionen? [gɪpt əs aʊx ˈkɪndɐpɔˈtsjo:nn]

How would you like your steak?
Wie möchten Sie Ihr Steak haben? [vi møçtn zi ˀiɐ ˈste:k ha:bm]

well-done
gut durch [gu:t dʊɐç]
medium
halb durch [halp dʊɐç]
rare
englisch [ˈˀɛŋlɪʃ]

What would you like to drink?
Was möchten Sie trinken? [vas møçtn zi ˈtʀɪŋkŋ]

A glass of ..., please.
Bitte ein Glas ... [ˈbɪtə ˀaɪn gla:s]

A bottle of/Half a bottle of ..., please.
Bitte eine Flasche/eine halbe Flasche ...
[ˈbɪtə ˈˀaɪnə ˈflaʃə/ˌˀaɪnə ˈhalbə ˈflaʃə]

With ice, please.
Mit Eis, bitte. [mɪt ˀaɪs ˈbɪtə]

Enjoy your meal!
Guten Appetit! [ˈgu:tn ˀapəˈti:t]

Would you like anything else?
Haben Sie sonst noch einen Wunsch?
[ha:bm zi ˈzɔnst nɔx aɪnn vʊnʃ]

Bring us ..., please.
Bitte bringen Sie uns ... [ˈbɪtə brɪŋŋ zi ˀʊns]

Could we have some more bread/water/wine, please?
Könnten wir noch etwas Brot/ Wasser/Wein bekommen?
[ˈkøntn viɐ nɔx ˌɛtvas ˈbʀoːt/ˈvasɐ/ˈvaɪn bəˈkɔmm]

Cheers!
Zum Wohl! [tsʊm ˈvoːl]

Complaints

We need another ...
Wir brauchen noch ein ... [viɐ bʀaʊxn nɔx ˀaɪn]

Have you forgotten my ...?
Haben Sie mein ... vergessen? [haːbm zi ˌmaɪn … fɐˈgɛsn]

I didn't order that.
Das habe ich nicht bestellt. [das haːb ɪç nɪçt bəˈʃtɛlt]

The food is cold.
Das Essen ist kalt. [das ˀɛsn ˀɪst kalt]

There's too much salt in the soup.
Die Suppe ist versalzen. [di ˈzʊpə ˀɪst fɐˈzaltsn]

The meat's tough/too fatty.
Das Fleisch ist zäh/zu fett. [das flaɪʃ ɪst ˈtsɛː/tsʊ ˈfɛt]

The fish is not fresh.
Der Fisch ist nicht frisch.
[dɐ fɪʃ ˀɪst nɪçt fʀɪʃ]

I'm afraid the wine is corked.
Es tut mir leid, aber der Wein schmeckt nach Korken.
[ˀəs tuːt miɐ laɪt ˈˀabɐ dɐ vaɪn ʃmɛkt nax ˈkɔɐkŋ]

Take it back, please.
Nehmen Sie es bitte zurück. [ˈneːmm zi əs ˈbɪtə tsʊˈʀʏk]

Fetch the manager, please.
Holen Sie bitte den Chef. [ˈhoːln zi ˈbɪtə den ˈʃɛf]

Don't confuse German *Chef* (= manager) with English "chef" (= *Koch*).

The bill

Could I have the bill, please?
Die Rechnung, bitte. [di ˈʀɛçnʊŋ ˈbɪtə]/
Bezahlen, bitte. [bəˈtsa:ln ˈbɪtə]

All together, please.
Bitte alles zusammen. [ˈbɪtə ˈʔaləs tsʊˈsamm]

Separate bills, please.
Getrennte Rechnungen, bitte. [gəˈtʀɛntə ˈʀɛçnʊŋŋ ˈbɪtə]

There seems to be a mistake on the bill.
Die Rechnung scheint mir nicht zu stimmen.
[di ˈʀɛçnʊŋ ʃaɪnt miɐ nɪçt tsʊ ˈʃtɪmm]

I didn't have that. I had ...
Das habe ich nicht gehabt. Ich hatte ...
[das ˈha:bə ɪç nɪçt gəˈhapt ʔɪç ˈhatə ...]

Did you enjoy your meal?
Hat es geschmeckt? [hat ʔɛs gəˈʃmɛkt]

The food was excellent.
Das Essen war ausgezeichnet. [das ʔɛsn va: ʔaʊsgəˈtsaɪçnət]

That's for you.
Das ist für Sie. [das ɪst fyɐ ˈzi:]

Keep the change.
(Es) Stimmt so. [(ʔəs) ˈʃtɪmt zo:]

Drinks will be included on the bill with food. Service of 10% is included and it is customary to round up the bill by about 10% or so.

Zum Weißen Adler – Meeting people

After arriving at the airport or driving through a city centre, you may be wondering what became of the German-speaking Old World. To find that and real-time natives, head to the nearest *Gasthaus*. They usually have a name beginning with *zum* or *zur: Zum Weißen Adler* – to the white eagle, *Zum Roten Ochsen* – to the red ox, or *Zur Post* – to the post office. The *Gasthaus* was traditionally an inn for travellers and anyone else looking for a place to eat or sleep. They also became good places to drink beer or wine, to meet people and socialize. This they have remained to the present day.

Even if they appear often quite reserved, Germans, Austrians and the Swiss pride themselves on being open and willing to exchange ideas. Furthermore, in any non-posh eating-and-drinking establishment any seat not taken is yours to sit down in for the asking: *„Ist hier noch frei?"* You can now strike up a conversation by asking about tomorrow's weather, satisfaction with the government, or what happened today in football. Sitting together with strangers is normal, unless you run into a couple who insist on being by themselves.

Don't be turned off if there aren't cuckoo clocks and alpine horns hanging from every wall. Some of these places can be very simple in decoration. There'll always be a small bar with beer on tap and dozens of bottles of schnapps and other forms of liquor above and below the bar. Somewhere not far away you'll also see that quintessence of Germanic drinking culture, the *Stammtisch* regulars' table, that means a no-go area for any stranger.

Good evening.
Guten Abend! [ˈguːtn ˀaːbmt]

Can I sit here?
Ist hier noch frei? [ˀɪst hiɐ nɔx fʀaɪ]

Where are you from?
Wo kommen Sie her? [voː kɔmm zi ˈheɐ]

I come from England/the States.
Ich komme aus England/den USA.
[ˀɪç kɔmə aʊs ˈˀɛŋlant/den uːɛsˈˀaː]

What'll it be?
Was darf es sein? [vas daːf əs zaɪn]

I'd like a beer/a wine/a schnapps.
Ich hätte gern ein Bier/einen Wein/ einen Schnaps.
[ˀɪç ˈhɛtə gɛɐn ˀaɪn biɐ/ˀaɪnn vaɪn/ˀaɪnn ʃnaps]

What flavour?
Welche Geschmacksrichtung? [ˈvɛlçə gəˈʃmaksˌʀɪçtʊŋ]

A pint of mild (dark beer).
Ein großes Dunkles. [ˀaɪn ˈgʀoːsəs dʊŋkləs]

A half-pint of lager.
Ein kleines Helles. [ˀaɪn ˈklaɪnəs ˈhɛləs]

Would you like another drink?
Möchten Sie noch etwas trinken? [ˈmøçtn zi nɔx ˀɛtvas ˈtʀɪŋkŋ]

Same again.
Das Gleiche noch einmal. [das ˈglaɪçə nɔx ˀaɪnmaːl]

Here's to your health!
Zum Wohl! [tsʊm voːl]

Cheers!
Prost! [pʀoːst]

What do you drink where you're from?
Was trinkt man bei Ihnen zu Hause?
[vas ˈtʀɪŋkt man baɪ ˈˀiːnn tsʊ haʊzə]

Did you see that game on TV between ... and ...?
Haben Sie das Spiel im Fernsehen zwischen ... und ... gesehen? [ˈhaːbm zi das ʃpiːl ˀɪm ˈfɛɐnzeːn ˈtsvɪʃn ... ˀʊnt ... gəˈzeːn]

What's your opinion of ...?
Was halten Sie von ...? [vas ˈhaltn zi fɔn]

I don't understand politics. I only pay taxes.
Ich verstehe nichts von Politik. Ich zahle nur Steuern.
[ˀɪç fɐˈʃteː nɪçts fɔn pɔlɪˈtiːk ˀɪç ˈtsaːlə nuɐ ˈʃtɔjɐn]

I'd like the bill, please.
Die Rechnung, bitte. [di ˈʀɛçnʊŋ ˈbɪtə]

This round is on me.
Diese Runde übernehme ich. [ˈdiːzə ˈʀʊndə ˀybɐˈneːmə ˈˀɪç]

➢ also Groceries

appetizer	die Vorspeise [di ˈfoɐʃpaɪzə]
ashtray	der Aschenbecher [dɐ ˈˀaʃnbɛçɐ]
bone	der Knochen [dɐ knɔxn]
bowl	die Schüssel [di ʃʏsl]
breakfast	das Frühstück [das ˈfʀyːʃtʏk]
children's portion	der Kinderteller [dɐ ˈkɪndɐtɛlɐ]
cook	der Koch [dɐ kɔx]
corkscrew	der Korkenzieher [dɐ ˈkɔɐkŋtsiːɐ]
course	der Gang [dɐ gaŋ]
cover *(setting)*	das Gedeck [das gəˈdɛk]
cup	die Tasse [di ˈtasə]
cutlery	das Besteck [das bəˈʃtɛk]

dessert .... der Nachtisch [dɐ ˈnaːxtɪʃ]
diabetic .... diabetisch [diaˈbeːtɪʃ]
diabetic *(person)* .... der Diabetiker/die Diabetikerin [dɐ diaˈbeːtɪkɐ/dɪ diaˈbeːtɪkəʀɪn]
diet .... die Schonkost [di ˈʃoːnkɔst]
dinner .... das Abendessen [das ˈʔaːbmtʔɛsn]
dish .... das Gericht [das gəˈʀɪçt]
dish of the day .... das Tagesgericht [das ˈtaːgəsgəʀɪçt]
draught .... vom Fass [fɔm fas]
dressing .... das Dressing [das ˈdʀɛsɪŋ]
drink .... das Getränk [das gəˈtʀɛŋk]
fishbone .... die Gräte [di ˈgʀɛːtə]
fork .... die Gabel [di ˈgaːbl]
glass .... das Glas [das glaːs]
gourmet restaurant .... das Feinschmeckerlokal [das ˈfaɪnʃmɛkɐloˌkaːl]
gravy .... die (Braten)Soße [di (ˈbʀaːtn)zoːsə]
grill .... der Rost [dɐ ʀɔst]
hard-boiled .... hart gekocht [ˈhaːt gəˌkɔxt]
home-made .... hausgemacht [ˈhaʊsgəmaxt]
hors d'œuvre .... die Vorspeise [di ˈfoɐʃpaɪzə]
hot *(temperature)* .... heiß [haɪs]
hot *(spicy)* .... scharf [ʃaːf]
hungry .... hungrig [ˈhuŋʀɪç]
ketchup .... das Ketschup [das ˈkɛtʃap]
knife .... das Messer [das ˈmɛsɐ]
low-calorie .... kalorienarm [kaloˈʀiːnʔaːm]
low-fat .... fettarm [ˈfɛtʔaːm]
lunch .... das Mittagessen [das ˈmɪtakˌʔɛsn]
main course .... die Hauptspeise [di ˈhaʊptʃpaɪzə]
mayonnaise .... die Mayonnaise [di majoˈnɛːzə]
menu .... die Speisekarte [di ˈʃpaɪzəkaːtə]
mustard .... der Senf [dɐ zɛnf (zɛmf)]
napkin .... die Serviette [di zɐˈvjɛtə]
non-alcoholic .... alkoholfrei [ˈʔalkoˈhoːlfʀaɪ]
oil .... das Öl [das ˈʔøːl]
on tap .... vom Fass [fɔm fas]
order .... die Bestellung [di bəˈʃtɛlʊŋ]
pepper .... der Pfeffer [dɐ ˈpfɛfɐ]
plate .... der Teller [dɐ ˈtɛlɐ]
portion .... die Portion [di pɔˈtsjoːn]
salad bar .... das Salatbüfett [das zaˈlaːtbʏˈfeː]
salt .... das Salz [das zalts]
sauce .... die Soße [di ˈzoːsə]
saucer .... die Untertasse [di ˈʔʊntɐtasə]
season .... würzen [vʏʁtsn]
seasoning .... das Gewürz [das gəˈvʏʁts]

serviette	die Serviette [di zɐˈvjɛtə]
set meal	das Menü [das meˈnyː]
slice	die Scheibe [di ˈʃaɪbə]
soup	die Suppe [di ˈzʊpə]
soup plate	der Suppenteller [dɐ ˈzʊpmtɛlɐ]
special (of the day)	das Tagesmenü [das ˈtaːgəsmeˌnyː]
speciality	die Spezialität [di ʃpetsjaliˈtɛːt]
spice	das Gewürz [das gəˈvʏɐts]
spoon	der Löffel [dɐ løfl]
stain	der Fleck [dɐ flɛk]
starter	die Vorspeise [di ˈfoɐʃpaɪzə]
straw	der Strohhalm [dɐ ˈʃtʀoːhalm]
sugar	der Zucker [dɐ ˈtsʊkɐ]
sweet	der Nachtisch [dɐ ˈnaːxtɪʃ]
sweetener	der Süßstoff [dɐ ˈzyːʃtɔf]
tablecloth	das Tischtuch [das ˈtɪʃtuːx]
teaspoon	der Teelöffel [dɐ ˈteːløfl]
tip	das Trinkgeld [das ˈtʀɪŋkgɛlt]
toothpick	der Zahnstocher [dɐ ˈtsaːnʃtɔxɐ]
tumbler	das Wasserglas [das ˈvasɐglaːs]
vegetarian	vegetarisch [vegəˈtaːʀɪʃ]
vegetarian *(person)*	der Vegetarier/die Vegetarierin [dɐ vegəˈtaːʀɪɐ/dɪ vegəˈtaːʀɪəʀɪn]
vinegar	der Essig [dɐ ˈʔɛsɪç]
waiter/waitress	der Kellner/die Kellnerin [dɐ ˈkɛlnɐ/di ˈkɛlnəʀɪn]
water	das Wasser [das ˈvasɐ]
water glass	das Wasserglas [das ˈvasɐglaːs]
wineglass	das Weinglas [das ˈvaɪnglaːs]

Preparation/Cooking style

au gratin	überbacken [ˈʔybɐˈbakŋ]
baked	gebacken [gəˈbakŋ]
boiled	gekocht [gəˈkɔxt]
braised	geschmort [gəˈʃmoɐt]
broiled	gegrillt [gəˈgʀɪlt]
cooked/done	gar [gaː]
fried	in der Pfanne gebraten [ˈʔɪn dɐ ˈpfanə gəˈbʀaːtn]
grilled	vom Grill [fɔm ˈgʀɪl]
hot (spicy)	scharf [ʃaːf]
juicy	saftig [ˈzaftɪç]
lean	mager [ˈmaːgɐ]
raw	roh [ʀoː]
roasted	gebraten [gəˈbʀaːtn]

smoked	geräuchert [gəˈʀɔɪçɐt]
soft-boiled	weich gekocht [ˈvaɪç gəˌkɔxt]
sour	sauer [ˈzaʊɐ]
spit-roasted	am Spieß gebraten [am ʃpiːs gəˈbʀaːtn]
steamed	gedämpft [gəˈdɛmpft], gedünstet [gəˈdʏnstət]
stuffed	gefüllt [gəˈfʏlt]
sweet	süß [zyːs]
tender	zart [tsaːt]
tough	zäh [tsɛː]
well-done	durchgebraten [ˈdʊɐçgəbʀaːtn]

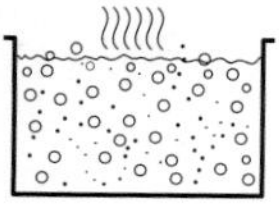

boiled
gekocht

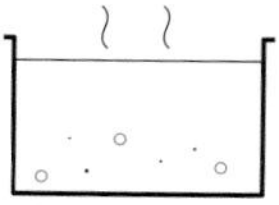

simmered/cooked
gegart

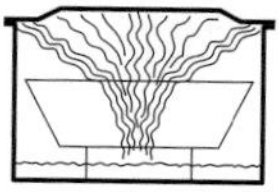

steamed
gedämpft

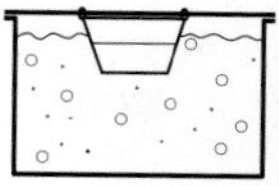

in a bain-marie
im Wasserbad

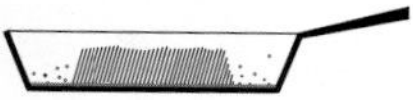

fried
gebraten

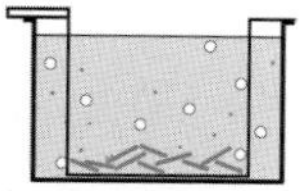

deep fried
frittiert

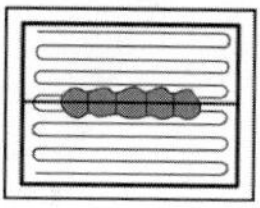

grilled
gegrillt

I'd like
Ich hätte gern ...

ginger der Ingwer [dɐ ˈʔɪŋvɐ]

garlic
der Knoblauch
[dɐ ˈkno:blaʊx]

onion
die Zwiebel
[di tsvi:bl]

dill
der Dill [dɐ dɪl]

bay-leaves
die Lorbeerblätter *n pl*
[di ˈlɔɐbeɐˌblɛtɐ]

rosemary
der Rosmarin
[dɐ ˈʀo:smaʀi:n]

marjoram
der Majoran
[dɐ ˈma:joʀa:n]

coriander
der Koriander
[dɐ ko:ri:ˈandə]

parsley
die Petersilie
[di pe:tɐˈzi:ljə]

basil
das Basilikum
[das baˈzi:lɪkʊm]

nutmeg die Muskatnuss [di mʊsˈkaːtnʊs]

chilli
der Chili
[dɐ ˈtsɪli]

pepperoni
die Peperoni
[di pɛpəˈroːni]

chives
der Schnittlauch
[dɐ ˈʃnɪtlaʊx]

sage
der Salbei
[dɐ ˈzalbaɪ]

chervil
der Kerbel
[dɐ kɛɐbl]

thyme
der Thymian
[dɐ ˈtyːmiaːn]

savory
das Bohnenkraut
[das ˈboːnnkʀaʊt]

lovage
der/das Liebstöckl
[dɐ/das ˈliːpʃtøkl]

I'd like
Ich hätte gern ...

I'd like
Ich hätte gern ...

Speisekarte — Menu

Frühstück	Breakfast
Schwarzer Kaffee [ˌʃvaːtsɐ ˈkafeː]	black coffee
Kaffee mit Milch [ˈkafeː mɪt ˈmɪlç]	white coffee
Koffeinfreier Kaffee [kɔfeˈʔiːnfʀaɪɐ ˈkafeː]	decaffeinated coffee
Tee mit Milch/Zitrone [teː mɪt ˈmɪlç/tsɪˈtʀoːnə]	tea with milk/lemon
Schokolade [ʃokoˈlaːdə]	hot chocolate
Fruchtsaft [ˈfʀʊxtzaft]	fruit juice
Weiches Ei [vaɪçəs ʔaɪ]	soft-boiled egg
Rühreier [ˈʀyɐʔaɪɐ]	scrambled eggs
Brot/Brötchen [bʀoːt/bʀøːtçn]	bread/rolls
Toast [toːst]	toast
Butter [ˈbʊtɐ]	butter
Honig [ˈhoːnɪç]	honey
Marmelade [maməˈlaːdə]	jam
Orangenmarmelade [oˈʀaŋʒnmaməˌlaːdə]	marmalade
Müsli [ˈmyːsli]	muesli
Jogurt [ˈjoːgʊɐt]	yoghurt
Obst [ˈʔoːpst]	fruit

Most hotels have a breakfast buffet with a large selection of cheese, sausage, fruit, breakfast cereal, and juice. Bacon-and-eggs style breakfast can only be found in large international hotels. Smaller hotels may still offer "continental breakfast" – bread rolls, cheese, and jam. Tea is usually served with a slice of lemon; if you take milk, ask for it.

Vorspeisen	Hors d'œuvres
Austern *f pl* [ˈʔaʊstɐn]	oysters
Avocado [ʔavoˈkaːdo]	avocado
Garnelencocktail [gaˈneːlnˌkɔktɛɪl]	prawn cocktail
Hummer [ˈhʊmɐ]	lobster
Krabbencocktail [ˈkʀabmˌkɔktɛɪl]	shrimp cocktail
Melone mit Schinken [meˈloːnə mɪt ˈʃɪŋkŋ]	melon with ham
Muscheln *f pl* [mʊʃln]	mussels
Räucherlachs [ˈʀɔɪçɐlaks]	smoked salmon
Schinken [ʃɪŋkŋ]	ham
Weinbergschnecken [ˈvaɪnbɛɐkˌʃnɛkŋ]	snails in garlic butter

Salate	Salads
Bohnensalat [ˈboːnnzalaːt]	bean salad
Gemischter Salat [gəˈmɪʃtɐ zaˈlaːt]	mixed salad
Gurkensalat [ˈgʊʁkŋzalaːt]	cucumber salad
Karottensalat [kaˈʀɔtnzalaːt]	carrot salad
Kartoffelsalat [kaˈtɔflzalaːt]	potato salad
Krautsalat [ˈkʀaʊtzalaːt]	coleslaw

Suppen	Soups
Bouillon [bʊlˈjɔŋ]	clear soup/consommé
Champignoncremesuppe [ˈʃampɪnjɔŋˌkʀɛːmzʊpə]	cream of mushroom soup
Erbsensuppe [ˈˀɛɐpsnˌzʊpə]	pea soup
Fleischbrühe [ˈflaɪʃbʀyə]	clear soup/consommé
Französische Zwiebelsuppe [fʀanˈtsøːzɪʃə ˈtsviːblzʊpə]	French onion soup
Gemüsesuppe [gəˈmyːzəzʊpə]	vegetable soup
Gulaschsuppe [ˈgʊlaʃzʊpə]	goulash soup
Hühnersuppe [ˈhyːnɐzʊpə]	chicken soup
Ochsenschwanzsuppe [ˈˀɔksnʃvantsˌzʊpə]	oxtail soup
Spargelcremesuppe [ˈʃpaːglkʀɛːmˌzʊpə]	cream of asparagus soup
Tomatencremesuppe [toˈmaːtnkʀɛːmˌzʊpə]	cream of tomato soup

Eierspeisen	Egg dishes
(Käse-/Champignon-/Tomaten-) Omelett [(ˈkɛːzə/ˈʃampɪnjɔŋ/toˈmaːtn)ˌˀɔmlɛt]	(cheese/mushroom/tomato) omelette
Rühreier [ˈʀyɐˀaɪɐ]	scrambled eggs
Spiegeleier [ˈʃpiːglˀaɪɐ]	fried eggs
Spiegeleier mit Schinken [ˈʃpiːglˀaɪɐ mɪt ˈʃɪŋkŋ]	ham and eggs
Verlorene Eier [vɐˈloːʀənə ˈˀaɪɐ]	poached eggs

Fisch	Fish
Aal [ˀa:l]	eel
Austern [ˈˀaʊstɐn]	oysters
Bückling [ˈbʏklɪŋ]	kipper
Forelle [foˈʀɛlə]	trout
Garnelen [gaˈne:ln]	prawns
Hummer [ˈhʊmɐ]	lobster
Kabeljau [ˈka:bljaʊ]	cod
Karpfen [ka:pfn]	carp
Krabben [kʀabm]	shrimps
Krebs [kʀe:ps]	crab
Lachs [laks]	salmon
Makrele [maˈkʀe:lə]	mackerel
Matjesfilet [ˈmatçəsfɪˌle:]	salted young herring
Muscheln [mʊʃln]	mussels
Räucherhering [ˈʀɔɪçɐhe:ʀɪŋ]	smoked herring, kipper
Scholle [ˈʃɔlə]	plaice
Schwertfisch [ʃveɐtfɪʃ]	swordfish
Seezunge [ˈze:tsʊŋə]	sole
T(h)unfisch [ˈtu:nfɪʃ]	tuna
Tintenfisch [ˈtɪntnfɪʃ]	squid

Geflügel	Poultry
Ente [ˈˀɛntə]	duck
Fasan [faˈza:n]	pheasant
Gans [gans]	goose
Hähnchen/Huhn [ˈhɛ:nçn/hu:n]	chicken
Pute [ˈpu:tə]	turkey
Rebhuhn [ˈʀe:phu:n]	partridge
Truthahn [ˈtʀu:tha:n]	turkey
Wachtel [vaxtl]	quail

Fleisch	Meat
Filet(steak) [fɪˈle:ste:k]	fillet/filet (steak)
Frikadellen [fʀɪkaˈdɛln]	meat balls
Hackfleisch (vom Rind) [ˈhakflaɪʃ (fɔm ˈʀɪnt)]	minced beef/ground beef
Hamburger [ˈhambʊɐgɐ]	hamburger
Hirsch [hɪɐʃ]	venison (red deer)

Kalbfleisch [ˈkalpflaɪʃ]	veal
Kaninchen [kaˈniːnçn]	rabbit
Kotelett [ˈkɔtlɛt]	chop/cutlet
Kutteln [kʊtln]	tripe
Lamm [lam]	lamb
Leber [ˈleːbɐ]	liver
Nieren [ˈniːʀən]	kidneys
Reh [ʀeː]	venison (roe deer)
Rindfleisch [ˈʀɪntflaɪʃ]	beef
Rumpsteak [ˈʀʊmpsteːk]	rump steak
Schinken [ʃɪŋkŋ]	ham
Schweinefleisch [ˈʃvaɪnəflaɪʃ]	pork
Spanferkel [ˈʃpaːnfɛɐkl]	sucking pig
Wildschwein [ˈviltʃvaɪn]	wild boar
Würstchen [ˈvʏɐstçn]	sausages
Zunge [ˈtsʊŋə]	tongue

Gemüse	**Vegetables**
Blumenkohl [ˈbluːmmkoːl]	cauliflower
Bratkartoffeln [ˈbʀaːtkaˌtɔfln]	fried potatoes
Brokkoli [ˈbʀɔkoli]	broccoli
Champignons [ˈʃampɪnjɔŋs]	mushrooms
Chicorée [ˈʃɪkoʀe]	chicory
Erbsen [ˀɛɐpsn]	peas
Fenchel [fɛnçl]	fennel
Folienkartoffel [ˈfoːljənkaˌtɔfl]	baked potato
Frühlingszwiebeln [ˈfʀyːlɪŋstsviːbln]	spring/green onions
grüne Bohnen [ˌgʀyːnə ˈboːnn]	French beans
Gurke [ˈgʊɐkə]	cucumber
Karotten [kaˈʀɔtn]	carrots
Kartoffelbrei [kaˈtɔflbʀaɪ]	mashed potato(es)
Kartoffeln [kaˈtɔfln]	potatoes
Knoblauch [ˈknoːblaʊx]	garlic
Kresse [ˈkʀɛsə]	cress
Kürbis [ˈkʏɐbɪs]	pumpkin
Lauch [laʊx]	leek
Maiskolben [ˈmaiskɔlbm]	corn-on-the-cob
Möhren [ˈmøːʀən]	carrots
Ofenkartoffel [ˈˀoːfnkaˌtɔfl]	baked potato
Paprikaschoten [ˈpapʀɪkaˌʃoːtn]	peppers
Pommes frites [pɔmˈfʀɪts]	chips/French fries

Rosenkohl ['ʀoːznkoːl]	Brussel sprouts
Rösti ['ʀøsti]	hash brown potatoes
Rote Bete [ˌʀoːtə 'beːtə]	beetroot/beets
Rotkohl ['ʀoːtkoːl]	red cabbage
Salzkartoffeln ['zaltskaˌtɔfln]	boiled potatoes
Schwenkkartoffeln ['ʃvɛŋkaˌtɔfln]	sauté(ed) potatoes
Spargel [ʃpaːgl]	asparagus
Spinat [ʃpɪ'naːt]	spinach
Stangensellerie ['ʃtaŋŋˌzɛləʀi]	celery
Tomaten [to'maːtn]	tomatoes
Weißkohl ['vaɪskoːl]	cabbage
Zucchini [tsʊ'kiːni]	courgettes/zucchini
Zwiebeln [tsviːbln]	onions

Some vegetable names vary from region to region, for example *Karfiol* ("cauliflower" in Austria) and *Erdäpfel* ("potato" in Austria and Switzerland); "carrots" are *Möhren* and *Mohrrüben* in northern Germany, and *Karotten* elsewhere.

Käse	Cheese
Blauschimmelkäse ['blaʊʃɪmlˌkɛːzə]	blue cheese
Frischkäse ['fʀɪʃkɛːzə]	cream cheese
Hüttenkäse ['hʏtnkɛːzə]	cottage cheese
Schafskäse ['ʃaːfskɛːzə]	sheep's milk cheese
Ziegenkäse ['tsiːgŋkɛːzə]	goat's milk cheese

The German-speaking countries are also becoming important producers of cheese. Typical hard cheeses are *Emmentaler* or, more tasty, *Appenzeller, Greyerzer (Gruyère)* and *Bergkäse*. Particularly pungent are *Harzer, Limburger* and *Handkäse*. Soft cheeses from France (*Camembert, Brie*) have become very popular and are also being produced domestically. A traditional dish of cheese is *Handkäse mit Musik*, served with caraway seeds, onions and vinegar.

Nachtisch/Obst	Dessert/Fruit
Ananas ['ʔananas]	pineapple
Birnen [bɪʀnn]	pears
Eis [ʔaɪs]	ice-cream
Eisbecher ['ʔaɪsbɛçɐ]	sundae

Erdbeeren ['ˀeɐtbeːʀən]	strawberries
Gebäck [gəˈbɛk]	pastries
Kirschen [kɪɐʃn]	cherries
Kompott [kɔmˈpɔt]	stewed fruit
Obstsalat ['ˀoːpstzaˌlaːt]	fruit salad
Pfannkuchen ['pfankuːxn]	pancakes
Pfirsiche ['pfɪɐzɪçə]	peaches
Pflaumen [pflaʊmm]	plums
Rhabarber [ʀaˈbaːbɐ]	rhubarb
Schlagsahne ['ʃlaːkzaːnə]; *(Austria)* Schlagobers ['ʃlagobɐs]	whipped cream
Stachelbeeren ['ʃtaxlbeːʀən]	gooseberries
Vanillesoße [vaˈnɪlzoːsə]	custard

Germany, Switzerland and Austria are a cake-eater's paradise. The range of cakes and pastries is overwhelming. As well as different types of fruit cakes such as *Apfelkuchen, Käsekuchen* (cheesecake), there are many *Torten* (with layers of cream), e.g. *Schwarzwälder Kirschtorte* (Black Forest Cake). People like to go to a Café for their cake, or buy some to bring back home for coffee. In a restaurant, on the other hand, the choice of desserts may seem limited – ice cream or fruit salad, but also typical desserts, such as *Rote Grütze,* stewed red summer fruit served cold with cream or custard.

Getränke — Beverages

Alkoholische Getränke — Alcoholic drinks

Apfelwein ['ˀapflvaɪn]	cider
Bier [biɐ]	beer

There are many different types of beer, and the names can vary, depending on the region. The most popular ones are *Export* or *Helles* (lager), *Pils* (a strong lager), *Alt* or *Bockbier* (dark beer) and *Weizenbier* (a light summer beer made from wheat). *Radler* or *Alsterwasser* is beer diluted with lemonade/ lemon soda.

Wein [vaɪn]	wine
Champagner [ʃamˈpanjɐ]	champagne (from France)
Sekt [zɛkt]	champagne style wine (from outside France)
leicht [laɪçt]	light
lieblich ['liːplɪç]	sweet

rosé [ʀoˈzeː]	rosé
rot [ʀoːt]	red
trocken [tʀɔkŋ]	dry
weiß [vais]	white
Weinschorle sauer [ˈvaɪnʃɔːlə ˈzauɐ]	wine diluted with mineral water
Weinschorle süß [ˈvaɪnʃɔːlə ˈzyːs]	wine diluted with lemonade/lemon soda
Weinbrand [ˈvaɪnbʀant]	brandy
Most [mɔst]	cider
Kognak [ˈkɔnjak]	cognac
Likör [lɪˈkøɐ]	liqueur
Gin [dʒɪn]	gin
Rum [ʀʊm]	rum
Whisky [ˈvɪski]	whisky
Wodka [ˈvɔtka]	vodka

After a meal you may be offered a *Schnaps*, a spirit often distilled from pears, cherries or plums. A sweeter variation is *Obstler*, a mixed fruit schnapps.
Germany is famous for its white wines. The red wines and rosé tend to be light. There are two basic wine categories: *Tafelwein* (table wine) and *Qualitätswein* (quality wine). *QbA* (*Qualitätswein besonderer Anbaugebiete*) means that the wine comes from one of eleven special regions. Further designations are: *Kabinett* (premium quality), *Spätlese* (late harvest, with a richer flavour), *Auslese* (from selected grapes). A rare speciality is *Eiswein* (ice wine) made from frost-bitten grapes.

Alkoholfreie Getränke	Non-alcoholic drinks
Alkoholfreies Bier [ˀalkoˈhoːlfʀaɪəs biɐ]	non-alcoholic/alcohol-free beer
Apfelsaft [ˈˀapflzaft]	apple juice

Apple juice is often drunk diluted with mineral water (*eine Apfelsaftschorle* or *ein gespritzter Apfelsaft*). Another popular drink is *Spezi* (a mixture of cola and orange). American children will be disappointed that lemonade as in the US is unknown.

Cola [ˈkoːla]	coke
Eistee [ˈˀaɪsteː]	iced tea
Fruchtsaft [ˈfʀʊxtzaft]	fruit juice
Limonade [lɪmoˈnaːdə]	lemonade/soda pop

Mineralwasser [mɪnəˈʀaːlvasɐ]	mineral water
mit Kohlensäure [mɪt ˈkoːlnzɔɪʀə]	carbonated
ohne Kohlensäure [ˈʔoːnə ˈkoːlnzɔɪʀə]	still
Orangensaft [ʔoˈʀaŋʒnzaft/ʔoˈʀaːʒnzaft]	orange juice
Tomatensaft [toˈmaːtnzaft]	tomato juice
Tonic [ˈtɔnɪk]	tonic water
Eiskaffee [ˈʔaɪskafeː]	iced coffee
Früchtetee [ˈfʀʏçtəteː]	fruit tea
(eine Tasse) Kaffee [(ˈʔaɪnə ˈtasə) kaˈfeː]	(a cup of) coffee
Koffeinfreier Kaffee [kɔfeˈʔiːnfʀaɪɐ kaˈfeː]	decaffeinated coffee
Kräutertee [ˈkʀɔɪtɐteː]	herbal tea
Milch [mɪlç]	milk
Pfefferminztee [ˈpfɛfɐmɪntsteː]	peppermint tea
Sahne [ˈzaːnə]	cream
(eine Tasse/ein Glas) Tee [(ˈʔaɪnə ˈtasə/ʔaɪn glaːs) ˈteː]	(a cup/glass of) tea

Coffee is usually served with evaporated milk, normal milk, or cream. In Germany, when sitting outside, often you can only order *ein Kännchen*, a small pot for two cups. *Schümli* is Swiss-style frothy coffee. Italian coffees such as *Cappuccino* and *Espresso* are very popular. Austrian coffee houses offer a wide range of specialities such as *Melange* (milk coffee), *Schwarzer* (black coffee) or *kleiner Brauner* (small cup of coffee with milk or cream).

Österreichische Spezialitäten
Austrian specialities

G'spritzter [ˈkʃpʀɪtstɐ]	1/8 litre of wine diluted with the same amount of mineral water
Heuriger [ˈhɔɪʀɪgɐ]	young wine less than a year old
Backhendl [ˈbakhendl]	whole roast chicken
Brettljause [ˈbʀɛtljaʊzə]	a selection of cheeses and sliced cold meat
Cevapcici [tʃeˈvaptʃitʃi]	spicy, grilled minced meat fingers
Dampfnudeln [ˈdampfnuːdln]	yeast dumplings often eaten with custard

Erdäpfel [ˈʔeɐdepfl]	potatoes
Faschiertes [faˈʃiɐtəs]	minced/ground meat
Frittatensuppe [frɪˈdaːtnsupːe]	clear soup with strips of pancake
Germknödel [ˈgɛɐmkneːdl]	a yeast dumpling filled with plum jam
Geselchtes [ˈkselçtes]	smoked meat
Haxe [haksə]	pork knuckles
Jause [ˈjaʊzə]	afternoon snack
Kaiserschmarren [ˈkɛːzɐʃmoɐn]	Austrian pancakes with almonds and raisins
Kren [kʀeːn]	horseradish
Marillen [maˈʀɪln]	apricots
Nockerl [ˈnɔkɐl]	dumpling
Schlagobers [ˈʃlagobɐs]	whipped cream
Palatschinken [ˈpalatˌʃɪŋkŋ]	pancakes with chocolate sauce
Paradeiser [paʀaˈdaɪzɐ]	tomatoes
Sachertorte [ˈzaxɐtɔɐtə]	rich chocolate cake with a thin layer of apricot jam
Schwammerl [ˈʃvamɐl]	mushrooms
Semmel [semːl]	bread roll
Surstelze [ˈsuːrstəltsə]	pork knuckle
Tafelspitz [ˈtaːflʃpɪts]	boiled beef served with horseradish
Topfen [ˈtɔpfn]	*Quark:* thick, creamy dairy product
Topfenstrudel [ˈtɔpfnʃtʀuːdl]	similar to apple strudel, but filled with *Topfen*

Schweizer Spezialitäten
Swiss specialities

Café crème [kaˈfeː ˈkʀɛːm]	coffee with cream
Schale [ˈʃaːlə]	coffee with milk
Berner Platte [ˈbærnər ˈplatːe]	platter with different kinds of meat, boiled tongue, sausages and beans
Bündner Fleisch [ˈbyndnər flaɪʃ]	paper thin slices of air-dried beef
Bürli [ˈbyrli]	bread rolls
Fladen [flaːdn]	cake

Fondue [fɔn'dy:]	small pieces of fillet of pork/beef on skewers dipped in hot oil, served with various sauces
Glacé [gla'se:]	ice cream
Kabis ['xabis)]	cabbage
Käsefondue ['kɛzəfɔndy:]	cheese fondue: hot melted cheese into which pieces of bread are dipped
Raclette ['raxlet)]	slices of melted raclette cheese served with potatoes
Rahm [ʀa:m]	whipped cream
Rösti ['røʃti)]	hash brown potatoes
Rübli ['ʀy:bli]	carrots
Züricher Rahmgeschnetzeltes ['tsyrxər 'ʀa:mgʃnɛtsltəs]	strips of veal in a creamy wine and mushroom sauce

Sightseeing and excursions

Tourists love it here
The German-speaking countries are in many ways a tourist's dream. The countries are filled with old, romantic castles and other wonders of bygone days; the countryside is very pretty and remarkably varied; there is an abundance of cultural attractions such as festivals and concerts. Connecting all of this is an excellent system of roads and public transportation. Only the weather can be somewhat disappointing at times. Tourist high-season is the summer, of course. If you come earlier, the crowds of tourists will be smaller, but the weather more unpredictable. The crowds also get smaller starting in September, and the weather is usually quite good on into October – but the days will be shorter.
For information about interesting sights, festivals and events follow the L-sign to the *Fremdenverkehrsamt* (tourist office). There is one in nearly every town. Before you leave, you can also check ahead by looking at a city's web page. Frankfurt, for example, is **www.frankfurt.de**.

Tourist Information

Where's the tourist office?
Wo ist das Fremdenverkehrsamt? [vo: ˀɪst das fʀɛmdnfɐˈkeɐsˀamt]

I'd like a map of ..., please.
Ich hätte gern einen Stadtplan von ...
[ˀɪç ˈhɛtə gɛɐn ˀaɪnn ˈʃtatpla:n fɔn]

Have you got a calendar of events for this week?
Haben Sie einen Veranstaltungskalender für diese Woche?
[ha:bm zi ˀaɪnn fɐˈˀanʃtaltʊŋskaˌlɛndɐ fyɐ ˈdi:zə ˈvɔxə]

Are there sightseeing tours of the town?
Gibt es Stadtrundfahrten? [gɪpt əs ˈʃtatʀʊntfa:tn]

Cultural attractions

Opening hours, guided tours, admission

Can you tell me what special attractions there are here?
Können Sie mir bitte sagen, welche Sehenswürdigkeiten es hier gibt?
[kønn zi miɐ ˈbɪtə za:gŋ ˈvɛlçə ˈze:nsvʏɐdɪçkaɪtn əs hiɐ gɪpt]

You really must visit ...
Sie müssen unbedingt ... besichtigen.
[zi mʏsn ˈˀʊnbədɪŋt … bəˈzɪçtɪgŋ]

When's the museum open?
Wann ist das Museum geöffnet? [ˈvan ɪst das muˈzeʊm gəˈˀøfnət]

Most museums and art galleries are closed on Mondays.

When does the tour start?
Wann beginnt die Führung? [van bəˈgɪnt di ˈfy:ʀʊŋ]

Is there a tour in English, too?
Gibt es auch eine Führung auf Englisch?
[gɪpt əs aʊx ˀaɪnə ˈfy:ʀʊŋ ˀaʊf ˈˀɛŋlɪʃ]

Two tickets, please.
Zwei Eintrittskarten, bitte! [tsvaɪ ˈˀaɪntʀɪtska:tn ˈbɪtə]

Two adults and one child.
Zwei Erwachsene und ein Kind. [tsvaɪ ˀɐˈvaksənə ˀʊnt ˀaɪn ˈkɪnt]

Are there reductions for ...
Gibt es Ermäßigungen für ... [gɪpt əs ˀɐˈmɛ:sɪgʊŋŋ fyɐ]
children?
Kinder? [ˈkɪndɐ]
students?
Studenten? [ʃtʊˈdɛntn]
senior citizens?
Senioren? [zenˈjo:ʀən]
groups?
Gruppen? [ˈgʀʊpm]

Is there an exhibition catalogue?
Gibt es einen Katalog zur Ausstellung?
[gɪpt əs aɪnn kataˈlo:k tsʊɐ ˈˀaʊʃtɛlʊŋ]

What? Who? When?

Is this/that ...?
Ist das ...? [ˀɪst das]

When was the church built?
Wann wurde die Kirche erbaut? [ˈvan ˌvʊɐdə di: ˈkɪɐçə ˀɐˈbaʊt]

When was this building restored?
Wann wurde dieses Gebäude restauriert?
[van ˌvʊɐdə ˈdi:zəs gəˈbɔɪdə ʀɛstaʊˈʀiɐt]

Who painted this picture?
Von wem ist dieses Bild? [fɔn ve:m ˀɪst ˈdi:zəs bɪlt]

Have you got a poster of this picture?
Haben Sie das Bild als Poster? [ˈha:bm zi das bɪlt ˀals ˈpo:stɐ]

Cultural attractions

alley	die Gasse [di ˈgasə]
art	die Kunst [di kʊnst]
city centre	das Stadtzentrum [das ˈʃtattsɛntʀʊm]
district	der Stadtteil [dɐ ˈʃtataɪl]

Sightseeing and excursions

emblem	das Wahrzeichen [das ˈvaːtsaɪçn]
emperor/empress	der Kaiser/die Kaiserin [dɐ ˈkaɪzɐ/di ˈkaɪzəʀɪn]
findings	die Funde *m pl* [di fʊndə]
guide	der Fremdenführer/die Fremdenführerin [dɐ ˈfʀɛmdnfyːʀɐ/ˈfʀɛmdnfyːʀəʀɪn]
guided tour	die Führung [di ˈfyːʀʊŋ]
history	die Geschichte [di gəˈʃɪçtə]
home town	die Geburtsstadt [di gəˈbʊɐtʃtat]′ die Heimatstadt [di ˈhaɪmaːtʃtat]
house	das Haus [das haʊs]
king	der König [dɐ ˈkøːniç]
lane	die Gasse [di ˈgasə]
market	der Markt [dɐ maːkt]
museum	das Museum [das muˈzeːʊm]
ethnic museum of mankind	das Volkskundemuseum [das ˈfɔlkskʊndəmuˌzeʊm]
park	der Park [dɐ paːk]
pedestrian precinct/zone	die Fußgängerzone [di ˈfuːsgɛŋɐˌtsoːnə]
queen	die Königin [di ˈkøːnɪgɪn]
to reconstruct	rekonstruieren [ʀekɔnstʀʊˈʔiːʀən]
religion	die Religion [di ʀelɪˈgjoːn]
remains	die Überreste *m pl* [di ˈʔyːbɐʀɛstə]
to restore	restaurieren [ʀɛstaʊˈʀiːʀən]
road	die Straße [di ˈʃtʀaːsə]
sights	die Sehenswürdigkeiten *f pl* [di ˈzeːnsvʏɐdɪçkaɪtn]
sightseeing tour of the town/city	die Stadtrundfahrt [di ˈʃtatʀʊntfaːt]
street	die Straße [di ˈʃtʀaːsə]
suburb	der Vorort [dɐ ˈfoɐʔɔɐt]
symbol	das Wahrzeichen [das ˈvaːtsaɪçn]
tour	die Besichtigung [di bəˈzɪçtɪgʊŋ]
town centre/downtown	das Stadtzentrum [ˈʃtattsɛntʀʊm]

Architecture

abbey	die Abtei [di ʔapˈtaɪ]
altar	der Altar [dɐ ʔalˈtaː]
arch	der Bogen [dɐ ˈboːgŋ]
archaeology	die Archäologie [di ʔaːçeoloˈgiː]
architect	Architekt/Architektin [ʔaːçɪˈtɛkt/ʔaːçɪˈtɛkt ɪn]
architecture	die Architektur [di ʔaːçitɛkˈtuɐ]
bay	der Erker [dɐ ˈʔɛɐkɐ]
bay window	das Erkerfenster [das ˈʔɛɐkɐfɛnstɐ]
bridge	die Brücke [di ˈbʀʏkə]
building	das Gebäude [das gəˈbɔɪdə]

castle (*fortress*)	die Burg [di bʊɐk]
castle (*palace*)	das Schloss [das ʃlɔs]
cathedral	die Kathedrale [di kateˈdʀaːlə]
ceiling	die Decke [di ˈdɛkə]
cemetery	der Friedhof [dɐ ˈfʀiːtoːf]
chapel	die Kapelle [di kaˈpɛlə]
church	die Kirche [di ˈkɪɐçə]
cloister	der Kreuzgang [dɐ ˈkʀɔɪtsgaŋ]
column	die Säule [di ˈzɔɪlə]
convent	das(Nonnen)Kloster [das (ˈnɔnn)ˌkloːstɐ]
covered market	die Markthalle [di ˈmaːkthalə]
crypt	die Krypta [di kʀʏpta]
dome	die Kuppel [di kʊpl]
excavations	die Ausgrabungen *f pl* [di ˈʔaʊsgʀaːbʊŋŋ]
façade	die Fassade [di faˈsaːdə]
fortress	die Festung [di ˈfɛstʊŋ]
fountain	der (Spring)Brunnen [dɐ (ˈʃpʀɪŋ)bʀʊnn]
gable	der Giebel [dɐ giːbl]
gate	das Tor [das toɐ]
grave	das Grab [das gʀaːp]
graveyard	der Friedhof [dɐ ˈfʀiːtoːf]
inner courtyard	der Innenhof [dɐ ˈʔɪnnhoːf]
inscription	die Inschrift [di ˈʔɪnʃʀɪft]
mausoleum	das Mausoleum [das maʊzoˈleʊm]
memorial	die Gedenkstätte [di gəˈdɛŋkʃtɛtə]
monastery	das (Mönchs)Kloster [das (ˈmønçs)ˌkloːstɐ]
monument (*memorial edifice*)	das Denkmal [das ˈdɛŋkmaːl]
monument (*tomb*)	das Grabmal [ˈgʀaːbmaːl]
opera	die Oper [di ˈʔoːpɐ]
palace	der Palast [dɐ paˈlast]
pilgrimage church	die Wallfahrtskirche [di ˈvalfaːtsˌkɪɐçə]
pillar	die Säule [di ˈzɔɪlə], der Pfeiler [dɐ ˈpfaɪlɐ]
portal	das Portal [das pɔ(ɐ)ˈtaːl]
pulpit	die Kanzel [di kantsl]
to rebuild	wieder aufbauen [viːdɐ ˈʔaʊfbaʊən]
roof	das Dach [das dax]
ruin	die Ruine [di ʀuˈʔiːnə]
square	der Platz [dɐ plats]
steeple	der Kirchturm [dɐ ˈkɪɐçtʊɐm]
temple	der Tempel [dɐ tɛmpl]
theatre	das Theater [das teˈʔaːtɐ]
tomb	das Grab [das gʀaːp]
tower	der Turm [dɐ tʊɐm]

town centre	die Innenstadt [di ˈˀɪnnʃtat]
the old town	die Altstadt [di ˈˀaltʃtat]
town hall	das Rathaus [das ˈʀa:thaʊs]
town walls	die Stadtmauern *f pl* [di ˈʃtatmaʊɐn]
treasure chamber	die Schatzkammer [di ˈʃatskamɐ]
triumphal arch	der Triumphbogen [dɐ tʀiˈʊmpfbo:gŋ]
university	die Universität [di ˀʊnivɛɐziˈtɛ:t]
vault(s)	das Gewölbe [das gəˈvølbə]
wall (*supportive structure*)	die Mauer [di ˈmaʊɐ]
wall (*inside partition of house*)	die Wand [di vant]
window	das Fenster [das ˈfɛnstɐ]
wing	der Flügel [dɐ fly:gl]

Arts and artefacts

arts and crafts	das Kunstgewerbe [das ˈkʊnstgəvɛɐbə]
bronze	die Bronze [di ˈbʀɔŋsə]
carpet	der Teppich [dɐ ˈtɛpɪç]
ceramics	die Keramik [di keˈʀa:mɪk]
china	das Porzellan [das pɔɐtsəˈla:n]
copperplate	der Kupferstich [dɐ ˈkʊpfɐʃtɪç]
copy	die Kopie [di koˈpi:]
cross	das Kreuz [das ˈkʀɔɪts]
crucifix	das Kruzifix [das ˈkʀʊtsifɪks]
drawing	die Zeichnung [di ˈtsaɪçnʊŋ]
etching	die Radierung [di ʀaˈdi:ʀʊŋ]
exhibit	das Exponat [das ˀɛkspoˈna:t]
exhibition	die Ausstellung [di ˈˀaʊʃtɛlʊŋ]
gallery	die Galerie [di galəˈʀi:]
glass painting	die Glasmalerei [di ˈgla:sma:ləˌʀaɪ]
gold work	die Goldschmiedekunst [di ˈgɔltʃmi:dəˌkʊnst]
graphic arts	die Grafik [di ˈgʀa:fɪk]
lithograph; lithography	die Lithografie [di litograˈfi:]
model	das Modell [das moˈdɛl]
mosaic	das Mosaik [das mozaˈˀi:k]
nude (*painting*)	der Akt [dɐ ˀakt]
original (*version*)	das Original [das ˀɔʀigiˈna:l]
painter	der Maler/die Malerin [dɐ ˈma:lɐ/di ˈma:ləʀɪn]
painting (*picture or portrait*)	das Gemälde [das gəˈmɛ:ldə]
painting (*type of art*)	die Malerei [di ma:ləˈʀaɪ]
photography	die Fotografie [di fotogʀaˈfi:]
picture	das Bild [das bɪlt]
porcelain	das Porzellan [das pɔ(ɐ)tsəˈla:n]
portrait	das Porträt [das pɔ(ɐ)ˈtʀɛ:]
poster	das Plakat [das plaˈka:t]
pottery	die Töpferei [di tøpfəˈʀaɪ]

sculptor	der Bildhauer/die Bildhauerin [dɐ ˈbɪlthaʊɐ/di ˈbɪlthaʊəʀɪn]
sculpture	die Skulptur [di skʊlpˈtuɐ]
silk-screen print	der Siebdruck [dɐ ˈziːpdʀʊk]
statue	die Statue [di ˈʃtaːtuə]
still life	das Stillleben [das ˈʃtɪleːbm]
tapestry	der Wandteppich [dɐ ˈvanttɛpɪç]
terracotta	die Terrakotta [di tɛʀaˈkɔta]
torso	der Torso [dɐ ˈtɔɐzo]
vase	die Vase [di ˈvaːzə]
water-colour (picture)	das Aquarell [das ˀakvaˈʀɛl]
wood carving	die Schnitzerei [di ʃnɪtsəˈʀaɪ]
woodcut	der Holzschnitt [dɐ ˈhɔltʃnɪt]

Styles and ages

ancient	antik [ˀanˈtiːk]
art nouveau	der Jugendstil [dɐ ˈjuːgŋtstiːl]
baroque	barock [baˈʀɔk]
bronze age	die Bronzezeit [di ˈbʀɔŋsətsaɪt]
Celtic	keltisch [ˈkɛltɪʃ]
century	das Jahrhundert [das jaˈhʊndɐt]
Christianity	das Christentum [das ˈkʀɪstntuːm]
classicism	der Klassizismus [dɐ klasɪˈtsɪsmʊs]
dynasty	die Dynastie [di dʏnasˈtiː]
epoch	die Epoche [di ˀeˈpɔxə]
expressionism	der Expressionismus [dɐ ˀɛkspʀɛsjoˈnɪsmus]
Gothic	die Gotik [di ˈgoːtik]
Greek	griechisch [ˈgʀiːçɪʃ]
heathen	heidnisch [ˈhaɪtnɪʃ]
impressionism	der Impressionismus [dɐ ˀɪmpʀɛsjoˈnɪsmʊs]
mannerism	der Manierismus [dɐ ˌmaniːˈʀɪsmʊs]
Middle Ages	das Mittelalter [das ˈmɪtlˀaltɐ]
modern	modern [moˈdɛɐn]
pagan	heidnisch [ˈhaɪtnɪʃ]
prehistoric	vorgeschichtlich [ˈfoɐgəʃɪçtlɪç]
prime	die Blütezeit [di ˈblyːtətsaɪt]
Renaissance	die Renaissance [di ʀənɛˈsa)ːs]
rococo	das Rokoko [das ˈʀɔkoko]
Romanesque style/period	die Romanik [di ʀoˈmaːnɪk]
Romanticism	die Romantik [di ʀoˈmantɪk]
Stone Age	die Steinzeit [di ˈʃtaɪntsaɪt]

Excursions

When do we meet?
Wann treffen wir uns? [van ˈtʀɛfn viɐ ˀʊns]

Where do we leave from?
Wo fahren wir los? [vo: ˈfa:ʀən viɐ lo:s]

Will we pass ...?
Kommen wir an ... vorbei? [kɔmm viɐ ˀan … fɔˈbaɪ]

Are we going to see ..., too?
Besichtigen wir auch ...? [bəˈzɪçtɪgŋ viɐ ˀaʊx …]

amusement park	der Freizeitpark [dɐ ˈfʀaɪtsaɪtˌpa:k]
botanic gardens	der botanische Garten [dɐ boˈtanɪʃə ˈga:tn]
cave	die Höhle [di ˈhø:lə]
cliff	die Klippe [di ˈklɪpə]
country(side)	das Land [das ˈlant]
day trip	der Tagesausflug [dɐ ˈta:gəsˌˀaʊsflu:k]
dripstone cave	die Tropfsteinhöhle [di ˈtʀɔpfʃtaɪnˌhø:lə]
excursion	der Ausflug [dɐ ˈˀaʊsflu:k]
fishing port	der Fischerhafen [dɐ ˈfɪʃɐha:fn]
forest	der Wald [dɐ valt]
island	die Insel [di ˀɪnzl]
lake	der See [dɐ ze:]
market	der Markt [dɐ ma:kt]
mountains	das Gebirge [das gəˈbɪɐgə]
mountain village	das Bergdorf [das ˈbɛɐkdoɐf]
national park	der Nationalpark [dɐ natsjoˈna:lpa:k]
nature reserve	das Naturschutzgebiet [das naˈtuɐʃʊtsgəbi:t]
observatory	die Sternwarte [di ˈʃtɛɐnva:tə]
open-air museum	das Freilichtmuseum [das ˈfʀaɪlɪçtmuˌzeʊm]
place of pilgrimage	der Wallfahrtsort [dɐ ˈvalfa:tsˌˀɔɐt]
ravine	die Schlucht [di ˈʃlʊxt]
scenery	die Landschaft [di ˈlantʃaft]
surroundings	die Umgebung [di ˀʊmˈge:bʊŋ]
tour	die Rundfahrt [di ˈʀʊntfa:t]
trip	der Ausflug [dɐ ˈˀaʊsflu:k]
valley	das Tal [das ta:l]
vantage point	der Aussichtspunkt [dɐ ˈˀaʊsɪçtspʊŋt]
view	die Aussicht [di ˈˀaʊsɪçt]
waterfall	der Wasserfall [dɐ ˈvasɐfal]
wildlife park	der Wildpark [dɐ ˈvɪltpa:k]
woods	der Wald [dɐ valt]
zoo	der Zoo [dɐ tso:]

Active and creative holidays

Lots of opportunities
Germany is a very popular country. It offers fine scenery, from high mountains to beaches on the sea, and noteworthy cultural attractions. The weather in the summer is usually mild, although there can be rather high humidity in some areas. Regardless of the time of year, you'll have a lot to choose from, and you can take advantage of numerous sporting and cultural opportunities, from swimming and hiking to booking a language course to improve your German.

Bathing and swimming

Excuse me, is there a ... here?
Entschuldigen Sie bitte, gibt es hier ein ...
[ˀɛntˈʃʊldɪgŋ zi ˈbɪtə gɪpt ɛs hiɐ ˀaɪn ...]
  swimming pool
  Schwimmbad? [ˈʃvɪmba:t]
  outdoor pool
  Freibad? [ˈfʀaɪba:t]
  indoor pool
  Hallenbad? [halnba:t]

A/One ticket, please.
Eine Eintrittskarte, bitte! [ˈˀaɪnə ˈˀaɪntʀɪtska:tə ˈbɪtə]

Can you tell me where the ... are, please?
Können Sie mir bitte sagen, wo die ... sind?
[kønn zi miɐ ˈbɪtə za:gŋ vo: di ... zɪnt]
  showers
  Duschen [ˈdu:ʃn]
  changing rooms
  Umkleidekabinen [ˈˀʊmklaɪdəkaˌbi:nn]

Is the beach ...
Ist der Strand ... [ˀɪst dɐ ʃtʀant ...]
  sandy?
  sandig? [ˈzandɪç]
  pebbled/stony?
  steinig? [ˈʃtaɪnɪç]

Are there any sea urchins/jellyfish here?
Gibt es hier Seeigel/Quallen? [gɪpt əs hiɐ ˈze:ˀi:gl/ˈkvaln]

Is the current strong?
Ist die Strömung stark? [ˀɪst di ˈʃtʀø:mʊŋ ʃta:k]

Is it dangerous for children?
Ist es für Kinder gefährlich? [ˀɪst əs fyɐ ˈkɪndɐ gəˈfeɐlɪç]

When's low tide/high tide?
Wann ist Ebbe/Flut? [van ɪst ˈˀɛbə/ˈflu:t]

I'd like to rent ...
Ich möchte ... mieten. [ˀɪç ˈmøçtə ... miːtn]
a deck chair.
einen Liegestuhl [ˀaɪnn ˈliːgəʃtuːl]
a sunshade.
einen Sonnenschirm [ˀaɪnn ˈzɔnnʃɪɐm]
a boat.
ein Boot [ˀaɪn ˈboːt]
a pair of water skis.
ein Paar Wasserski [ˀaɪn paː ˈvasɐʃiː]

How much is it per hour/day?
Was kostet das pro Stunde/Tag? [vas ˈkɔstət das pʀo ˈʃtʊndə/taːk]

air mattress	die Luftmatratze [di ˈlʊftmaˌtʀatsə]
boat-hire	der Bootsverleih [dɐ ˈboːtsfɐlaɪ]
children's pool	das Kinderbecken [das ˈkɪndɐbɛkŋ]
lifeguard	der Bademeister/die Bademeisterin [dɐ ˈbaːdəmaɪstɐ/ˈbaːdəmaɪstəʀɪn]
non-swimmer	der Nichtschwimmer [dɐ ˈnɪçtʃvɪmɐ]
nudist beach	der FKK-Strand [dɐ ˀɛfkaˈkaːʃtʀant]
pedal boat/pedalo	das Tretboot [das ˈtʀeːtboːt]
swimmer	der Schwimmer/die Schwimmerin [dɐ ˈʃvɪmɐ/di ˈʃvɪməʀɪn]
to swim	schwimmen [ʃvɪmm]
volleyball	der Volleyball [dɐ ˈvɔlɪbal]
to go water skiing	Wasserski fahren [ˈvasɐʃiː ˈfaːʀən]
water wings	die Schwimmflügel *m pl* [di ˈʃvɪmflyːgl]
windbreak	der Windschirm [dɐ ˈvɪntʃɪɐm]

Other sporting activities

Popular sports are soccer, tennis and cycling in summer and skiing in winter. Golf is becoming quite popular now, although golf courses are usually for members only.
The national pastime-sport is *Wandern,* something between hiking and walking. In almost any larger wooded area there'll be a parking area *(Wanderparkplatz),* complete with a map on a signboard showing possible routes and walking time.

What sort of sports facilities are there here?
Welche Sportmöglichkeiten gibt es hier?
[ˈvɛlçə ˈʃpɔɐtmøːklɪçkaɪtn gɪpt əs hiɐ]

Is there ... here?
Gibt es hier ... [gɪpt əs hiɐ ...]

a golf course
einen Golfplatz? [ˀaɪnn ˈgɔlfplats]
a tennis court
einen Tennisplatz? [ˀaɪnn ˈtɛnɪsplats]

Where can I go ... here?
Wo kann man hier ... [vo: kan man hiɐ ...]
fishing
angeln? [ˈˀaŋln]
hiking
wandern? [ˈvandɐn]

Where can I hire/rent ...?
Wo kann ich ... ausleihen? [vo: ˈkan ɪç ... ˈˀaʊslaɪn]

I'd like to take a beginner's course/an advanced course.
Ich möchte einen Kurs für Anfänger/Fortgeschrittene machen.
[ˀɪç ˈmøçtə ˀaɪnn kʊɐs fyɐ ˈˀanfɛŋɐ/ˈfɔɐtgəʃʀɪtənə maxn]

Water sport

canoe	das Kanu [das ˈka:nu]
inflatable (boat)	das Schlauchboot [das ˈʃlaʊxbo:t]
motorboat	das Motorboot [das ˈmo:tɔbo:t]
pick-up service	der Rückholservice [dɐ ˈʀʏkho:løsøɐvɪs]
regatta	die Regatta [di ʀeˈgata]
to row	rudern [ˈʀu:dɐn]
rowing boat	das Ruderboot [das ˈʀu:dɐbo:t]
rubber dinghy	das Schlauchboot [das ˈʃlaʊxbo:t]
to sail	segeln [ˈze:gln]
sailing boat	das Segelboot [das ˈze:glbo:t]
to surf	surfen [ˈsøɐfn]
surfboard	das Surfbrett [das ˈsøɐfbʀɛt]
wind conditions	die Windverhältnisse *n pl* [di ˈvɪntfɐˌhɛltnɪsə]
windsurfing	das Windsurfen [das ˈvɪntsøɐfn]

Diving

to dive	tauchen [taʊxn]
diving equipment	die Taucherausrüstung [di ˈtaʊxɐˀaʊsʀʏstʊŋ]
diving goggles	die Taucherbrille [di ˈtaʊxɐbʀɪlə]
snorkel	der Schnorchel [dɐ ʃnɔɐçl]
to go snorkelling	schnorcheln [ʃnɔɐçln]
wetsuit	der Neoprenanzug [dɐ neoˈpʀe:nˌˀantsu:k]

Fishing

bait	der Köder [dɐ ˈkø:dɐ]
fishing licence	der Angelschein [dɐ ˈʔaŋlʃaɪn]
fishing rod	die Angel [di ʔaŋl]
fresh water	das Süßwasser [das ˈzy:svasɐ]
to go fishing	angeln [ˈʔaŋln]
off season	die Schonzeit [di ˈʃo:ntsaɪt]
salt water	das Salzwasser [das ˈzaltsvasɐ]

Ball games

ball	der Ball [dɐ bal]
basketball	der Basketball [dɐ ˈba:skətbal]
football	der Fußball [dɐ ˈfu:sbal]
football pitch/football field	der Fußballplatz [dɐ ˈfu:sbalˌplats]
football match	das Fußballspiel [das ˈfu:sbalˌʃpi:l]
goal	das Tor [das toɐ]
goalkeeper	der Torwart [dɐ ˈtoɐva:t]
half-time	die Halbzeit [di ˈhalptsaɪt]
handball	der Handball [ˈhantbal]
team	die Mannschaft [di ˈmanʃaft]
volleyball	der Volleyball [dɐ ˈvɔlɪbal]

Tennis and badminton

badminton (sport)	das Badminton [das ˈbɛtmɪntn]
doubles	das Doppel [das dɔpl]
floodlight(s)	das Flutlicht [das flu:tlɪçt]
racquet	der Schläger [dɐ ˈʃlɛ:gɐ]
shuttlecock	der Federball [dɐ ˈfe:dɐbal]
singles	das Einzel [das ˈʔaɪntsəl]
squash	das Squash [das skvɔʃ]
table tennis	das Tischtennis [das ˈtiʃtɛnɪs]
tennis	das Tennis [das ˈtɛnɪs]
tennis racquet	der Tennisschläger [dɐ ˈtɛnɪʃlɛ:gɐ]

Fitness and working out

aerobics	das Aerobic [das ʔɛˈʀɔbɪk]
body-building	das Bodybuilding [das ˈbɔdɪbɪldɪŋ]
fitness centre	das Fitnesscenter [das ˈfɪtnəsˌtsɛntɐ]
fitness training	das Konditionstraining [das kɔndɪˈtsjo:nstʀɛ:nɪŋ]
gymnastics	die Gymnastik [di gʏmˈnastɪk]

jazz aerobics	die Jazzgymnastik [di ˈdʒɛsgʏmˌnastɪk]
jogging	das Jogging [das ˈdʒɔgɪŋ]
to jog	joggen [ˈdʒɔgŋ]
weight training	das Krafttraining [das ˈkʀaftʀɛːnɪŋ]

Cycling

bicycle/bike	das Fahrrad [das ˈfaːʀat]
crash helmet	der Fahrradhelm [dɐ ˈfaːʀatˌhɛlm]
to cycle	Rad fahren [ˈʀaːt ˈfaːʀən]
cycle path	der Fahrradweg [dɐ ˈfaːʀatveːk]
cycle tour	die Radtour [di ˈʀaːttuɐ]
cycling	der Radsport [dɐ ˈʀaːtʃpɔɐt]
flat tyre/tire	die Panne [di ˈpanə]
mountain bike	das Mountainbike [das ˈmaʊntnbaɪk]
pump	die Luftpumpe [di ˈlʊftpʊmpə]
racing bike	das Rennrad [das ˈʀɛnʀaːt]
repair kit	das Flickzeug [das ˈflɪktsɔɪk]
touring bike	das Tourenrad [das ˈtuːʀənʀaːt]
trekking bike	das Trekkingrad [das ˈtʀɛkɪŋʀaːt]

Hiking and mountaineering

I'd like to go for a hike in the mountains.
Ich möchte eine Bergtour machen.
[ˀɪç ˈmøçtə ˌˀaɪnə ˈbɛɐktuɐ maxn]

Can you show me an interesting route on the map?
Können Sie mir eine interessante Route auf der Karte zeigen?
[kønn zi miɐ ˌˀaɪnə ˀɪntʀəˈsantə ˈʀuːtə ˀaʊf dɐ ˈkaːtə tsaɪgŋ]

day trip	die Tagestour [di ˈtaːgəstuɐ]
freeclimbing	das Freeclimbing [das ˈfʀiːklaɪmbɪŋ]
to hike	wandern [ˈvandɐn]
hiking map	die Wanderkarte [di ˈvandɐkaːtə]
hiking trail	der Wanderweg [dɐ ˈvandɐveːk]
mountaineering	das Bergsteigen [das ˈbɛɐkʃtaɪgŋ]
path	der Pfad [dɐ pfaːt]
refuge hut/shelter	die Schutzhütte [di ˈʃʊtshʏtə]

Riding

horse	das Pferd [das pfeɐt]
ride, horse ride	der Ausritt [dɐ ˈaʊsʀɪt]
to ride	reiten [ˈʀaɪtn]

riding holiday	die Reiterferien *pl* [di ˈʀaɪtɐˌfeːʀiən]
riding school	die Reitschule [ˈʀaɪtʃuːlə]
saddle	der Sattel [dɐ zatl]

Golf

18-hole course	der 18-Loch-Platz [dɐ ˈaxtseːn lɔx plats]
club member	das Clubmitglied [das ˈklʊpˌmɪtgliːt]
clubhouse	das Clubhaus [das ˈklʊphaʊs]
day guest	der Tagesbesucher [dɐ ˈtaːgəsbəzuːxɐ]
golf	das Golf [das gɔlf]
golf club *(implement)*	der Golfschläger [dɐ ˈgɔlfʃlɛːgɐ]
golf course	der Golfplatz [dɐ ˈgɔlfplats]
to play a round of golf	eine Runde Golf spielen [ˀaɪnə ˈʀʊndə gɔlf ˈʃpiːln]
tee	das Tee [das tiː]
tee-off	der Abschlag [dɐ apʃlaːk]

Gliding

glider	das Segelflugzeug [das ˈzeːglˌfluːktsɔɪk]
gliding	das Segelfliegen [das ˈzeːglfliːgŋ]
hang-gliding	das Drachenfliegen [das ˈdʀaxnfliːgŋ]
parachute	der Fallschirm [dɐ ˈfalʃɪɐm]
parachuting	das Fallschirmspringen [das ˈfalʃɪɐmʃpʀɪŋŋ]
paraglider	der Gleitschirm [dɐ ˈglaɪtʃɪɐm]
take-off area	der Startplatz [dɐ ˈʃtaːtplats]

Winter holidays

A day ticket, please.
Eine Tageskarte, bitte. [ˀaɪnə ˈtaːgəskaːtə ˈbɪtə]

How many points does this ski lift cost?
Wie viele Punkte kostet dieser Skilift?
[ˈviː filə ˈpʊŋktə ˈkɔstət diːzɐ ˈʃiːlɪft]

What time is the last trip up the mountain?
Um wie viel Uhr ist die letzte Bergfahrt?
[ˀʊm ˈviː fil ˀuɐ ˀɪst di ˈlɛtstə ˈbɛɐkfaːt]

baby lift	Babylift [ˈbeːbilɪft]
bottom station, base terminal	die Talstation [di ˈtaːlʃtaˌtsjoːn]
cable car	die Seilbahn [di ˈzaɪlbaːn]

cable railway	die (Stand)Seilbahn [di (ˈʃtant)ˌzaɪlbaːn]
chair-lift	der Sessellift [dɐ ˈzɛslɪft]
cross-country ski course	die Loipe [di lɔɪpə]
cross-country skiing	der Langlauf [dɐ ˈlaŋlaʊf]
curling	das Curling [das ˈkəːlɪŋ]
day pass	der Tagespass [dɐ ˈtaːgəspas]
downhill skiing	Ski alpin [ʃiː ˀalˈpiːn]
drag lift	der Schlepplift [dɐ ˈʃlɛplɪft]
funicular	die (Stand)Seilbahn [di (ˈʃtant)ˌzaɪlbaːn]
ice hockey	das Eishockey [das ˈˀaɪshɔkeː]
ice rink	die Eisbahn [di ˈˀaɪsbaːn]
to go ice skating	Schlittschuh laufen [ˈʃlɪtʃuː laʊfn]
ice skates	die Schlittschuhe *m pl* [di ˈʃlɪtʃuːə]
middle station	die Mittelstation [di ˈmɪtlʃtaˌtsjoːn]
ski	der Ski [dɐ ʃiː]
ski bindings	die Skibindungen *f pl* [di ˈʃiːbɪndʊŋŋ]
ski goggles	die Skibrille [di ˈʃiːbʀɪlə]
ski instructor	der Skilehrer/die Skilehrerin [dɐ ˈʃiːleːʀɐ/ˈʃiːleːʀəʀɪn]
ski poles	die Skistöcke *m pl* [di ˈʃiːˈʃtøkə]
ski slope	die Skipiste [di ˈʃiːpɪstə]
to go skiing	Ski laufen [ˈʃiː laʊfn]
skiing course	der Skikurs [dɐ ˈʃiːkʊɐs]
sledge	der Schlitten [dɐ ʃlɪtn]
snowboard	das Snowboard [das ˈsnoːbɔɐt]
summit station/top station	die Bergstation [di ˈbɛɐkʃtaˌtsjoːn]
toboggan	der Schlitten [dɐ ʃlɪtn]
week('s) pass	der Wochenpass [dɐ ˈvɔxnpas]

Other sports

athletics	die Leichtathletik [di ˈlaɪçtˀatˌleːtɪk]
bowling (tenpin)	das Bowling [das ˈboːlɪŋ]
bowling (ninepin)	das Kegeln [das keːgln]
crazy golf	das Minigolf [das ˈmɪnigɔlf]
inline skating	das Inlineskating [das ˈˀɪnlaɪnˌskɛɪtɪŋ]
motor-racing	der Motorsport [dɐ ˈmoːtɔʃpɔɐt]
to go roller-skating	Rollschuh fahren [ˈʀɔlʃuː ˈfaːʀən]
skateboard	das Skateboard [das ˈskɛɪtbɔɐt]
to skateboard	Skateboard fahren [ˈskɛɪtbɔɐt ˈfaːʀən]

Sporting events

Can you tell me what sort of sporting events there are here?
Können Sie mir bitte sagen, welche Sportveranstaltungen es hier gibt?
[kønn zi miɐ ˈbɪtə zaːgŋ ˈvɛlçə ˈʃpɔɐtfɐˌʔanʃtaltʊŋŋ əs hiɐ gɪpt]

I'd like to see the football match.
Ich möchte mir das Fußballspiel ansehen.
[ʔɪç ˈmøçtə miɐ das ˈfuːsbalʃpiːl ˈʔanzeːn]

When/Where is it?
Wann/Wo findet es statt? [van/voː fɪndət əs ˈʃtat]

What's the score?
Wie steht's? [viː ʃteːts]

Two-one.
Zwei zu eins. [tsvaɪ tsʊ ʔaɪns]

Three all/three tied.
Drei-drei. [dʀaɪ dʀaɪ]

Foul!
Foul! [faʊl]

Good shot!
Schöner Schuss! [ˈʃøːnɐ ʃʊs]

Goal!
Tor! [toɐ]

athlete	der Sportler/die Sportlerin [dɐ ˈʃpɔɐtlɐ/di ˈʃpɔɐtləʀɪn]
championship	die Meisterschaft [di ˈmaɪstɐʃaft]
contest	der Wettkampf [dɐ ˈvɛtkamf]
corner kick	der Eckstoß [dɐ ˈʔɛkʃtoːs]
cross	die Flanke [di flaŋkə]
cycle racing	das Radrennen [das ˈʀaːtʀɛnn]
defeat	die Niederlage [di ˈniːdɐlaːgə]
draw	unentschieden [ˈʔʊnɛntˌʃiːdn]
free kick	der Freistoß [dɐ ˈfʀaɪʃtoːs]
game	das Spiel [ʃpiːl]
kickoff	der Anstoß [dɐ ˈanʃtoːs]
to lose	verlieren [fɐˈliːʀən]
match	das Spiel [ʃpiːl]
offside	abseits [ˈʔapzaɪts]
pass	der Pass [dɐ pas]
penalty kick	der Elfmeter [dɐ ʔɛlfˈmeːtɐ]
penalty box	der Strafraum [dɐ ˈʃtʀaːfʀaʊm]
program(me)	das Programm [das pʀoˈgʀam]
race	das Rennen [das ʀɛnn]

referee	der Schiedsrichter [dɐ ˈʃiːtsʀɪçtɐ]
to score a goal	ein Tor schießen [ˀaɪn toɐ ʃiːsn]
sports ground	der Sportplatz [dɐ ˈʃpɔɐtplats]
stadium	das Stadion [das ˈʃtaːdjon]
ticket	die Eintrittskarte [di ˈˀaɪntʀɪtsˌkaːtə]
ticket office	die Kasse [di ˈkasə]
umpire	der Schiedsrichter [dɐ ˈʃiːtsʀɪçtɐ]
victory/win	der Sieg [dɐ ziːk]
to win	gewinnen [gəˈvɪnn]

Wellness

How many more treatments do I get?
Wie viele Anwendungen bekomme ich noch?
[ˈviː fiːlə ˈˀanvɛndʊŋŋ bəˈkɔmə ɪç nɔx]

I'd like a number of additional ...
Ich möchte noch einige zusätzliche ...
[ˀɪç ˈmœçtə nɔx ˈˀaɪnɪgə ˈtsuːzɛtslɪçə]

Could I have another appointment?
Könnte ich einen anderen Termin bekommen?
[ˈkœntə ɪç ˀaɪnn ˈˀandəʁən tɛɐˈmiːn bəˈkɔmm]

Are you also having a ...?
Machen Sie auch ein(e) ... [ˈmaxn zi ˀaʊx ˈˀaɪn(ə)]

I suffer from ...
Ich leide unter ... [ˀɪç ˈlaɪdə ˈˀʊntɐ]

aqua jogging	das Aqua-Jogging [das ˈˀakvaˌdʒɔgɪŋ]
acupuncture	die Akupunktur [di ˀakupʊŋ(k)ˈtuɐ]
aroma bath	das Aromabad [das ˀaˈʁoːmabaːt]
Ayurveda	Ayurveda [ˀajʊˈveːda]
treatment	die Behandlung [di bəˈhandlʊŋ]
purify, detoxify	die Entschlacken, die Entgiftung [di ˀɛntˈʃlakuŋ/di ˀɛntˈgɪftuŋ]
fango	der Fango [dɐ ˈfaŋgo]
reflexology (foot) massage	die Fuß(reflexzonen)massage [di ˈfuːs(ʁeˈflɛkstsoːnn)maˌsaːʒə]
full body massage	die Ganzkörpermassage [di ˈgantsˌkœɐpɐmaˌsaːʒə]
face treatment	die Gesichtsbehandlung [di gəˈzɪçtsbəˌhandlʊŋ]
therapeutic bath	das Heilbad [das ˈhaɪlbaːt]
fasting cure	das Heilfasten [das ˈhaɪlfastn]
hay bath	das Heu-Bad [das ˈhɔɪbaːt]

kneipism	die Kneipp-Anwendung [di 'knaɪpanˌvɛndʊŋ]
visitor's tax	die Kurtaxe [di 'kuɐtaksə]
lymphatic drainage	die Lymphdrainage [di 'lʏmfdʁɛˌna:ʒə]
massage	die Massage [di ma'sa:ʒə]
meditation	die Meditation [di ˌmedita'tsjo:n]
therapy	die Therapie [di teʁa'pi:]
thermal baths	das Thermalbad [das tɛɐ'ma:lba:t]
treatments	die Anwendungen *f pl* [di 'anˌvɛndʊŋŋ]
wave pool	das Wellenbad [das 'vɛlnba:t]
yoga	das Yoga [das 'jo:ga]

Creative holidays

I'm interested in ...
Ich interessiere mich für ... [ˀɪç ˀɪntʀə'si:ʀə mɪç fyɐ ...]
a pottery course.
einen Töpferkurs. [ˀaɪnn 'tøpfɐkʊɐs]
a German course.
einen Deutschkurs. [ˀaɪnn 'dɔɪtʃkʊɐs]
for beginners
für Anfänger [fyɐ 'ˀanfɛŋɐ]
for advanced learners
für Fortgeschrittene [fyɐ 'fɔɐtgəʃʀɪtnə]

How many hours per day are we together?
Wie viele Stunden pro Tag arbeiten wir zusammen?
['vi: fi:lə 'ʃtʊndn pʀo ta:k 'ˀa:baɪtn viɐ tsʊ'zamm]

Is the number of participants limited?
Ist die Teilnehmerzahl begrenzt? [ˀɪst di 'taɪlne:mɐtsa:l bə'gʀɛntst]

When do I have to enrol(l) by?
Bis wann muss man sich anmelden?
[bis van mʊs man zɪç 'ˀanmɛldn]

Are the costs of materials included?
Sind die Materialkosten inklusive?
[zɪnt di mateʀɪ'a:lkɔstn ˀɪŋklʊ'zi:və]

What should I bring along?
Was soll ich mitbringen? [vas zɔl ɪç 'mɪtbrɪŋŋ]

carpentry workshop	die Holzwerkstatt [di 'hɔltsˌvɛɐkʃtat]
to cook	kochen ['kɔxn]
course	der Kurs [dɐ kʊɐs]
dance theatre	das Tanztheater [das 'tantsteˌˀa:tɐ]
drama workshop	der Schauspielworkshop [dɐ 'ʃaʊʃpi:lˌwə:kʃɔp]

to draw	zeichnen [ˈtsaɪçnn]
drumming	das Trommeln [das ˈtʀɔmln]
meditation	die Meditation [di meditaˈtsjoːn]
oil painting	die Ölmalerei [di ˈʔøːlmaːləˌʀaɪ]
to paint	malen [maːln]
silk painting	die Seidenmalerei [di ˈzaɪdnmaːləˌʀaɪ]
to photograph	fotografieren [ˌfotoɡʀaˈfiːʀən]
workshop	der Workshop [dɐ ˈwəːkʃɔp]
yoga	das Yoga [das ˈjoːga]

Entertainment

Culture, fun and diversion
All year long you'll find countless opportunities for entertainment. The normal concert and theatre season is from autumn to spring, but during the summer there are numerous festivals, including outdoor performances. Most cities and larger towns have websites (e.g. www.heidelberg.de for Heidelberg) where you can find out what's going on and get valuable tips for booking or planning your stay.

Theatre - Concert - Cinema

Could you tell me what's on at the theatre tonight, please?
Könnten Sie mir bitte sagen, welches Stück heute Abend im Theater gespielt wird? [køntn zi miɐ ˈbɪtə zaːgŋ ˈvɛlçəs ʃtʏk ˈhɔɪtə ˀaːbmt ˀɪm teˈˀaːtɐ gəˈʃpiːlt vɪɐt]

What's on at the cinema/movies tomorrow night?
Was läuft morgen Abend im Kino?
[vas lɔɪft ˌmɔɐgŋ ˈˀaːbmt ˀɪm ˈkiːno]

Are there concerts in the cathedral?
Werden im Dom Konzerte veranstaltet?
[veɐdn ˀɪm ˈdoːm kɔnˈtsɛɐtə fɐˈˀanʃtaltət]

Can you recommend a good play?
Können Sie mir ein gutes Theaterstück empfehlen?
[ˈkønn zi miɐ ˀaɪn ˈguːtəs teˈˀaːtɐʃtʏk ˀɛmpˈfeːln]

When does the performance start?
Wann beginnt die Vorstellung? [van bəˈgɪnt di ˈfoɐʃtɛlʊŋ]

Where can I get tickets?
Wo bekommt man Karten? [voː bəˈkɔmt man ˈkaːtn]

Two tickets for this evening, please.
Bitte zwei Karten für heute Abend.
[ˈbɪtə tsvaɪ ˈkaːtn fyɐ ˈhɔɪtə ˀaːbmt]

Two seats at ..., please.
Bitte zwei Plätze zu ... [ˈbɪtə ˈtsvaɪ ˈplɛtsə tsʊ]

Can I have a programme, please?
Kann ich bitte ein Programm haben?
[kan ɪç ˈbɪtə ˀaɪn pʀoˈgʀam ˈhaːbm]

advance booking	der Vorverkauf [dɐ ˈfoɐfɐkaʊf]
box office	die Kasse [di ˈkasə]
cloakroom	die Garderobe [di gaˈdʀoːbə]
festival	das Festival [das ˈfɛstɪval]
interval/intermission	die Pause [di ˈpaʊzə]
performance	die Vorstellung [di ˈfoɐʃtɛlʊŋ]

program(me)	das Programmheft [das pʀoˈgʀamhɛft]
ticket	die Eintrittskarte [di ˈʔaɪntʀɪtskaːtə]

Theatre

1st/2nd row	erster/zweiter Rang [ˈeɐstɐ/ˈtsvaɪtɐ ʀaŋ]
act	der Akt [dɐ ʔakt]
actor/actress	Schauspieler/Schauspielerin [ˈʃaʊʃpiːlɐ/ ˈʃaʊʃpiːləʀɪn]
ballet	das Ballett [das baˈlɛt]
box	die Loge [di ˈloːʒə]
cabaret	das Kabarett [das kabaˈʀeː]
comedy	die Komödie [di koˈmøːdiə]
dancer	der Tänzer/die Tänzerin [dɐ təntsɐ/ di təntsɐˈʀɪn]
drama	das Drama [das ˈdʀaːma]
encore	die Zugabe [di ˈtsuːgaːbə]
music hall	das Varietee [das vaʀiəˈteː]
musical	das Musical [das ˈmjuːzɪkl]
open-air theatre	das Freilufttheater [das ˈfʀaɪlʊfteˌʔaːtɐ]
opera	die Oper [di ˈʔoːpɐ]
operetta	die Operette [di ʔopəˈʀɛtə]
performance	die Aufführung [di ʔaʊfyːʀʊŋ]
play	das Schauspiel [das ˈʃaʊʃpiːl]
play	das Theaterstück [das teˈʔaːtɐˌʃtʏk]
premiere	die Premiere [di pʀəmˈjeːʀə]
production	die Inszenierung [di ʔɪntsəˈniːʀʊŋ]
programme (*booklet*)	das Programmheft [das pʀoˈgʀamhɛft]
revue	das Kabarett [das kabaˈʀeː]
stalls	das Parkett [das paˈkɛt]
tragedy	die Tragödie [di tʀaˈgøːdiə]
variety theatre	das Varietee [das vaʀiəˈteː]

Concerts

blues	der Blues [dɐ bluːs]
choir	der Chor [dɐ koɐ]
classical	die Klassik [di ˈklasɪk]
composer	der Komponist/die Komponistin [dɐ kɔmpoˈnɪst/di kɔmpoˈnɪstɪn]
concert	das Konzert [das kɔnˈtsɛɐt]
chamber music concert	das Kammerkonzert [das ˈkamɐkɔnˌtsɛɐt]
church concert	das Kirchenkonzert [das ˈkɪɐçnkɔnˌtsɛɐt]
symphony concert	das Sinfoniekonzert [das zɪmfoˈniːkɔnˌtsɛɐt]
piano recital	der Klavierabend [dɐ klaˈviɐaːbmt]

conductor	der Dirigent/die Dirigentin [dɐ diʀiˈgɛnt/di diʀiˈgɛntɪn]
jazz	der Jazz [dɐ ˈdʒɛs]
orchestra	das Orchester [das ˀɔɐˈkɛstɐ]
pop	der Pop [dɐ pɔp]
reggae	der Reggae [dɐ ˈʀɛge:]
rock	der Rock [dɐ ʀɔk]
singer	der Sänger/die Sängerin [dɐ ˈzɛŋɐ/di ˈzɛŋəʀɪn]
soloist	der Solist/die Solistin [dɐ zoˈlɪst/di zoˈlɪstɪn]
traditional music	die Volksmusik [di ˈfɔlksmuˌzi:k]
folk music	der Folk [dɐ fo:k]

Cinema/Movie Theater

cast	die Besetzung [di bəˈzɛtsʊŋ]
cinema/movie theater	das Kino [das ˈki:no]
drive-in cinema	das Freilichtkino [das ˈfʀaɪlɪçtki:no]
arts cinema	das Programmkino [das pʀoˈgʀamki:no]
directed by	die Regie [di ʀəˈʒi:]
dubbed	synchronisiert [zʏŋkroniˈziɐt]
film (*Am* movie)	der Film [dɐ fɪlm]
action film	der Actionfilm [dɐ ˈˀɛktʃnfɪlm]
black-and-white film	der Schwarzweißfilm [dɐ ʃva:tsˈvaɪsfɪlm]
cartoon	der Zeichentrickfilm [dɐ ˈtsaɪçnˌtʀɪkfɪlm]
classic film	der Klassiker [dɐ ˈklasɪkɐ]
comedy	die Komödie [di koˈmø:diə]
documentary	der Dokumentarfilm [dɐ dɔkumɛnˈta:fɪlm]
drama	das Drama [das ˈdʀa:ma]
science fiction film	der Sciencefictionfilm [dɐ saɪnsˈfɪktʃnfɪlm]
short film	der Kurzfilm [dɐ kʊɐtsfɪlm]
thriller	der Thriller [dɐ ˈθʀɪlɐ]
western	der Western [dɐ ˈvɛstɐn]
film/movie actor	der Filmschauspieler [dɐ ˈfɪlmʃaʊʃpi:lɐ]
film/movie actress	die Filmschauspielerin [di ˈfɪlmʃaʊʃpi:ləʀɪn]
leading role	die Hauptrolle [di ˈhaʊptʀɔlə]
movie	der Film [dɐ fɪlm]
original version	die Originalfassung [di ˀoʀɪgɪˈna:lfasʊŋ]
screen	die Leinwand [di ˈlaɪnvant]
screenplay, script	das Drehbuch [das ˈdʀe:bu:x]

special effects	die Spezialeffekte *m pl* [di ʃpeˈtsjaːleˌfɛktə]
subtitles	der Untertitel [dɐ ˈˀʊntɐtɪtl]
supporting role	die Nebenrolle [di ˈneːbmʀɔlə]

Nightlife

What is there to do here in the evenings?
Was kann man hier abends unternehmen?
[vas kan man hiɐ ˈˀaːbmts ˀʊntɐˈneːmm]

Is there a nice pub here?
Gibt es hier eine gemütliche Kneipe?
[gɪpt əs hiɐ ˌˀaɪnə gəˈmyːtlɪçə ˈknaɪpə]

How long are you open today?
Bis wann haben Sie heute auf? [bɪs van ˈhaːbm zi ˈhɔɪtə ˀaʊf]

Where can we go dancing?
Wo kann man hier tanzen gehen? [voː kan man hiɐ ˈtantsn geːn]

Shall we have another dance?
Wollen wir noch einmal tanzen? [vɔln viɐ nɔx ˈˀaɪnmaːl ˈtantsn]

In pubs and bars you don't normally pay for each individual drink. The waiter or barkeeper keeps a record of your orders (sometimes on your beer mat) and presents you with the total when you leave. Closing times vary considerably; ask if in doubt. In larger cities pubs and bars are often open until well after midnight.

band	die Band [di bɛ(ː)nt]
bar	die Bar [di baː]
casino	das Spielkasino [das ˈʃpiːlkaˌziːno]
to dance	tanzen [tantsn]
dance band	die Tanzkapelle [di ˈtantskaˌpɛlə]
discotheque	die Diskothek [di dɪskoˈteːk]
folklore evening	der Folkloreabend [dɐ fɔlkˈloːʀəˀaːbmt]
gambling	das Glücksspiel [das ˈglʏkʃpiːl]
to go out	ausgehen [ˈˀaʊsgeːn]
night club	der Nachtklub [dɐ ˈnaxtklʊp]
pub	die Kneipe [di ˈknaɪpə]
show	die Show [di ʃoː]

Festivals and events

Could you tell me when the music festival takes place, please?
Könnten Sie mir bitte sagen, wann das Musikfestival stattfindet?
[køntn zi miɐ ˈbɪtə zaːgŋ van das muˈziːkfɛstɪval ˈʃtatfɪndət]
from June to September
von Juni bis September [fɔn ˈjuːni bɪs zɛpˈtɛmbɐ]

every year in August
jedes Jahr im August [ˈjeːdəs jaː ˀɪm aʊˈgʊst]
every 2 years
alle zwei Jahre [ˈˀalə tsvaɪ ˈjaːʀə]

Can anyone take part?
Kann jeder teilnehmen? [kan ˈjeːdɐ ˈtaɪlneːmm]

Typical festivals and events

ball	der Ball [dɐ bal]
barbecue	das Grillfest [das ˈgʀɪlfɛst]
brass band	die Blaskapelle [di ˈblaːskaˌpɛlə]
carnival	der Fasching [dɐ ˈfaʃiŋ]
Christmas market	der Weihnachtsmarkt [dɐ ˈvaɪnaxtsˌmaːkt]
circus	der Zirkus [dɐ ˈtsɪɐkʊs]
dance (party)	das Tanzfest [das ˈtantsfɛst]
event	die Veranstaltung [di fɐˈˀanʃtaltʊŋ]
fair	die Kirmes [di ˈkɪɐməs]
fireworks display	das Feuerwerk [das ˈfɔɪɐvɛɐk]
flea market	der Flohmarkt [dɐ ˈfloːmaːkt]
flower show	die Gartenschau [di ˈgaːtnʃaʊ]
funfair	der Jahrmarkt [dɐ ˈjaːmaːkt]
garden party	das Gartenfest [das ˈgaːtnfɛst]
New Year's Eve party	die Silvester-Party [di zɪlˈvɛstɐpaːti]
parade	der Umzug [dɐ ˈˀʊmtsuːk]
procession	die Prozession [di pʀotsɛsˈjoːn]
village fête	das Dorffest [das ˈdɔɐfɛst]

Shopping

Spending your money

Shopping is a natural activity, and you'll have no trouble doing it in the German-speaking countries. Restrictions in store hours have been liberalised recently, so you can take advantage of opportunities six days a week and well into the evening. If you're looking for clothes, a great time to shop is during the *Sommerschlussverkauf* (summer clearance sale), from the end of July to the middle of August. This is when stores clear out their summer lines and drop prices often by as much as 30% or 40% to do so.

Questions

I'm looking for ...

Are you being served?
Werden Sie schon bedient? [veɐdn zi ʃon bəˈdiːnt]

Thank you, I'm just looking (a)round.
Danke, ich sehe mich nur um. [daŋkə ˀɪç zeː mɪç nuɐ ˀʊm]

I'd like ...
Ich hätte gern ... [ˀɪç hɛtə gɛɐn]

Have you got ...?
Haben Sie ...? [ˈhaːbm zi]

Can I get you anything else?
Darf es sonst noch (et)was sein? [daːf əs zɔnst nɔx (ˀɛt)vas zaɪn]

Bargaining and buying

How much is it?
Wie viel kostet es? [ˈviː fil ˈkɔstət əs]

That's really expensive!
Das ist aber teuer! [das ɪst ˌˀabɐ ˈtɔɪɐ]

Do you grant a discount?
Geben Sie einen Rabatt? [ˈgeːbm zi ˀaɪnn ʁaˈbat]

Good. I'll take it.
Gut, ich nehme es. [guːt ˀɪç ˈneːm əs]

Do you take credit cards?
Nehmen Sie Kreditkarten? [ˈneːmm zi kʀeˈdiːtˌkaːtn]

Shops

Excuse me, where can I find ...?
Entschuldigen Sie bitte, wo finde ich ...?
[ˀɛntˈʃʊldɪgŋ zi ˈbɪtə voː fɪndə ˀɪç]

Öffnungszeiten – opening hours

offen	open
geschlossen	closed
Betriebsferien	closed for holidays

antique shop	das Antiquitätengeschäft [das ˀantɪkvɪˈtɛːtngəʃɛft]
art dealer	der Kunsthändler [dɐ ˈkʊnstˌhɛntlɐ]
baker's	die Bäckerei [di bɛkəˈʀaɪ]
barber's	der (Herren)Friseur [dɐ(ˈhɛʀən)fʀɪˈzøɐ]
book shop	die Buchhandlung [di ˈbuːxhantlʊŋ]
boutique	die Boutique [di buˈtiːk]
butcher's	die Metzgerei [di mɛtsgəˈʀaɪ]
cake shop	die Konditorei [di kɔnditoˈʀaɪ]
candy store	das Süßwarengeschäft [das ˈzyːsvaːʀəngəˌʃɛft]
chemist's (*pharmacy*)	die Apotheke [di ˀapoˈteːkə]
cobbler	der Schuhmacher [dɐ ˈʃuːmaxɐ]
computer shop	das Computerfachgeschäft [das kɔmˈpjuːtɐˌfaxgəʃɛft]
delicatessen	das Feinkostgeschäft [das ˈfaɪnkɔstgəˌʃɛft]
department store	das Kaufhaus [das ˈkaʊfhaʊs]
dressmaker	der Schneider/die Schneiderin [dɐ ˈʃnaɪdɐ/ ˈʃnaɪdəʀɪn]
drugstore (*shop for toiletries*)	die Drogerie [di dʀogəˈʀiː]
dry cleaner's	die Reinigung [di ˈʀaɪnɪgʊŋ]
fishmonger's/fish dealer	das Fischgeschäft [das ˈfɪʃgəʃɛft]
flea market	der Flohmarkt [dɐ ˈfloːmaːkt]
florist's	das Blumengeschäft [das ˈbluːmmgəʃɛft]
food/grocery store	das Lebensmittelgeschäft [das ˈleːbmsmɪtlgəˌʃɛft]
greengrocer('s)	der Obst- und Gemüsehändler [dɐ ˀoːpst ʊnt gəˈmyːzəˌhɛndlɐ]
hairdresser's	der Friseur [dɐ fʀɪˈzøɐ]
health food shop	das Reformhaus [das ʀeˈfɔɐmhaʊs]
jeweller's	der Juwelier [dɐ juveˈliɐ]
launderette	der Waschsalon [dɐ ˈvaʃzaˌlɔŋ]

laundry	die Wäscherei [di vɛʃəˈʀaɪ]
liquor store	das Spirituosengeschäft [das ʃpiʀituˈo:zngəʃɛft]
market	der Markt [dɐ ma:kt]
mobile communications centre	das Handygeschäft [das ˈhɛndigəˌʃɛft]
music shop	der Plattenladen [dɐ ˈplatnla:dn]
newsagent's	der Zeitungshändler [dɐ ˈtsaɪtʊŋshɛntlɐ]
off-licence	das Spirituosengeschäft [das ʃpiʀituˈo:zngəʃɛft]
optician's	der Optiker [dɐ ˈʔɔptɪkɐ]
organic food shop	der Bioladen [der ˈbiola:dn]
perfumery	die Parfümerie [di pafʏməˈʀi:]
photographic materials	die Fotoartikel *m pl* [di ˈfo:toʔaˌtɪkl]
second-hand shop	der Trödelladen [dɐ ˈtʀø:dlla:dn]
shoe shop	das Schuhgeschäft [das ˈʃu:gəʃɛft]
shoemaker's	der Schuhmacher [dɐ ˈʃu:maxɐ]
souvenir shop	der Souvenirladen [dɐ zuvəˈniɐla:dn]
sports shop	das Sportgeschäft [das ˈʃpɔɐtgəʃɛft]
stationer's	das Schreibwarengeschäft [das ˈʃʀaɪpva:ʀəngəˌʃɛft]
supermarket	der Supermarkt [dɐ ˈzu:pɐma:kt]
sweet shop	das Süßwarengeschäft [das ˈzy:sva:ʀəngəˌʃɛft]
tailor	der Schneider/die Schneiderin [dɐ ˈʃnaɪdɐ/ ˈʃnaɪdəʀɪn]
tobacconist's/tobacco shop	der Tabakladen [dɐ ˈtabakla:dn]
toy shop	das Spielwarengeschäft [das ˈʃpi:lva:ʀəngəˈʃɛft]
travel agency	das Reisebüro [das ˈʀaɪzəbyˌʀo:]
watchmaker's	der Uhrmacher [dɐ ˈʔuɐmaxɐ]
wine merchant's	die Weinhandlung [di ˈvaɪnhantlʊŋ]

Books, magazines and stationery

I'd like ...
Ich hätte gern ... [ʔɪç hɛtə gɛɐn ...]

a German newspaper.
eine deutsche Zeitung. [ʔaɪnə ˈdɔɪtʃə ˈtsaɪtʊŋ]

a magazine.
eine Zeitschrift. [ʔaɪnə ˈtsaɪtʃʀɪft]

a travel guide.
einen Reiseführer. [ʔaɪnn ˈʀaɪzəfy:ʀɐ]

a hiking map for this area.
eine Wanderkarte dieser Gegend. [ʔaɪnə ˈvandɐka:tə di:zɐ ˈge:gŋt]

Books, magazines and newspapers

comic	das Comicheft [das 'kɔmɪkhɛft]
cookbook	das Kochbuch [das 'kɔxbu:x]
daily paper	die Tageszeitung [di 'ta:gəstsaɪtʊŋ]
detective novel	der Kriminalroman [dɐ kʀɪmi'na:lʀoˌma:n]
dictionary	das Wörterbuch [das 'vøɐtɐbu:x]
(glossy) magazine	die Illustrierte [di ɪlʊ'stʀiɐtə]
(news) magazine	die Zeitschrift [di 'tsaɪtʃʀɪft]
map *(of country area)*	die Landkarte [di 'lantka:tə]
newspaper	die Zeitung [di 'tsaɪtʊŋ]
novel	der Roman [dɐ ʀo'ma:n]
paperback	das Taschenbuch [das 'taʃnbu:x]
road map	die Straßenkarte [di 'ʃtʀa:snka:tə]
thriller	der Kriminalroman [dɐ kʀɪmi'na:lʀoma:n]
town map	der Stadtplan [dɐ 'ʃtatpla:n]
travel guide	der Reiseführer [dɐ 'ʀaɪzəfy:ʀɐ]
women's magazine	die Frauenzeitschrift [di 'fʀaʊntsaɪtʃʀɪft]

Stationery

ball-point pen	der Kugelschreiber [dɐ 'ku:glʃʀaɪbɐ]
biro	der Kuli [dɐ 'ku:li]
coloured pencil	der Farbstift [dɐ 'fa:pʃtɪft]
colouring book	das Malbuch [das 'ma:lbu:x]
envelope	der Briefumschlag [dɐ 'bʀi:fʊmʃla:k]
eraser	der Radiergummi [dɐ ʀa'diɐˌgʊmi]
felt-tip pen	der Filzstift [dɐ 'fɪltʃɪft]
floppy disks	die Disketten *f pl* [di dɪs'kɛtn]
glue	der Klebstoff [dɐ 'kle:pʃtɔf]
notepad	der Notizblock [dɐ no'ti:tsblɔk]
paper	das Papier [das pa'piɐ]
pencil	der Bleistift [dɐ 'blaɪʃtɪft]
picture postcard	die Ansichtskarte [di 'ʔanzɪçtska:tə]
sellotape®/scotch tape®	der Tesafilm® [dɐ 'te:safɪlm]
writing pad	der Block [dɐ blɔk]
writing paper	das Briefpapier [das 'bʀi:fpaˌpiɐ]

CDs and cassettes

➣ **also "Electrical goods/Computer" and "Concert"**

Do you have any CDs/cassettes by ...?
Haben Sie CDs/Kassetten von ...? ['ha:bm zi tse'de:s/ka'sɛtn fɔn ...]

I'd like a CD of typical Swiss music.
Ich hätte gern eine CD mit typisch Schweizer Musik.
[ˀɪç hɛtə gɛɐn ˀaɪnə tse'de: mɪt 'ty:pɪʃ ˌʃvaɪtsɐ mu'zi:k]

Can I have a quick listen to this, please?
Kann ich hier bitte kurz reinhören?
[kan ˀɪç hiɐ 'bɪtə kʊɐts 'ʀaɪnhø:ʀən]

cassette	die Kassette [di ka'sɛtə]
CD	die CD [di tse'de:]
CD player	der CD-Spieler [dɐ tse'de:ʃpi:lɐ]
Discman®	der tragbare CD-Spieler [dɐ 'tʀa:kba:ʀə tse'de: ʃpi:lɐ]
DVD	die DVD [di defaʊ'de:]
headphones	der Kopfhörer [dɐ 'kɔpfhø:ʀɐ]
personal stereo	der Walkman® [dɐ 'wɔ:kmɛn]
portable CD player	der tragbare CD-Spieler [dɐ 'tʀa:kba:ʀə tse'de:ʃpi:lɐ]
speaker	der Lautsprecher [dɐ 'laʊtʃpʀɛçɐ]
Walkman®	der Walkman® [dɐ 'wɔ:kmɛn]

Electrical goods/Computer

➢ **also "Photographic materials", "CDs and cassettes"**

adapter	der Adapter [dɐ ˀa'daptɐ]
alarm clock	der Wecker [dɐ 'vɛkɐ]
battery	die Batterie [di batə'ʀi:]
battery charger	das Ladegerät [das 'la:dəgəʀɛ:t]
blank	der Rohling [dɐ 'ʁo:lɪŋ]
CD/DVD	die CD/die DVD [di tse'de:/di defaʊ'de:]
extension lead/cord	die Verlängerungsschnur [di fɐ'lɛŋəʀʊŋˌʃnuɐ]
flashlight, torch	die Taschenlampe [di 'taʃnlampə]
hair dryer	der Föhn [dɐ fø:n]
laptop	der Laptop [dɐ 'lɛptɔp]
light bulb	die Glühbirne [di 'gly:bɪɐnə]
memory card	die Speicherkarte [di 'ʃpaɪçɐˌka:tə]
memory stick	der Memorystick [dɐ 'mɛmoʁistɪk]
MP3 player/iPod	der MP3Player/der iPod [dɐ ˀɛmpe'dʁaɪplɛɪɐ/ dɐ 'ˀaɪpɔt]
pager	der Piepser [dɐ 'pi:psɐ]
pocket calculator	der Taschenrechner [dɐ 'taʃnʀɛçnɐ]
printer	der Drucker [dɐ 'dʁʊkɐ]
radio	das Radio [das 'ʁa:djo]
rechargeable battery	der Akku [dɐ 'ˀaku]
scanner	der Scanner [dɐ 'skɛnɐ]

Fashion

➣ also Colours

Clothing

Can you please show me ...?
Können Sie mir bitte ... zeigen? [ˈkønn zi miɐ ˈbɪtə … ˈtsaɪgŋ]

Can I try it on?
Kann ich es anprobieren? [kan ɪç əs ˈʔanpʀobiːʀən]

What size do you take?
Welche Größe haben Sie? [ˈvɛlçə ˈgrøːsə ˈhaːbm ziː]

It's too ...
Das ist mir zu ... [ˈdas ʔɪst miɐ tsʊ ˈ…]
  tight/big.
  eng/weit. [ʔɛŋ/vaɪt]
  short/long.
  kurz/lang. [kʊɐts/laŋ]
  small/big.
  klein/groß. [klaɪn/gʀoːs]

It's a good fit. I'll take it.
Das passt gut. Ich nehme es. [das past ˈguːt ʔɪç ˈneːm əs]

It's not quite what I want(ed).
Das ist nicht ganz, was ich möchte.
[das ʔɪst nɪçt gants vas ɪç ˈmøçtə]

anorak	der Anorak [dɐ ˈʔanoʀak]
bathing-cap	die Bademütze [di ˈbaːdəmʏtsə]
bathrobe	der Bademantel [dɐ ˈbaːdəmantl]
bikini	der Bikini [dɐ biˈkiːni]
blazer	der Blazer [dɐ ˈbleːzɐ]
blouse	die Bluse [di ˈbluːzə]
body stocking/body suit	der Body [dɐ ˈbɔdi]
bow-tie	die Fliege [di ˈfliːgə]
bra	der Büstenhalter [dɐ ˈbʏstnhaltɐ]
briefs	der (Herren)Slip [dɐ (ˈhɛʀən)slɪp]
cap	die Mütze [di ˈmʏtsə]
cardigan	die Strickjacke [di ˈʃtʀɪkjakə]
coat	der Mantel [dɐ mantl]
cotton	die Baumwolle [di ˈbaʊmvɔlə]
dress	das Kleid [das klaɪt]
gloves	die Handschuhe *m pl* [di ˈhantʃuːə]
hat	der Hut [dɐ huːt]
jacket	die Jacke [di ˈjakə]
jeans	die Jeans [di ˈdʒiːns]

jumper	der Pullover [dɐ pʊˈloːvɐ]
leggings	die Leggings [di ˈlɛgɪŋs]
linen	das Leinen [das laɪnn]
panties	der (Damen)Slip [dɐ (ˈdaːmən)slɪp]
pants (*Am*)	die Hose [di ˈhoːzə]
pants (*underwear*)	die Unterhose [di ˈʊntɐhoːzə]
parka	der Anorak [dɐ ˈʔanoʀak]
pullover	der Pullover [dɐ pʊˈloːvɐ]
raincoat	der Regenmantel [dɐ ˈʀeːgŋmantl]
scarf (*decorative*)	das Halstuch [das ˈhalstuːx]
scarf (*for keeping warm*)	der Schal [dɐ ʃaːl]
shirt	das Hemd [das hɛmt]
shorts	die kurze Hose [di ˈkʊɐtsə ˈhoːzə]
silk	die Seide [di ˈzaɪdə]
silk stockings	die Seidenstrümpfe *m pl* [di ˈzaɪdnʃtʀʏmpfə]
silk tights	die Seidenstrumpfhose [di ˈzaɪdnˌʃtʀʊmpfhoːze]
skirt	der Rock [dɐ ʀɔk]
sleeve	der Ärmel [dɐ ˀɛɐml]
socks	die Socken *f pl* [di ˈzɔkŋ]
stockings	die Strümpfe *m pl* [di ˈʃtʀʏmpfə]
suit (*for men*)	der Anzug [dɐ ˈʔantsuːk]
suit (*for women*)	das Kostüm [das kɔsˈtyːm]
sun hat	der Sonnenhut [dɐ ˈzɔnnhuːt]
sweater	der Pullover [dɐ pʊˈloːvɐ]
swimming trunks	die Badehose [di ˈbaːdəhoːzə]
swimsuit	der Badeanzug [dɐ ˈbaːdəˌʔantsuːk]
tee-shirt	das T-Shirt [das ˈtiːʃøɐt]
tie	die Krawatte [di kʀaˈvatə]
tights	die Strumpfhose [di ˈʃtʀʊmpfhoːzə]
tracksuit	der Trainingsanzug [dɐ ˈtʀɛːnɪŋsˌʔantsuːk]
trousers	die Hose [di ˈhoːzə]
umbrella	der Schirm [dɐ ʃɪɐm]
underpants	die Unterhose [di ˈʊntɐhoːzə]
underwear	die Unterwäsche [di ˈʔʊntɐvɛʃə]
waistcoat, (*US*) vest	die Weste [di ˈvɛstə]
vest (*undershirt*)	das Unterhemd [das ˈʊntɐhɛmt]
wool	die Wolle [di ˈvɔlə]

Dry cleaning

I'd like to have these things cleaned/washed.
Ich möchte diese Sachen reinigen/ waschen lassen.
[ˀɪç ˈmøçtə ˌdiːzə ˈzaxn ˈʀaɪnɪgŋ/vaʃn lasn]

When will they be ready?
Wann sind sie fertig? [van zɪnt zi ˈfɛɐtɪç]

to dry-clean	chemisch reinigen [ˈçe:mɪʃ ˈʀaɪnɪgŋ]
to iron	bügeln [by:gln]
to press	plätten [plɛtn]

Groceries

What can I get you?
Was darf es sein? [vas da:f əs ˈzaɪn]

I'd like ..., please.
Geben Sie mir bitte ... [ge:bm zi miɐ ˈbɪtə]
a pound of ...
ein Pfund ... [ˈʔaɪn pfʊnt]
ten slices of ...
10 Scheiben ... [ˈtse:n ʃaɪbm]
a piece of ...
ein Stück von ... [ʔaɪn ˈʃtʏk fɔn]
a packet of ...
eine Packung ... [ˈʔaɪnə ˈpakʊŋ]
a jar of ...
ein Glas ... [ʔaɪn gla:s]
a tin of ...
eine Dose ... [ˈʔaɪnə ˈdo:zə]
a bottle of ...
eine Flasche ... [ˈʔaɪnə ˈflaʃə]
a bag, please.
eine (Einkaufs)tüte. [ˈʔaɪnə (ˈʔaɪnkaʊfs)ˌty:tə]

Please cut it in slices.
Bitte schneiden Sie es in Scheiben. [ˈbɪtə ˈʃnaɪdn zi əs ɪn ˈʃaɪbm]

Could I try some of this?
Dürfte ich vielleicht etwas hiervon probieren?
[dʏɐft ɪç fiˌlaɪçt ˌɛtvas ˈhiɐfɔn pʀoˈbi:ʀən]

Would a little bit more be OK?
Darf es auch etwas mehr sein? [da:f əs aʊx ˌʔɛtvas ˈmeɐ zaɪn]

No, thank you. That's all.
Danke, das ist alles. [ˈdaŋkə das ɪst ˈʔaləs]

past the sell-by date	abgelaufen [ʔapgəlaʊfn]
sell-by date/best before	die Haltbarkeit [di ˈhaltba(:)kaɪt]

Fruit	Obst
apples	die Äpfel *m pl* [di ˀɛpfl]
apricots	die Aprikosen *f pl* [di ˀapʀɪˈkoːzn]
bananas	die Bananen *f pl* [di baˈnaːnn]
blackberries	die Brombeeren *f pl* [di ˈbʀɔmbeːʀən]
blackcurrants	die schwarzen Johannisbeeren *f pl* [di ˈʃvaːtsn joˈhanɪsbeːʀən]
blueberries	die Heidelbeeren *f pl* [di ˈhaɪdlbeːʀən]
cherries	die Kirschen *f pl* [di kɪɐʃn]
coconut	die Kokosnuss [di ˈkoːkosnʊs]
cranberries	die Preiselbeeren *f pl* [di ˈpʀaɪzlbeːʀən]
dried	getrocknet [gəˈtʀɔknət]
fruit	das Obst [das ˀoːpst]
gooseberries	die Stachelbeeren *f pl* [di ˈʃtaxlbeːʀən]
grapefruit	die Grapefruit [di ˈgreːpfruːt]
grapes	die Weintrauben *f pl* [di ˈvaɪntʀaʊbm]
lemons	die Zitronen *f pl* [di tsɪˈtʀoːnn]
mandarins	die Mandarinen *f pl* [di mandaˈʀiːnn]
melon	die Melone [di meˈloːnə]
oranges	die Apfelsinen *f pl* [di ˀapflˈziːnn]
peaches	die Pfirsiche *m pl* [di ˈpfɪɐzɪçə]
pears	die Birnen *f pl* [di bɪɐnn]
pineapple	die Ananas [ˈˀananas]
plums	die Pflaumen *f pl* [di pflaʊmm]
raspberries	die Himbeeren *f pl* [di ˈhɪmbeːʀən]
redcurrants	die roten Johannisbeeren *f pl* [di ʀoːtn joˈhanɪsbeːʀən]
strawberries	die Erdbeeren *f pl* [di ˈˀeɐtbeːʀən]
tangerines	die Tangerinen *f pl* [di tangəˈʀiːnn]

Vegetables	Gemüse
artichokes	die Artischocken *f pl* [di ˀaːtɪˈʃɔkŋ]
asparagus	der Spargel [ʃpaːgl]
aubergines	die Auberginen *f pl* [di ˀobɐˈʒiːnn]
avocado	die Avocado [di ˀavoˈkaːdo]
beans	die Bohnen *f pl* [di boːnn]
green beans	grüne Bohnen [ˌgʀyːnə ˈboːnn]
haricot beans	weiße Bohnen [ˌvaɪsə ˈboːnn]
kidney beans	rote Bohnen [ˌʀoːtə ˈboːnn]
beetroot/beet(s)	Rote Bete [ˌʀoːtə ˈbeːtə]
cabbage	der Kohl [dɐ koːl]
carrots	die Karotten *f pl* [di kaˈʀɔtn]
cauliflower	der Blumenkohl [ˈbluːmmkoːl]
celeriac	der Sellerie [dɐ ˈzɛləʀiː]
celery	der Stangensellerie [dɐ ˈʃtaŋŋˌzɛləʀiː]

corn, maize	der Mais [dɐ maɪs]
cucumber	die Gurke [di ˈgʊɐkə]
fennel	der Fenchel [dɐ fɛnçl]
garlic	der Knoblauch [dɐ ˈkno:blaʊx]
horseradish	der Meerrettich [dɐ ˈme:ʀɛtɪç]
leek	der Lauch [dɐ laʊx]
lentils	die Linsen *f pl* [di lɪnzn]
lettuce	der Kopfsalat [dɐ ˈkɔpfsaˌla:t]

Salat means: (1) "salad" as in "potato salad", "green salad", etc., and (2) "lettuce". To clarify, use *Kopfsalat* (lettuce) or *Kartoffelsalat, grüner Salat*, etc.
Don't be surprised if you encounter regional dialect words, different from those in this list, especially for sausages, bread rolls and cakes.

olives	die Oliven *f pl* [di ˀoˈli:vn]
onions	die Zwiebeln *f pl* [di tsvi:bln]
peas	die Erbsen *f pl* [di ˀɛɐpsn]
peppers	die Paprikaschoten *f pl* [di ˈpapʀɪkaˌʃo:tn]
potatoes	die Kartoffeln *f pl* [di kaˈtɔfln]
pumpkin	der Kürbis [dɐ ˈkʏɐbɪs]
spinach	der Spinat [dɐ ʃpɪˈna:t]
tomatoes	die Tomaten *f pl* [di toˈma:tn]
zucchini *(Am)*/courgette *(GB)*	die Zucchini [di tsʊˈki:ni]

Herbs and spices — Kräuter und Gewürze

basil	das Basilikum [das baˈzi:lɪkʊm]
bay-leaves	die Lorbeerblätter *n pl* [di ˈlɔɐbeɐˌblɛtɐ]
borage	der Borretsch [dɐ ˈbɔʀɛtʃ]
caraway seed(s)	der Kümmel [dɐ kʏml]
chervil	der Kerbel [dɐ kɛɐbl]
chilli	der Chili [dɐ ˈtsɪli]
chives	der Schnittlauch [dɐ ˈʃnɪtlaʊx]
cinnamon	der Zimt [dɐ tsɪmt]
cloves	die Nelken *f pl* [di nɛlkŋ]
coriander	der Koriander [dɐ koʀiˈandɐ]
dill	der Dill [dɐ dɪl]
garlic	der Knoblauch [dɐ ˈkno:blaʊx]
ginger	der Ingwer [dɐ ˈˀɪŋvɐ]
herbs	die Kräuter *n pl* [di ˈkʀɔɪtɐ]
lovage	der/das Liebstöckel [dɐ/das ˈli:pʃtøkl]
marjoram	der Majoran [dɐ ˈma(:)joʀa:n]
mint	die Minze [di ˈmɪntsə]

nutmeg	die Muskatnuss [di mʊsˈkaːtnʊs]
oregano	der Oregano [dɐ ˀoʀeˈgaːno]
paprika	der Paprika [dɐ ˈpapʀɪka]
parsley	die Petersilie [di peːtɐˈziːljə]
pepper	der Pfeffer [dɐ ˈpfɛfɐ]
pepperoni	die Peperoni [di pɛpəˈroːni]
rosemary	der Rosmarin [dɐ ˈʀoːsmaʀiːn]
saffron	der Safran [dɐ ˈzafraːn]
sage	der Salbei [dɐ ˈzalbaɪ]
savory	das Bohnenkraut [das ˈboːnnkʀaʊt]
tarragon	der Estragon [dɐ ˈˀɛstʀagɔn]
thyme	der Thymian [dɐ ˈtyːmiaːn]

Bread, cakes and sweets — Backwaren und Süßwaren

The German-speaking countries undoubtedly set the benchmark for bakery goods. What you'll find in every town and city is worthy of any hungry person's attention and would go far beyond the limits of this book. Follow your nose, go in and point, saying *Was ist das, bitte? Kuchen* is something baked that is sweet, often combined with other words, like *Apfelkuchen* (apple pastry). *Torte* is roughly like a pie, that is, something sweet is spread over baked dough. *Gebäck* is a collective term used for small baked items, much like biscuits/cookies. *Brot* always means literally bread, and comes in countless delicious variations.

bread	das Brot [das bʀoːt]
brown rye bread	das Schwarzbrot [das ˈʃvaːtsbʀoːt]
white bread	das Weißbrot [das ˈvaɪsbʀoːt]
wholemeal bread	das Vollkornbrot [das ˈfɔlkɔɐnˌbʀoːt]
biscuits/cookies	die Kekse *m pl* [di keːksə]
cake	der Kuchen [dɐ kʊːxn]
candy	die Süßigkeiten *f pl* [di ˈzyːsɪçkaɪtn]
chocolate	die Schokolade [di ʃokoˈlaːdə]
chocolate bar	der Schokoriegel [dɐ ˈʃoːkoʀiːgl]
chocolates	die Pralinen *f pl* [di pʀaˈliːnn]
ice-cream	das Eis [das ˈˀaɪs]
jam/marmalade	die Marmelade [di mamaˈlaːdə]

Marmelade in German means any kind of jam. If you want orange marmelade, ask for *Orangenmarmelade*.

muesli	das Müsli [das ˈmyːsli]
rolls	die Brötchen *n pl* [di bʀøːtçn]
filled rolls	belegte Brötchen [bəˈleːktə bʀøːtçn]

sweets	die Süßigkeiten *f pl* [di ˈzy:siçkaɪtn]
toast	der Toast [dɐ to:st]

Eggs and milk products	Eier und Milchprodukte
butter	die Butter [di ˈbʊtɐ]
buttermilk	die Buttermilch [di ˈbʊtɐmɪlç]
cheese	der Käse [dɐ ˈkɛ:zə]
cottage cheese	der Hüttenkäse [dɐ ˈhʏtnkɛ:zə]
cream	die Sahne [ˈza:nə]
sour cream	die saure Sahne [di zaʊʀə ˈza:nə]
whipping cream	die Schlagsahne [ˈʃla:kza:nə]
cream cheese	der Frischkäse [dɐ ˈfʀɪʃkɛ:zə]
eggs	die Eier *n pl* [di ˈʔaɪɐ]
milk	die Milch [mɪlç]
low-fat milk	fettarme Milch [ˈfɛtʔa:mə mɪlç]
yoghurt	der Joghurt [dɐ ˈjo:gʊɐt]

Meat	Fleisch und Wurst
beef	das Rindfleisch [ˈʀɪntflaɪʃ]
chicken	das Hähnchen [das hɛ:nçn]
chop	das Kotelett [ˈkɔtlɛt]
cold cuts/lunch meat	der Aufschnitt [dɐ ˈʔaʊfʃnɪt]
cutlet	das Kotelett [das ˈkɔtlɛt]
goulash	das Gulasch [das ˈgʊlaʃ]
ham	der Schinken [dɐ ʃɪŋkŋ]
cooked ham	gekochter Schinken [gəˈkɔxtɐ ʃɪŋkŋ]
smoked ham	roher Schinken [ʀo:ɐ ʃɪŋkŋ]
lamb	das Lammfleisch [das ˈlamflaɪʃ]
liver sausage	die Leberwurst [di ˈle:bɐvʊɐst]
meat	das Fleisch [das flaɪʃ]
minced meat	das Hackfleisch [das ˈhakflaɪʃ]
pork	das Schweinefleisch [ˈʃvaɪnəflaɪʃ]
rabbit	das Kaninchen [kaˈni:nçn]
salami	die Salami [di zaˈla:mi]
sausage	die Wurst [di vʊɐst]
small sausages *(e.g., frankfurters)*	die Würstchen *n pl* [di vʏɐstçn]
veal	das Kalbfleisch [ˈkalpflaɪʃ]

Fish and seafood	Fisch und Meeresfrüchte
bream	die Brasse [di ˈbʀasə]
cod	der Kabeljau [dɐ ˈka:bljaʊ]
crab	der Krebs [dɐ kre:ps]

Shopping

eel	der Aal [dɐ ˀa:l]
herring	der Hering [dɐ ˈhe:ʀɪŋ]
lobster	der Hummer [dɐ ˈhʊmɐ]
mackerel	die Makrele [di maˈkʀe:lə]
mussels	die Muscheln *f pl* [di mʊʃln]
oysters	die Austern *f pl* [di ˈˀaʊstɐn]
perch	der Barsch [dɐ ba:ʃ]
plaice	die Scholle [di ˈʃɔlə]
prawns	die Garnelen *f pl* [di gaˈne:ln]
salmon	der Lachs [dɐ laks]
shrimps	die Krabben *f pl* [di kʀabm]
sole	die Seezunge [di ˈze:tsʊŋə]
squid	der Tintenfisch [dɐ ˈtɪntnfɪʃ]
swordfish	der Schwertfisch [dɐ ˈʃveɐtfɪʃ]
trout	die Forelle [di foˈʀɛlə]
tuna	der Thunfisch [dɐ ˈtu:nfɪʃ]

Miscellaneous — Dies und das

almonds	die Mandeln *f pl* [di ˈmandln]
butter	die Butter [di ˈbʊtɐ]
flour	das Mehl [das me:l]
honey	der Honig [dɐ ˈho:nɪç]
margarine	die Margarine [di magaˈʀi:nə]
mayonnaise	die Mayonnaise [di maɪoˈne:zə]
mustard	der Senf [dɐ zɛnf/zɛmf]
noodles	die Nudeln *f pl* [di nu:dln]
nuts	die Nüsse *f pl* [di ˈnʏsə]
oil	das Öl [das ˀø:l]
olive oil	das Olivenöl [das ˀoˈli:vnˀø:l]
pasta	die Nudeln *f pl* [di nu:dln]
rice	der Reis [dɐ ʀaɪs]
salt	das Salz [das zalts]
sugar	der Zucker [dɐ ˈtsʊkɐ]
vegetable stock cube	der Gemüsebrühwürfel [dɐ gəˈmy:zəˌbʀy:vʏɐfl]
vinegar	der Essig [dɐ ˈˀɛsɪç]

Drink — Getränke

Wine and spirits are sold openly in all shops offering food or drink. The only restriction is that the buyer must be of age. Identification is rarely, if ever, demanded. If you are looking for especially good wine, there are specialist shops (*Weinhändler* – wine dealer) in almost every larger town or city.

apple juice	der Apfelsaft [dɐ ˈˀapflzaft]
beer	das Bier [das biɐ]
champagne	der Champagner [dɐ ʃamˈpanjɐ]
coffee	der Kaffee [dɐ ˈkafeː/kaˈfeː]
decaffeinated coffee	der koffeinfreie Kaffee [dɐ kɔfeˈˀiːnfraɪə ˈkafeː]
cocoa	der Kakao [dɐ kaˈkaʊ]
lemonade	die Limonade [lɪmoˈnaːdə]
mineral water	das Mineralwasser [das mɪnəˈʀaːlvasɐ]
sparkling	mit Kohlensäure [mɪt ˈkoːl(ə)nzɔɪʀə]
still	ohne Kohlensäure [ˈˀoːnə ˈkoːl(ə)nzɔɪʀə]
orange juice	der Orangensaft [dɐ ˀoˈʀaŋʒnzaft]
tea	der Tee [dɐ teː]
green tea	der grüne Tee [dɐ ˈgryːnə ˈteː]
fruit tea	der Früchtetee [dɐ ˈfʀʏçtəteː]
rosehip tea	der Hagebuttentee [dɐ hagəˈbʊtnteː]
camomile tea	der Kamillentee [dɐ kaˈmɪl(ə)nteː]
herbal tea	der Kräutertee [dɐ ˈkʀɔɪtɐteː]
peppermint tea	der Pfefferminztee [dɐ ˈpfɛfɐmɪntsteː]
black tea	der Schwarztee [dɐ ˈʃvaːtsteː]
tea bags	der Teebeutel [dɐ ˈteːbɔɪtl]
wine	der Wein [dɐ vaɪn]
rosé wine	Rosé(wein) [ʀoˈzeː(vaɪn)]
red wine	Rotwein [ˈʀoːtvaɪn]
white wine	Weißwein [ˈvaɪsvaɪn]
mulled wine	Glühwein [ˈglyːvaɪn]

Hairdresser/Barber

Shampoo and blow dry, please.
Waschen und föhnen, bitte. [ˈvaʃn ˀʊnt føːnn ˈbɪtə]

Wash and cut, please.
Schneiden mit Waschen, bitte. [ˈʃnaɪdn mɪt ˈvaʃn ˈbɪtə]

Dry cut.
Schneiden ohne Waschen. [ˈʃnaɪdn ˈˀoːnə ˈvaʃn]

I'd like ...
Ich möchte ... [ˀɪç ˈmøçtə ...]

Just trim the ends.
Nur die Spitzen. [nuɐ di ˈʃpɪtsn]

Not too short, please.
Nicht zu kurz, bitte. [nɪçt tsʊ ˈkʊɐts ˈbɪtə]

A bit shorter.
Etwas kürzer. [ˈʔɛtvas ˈkʏɐtsɐ]

Thank you. That's fine.
Vielen Dank. So ist es gut. [ˌfiln ˈdaŋk ˈzoː ʔɪst əs ˈguːt]

fringe/bangs *(Am)*	der Pony [dɐ ˈpɔni]
beard	der Bart [dɐ baːt]
blond(e)	blond [blɔnt]
to blow dry	föhnen [føːnn]
to comb	kämmen [kɛmm]
curls	die Locken *f pl* [di lɔkŋ]
to cut the ends	Spitzen schneiden [ˈʃpɪtsn ˈʃnaɪdn]
dandruff	die Schuppen *f pl* [di ʃʊpm]
to do someone's hair	frisieren [fʀɪˈziɐn]
to dye	färben [fɛɐbm]
fringe	der Pony [dɐ ˈpɔni]
hair	das Haar [das haː]
greasy hair	fettiges Haar [ˈfɛtɪgəs haː]
dry hair	trockenes Haar [ˈtʀɔknəs haː]
hairstyle	die Frisur [di fʀɪˈzuɐ]
highlights	die Strähnchen *n pl* [di ˈʃtʀɛːnçn]
layers	die Stufen [di ˈʃtuːfn]
moustache	der Schnurrbart [dɐ ˈʃnʊɐbaːt]
parting	der Scheitel [dɐ ʃaɪtl]
pluck (your) eyebrows	Augenbrauen zupfen [ˈʔaʊgŋbʁaʊn ˈtsʊpfn]
shampoo	das Shampoo [das ˈʃampu]
to tint	tönen [tøːnn]

Household goods

bin liner	der Abfallbeutel [dɐ ˈʔapfalbɔɪtl]
bottle opener	der Flaschenöffner [dɐ ˈflaʃnʔøfnɐ]
can opener	der Dosenöffner [dɐ ˈdoːznʔøfnɐ]
candles	die Kerzen *f pl* [di kɛɐtsn]
charcoal	die Grillkohle [di ˈgʀɪlkoːlə]
cling film	die Frischhaltefolie [di ˈfʀɪʃhaltəˌfoːljə]
clothes line	die Wäscheleine [di ˈvɛʃəlaɪnə]
clothes pegs	die Wäscheklammern *f pl* [di ˈvɛʃəklamɐn]
corkscrew	der Korkenzieher [dɐ ˈkɔɐkŋtsiːɐ]
fire-lighter	der Grillanzünder [dɐ ˈgʀɪlantsʏndɐ]
fork	die Gabel [di ˈgaːbl]
garbage bag	der Abfallbeutel [dɐ ˈʔapfalbɔɪtl]
glass	das Glas [das glaːs]
grill	der Grill [dɐ gʀɪl]

ice box	die Kühltasche [di ˈkyːltaʃə]
ice pack	das Kühlelement [das ˈkyːlɛləˌmɛnt]
knife	das Messer [das ˈmɛsɐ]
methylated spirits	der Brennspiritus [dɐ ˈbʀɛnˌʃpiʀitʊs]
paper napkins/serviettes	die Papierservietten *f pl* [di paˈpiɐzɐˌvjɛtn]
paraffin	das Petroleum [das peˈtʀoːleʊm]
plastic bag	der Plastikbeutel [dɐ ˈplastɪkbɔɪtl]
plastic cup/mug	der Plastikbecher [dɐ ˈplastɪkbɛçɐ]
plastic wrap	die Frischhaltefolie [di ˈfʀɪʃhaltəˌfoːljə]
pocket knife	das Taschenmesser [das ˈtaʃnmɛsɐ]
spoon	der Löffel [dɐ løfl]
thermos (flask)	die Thermosflasche® [di ˈtɛɐmɔsflaʃə]
tin foil	die Alufolie [di ˈˀalufoːljə]
tin opener	der Dosenöffner [dɐ ˈdoːznˀøfnɐ]

Jewellery shop

bracelet	das Armband [das ˈˀaːmbant]
brooch	die Brosche [di ˈbʀɔʃə]
costume jewellery	der Modeschmuck [dɐ ˈmoːdəʃmʊk]
crystal	der Kristall [dɐ kʀɪsˈtal]
earrings	die Ohrringe *m pl* [di ˈˀoːʀɪŋə]
earstud	der Ohrstecker [dɐ ˈˀoɐʃtɛkɐ]
gold	das Gold [das ˈgɔlt]
jewellery	der Schmuck [dɐ ʃmʊk]
necklace	die Kette [di ˈkɛtə]
pearl	die Perle [di ˈpɛɐlə]
pendant	der Anhänger [dɐ ˈˀanhɛŋɐ]
platinum	das Platin [das ˈplaːtiːn]
ring	der Ring [dɐ ʀɪŋ]
silver	das Silber [das ˈzɪlbɐ]
stud earring	der Ohrstecker [dɐ ˈˀoɐʃtɛkɐ]
tiepin	die Krawattennadel [di kʀaˈvatnnaːdl]
travel alarm	der Reisewecker [dɐ ˈʀaɪəvɛkɐ]
waterproof watch	die wasserdichte Uhr [di ˈvasɐdɪçtə ˈˀuɐ]
wristwatch	die Armbanduhr [di ˈˀaːmbantˌˀuɐ]
ladies'	für Damen [fyɐ ˈdaːmən]
men's	für Herren [fyɐ ˈhɛʀən]

Shopping

Optician

Could you repair these glasses for me, please.
Würden Sie mir bitte diese Brille reparieren?
[ˈvʏɐdn zi miɐ ˈbɪtə ˈdiːzə ˈbʀɪlə rɛpaˈʀiɐn]

I'm short-sighted/near-sighted.
Ich bin kurzsichtig. [ˀɪç bɪn ˈkʊɐtsɪçtɪç]

I'm long-sighted/far-sighted.
Ich bin weitsichtig. [ˀɪç bɪn ˈvaɪtsɪçtɪç]

What's your (visual) acuity?
Wie ist Ihre Sehstärke? [ˈvi ɪst iʀə ˈzeːʃtɛɐkə]

... in the right eye, ... in the left eye.
rechts ..., links ... [ʀɛçts ... lɪŋks ...]

When can I pick up the glasses?
Wann kann ich die Brille abholen? [van kan ɪç di ˈbʀɪlə ˈˀaphoːln]

I'd like ...
Ich hätte gern ... [ˀɪç ˈhɛtə ˈgɛɐn ...]
some storage solution
eine Aufbewahrungslösung [ˌˀaɪnə ˈˀaʊfbəvaːʀʊŋsˌløːzʊŋ]
some cleansing solution
eine Reinigungslösung [ˌˀaɪnə ˈʀaɪnɪgʊŋsˌløːzʊŋ]
for hard/soft contact lenses.
für harte/weiche Kontaktlinsen. [fyɐ ˈhaːtə/ˈvaɪçə kɔnˈtaktlɪnzn]
some sunglasses.
eine Sonnenbrille. [ˈˀaɪnə ˈzɔnnbʀɪlə]
some binoculars.
ein Fernglas. [ˀaɪn ˈfɛɐnglaːs]

Photographic materials

➢ **also Photos**

I'd like ...
Ich hätte gern ... [ˀɪç ˈhɛtə gɛɐn]
a film for this camera.
einen Film für diesen Fotoapparat.
[ˀaɪnn ˈfɪlm fyɐ ˈdiːzn ˈfoːtoˀapaˌʀaːt]
a colour film (for slides).
einen Farbfilm (für Dias). [ˀaɪnn ˈfaːpfɪlm (fyɐ ˈdiaːs)]
a film with 36/24/12 exposures.
einen Film mit sechsunddreißig/ vierundzwanzig/zwölf Aufnahmen.
[ˀaɪnn ˈfɪlm mɪt ˈzɛksʊnˌdʀasɪç/ ˈfiɐʊnˌtsvantsɪç/tsvølf ˈˀaʊfnaːmm]

... doesn't work/is broken.
... funktioniert nicht/ist kaputt. [fʊŋktsjoˈniɐt nɪçt/ɪst kaˈpʊt]

Can you repair/fix it?
Können Sie es reparieren? [ˈkønn zi əs ʀɛpaˈʀiɐn]

black-and-white film	der Schwarzweiß-Film [dɐ ʃvaːtsˈvaɪsfɪlm]
camcorder	der Camcorder [dɐ ˈkamkhɔɐdɐ]
digital camera	die Digitalkamera [di digiˈtaːlˌkaməʀa]
DVD	die DVD [di defaʊˈdeː]
film speed	die Filmempfindlichkeit [di ˈfɪlmɛmpfɪntlɪçkaɪt]
flash	das Blitzgerät [das ˈblɪtsgəʀɛːt]
lens	das Objektiv [das ˀɔbjɛkˈtiːf]
light meter	der Belichtungsmesser [dɐ bəˈlɪçtʊŋsˌmɛsɐ]
Polaroid® camera	die Sofortbildkamera [di zoˈfɔɐtbɪltˌkaməʀa]
self-timer	der Selbstauslöser [dɐ ˈzɛlpstaʊsløːzɐ]
shutter	der Auslöser [dɐ ˈˀaʊsløːzɐ]
slide	das Dia [das ˈdia]
telephoto lens	das Teleobjektiv [das ˈteːləˀɔbjɛkˌtiːf]
tripod	das Stativ [das ʃtaˈtiːf]
underwater camera	die Unterwasserkamera [di ˀʊntɐˈvasɐˌkaməʁa]
video camera	die Videokamera [di ˈviːdeoˌkaməʀa]
video cassette	die Videokassette [di ˈviːdeokaˌsɛtə]
video film	der Videofilm [dɐ ˈviːdeofɪlm]
video recorder	der Videorekorder [dɐ ˈviːdeoʀeˌkɔɐdɐ]
viewfinder	der Sucher [dɐ ˈzuːxɐ]

Shoes and leather goods

I'd like a pair of shoes.
Ich hätte gern ein Paar Schuhe. [ˀɪç ˈhɛtə gɛɐn ˀaɪn paː ˈʃuə]

I take (shoe) size ...
Ich habe Schuhgröße ... [ˀɪç ˈhaːbə ˈʃuːgrøːsə]

They're too tight
Sie sind zu eng. [zi zɪnt tsʊ ˈˀɛŋ]

They're too big.
Sie sind zu groß. [zi zɪnt tsʊ gʀoːs]

backpack	der Rucksack [dɐ ˈʀʊkzak]
bag	die Tasche [di ˈtaʃə]
bathing shoes	die Badeschuhe *m pl* [di ˈbaːdəʃuə]
beach shoes	die Strandschuhe *m pl* [di ˈʃtʀantʃuə]
belt	der Gürtel [dɐ gʏɐtl]

boots	die Stiefel *m pl* [di ʃtiːfl]
bumbag/fanny pack	die Gürteltasche [di gʏʁtltaʃə]
flip-flops	die Flipflops [di ˈflɪpflɔps]
gym shoes	die Turnschuhe *m pl* [di ˈtʊʁnʃuə]
handbag	die Handtasche [di ˈhan(t)taʃə]
hiking boots	der Wander-/der Trekkingschuh [dɐ ˈvandɐ-/ dɐ ˈtʁɛkɪŋ-ʃuː]
leather coat	der Ledermantel [dɐ ˈleːdɐmantl]
leather jacket	die Lederjacke [di ˈleːdɐjakə]
leather trousers	die Lederhose [di ˈleːdɐhoːzə]
rubber boots	die Gummistiefel *m pl* [di ˈgʊmiʃtiːfl]
rucksack	der Rucksack [dɐ ˈʀʊkzak]
sandals	die Sandalen *f pl* [di zanˈdaːln]
shoe	der Schuh [dɐ ʃuː]
shoe brush	die Schuhbürste [di ˈʃuːbʏʁstə]
shoe cream	die Schuhcreme [di ˈʃuːkʀɛːm]
shoelaces	die Schnürsenkel *m pl* [di ˈʃnyɐzɛŋkl]
shoulder bag	die Umhängetasche [di ˈʔʊmhɛŋəˌtaʃə]
shoulder strap	der Schulterriemen [də ˈʃʊltɐʀiːmm]
ski boots	die Skistiefel *m pl* [di ˈʃiːʃtiːfl]
sneakers *(US)*	die Turnschuhe *m pl* [di ˈtʊʁnʃuə]
sole	die Sohle [di ˈzoːlə]
suitcase	der Koffer [dɐ ˈkɔfɐ]
travelling bag	die Reisetasche [di ˈʀaɪzətaʃə]
trolley case	der Trolleykoffer/die Trolleytasche [dɐ ˈtʀɔlɪkɔfɐ/di ˈtʀɔlɪtaʃə]
wellingtons	die Gummistiefel *m pl* [di ˈgʊmiʃtiːfl]

Souvenirs

I'd like ...
Ich hätte gern ... [ˀɪç ˈhɛtə gɛɐn]
a nice souvenir.
ein hübsches Andenken. [ˀaɪn ˈhʏpʃəs ˈˀandɛŋkŋ]
something typical of this area.
etwas Typisches aus dieser Gegend.
[ˀɛtvas ˈtyːpɪʃ ˀaʊs diːzɐ ˈgeːgɛnt]

How much do you want to spend?
Wie viel wollen Sie ausgeben? [ˈviː fiːl vɔln zi ˈˀaʊsgeːbm]

I'd like something that's not too expensive.
Ich möchte etwas nicht zu Teures.
[ˀɪç ˈmøçtə ˌˀɛtvas ˈnɪç(t) tsʊ ˈtɔɪrəs]

That's lovely.
Das ist aber hübsch. [das ɪst ˈˀabɐ hʏpʃ]

Thanks, but I didn't find anything (I liked).
Danke schön, ich habe nichts gefunden(, das mir gefällt).
['daŋkə ʃøːn ˀɪç 'haːbə nɪçts gə'fʊndn (das miɐ gə'fɛlt)]

ceramics	die Keramik [di ke'ʀaːmɪk]
genuine	echt [ˀɛçt]
hand-made	handgemacht ['hantgəmaxt]
jewellery	der Schmuck [dɐ ʃmʊk]
local specialities	die regionalen Spezialitäten [di ʀegio'naːln ʃpɛtsjali'tɛːtn]
pottery	die Töpferwaren *f pl* [di 'tøpfɐvaːʀən]
souvenir	das Souvenir [das zʊvə'niɐ]
wood-carving	die Schnitzerei [di ʃnɪtsə'ʀaɪ]

Tobacco

A packet/pack of filter-tipped ..., please.
Eine Schachtel ... mit Filter, bitte! [ˀaɪnə ʃaxtl … mɪt 'fɪltɐ 'bɪtə]

A carton of plain ..., please.
Eine Stange ... ohne Filter, bitte! ['ˀaɪnə 'ʃtaŋə …'ˀoːnə 'fɪltɐ 'bɪtə]

Ten cigars/cigarillos, please.
Zehn Zigarren/Zigarillos, bitte. [tseːn tsɪ'gaʀən/tsɪga'ʀɪloːs 'bɪtə]

A packet of cigarette tobacco, please.
Ein Päckchen Zigarettentabak, bitte.
['ˀaɪn pɛkçn 'tsɪgaʀɛtn͵tabak 'bɪtə]

A tin of pipe tobacco, please.
Eine Dose Pfeifentabak, bitte. [ˀaɪnə 'doːzə '(p)faɪfn͵tabak 'bɪtə]

ashtray	der Aschenbecher [dɐ 'ˀaʃnbɛçɐ]
cigar	die Zigarre [di tsɪ'gaʀə]
cigarette	die Zigarette [di tsɪga'ʀɛtə]
cigarillo	das Zigarillo [das tsɪga'ʀɪlo]
lighter	das Feuerzeug [das 'fɔɪɐtsɔɪk]
matches	die Streichhölzer *n pl* [di 'ʃtʀaɪçhøltsɐ]
pipe	die Pfeife [di 'pfaɪfə]

Toiletries

after-shave lotion	das Rasierwasser [das ʀa'ziɐvasɐ]
brush	die Bürste [di 'bʏɐstə]
button	der Knopf [dɐ knɔpf]
comb	der Kamm [dɐ kam]
condom	das Kondom [kɔn'doːm]

I'd like
Ich hätte gern ...

cotton swabs	das Wattestäbchen [das 'vatəʃtɛ:pçn]
cotton wool	die Watte [di 'vatə]
cream	die Creme [di kʀɛ:m]
dental floss	die Zahnseide [di 'tsa:nzaɪdə]
deodorant	das Deo [das 'deo]
detergent *(dishes)*	das Spülmittel [das 'ʃpy:lmɪtl]
detergent *(clothes)*	das Waschmittel [das 'vaʃmɪtl]
dishcloth	das Spültuch [das 'ʃpy:ltu:x]
flannel	der Waschlappen [dɐ 'vaʃlapm]
hair gel	das Haargel [das 'ha:ge:l]
hairpins	die Haarklammern *f pl* [di 'ha:klamɐn]
Kleenex®	das Tempo(taschentuch)® [das 'tɛmpo͵taʃntu:x]
lip balm	die Lippenpomade [di 'lɪpmpoma:də]
lipstick	der Lippenstift [dɐ 'lɪpmʃtɪft]
mascara	die Wimperntusche [di 'vɪmpɐntʊʃə]
mirror	der Spiegel [dɐ ʃpi:gl]
moisturizing cream	die Feuchtigkeitscreme [di 'fɔɪçtɪçkaɪts͵kʀɛ:m]
nail scissors	die Nagelschere [di 'na:glʃe:ʀə]
nail varnish/polish	der Nagellack [dɐ 'na:gllak]
nail varnish/polish remover	der Nagellackentferner [dɐ 'na:gllakɛnt͵fɛɐnɐ]
needle	die Nadel [di na:dl]
night cream	die Nachtcreme [di 'naxtkrɛ:m]
panty liners	die Slipeinlagen *f pl* [di 'slɪpaɪnla:gŋ]
paper handkerchiefs	die Papiertaschentücher *n pl* [di pa'piɐ͵taʃnty:çɐ]
perfume	das Parfüm [das pa'fy:m]
plaster	das Pflaster [das 'pflastɐ]
powder	der Puder [dɐ 'pu:dɐ]
protection factor	der Lichtschutzfaktor [dɐ 'lɪçtʃʊts͵faktoɐ]
razor blade	die Rasierklinge [di ʀa'ziɐklɪŋə]
sanitary towels/napkins	die Damenbinden *f pl* [di 'da:mmbɪndn]
scent	das Parfüm [das pa'fy:m]
shampoo	das Schampoo [das 'ʃampo/'ʃampu]
shaver	der Rasierapparat [dɐ ʀa'ziɐˀapa͵ʀa:t]
shaving brush	der Rasierpinsel [dɐ ʀa'ziɐpɪnzl]
shaving foam	der Rasierschaum [dɐ ʀa'ziɐʃaʊm]
shower gel	das Duschgel [das 'du:ʃge:l]
soap	die Seife [di 'zaɪfə]
sun cream	die Sonnencreme [di 'zɔnnkʀɛ:m]
suntan lotion	die Sonnenmilch [di 'zɔnnmɪlç]
suntan oil	das Sonnenöl [das 'zɔnnˀø:l]

tampons	die Tampons *m pl* [di ˈtampɔŋs]
mini/regular/super/super plus	mini/normal/super/super plus [ˈmɪni/nɔɐˈmaːl/ˈzuːpɐ/ˌzuːpɐ ˈplʊs]
tea-tree oil	das Teebaumöl [das ˈteːbaʊmˀøːl]
thread	der Faden [dɐ faːdn]
toilet paper	das Toilettenpapier [das toˈlɛtnpaˌpiɐ]
toothbrush	die Zahnbürste [di ˈtsaːnbʏɐstə]
toothpaste	die Zahnpasta [di ˈtsaːnpasta]
toothpick	das Zahnstocher [dɐ ˈtsaːnʃtɔxɐ]
washcloth *(US)*	der Waschlappen [dɐ ˈvaʃlapm]
washing-up brush	die Spülbürste [di ˈʃpyːlbʏɐstə]

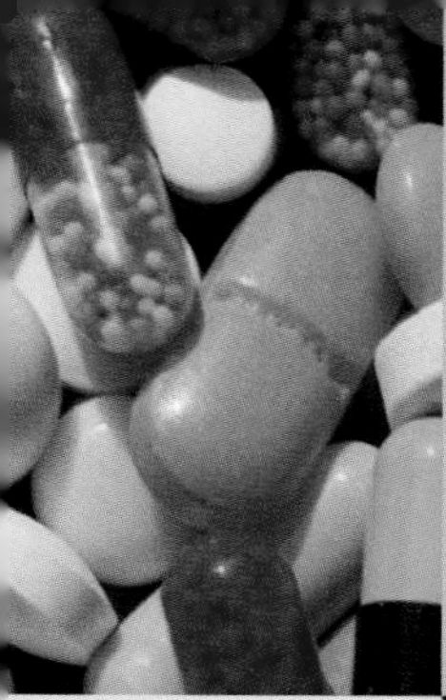

Health

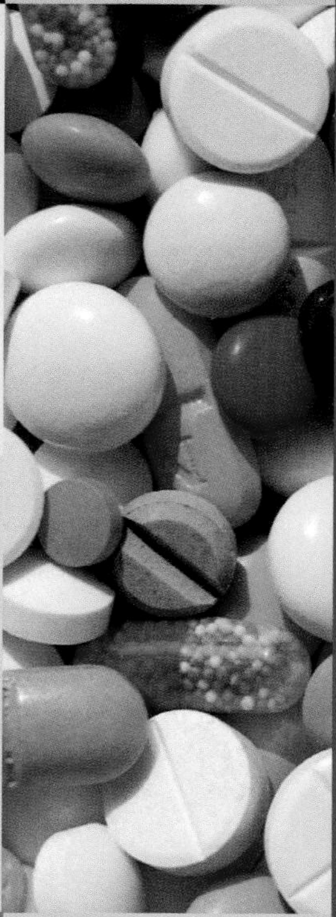

In an emergency
If you have any need of medical assistance, you will find first-rate facilities and medical personnel in all the German-speaking countries. As anywhere else, expect standards in large cities to be higher than those in small towns. Particularly noteworthy are the university clinics in most cities. Here you will find highly-motivated doctors and assistants who almost always speak good English, should you be worried that your German won't be sufficient.

At the chemist's/pharmacy

Can you tell me where the nearest chemist's (with all-night service) is, please?
Können Sie mir sagen, wo die nächste Apotheke (mit Nachtdienst) ist?
[kønn zi miɐ za:gŋ vo: di ˈnɛ:çstə ˀapoˈte:kə (mɪt ˈnaxtdi:nst) ˀɪst]

Could you give me something for ..., please?
Könnten Sie mir bitte etwas gegen ... geben
[køntn zi miɐ ˈbɪtə ˈˀɛtvas ge:gŋ … ge:bm]

You need a prescription for this.
Für dieses Mittel brauchen Sie ein Rezept.
[fyɐ ˈdi:zəs ˈmɪtl bʀaʊxn zi ˀaɪn ʀeˈtsɛpt]

➢ **also At the doctor's**

aftersun lotion	die Sonnenbrandlotion [di ˈzɔnnbʀantˌloʊʃən]
aspirin	das Aspirin [das ˀaspiˈʀi:n]
burns ointment	die Brandsalbe [di ˈbʀantzalbə]
cardiac stimulant	das Kreislaufmittel [das ˈkʀaɪslaʊfˌmɪtl]
condom	das Kondom [das kɔnˈdo:m]
cotton-wool/cotton	die Watte [di ˈvatə]
cough mixture/syrup	der Hustensaft [dɐ ˈhu:stnzaft]
disinfectant	das Desinfektionsmittel [das dezɪnfɛkˈtsjo:nsmɪtl]
drops	die Tropfen *m pl* [di ˈtʀɔpfn]
ear-drops	die Ohrentropfen *m pl* [di ˈˀo:ʀəntʀɔpfn]
elastic bandage	die Elastikbinde [di ˀeˈlastɪkbɪndə]
eye-drops	die Augentropfen *m pl* [di ˈˀaʊgŋtʀɔpfn]
gauze bandage	die Mullbinde [di ˈmʊlbɪndə]
glucose	der Traubenzucker [dɐ ˈtʀaʊbmtsʊkɐ]
headache tablets	die Kopfschmerztabletten *f pl* [di ˈkɔpfʃmɛɐtstaˌblɛtn]
insect repellent	das Mittel gegen Insektenstiche [das ˈmɪtl ge:gŋ ˀɪnˈzɛktnʃtɪçə]

insulin	das Insulin [das ˀɪnzʊˈliːn]
laxative	das Abführmittel [das ˈˀapfyɐˌmɪtl]
lice	die Läuse *f pl* [di ˈlɔɪzə]
treatment for lice	das Mittel gegen Läuse [das ˈmɪtl geːgŋ ˈlɔɪzə]
medicine	das Medikament [das medɪkaˈmɛnt]
ointment	die Salbe [di ˈzalbə]
pain-killing tablets	die Schmerztabletten *f pl* [di ˈʃmɛɐtstaˌblɛtn]
pill	die Tablette [di taˈblɛtə]
plaster	das Pflaster [das ˈpflastɐ]
powder	der Puder [dɐ ˈpuːdɐ]
prescription	das Rezept [das ʀeˈtsɛpt]
remedy	das Mittel [das ˈmɪtl]
sedative	das Beruhigungsmittel [das bəˈʀʊɪgʊŋsmɪtl]
sleeping pills	die Schlaftabletten *f pl* [di ˈʃlaːftaˌblɛtn]
sunburn lotion	die Sonnenbrandlotion [di ˈzɔnnbʀantˌloʊʃən]
suppository	das Zäpfchen [das ˈtsɛpfçn]
tablet	die Tablette [di taˈblɛtə]
thermometer	das Fieberthermometer [das ˈfiːbɐtɛɐmoˌmeːtɐ]
throat lozenges	die Halstabletten *f pl* [di ˈhalstaˌblɛtn]
tincture of iodine	die Jodtinktur [di ˈjoːtɪŋktuɐ]
tranquilliser	das Beruhigungsmittel [das bəˈʀʊɪgʊŋsmɪtl]
vitamin pills	die Vitamintabletten *f pl* [di vɪtaˈmiːntaˌblɛtn]

At the doctor's

➢ **also Travelling with children**

Could you recommend a/an ...?
Könnten Sie mir einen ... empfehlen?
[ˈkøntn zi miɐ ˀaɪnn ... ˀɛmpˈfeːln]

dentist
Zahnarzt [ˈtsaːnˀaːtst]

dermatologist
Hautarzt [ˈhaʊtˀaːtst]

doctor
Arzt/eine Ärztin [ˀaːtst/ˀaɪnə ˈˀɛɐtstɪn]

ear, nose and throat specialist
Hals-Nasen-Ohren-Arzt [hals-naːzn-ˈˀoːʀən-ˀaːtst]

eye specialist
Augenarzt [ˈˀaʊgŋˀaːtst]

general practitioner
praktischen Arzt [ˈpʀaktɪʃn ˀaːtst]
gynaecologist
Frauenarzt [ˈfʀaʊənˀaːtst]
pediatrician
Kinderarzt [ˈkɪndɐˀaːtst]
urologist
Urologen [ˀuʀoˈloːgŋ]

Beipackzettel	**Medicine information/ application leaflet**
Zusammensetzung	**Ingredients**
Anwendungsgebiete	Areas of application
Gegenanzeigen	Contraindications
Wechselwirkungen	Interactions
Nebenwirkungen	Side-effects
Dosierungsanleitung:	**Dosage:**
1 x/mehrmals täglich einnehmen	Take once/several times per day
1 Tablette	1 tablet
20 Tropfen	20 drops
1 Messbecher	1 measuring cup
vor dem Essen	before meals
nach dem Essen	after meals
auf nüchternen Magen	on an empty stomach
unzerkaut mit etwas Flüssigkeit einnehmen	Swallow whole with water
in etwas Wasser auflösen	Dissolve in a small amount of water
im Mund zergehen lassen	Dissolve in your mouth
dünn auf die Haut auftragen und einreiben	Apply thin layer to skin and rub in
Erwachsene	adults
Säuglinge	infants
Schulkinder	schoolchildren
Kleinkinder	toddlers
Jugendliche	young adults
Für Kinder unzugänglich aufbewahren!	Keep away from children!

Where's his/her surgery/the doctor's office?
Wo ist seine/ihre Praxis? [voː ˀɪst ˌzaɪnə/ˌˀiːʀə ˈpʀaksɪs]

I'd like to make an appointment.
Ich möchte einen Termin ausmachen.
[ˀɪç ˈmøçtə ˀaɪnn tɛɐˈmiːn ˈausmaxn]

Health

Medical complaints

What's the trouble?
Was für Beschwerden haben Sie? ['vas fyɐ bə'ʃveɐdn 'ha:bm zi:]

I've got a temperature.
Ich habe Fieber. [ʔɪç 'ha:bə 'fi:bɐ]

I often feel sick.
Mir ist oft schlecht. [miɐ ʔɪst ʔɔft 'ʃlɛçt]

Sometimes I feel dizzy.
Mir ist manchmal schwindlig. [miɐ ʔɪst 'mançma:l 'ʃvɪndlɪç]

I fainted.
Ich bin ohnmächtig geworden. [ʔɪç bɪn 'ʔo:nmɛçtɪç gə'vɔɐdn]

I've got a bad cold.
Ich bin stark erkältet. ['ʔɪç bɪn ʃta:k ʔɐ'kɛltət]

I've got ...
Ich habe ... [ʔɪç 'ha:bə]
  a headache.
  Kopfschmerzen. ['kɔpfʃmɛɐtsn]
  a sore throat.
  Halsschmerzen. ['halsʃmɛɐtsn]
  a cough.
  Husten. [hu:stn]

I've been stung.
Ich bin gestochen worden. [ʔɪç bɪn gə'ʃtɔxn 'vɔɐdn]

I've been bitten.
Ich bin gebissen worden. [ʔɪç bɪn gə'bɪsn 'vɔɐdn]

I've got an upset stomach.
Ich habe mir den Magen verdorben.
[ʔɪç ˌha:bə miɐ den 'ma:gŋ vɐ'dɔɐbm]

I've got diarrhoea.
Ich habe Durchfall. [ʔɪç 'ha:bə 'dʊɐçfal]

I'm constipated.
Ich habe Verstopfung. [ʔɪç 'ha:bə fɐ'ʃtɔpfʊŋ]

The food doesn't agree with me.
Ich vertrage das Essen nicht. [ʔɪç fɐ'tʀa:gə das 'ʔɛsn nɪçt]

I can't stand the heat.
Ich vertrage die Hitze nicht. [ʔɪç fɐ'tʀa:gə di 'hɪtsə nɪçt]

I've hurt myself.
Ich habe mich verletzt. [ʔɪç 'ha:bə mɪç fɐ'lɛtst]

I fell down.
Ich bin gestürzt. [ˀɪç bɪn gəˈʃtʏɐtst]

Can you prescribe something for ...?
Können Sie mir bitte etwas gegen ... verschreiben?
[ˈkønn zi miɐ ˈbɪtə ˈˀɛtvas ˈgeːgŋ ... fɐˈʃʀaɪbm]

I usually take ...
Normalerweise nehme ich ... [nɔˈmaːlɐvaɪzə ˈneːm ɪç]

I've got high/low blood pressure.
Ich habe einen hohen/niedrigen Blutdruck.
[ˀɪç ˌhaːbə ˀaɪnn ˈhoːn/ˈniːdʀɪgŋ ˈbluːtdʀʊk]

I'm a diabetic.
Ich bin Diabetiker/Diabetikerin. [ˀɪç bɪn diaˈbeːtɪkɐ/diaˈbeːtɪkəʀɪn]

I'm pregnant.
Ich bin schwanger. [ˀɪç bɪn ˈʃvaŋɐ]

I had ... recently
Ich hatte vor kurzem ... [ˀɪç ˌhatə foɐ ˈkʊɐtsm]

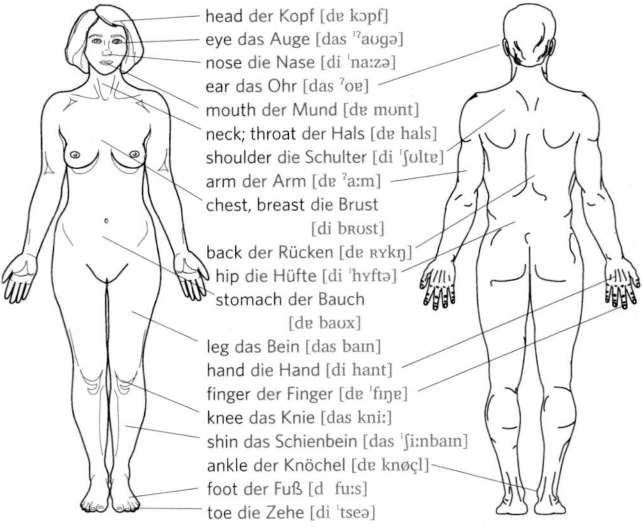

Check-up

What can I do for you?
Was kann ich für Sie tun? [vas kan ɪç fyɐ zi ˈtuːn]

Where does it hurt?
Wo tut es weh? [vo: ˈtu:t əs ˈve:]

I've got a pain here.
Ich habe hier Schmerzen. [ˀɪç ˈha:bə ˈhiɐ ˈʃmɛɐtsn]

Uncover your arm, please.
Bitte, machen Sie Ihren Arm frei. [ˈbɪtə maxn zi ˀiɐn ˈˀa:m fʀaɪ]

Take off your clothes, please.
Bitte, machen Sie sich frei. [ˈbɪtə maxn zi zɪç ˈfʀaɪ]

Take a deep breath.
Tief einatmen. [ti:f ˈˀaɪna:tmən]

Hold your breath.
Atem anhalten. [ˈˀa:təm ˈˀanhaltn]

I need to do a blood/urine test.
Ich brauche eine Blutprobe/ Urinprobe.
[ˀɪç ˌbʀaʊxə ˌˀaɪnə ˈblu:tpʀo:bə/ˀuˈʀi:npʀo:bə]

You need a few days in bed.
Sie brauchen ein paar Tage Bettruhe.
[zi bʀaʊxn aɪn pa: ˈta:gə ˈbɛtʀuə]

It's nothing serious.
Es ist nichts Ernstes. [ˀəs ɪst nɪçts (nɪks) ˈˀɛɐnstəs]

Have you got a vaccination card?
Haben Sie einen Impfpass? [ha(:b)m zi ˀaɪnn ˈˀɪmpfpas]

I've been vaccinated against ...
Ich bin gegen ... geimpft. [ˀɪç bɪn ge:gŋ … gəˈˀɪmpft]

EU nationals are covered free of charge for medical and dental treatment in Germany and Austria on production of an E111 form. Visitors from non-EU countries should take out medical insurance before travelling.

In hospital

How long will I have to stay here?
Wie lange muss ich hier bleiben? [vi ˈlaŋə mʊs ɪç ˈhiɐ blaɪbm]

I can't sleep.
Ich kann nicht einschlafen. [ˀɪç kan nɪçt ˈˀaɪnʃla:fn]

Could you give me ..., please.
Geben Sie mir bitte ... [ˈge:bm zi miɐ ˌbɪtə]
a glass of water
ein Glas Wasser. [ˀaɪn gla:s ˈvasɐ]

a pain-killing tablet
eine Schmerztablette. [ˌˀaɪnə ˈʃmɛɐtstaˌblɛtə]
a sleeping-pill
eine Schlaftablette. [ˌˀaɪnə ˈʃlaːftaˌblɛtə]
a hot-water bottle
eine Wärmflasche. [ˈˀaɪnə ˈvɛɐmflaʃə]

When can I get up?
Wann darf ich aufstehen? [van daːf ɪç ˈˀaʊfʃteːn]

Illnesses and afflictions

abscess	der Abszess [dɐ ˀapsˈɛs]
AIDS	das Aids [das ˀɛɪts]
be allergic to	allergisch sein gegen ... [ˀalɛˈgɪʃ zaɪn ˈgeːgŋ]
allergy	die Allergie [di ˀal(ɛ)ɐˈgiː]
angina	die Angina [di ˀaŋˈgiːna]
appendicitis	die Blinddarmentzündung [di ˈblɪntdaːmɛnˌtsʏndʊŋ]
asthma	das Asthma [das ˈˀastma]
attack	der Anfall [dɐ ˈˀanfal]
backache	die Rückenschmerzen *m pl* [di ˈʀʏkŋʃmɛɐtsn]
bleeding	die Blutung [di ˈbluːtʊŋ]
blood-poisoning	die Blutvergiftung [di ˈbluːtfɐgɪftʊŋ]
borreliosis	die Borreliose [di bɔʁɛlˈjoːzə]
broken	gebrochen [gəˈbʀɔxn]
bronchitis	die Bronchitis [di bʀɔnˈçiːtɪs]
bruise (*caused by hitting*)	die Prellung [di ˈpʀɛlʊŋ]
bruise (*caused by pinching*)	die Quetschung [di ˈkvɛtʃʊŋ]
burn	die Verbrennung [di fɐˈbʀɛnʊŋ]
cancer	der Krebs [dɐ kʀeːps]
cardiac infarction	der Herzinfarkt [dɐ ˈhɛɐtsɪnfaːkt]
circulatory disorder	die Kreislaufstörung [di ˈkʀaɪslaʊfˌʃtøːʀʊŋ]
cold	die Erkältung [di ˀɐˈkɛltʊŋ]
colic	die Kolik [di ˈkoːlɪk]
concussion	die Gehirnerschütterung [di gəˈhɪʁnɐˌʃʏtəʀʊŋ]
conjunctivitis	die Bindehautentzündung [di ˈbɪndəhaʊtɛnˌtsʏndʊŋ]
constipation	die Verstopfung [di fɐˈʃtɔpfʊŋ]
contagious	ansteckend [ˈˀanʃtɛkŋt]
cramp	der Krampf [dɐ kʀampf]
cut	die Schnittwunde [di ˈʃnɪtvʊndə]
cyst	die Zyste [di ˈtsʏstə]

diabetes	der Diabetes [dɐ diaˈbeːtəs]
diarrhoea	der Durchfall [dɐ ˈdʊɐçfal]
difficulty in breathing	die Atembeschwerden *f pl* [di ˈʔaːtmbəʃveɐdn]
diphtheria	die Diphtherie [di dɪftəˈʀiː]
dizziness	das Schwindelgefühl [das ˈʃvɪndlgəfyːl]
to faint	in Ohnmacht fallen [ʔɪn ˈʔoːnmaxt faln]
fever	das Fieber [das ˈfiːbɐ]
fit	der Anfall [dɐ ˈʔanfal]
flu	die Grippe [di ˈgʀɪpə]
food poisoning	die Lebensmittelvergiftung [di ˈleːbmsmɪtlfɐˌgɪftʊŋ]
fracture	der Knochenbruch [dɐ ˈknɔxnbʀʊx]
fungal infection	die Pilzinfektion [di ˈpɪltsɪnfɛkˌtsjoːn]
growth	die Geschwulst [di gəˈʃvʊlst]
haemorrhoids	die Hämorriden *f pl* [di hɛmoˈʀiːdn]
hay fever	der Heuschnupfen [dɐ ˈhɔɪʃnʊpfn]
headache	die Kopfschmerzen *m pl* [di ˈkɔpfʃmɛɐtsn]
heart attack	der Herzinfarkt [dɐ ˈhɛɐtsɪnfaːkt]
heart defect	der Herzfehler [dɐ ˈhɛɐtsfeːlɐ]
heart trouble	die Herzbeschwerden *f pl* [ˈhɛɐtsbəʃveɐdn]
heartburn	das Sodbrennen [das ˈzoːtbʀɛnn]
hernia	der Leistenbruch [dɐ ˈlaɪstnbʀʊx]
herpes	der Herpes [dɐ ˈhɛɐpəs]
high blood pressure	der Bluthochdruck [dɐ ˈbluːthoːxdrʊk]
HIV positive	HIV-positiv [haʔiˌfaʊ-ˈpoːzɪtiːf]
hoarse	heiser [ˈhaɪzɐ]
to hurt	wehtun [ˈveːtuːn]
to hurt oneself	sich verletzen [zɪç fɐˈlɛtsn]
ill	krank [kʀaŋk]
illness	die Krankheit [di ˈkʀaŋkhaɪt]
impaired balance	die Gleichgewichtsstörungen *f pl* [di ˈglaɪçgəvɪçtˌʃtøːʀʊŋŋ]
impaired vision	die Sehstörungen *f pl* [di ˈzeːʃtøːʀʊŋŋ]
indigestion	die Verdauungsstörung [di fɐˈdaʊʊŋʃtøːʀʊŋ]
infection	die Infektion [di ʔɪnfɛkˈtsjoːn]
inflammation	die Entzündung [di ʔɛnˈtsʏndʊŋ]
inflammation of the middle ear	die Mittelohrentzündung [di ˈmɪtlʔoɐɛnˌtsʏndʊŋ]
influenza	die Grippe [di ˈgʀɪpə]
to injure	verletzen [fɐˈlɛtsn]
injury	die Verletzung [di fɐˈlɛtsʊŋ]
insect bite	der Insektenstich [dɐ ʔɪnˈzɛktnʃtɪç]
insomnia	die Schlaflosigkeit [di ˈʃlaːflozɪçkaɪt]

jaundice	die Gelbsucht [di 'gɛlpzʊxt]
jellyfish	die Qualle [di 'kvalə]
kidney stone	der Nierenstein [dɐ 'niːʀənʃtaɪn]
lumbago	der Hexenschuss [dɐ 'hɛksnʃʊs]
meningitis	die Hirnhautentzündung [di 'hɪɐnhaʊtɛnˌtsʏndʊŋ]
migraine	die Migräne [di mi'gʀɛːnə]
miscarriage	die Fehlgeburt [di 'feːlgəbʊɐt]
nausea	der Brechreiz [dɐ 'bʀɛçʀaɪts]
nephritis	die Nierenentzündung [di 'niːʀənˀɛnˌtsʏndʊŋ]
nose bleed	das Nasenbluten [das 'naːznbluːtn]
pain	die Schmerzen *m pl* [di 'ʃmɛɐtsn]
painful	schmerzhaft ['ʃmɛɐtshaft]
paralysis	die Lähmung [di 'lɛːmʊŋ]
piles	die Hämorriden *f pl* [di hɛmoʀiːdn]
pneumonia	die Lungenentzündung [di 'lʊŋənˀɛnˌtsʏndʊŋ]
poisoning	die Vergiftung [di vɐ'gɪftʊŋ]
poisonous	giftig ['gɪftɪç]
polio	die Kinderlähmung [di 'kɪndɐlɛːmʊŋ]
pulled muscle	die Zerrung [di 'tsɛʀʊŋ]
rash	der Ausschlag [dɐ 'ˀaʊʃlaːk]
rheumatism	das Rheuma [das 'ʀɔɪma]
rupture	der Leistenbruch [dɐ 'laɪstnbʀʊx]
salmonella	die Salmonellen *pl* [zalmo'nɛln]
sciatica	der Ischias [dɐ 'ˀɪʃias]
shivering fit	der Schüttelfrost [dɐ 'ʃʏtlfʀɔst]
sick	krank [kʀaŋk]
sinusitis	die Stirnhöhlenentzündung [di 'ʃtɪɐnhøːlnˀɛnˌtsʏndʊŋ]
sleeplessness	die Schlaflosigkeit [di 'ʃlaːflozɪçkaɪt]
smallpox	die Pocken *f pl* [di pɔkŋ]
sore throat	die Halsschmerzen *m pl* [di 'halʃmɛɐtsn]
sprained	verstaucht [fɐ'ʃtaʊxt]
to sting	brennen [bʀɛnn]
stitch	das Seitenstechen [das 'zaɪtnʃtɛçn]
stomach-ache	die Magenschmerzen *m pl* [di 'maːgŋʃmɛɐtsn]
stroke	der Schlaganfall [dɐ 'ʃlaːkanfal]
sunburn	der Sonnenbrand [dɐ 'zɔnnbʀant]
sunstroke	der Sonnenstich [dɐ 'zɔnnʃtɪç]
swelling	die Schwellung [di 'ʃvɛlʊŋ]
swollen	geschwollen [gə'ʃvɔln]
tachycardia	das Herzrasen [das 'hɛɐtsʀaːzn]
temperature (*fever*)	das Fieber [das 'fiːbɐ]

tetanus	der Tetanus [dɐ ˈtɛtanʊs]
tick	die Zecke [di ˈtsɛkə]
tonsillitis	die Mandelentzündung [di ˈmandlˀɛnˌtsʏndʊŋ]
torn ligament	der Bänderriss [dɐ ˈbɛndɐʀɪs]
tumour	die Geschwulst [di gəˈʃvʊlst]
typhoid	der Typhus [dɐ ˈty:fʊs]
ulcer	das Geschwür [das gəˈʃvyɐ]
venereal disease	die Geschlechtskrankheit [di geˈʃlɛçtsˌkʀaŋkhaɪt]
whooping-cough	der Keuchhusten [dɐ ˈkɔɪçhu:stn]
wind	die Blähungen *f pl* [di ˈblɛ:ʊŋŋ]
wound	die Wunde [di ˈvʊndə]

Body – Doctor – Hospital

abdomen	der Unterleib [dɐ ˈˀʊntɐlaɪp]
anaesthetic	die Narkose [di naˈko:zə]
appendix	der Blinddarm [dɐ ˈblɪntda:m]
artificial limb	die Prothese [di pʀoˈte:zə]
bandage	der Verband [dɐ fɐˈbant]
bladder	die Blase [di ˈbla:zə]
to bleed	bluten [blu:tn]
blood	das Blut [das blu:t]
blood group	die Blutgruppe [di ˈblu:tgʀʊpə]
blood pressure (high/low)	der Blutdruck (hoher/niedriger) [dɐ ˈblutdrʊk (ˈhoɐ/ˈni:dʀɪgɐ)]
bone	der Knochen [dɐ knɔxn]
bowel movement	der Stuhlgang [dɐ ˈʃtu:lgaŋ]
brain	das Gehirn [das gəˈhɪɐn]
to breathe	atmen [ˈˀa:tmən]
bronchial tubes	die Bronchien *f pl* [di ˈbʀɔnçɪən]
bypass	der Bypass [dɐ ˈbaɪpa:s]
certificate	das Attest [das ˀaˈtɛst]
chest	die Brust [di bʀʊst]
collarbone	das Schlüsselbein [das ˈʃlʏslbaɪn]
cough	der Husten [dɐ hu:stn]
diagnosis	die Diagnose [di diaˈgno:zə]
diet	die Diät [di diˈɛ:t]
digestion	die Verdauung [di fɐˈdaʊʊŋ]
to disinfect	desinfizieren [dezɪnfɪˈtsi:ʀən]
to dress *(a wound)*	verbinden [fɐˈbɪndn]
dressing	der Verband [dɐ fɐˈbant]
eardrum	das Trommelfell [das ˈtʀɔmlfɛl]
examination	die Untersuchung [di ˀʊntɐˈzu:xʊŋ]
face	das Gesicht [das gəˈzɪçt]
gall-bladder	die Gallenblase [di ˈgalnbla:zə]
gullet	die Speiseröhre [di ˈʃpaɪzəʀø:ʀə]

health	die Gesundheit [di gəˈzʊnthaɪt]
health resort	der Kurort [dɐ ˈkuɐʔɔɐt]
hearing	das Gehör [das gəˈhøɐ]
heart	das Herz [das hɛɐts]
heart specialist	der Herzspezialist [dɐ ˈhɛɐtʃpɛtsjaˌlɪst]
hospital	das Krankenhaus [das ˈkʀaŋkŋhaʊs]
ill	krank [kʀaŋk]
infusion	die Infusion [di ʔɪnfʊˈzjoːn]
injection	die Spritze [di ˈʃpʀɪtsə]
intestines	der Darm [dɐ daːm]
joint	das Gelenk [das gəˈlɛŋk]
kidney	die Niere [di ˈniːʀə]
lip	die Lippe [di ˈlɪpə]
liver	die Leber [di ˈleːbɐ]
lungs	die Lunge [di ˈlʊŋə]
medical insurance card	die Versichertenkarte [dɪ fəˈzɪxəʀtənkaːtə]
menstruation	die Menstruation [di mɛnstʀuaˈtsjon]
muscle	der Muskel [dɐ ˈmʊskl]
nerve	der Nerv [dɐ nɛɐf]
nervous	nervös [nɐˈvøːs]
nurse	die Krankenschwester [di ˈkʀaŋkŋʃvɛstɐ]
oesophagus	die Speiseröhre [di ˈʃpaɪzəʀøːʀə]
operation	die Operation [di ʔɔpəʀaˈtsjoːn]
pacemaker	der Herzschrittmacher [dɐ ˈhɛɐt(s)ʃʀɪtmaxɐ]
to perspire	schwitzen [ˈʃvɪtsn]
pregnancy	die Schwangerschaft [di ˈʃvaŋɐʃaft]
to prescribe	verschreiben [fɐˈʃʀaɪbm]
pulse	der Puls [dɐ pʊls]
pus	der Eiter [dɐ ˈʔaɪtɐ]
rib	die Rippe [di ˈʀɪpə]
scar	die Narbe [di ˈnaːbə]
sexual organs	die Geschlechtsorgane *n pl* [di gəˈʃlɛçtsʔɔˌgaːnə]
sick	krank [kʀaŋk]
skin	die Haut [di haʊt]
sonogram	die Ultraschalluntersuchung [di ˈʔʊltʀaʃalʔʊntɐˌzuːxʊŋ]
specialist	der Facharzt [dɐ ˈfaxaːtst]
spine	die Wirbelsäule [di ˈvɪɐblzɔɪlə]
splint	die Schiene [di ˈʃiːnə]
sting	der Stich [dɐ ʃtɪç]
stitch (stitches)	die Naht [naːt]
to stitch (up)	nähen [nɛːn]
stomach	der Magen [dɐ maːgŋ]

surgeon	der Chirurg/die Chirurgin [dɐ çɪˈʀʊɐk/di çɪˈʀʊɐgɪn]
surgery *(hours)*	die Sprechstunde [di ˈʃpʀɛçʃtʊndə]
(operation)	die Operation [di ˀɔpəʀaˈtsjoːn]
to sweat	schwitzen [ˈʃvɪtsn]
throat	die Kehle [di keːlə]
tongue	die Zunge [ˈtsʊŋə]
tonsils	die Mandeln *f pl* [di ˈmandln]
ultrasound scan	die Ultraschalluntersuchung [di ˈˀʊltʀaʃalˀʊntɐˌzuːxʊŋ]
unconscious	bewusstlos [bəˈvʊstloːs]
urine	der Urin [dɐ ˀuˈʀiːn]
vaccination	die Impfung [di ˈˀɪmpfʊŋ]
vaccination card	der Impfpass [dɐ ˈˀɪmpfpas]
virus	das Virus [das ˈviːʀʊs]
visiting hours	die Besuchszeit [di bəˈzuːxstsaɪt]
to vomit	sich erbrechen [zɪç ˀɐˈbʀɛçn]
waiting room	das Wartezimmer [das ˈvaːtətsɪmɐ]
ward	die Station [di ʃtaˈtsjoːn]
windpipe	die Kehle [di keːlə]
X-ray	die Röntgenaufnahme [di ˈʀønçnˀaʊfnaːmə]
to X-ray	röntgen [ˈʀønçn]

At the dentist's

I've got (terrible) toothache.
Ich habe (starke) Zahnschmerzen. [ˀɪç ˈhaːbə (ˈʃtaːkə) ˈtsaːnʃmɛɐtsn]

This upper/bottom tooth hurts.
Dieser Zahn oben/unten tut weh. [ˈdiːzɐ tsaːn ˈˀoːbm/ˈˀʊntn tuːt ˈveː]

This front/back tooth hurts.
Dieser Zahn vorn/hinten tut weh. [ˈdiːzɐ tsaːn foɐn/ˈhɪntn tuːt ˈveː]

I've lost a filling.
Ich habe eine Füllung verloren. [ˀɪç ˈhaːbə ˈˀaɪnə ˈfʏlʊŋ fɐˈloɐn]

I've broken a tooth.
Mir ist ein Zahn abgebrochen. [miɐ ˀɪst ˀaɪn ˈtsaːn ˈˀapgəbʀɔxn]

I'll only do a temporary job.
Ich behandle ihn nur provisorisch.
[ˀɪç bəˈhandlə ˀin nuɐ pʀoviˈzoːʀɪʃ]

I'd like an injection, please.
Geben Sie mir bitte eine Spritze. [ˈgeːbm zi miɐ ˈbɪtə ˌˀaɪnə ˈʃpʀɪtsə]

I don't want an injection.
Geben Sie mir keine Spritze. [ˈgeːbm zi miɐ ˈkaɪnə ˈʃpʀɪtsə]

brace	die Zahnspange [di ˈtsaːnʃpaŋə]
bridge	die Brücke [di ˈbʀʏkə]
cavity	das Loch [das lɔx]
crown	die Krone [di ˈkʀoːnə]
dentures	die Zahnprothese [di ˈtsaːnpʀoˌteːzə]
to extract	ziehen [tsiːn]
filling	die Füllung [di ˈfʏlʊŋ], die Plombe [di ˈplɔmbə]
gums	das Zahnfleisch [das ˈtsaːnflaɪʃ]
incisor	der Schneidezahn [dɐ ˈʃnaɪdətsaːn]
jaw	der Kiefer [dɐ ˈkiːfɐ]
molar	der Backenzahn [dɐ ˈbakŋtsaːn]
tartar	der Zahnstein [dɐ ˈtsaːnʃtaɪn]
tooth	der Zahn [dɐ tsaːn]
tooth decay	die Karies [di ˈkaːʀiɛs]
toothache	die Zahnschmerzen *m pl* [di ˈtsaːnʃmɛɐtsn]
wisdom tooth	der Weisheitszahn [dɐ ˈvaɪshaɪtsaːn]

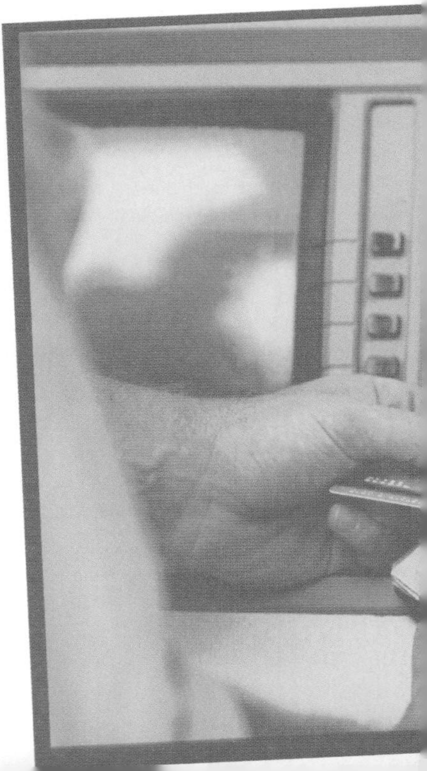

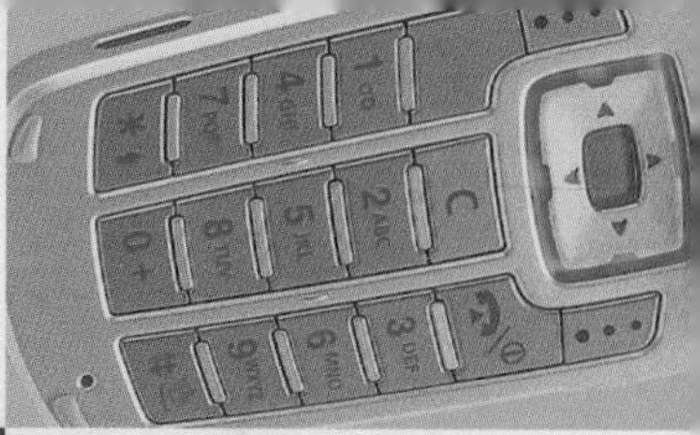

Essentials A to Z

Twenty-four hour language lab
Below you will find more practical phrases for situations "on the street". Keep in mind that a city's streets and walkways represent the world's greatest language lab. Get out there and try out your German. People are impressed if they see you're trying and will prove very helpful. *Viel Erfolg!* (Good luck!, literally, "much success")

Bank

Can you tell me where the nearest bank is, please?
Können Sie mir bitte sagen, wo hier eine Bank ist?
[kønn zi miɐ ˈbɪtə zaːgŋ voː hiɐ ˀaɪnə ˈbaŋk ˀɪst]

I'd like to change £100 into euros.
Ich möchte einhundert Pfund in Euro wechseln.
[ˀɪç møçtə ˈˀaɪnhʊndɐt pfʊnt ˀɪn ˈˀɔɪʀo ˈvɛksln]

I'd like to change $150 into Swiss francs.
Ich möchte einhundertfünfzig Dollar in Schweizer Franken wechseln.
[ˀɪç møçtə ˈˀaɪnhʊndɐtˌfʏnftsɪç ˈdɔlaː ˀɪn ˈʃvaɪtsɐ fʀaŋkŋ vɛksln]

Can you tell me what the exchange rate is today, please?
Können Sie mir bitte sagen, wie heute der Wechselkurs ist?
[kønn zi miɐ ˈbɪtə zaːgŋ viː hɔɪtə dɐ ˈvɛkslkʊɐs ˀɪst]

I'd like to cash this traveller's-cheque.
Ich möchte diesen Reisescheck einlösen.
[ˀɪç ˈmøçtə diːzn ˈʀaɪzəʃɛk ˈˀaɪnløːzn]

What's the maximum I can cash on one cheque?
Auf welchen Betrag kann ich ihn maximal ausstellen?
[ˀaʊf ˈvɛlçn bəˈtʀaːk kan ɪç ˀiːn maksiˈmaːl ˈˀaʊʃtɛln]

Can I see your cheque card, please?
Ihre Scheckkarte, bitte. [ˌˀiːʀə ˈʃɛkaːtə ˈbɪtə]

May I see ..., please?
Darf ich bitte ... sehen? [daːf ɪç ˈbɪtə … zeːn]
  your identity card
  Ihren Ausweis [ˈˀiːʀən ˈˀaʊsvaɪs]
  your passport
  Ihren Pass [ˈˀiːʀən ˈpas]

Sign here, please.
Unterschreiben Sie bitte hier. [ˀʊntɐˈʃʀaɪbm zi ˈbɪtə ˈhiɐ]

The cashpoint does not accept my card.
Der Geldautomat akzeptiert meine Karte nicht. [dɐ ˈgɛltˀautoˌmaːt ˀaktsɛpˈtiɐt ˌmaɪnə ˈkaːtə nɪçt]

The cashpoint has swallowed my card.
Der Geldautomat gibt meine Karte nicht mehr heraus.
[dɐ ˈgɛltˀautoˌmaːt gɪpt ˌmaɪnə ˈkaːtə nɪçt meɐ hɐˈʁaʊs]

account	das Konto [das ˈkɔnto]
amount	der Betrag [dɐ bəˈtʀa:k]
automated teller machine	der Geldautomat [dɐ ˈgɛltaʊtoˌma:t]
bank	die Bank [di baŋk]
banknote	der Geldschein [dɐ ˈgɛltʃaɪn]
cash	das Bargeld [das ˈba:gɛlt]
cashpoint	der Geldautomat [dɐ ˈgɛltaʊtoˌma:t]
cent	der Cent [dɐ sɛnt]
change	das Kleingeld [das ˈklaɪngɛlt]
to change	umtauschen [ˈʔʊmtaʊʃn]
cheque (*Am* check)	der Scheck [dɐ ʃɛk]
cheque card	die Scheckkarte [di ˈʃɛka:tə]
chip card	die Chipkarte [di ˈtʃɪpka:tə]
coin	die Münze [di ˈmʏntsə]
credit card	die Kreditkarte [di kʀedi:tka:tə]
currency	die Währung [di ˈvɛ:ʀʊŋ]
euro	der Euro [dɐ ˈʔɔɪʀo]
exchange	der Geldwechsel [dɐ ˈgɛltvɛksl]
exchange rate	der Wechselkurs [dɐ ˈvɛkslkʊɐs]
form	das Formular [das fɔmuˈla:]
money	das Geld [das gɛlt]
to pay out	auszahlen [ˈʔaʊstsa:ln]
payment	die Zahlung [di ˈtsa:lʊŋ]
Personal Identification Number (PIN)	die Geheimzahl [di gəˈhaɪmtsa:l]
receipt	die Quittung [di ˈkvɪtʊŋ]
remittance	die Überweisung [di ʔybɐˈvaɪzʊŋ]
service charge	die Bearbeitungsgebühr [di bəˈʔa:baɪtʊŋsgəˌbyɐ]
signature	die Unterschrift [di ˈʔʊntɐʃʀɪft]
Swiss francs	Schweizer Franken *m pl* [ˌʃvaɪtsɐ ˈfʀaŋkŋ]
telegraphic transfer	die telegrafische Überweisung [di teləˈgʀa:fɪʃə ʔy:bɐˈvaɪzʊŋ]
transfer	die Überweisung [di ʔybɐˈvaɪzʊŋ]
traveller's cheque	der Reisescheck [dɐ ˈʀaɪzəʃɛk]
to write a cheque	einen Scheck ausstellen [ʔaɪnn ˈʃɛk ˈʔaʊʃtɛln]

Internet café

Is there an Internet café near here?
Wo gibt es in der Nähe ein Internetcafé?
[ˈvo: gɪpt əs ɪn dɐ ˈnɛə ʔaɪn ˈʔɪntɐnɛtkaˌfe:]

What does it cost for an hour/a quarter of an hour?
Wieviel kostet eine Stunde?/Viertelstunde?
[ˈvi: fi:l ˌkɔstət ˌʔaɪnə ˈʃtʊndə/ˌfɪɐtlˈʃtʊndə]

I'd like to send an e-mail.
Ich möchte eine E-Mail senden. [ˀɪç ˈmœçtə ˀaɪnə ˈˀiːmɛɪl zɛndn]

Can I send a fax from here?
Kann ich von hier ein Fax versenden? [kan ɪç fɔn ˈhiɐ ˀaʊs aɪn ˈfaks fɐˈʃkɪkŋ]

Can I print out a page?
Kann ich eine Seite ausdrucken? [ˈkan ɪç ˌˀaɪnə ˈzaɪtə ˈˀaʊsdʁʊkŋ]

Can I download data?
Kann ich Daten herunterladen? [kan ɪç ˈdaːtn hɐˈʁʊtɐlaːdn]

Can I connect a memory stick/memory card/iPod/laptop/camera/microphone?
Kann ich einen Speicherstick/eine Speicherkarte/einen iPod/einen Laptop/eine Kamera/ein Mikrofon anschließen? [ˈkan ɪç ˀaɪnn ˈʃpaɪçɐstɪk/ˌˀaɪnə ˈʃpaɪçɐˌkaːtə/ˀaɪnn ˈˀaɪpɔt/ˀaɪnn ˈlɛptɔp/ˌˀaɪnə ˈkaməʁa/ˀaɪn mɪkʁoˈfoːn ˈˀanʃliːsn]

I don't have a connection.
Bei mir klappt die Verbindung nicht. [baɪ ˈmiɐ klapt di fɐˈbɪndʊŋ nɪçt]

I have a problem with the computer.
Ich habe Probleme mit dem Computer. [ˀɪç ˌhaːbə pʁoˈbleːmə mɪt dem kɔmˈpjuːtɐ]

There's a problem with the mouse/browser/monitor.
Es gibt Probleme mit der Maus/mit dem Browser/Monitor.
[ˀəs gɪpt pʁoˈbleːmə mɪt dɐ ˈmaʊs/mɪt dem ˈbʁaʊzɐ/ˈmoːnɪtoɐ]

Can I burn some photos from my digital camera onto CD here?
Kann ich bei Ihnen Fotos von meiner Digitalkamera auf CD brennen?
[kan ɪç baɪ ˈˀiːnn ˈfoːtos fɔn ˌmaɪnɐ digiˈtaːlkaməʁa ˀaʊf ˈtsedeː bʁɛnn]

Lost-property office

➢ **also Police**

Could you tell me where the lost-property office/lost-and-found is, please?
Könnten Sie mir bitte sagen, wo das Fundbüro ist?
[køntn zi miɐ ˈbɪtə zaːgŋ voː das ˈfʊntbyˌʁoː ˀɪst]

I've lost ...
Ich habe ... verloren. [ˀɪç ˈhaːbə … fɐˈloɐn]

I left my handbag on the train.
Ich habe meine Handtasche im Zug vergessen.
[ˀɪç ˈhaːbə ˈmaɪnə ˈhantaʃə ˀɪm tsuːk fɐˈgɛsn]

Would you let me know if it turns up, please?
Würden Sie mich bitte benachrichtigen, falls sie gefunden wurde?
[ˌvʏɐdn zi mɪç ˌbɪtə bəˈnaːxɪçtɪgŋ fals zi gəˈfʊndn vʊɐdə]

Here's the address of my hotel.
Hier ist meine Hotelanschrift. ['hiɐ ˀɪst 'maɪnə ho'tɛlanʃʀɪft]

Here's my home address.
Hier ist meine Heimatadresse. ['hiɐ ˀɪst 'maɪnə 'haɪmata͵dʀɛsə]

Photos

➢ **also Photographic materials**

Could you take a photo of us?
Könnten Sie ein Foto von uns machen?
['kœntn zi ˀaɪn 'fo:to fɔn ʊns maxn]

You only have to press this button.
Sie müssen nur auf diesen Knopf drücken.
[zi mʏsn nuɐ ˀaʊf 'di:zn 'knɔpf dʀʏkŋ]

You set the distance like this.
Die Entfernung stellt man so ein. [di ˀɛnt'fɛɐnʊŋ ʃtɛlt man 'zo: ˀaɪn]

May I take a photo of you?
Dürfte ich Sie wohl fotografieren? [dʏɐftə ˀɪç zi vo:l fotogʀa'fi:ʀən]

Smile, please.
Bitte lächeln. ['bɪtə 'lɛçln]

We'll have a lovely reminder of our holiday.
So haben wir eine schöne Erinnerung an unseren Urlaub.
[zo 'ha:bm viɐ ˀaɪnə 'ʃø:nə ˀɐ'ˀɪnəʀʊŋ ˀan ͵ˀʊnzɐn 'ˀuɐlaʊp]

snapshot....................	der Schnappschuss [dɐ 'ʃnapʃʊs]

Police

Could you tell me where the nearest police station is, please?
Könnten Sie mir bitte sagen, wo das nächste Polizeirevier ist? [kœntn zi miɐ 'bɪtə za:gŋ vo: das 'nɛ:çstə pɔlɪ'tsaɪʀe͵viɐ ˀɪst]

I'd like to report ...
Ich möchte ... anzeigen. [ˀɪç 'mœçtə ... 'ˀantsaɪgŋ]
a theft
einen Diebstahl [ˀaɪnn 'di:pʃta:l]
a robbery
einen Überfall [ˀaɪnn 'ˀy:bɐfal]

My ... has been stolen.
Mir ist ... gestohlen worden. [mɪɐ ˀɪst ... gə'ʃto:ln vɔɐdn]
wallet
meine Brieftasche ['maɪnə 'bʀi:ftaʃə]
camera
mein Fotoapparat [maɪn 'fotoˀapa͵ʀa:t]
car
mein Auto [maɪn 'ˀaʊto]

My car has been broken into.
Mein Auto ist aufgebrochen worden.
[maɪn ˈʔaʊto ʔɪst ˈʔaʊfgəbʀɔxn vɔɐdn]

... has been stolen from my car.
Aus meinem Auto ist ... gestohlen worden.
[ʔaʊs ˈmaɪ(nə)m ˈʔaʊto ʔɪst … gəˈʃto:ln vɔɐdn]

I've lost ...
Ich habe ... verloren. [ʔɪç ˈha:bə … fɐˈloɐn]

My son/daughter is missing.
Mein Sohn/Meine Tochter ist verschwunden.
[maɪn ˈzo:n/ˌmaɪnə ˈtɔxtɐ ʔɪst fɐˈʃvʊndn]

This man is pestering me.
Dieser Mann belästigt mich. [ˈdi:zɐ man bəˈlɛstɪçt mɪç]

Can you help me, please?
Können Sie mir bitte helfen? [ˈkønn zi miɐ ˈbɪtə ˈhɛlfn]

When exactly did this happen?
Wann genau ist das passiert? [van gəˈnaʊ ɪst das paˈsiɐt]

Your name and address, please.
Ihren Namen und Ihre Anschrift, bitte.
[ˈʔiʀən ˈna:mm ʊnt ˌiʀə ˈʔanʃʀɪft ˈbɪtə]

Please get in touch with your consulate.
Wenden Sie sich bitte an Ihr Konsulat.
[ˈvɛndn zi zɪç an iɐ kɔnzʊˈla:t]

to arrest	verhaften [fɐˈhaftn]
to beat up	zusammenschlagen [tsʊˈzammʃla:gŋ]
to break into/open	aufbrechen [ˈʔaʊfbʀɛçn]
car radio	das Autoradio [das ˈʔaʊtoˌʀa:djo]
car registration documents	der Kfz-Schein [dɐ kaʔefˈtsɛtʃaɪn]
cheque/check	der Scheck [dɐ ʃɛk]
cheque card	die Scheckkarte [di ˈʃɛka:tə]
court	das Gericht [das gəˈʀɪçt]
credit card	die Kreditkarte [di ˈkʀedi:tka:tə]
crime	das Verbrechen [das fɐˈbʀɛçn]
documents	die Papiere *n pl* [di paˈpi:ʀə]
drugs	das Rauschgift [das ˈʀaʊʃgɪft]
guilt	die Schuld [ʃʊlt]
to harass	belästigen [bəˈlɛstɪgŋ]
identity card	der Personalausweis [dɐ pɐzoˈna:laʊsvaɪs]
judge	der Richter/die Richterin [dɐ ˈʀɪçtɐ/di ˈʀɪçtəʀɪn]
key	der Schlüssel [dɐ ˈʃlʏsl]

lawyer	der Rechtsanwalt [dɐ ˈʀɛçtsanvalt]′ die Rechtsanwältin [dɪ ˈʀɛçtsanvɛltɪn]
to lose	verlieren [fɐˈliːʀən]
mugging	der Überfall [dɐ ˈˀyːbɐfal]
papers	die Papiere *n pl* [di paˈpiːʀə]
passport	der Reisepass [dɐ ˈʀaɪzəpas]
pickpocket	der Taschendieb [dɐ ˈtaʃndiːp]
police	die Polizei [di pɔlɪˈtsaɪ]
police car	der Polizeiwagen [dɐ pɔlɪˈtsaɪvaːgŋ]
police custody	die Untersuchungshaft [di ˀʊntɐˈzuːxʊŋshaft]
policeman/policewoman	der Polizist/die Polizistin [dɐ polɪˈtsɪst/di polɪˈtsɪstɪn]
prison	das Gefängnis [das gəˈfɛŋnɪs]
purse	die Geldbörse [di ˈgɛltbøɐzə]
rape	die Vergewaltigung [di fɐgəˈvaltɪgʊŋ]
to report	anzeigen [ˈˀantsaɪgŋ]
sexual harassment	die sexuelle Belästigung [di sɛksuˈɛlə bəˈlɛstɪgʊŋ]
to smuggle	schmuggeln [ʃmʊgln]
theft	der Diebstahl [dɐ ˈdiːpʃtaːl]
thief	der Dieb/die Diebin [dɐ diːp/di ˈdiːbɪn]

Post office

Can you tell me where ... is, please?
Können Sie mir bitte sagen, wo ... ist?
[kønn zi miɐ ˈbɪtə ˈzaːgŋ voː ... ˀɪst]
the nearest post office
das nächste Postamt [das ˈnɛːçstə ˈpɔstˀamt]
the nearest letterbox/mailbox
der nächste Briefkasten [dɐ ˈnɛːçstə ˈbʀiːfkastn]

How much does a letter/postcard cost ...
Was kostet ein Brief/eine Postkarte ...
[vas ˈkɔstət ˀaɪn ˈbʀiːf/ˌˀaɪnə ˈpɔstkaːtə nax ...]
to the US?
in die USA? [ˀɪn di ˀuɛsˈˀaː]
to England?
nach England? [nax ˈˀɛŋlant]

I'd like to send this letter ...
Diesen Brief bitte per ... [ˈdiːzn bʀifː ˌbɪtə pɛɐ]
by airmail.
Luftpost. [ˈlʊftpɔst]
express.
Express. [ˀɛksˈpʀɛs]

Three ... euro stamps, please.
Drei Briefmarken zu ... Euro, bitte!
[dʀaɪ ˈbʀiːfmaːkŋ tsʊ ... ˈʔɔɪʀo ˈbɪtə]

Do you have any special issue stamps?
Haben Sie Sondermarken? [haːbm zi ˈzɔndɐmaːkŋ]

➢ **also Bank**

address	die Adresse [di ʔaˈdʀɛsə]
addressee	der Empfänger [dɐ ʔɛmpˈfɛŋɐ]
by airmail	mit Luftpost [mɪt ˈlʊftpɔst]
charge	die Gebühr [di gəˈbyɐ]
collection (of mail)	die Leerung [di ˈleːʀʊŋ]
customs declaration	die Zollerklärung [di ˈtsɔlɐklɛːʀʊŋ]
declaration of value	die Wertangabe [di ˈveɐtangaːbə]
dispatch form	die Paketkarte [di paˈkeːtkaːtə]
express letter	der Eilbrief [dɐ ˈʔaɪlbʀiːf]
fax	das Telefax [das (ˈteːlə)faks]
fee	die Gebühr [di gəˈbyɐ]
to fill in	ausfüllen [ˈʔaʊsfʏln]
form	das Formular [das fɔmuˈlaː]
to forward	nachsenden [ˈnaːxzɛndn]
letter	der Brief [dɐ bʀiːf]
letterbox/mailbox	der Briefkasten [dɐ ˈbʀiːfkastn]
main post office	das Hauptpostamt [das ˈhaʊptˌpɔstʔamt]
parcel	das Paket [das paˈkeːt]
post code	die Postleitzahl [di ˈpɔstlaɪtsaːl]
post office	das Postamt [das ˈpɔstamt]
post office savings book	das Postsparbuch [das ˈpɔstʃpaːbuːx]
postage	das Porto [das ˈpɔɐto]
postcard	die Postkarte [di ˈpɔstkaːtə]
poste restante	postlagernd [ˈpɔstlaːgɐnt]
registered letter	der Einschreibebrief [dɐ ˈʔaɪnʃʀaɪbəbʀiːf]
to send on	nachsenden [ˈnaːxzɛndn]
sender	der Absender/die Absenderin [dɐ ˈʔapzɛndɐ/di ˈʔapzɛndəʀɪn]
small packet	das Päckchen [das pɛkçn]
special issue stamp	die Sondermarke [di ˈzɔndɐmaːkə]
stamp	die Briefmarke [di ˈbʀiːfmaːkə]
to stamp	frankieren [fʀaŋˈkiɐn]
stamp machine	der Briefmarkenautomat [dɐ ˈbʀiːfmaːkŋʔaʊtoˌmaːt]
telex	das Telex [das ˈteːlɛks]
weight	das Gewicht [das gəˈvɪçt]
zip code	die Postleitzahl [di ˈpɔstlaɪtsaːl]

Telephoning

Can you tell me where the nearest phone box/booth is, please?
Können Sie mir bitte sagen, wo die nächste Telefonzelle ist?
[kønn zi miɐ ˈbɪtə za:gŋ ˈvo di ˈnɛ:çstə teləˈfo:ntsɛlə ˀɪst]

I'd like a phonecard, please.
Ich möchte bitte eine Telefonkarte.
[ˀɪç ˈmøçtə bɪtə ˀaɪnə teləˈfo:nka:tə]

What's the area code for ...?
Wie ist bitte die Vorwahl von ...? [ˈvi: ˀɪst bɪtə di ˈfoɐva:l fɔn]

I'd like to make a call to ...
Bitte ein Ferngespräch nach ... [ˈbɪtə ˀaɪn ˈfɛɐngəʃpʀɛ:ç nax ...]

I'd like to make a reverse charge call/ collect call.
Ich möchte ein R-Gespräch anmelden.
[ˀɪç ˈmøçtə ˀaɪn ˈˀɛɐgəʃpʀɛ:ç ˈˀanmɛldn]

Use booth number four.
Gehen Sie in Kabine Nummer vier. [ˈge:n zi ˀɪn kaˈbi:nə ˌnʊmɐ ˈfiɐ]

A telephone call

This is ... speaking.
Hier spricht ... [ˈhiɐ ʃpʀɪçt ...]

Good morning/afternoon, my name is ...
Guten Tag, mein Name ist ... [gu:tn ˈta:k maɪn ˈna:mə ˀɪst]

Hello, who's speaking, please?
Hallo, mit wem spreche ich, bitte? [ˈhalo: mɪt ve:m ʃpʀɛç ɪç bɪtə]

Can I speak to Mr/Mrs ..., please?
Kann ich bitte Herrn/Frau ... sprechen?
[ˈkan ɪç ˈbɪtə hɛɐn/fʀaʊ ... ʃpʀɛçn]

I'm sorry, he's/she's not here.
Tut mir leid, er/sie ist nicht da. [tu:t mɪɐ ˈlaɪt ɛɐ/zi ˀɪst nɪçt da:]

Can he call you back?
Kann er Sie zurückrufen? [ˈkan (e)ɐ zi tsʊˈʀʏkʀu:fn]

Would you like to leave a message?
Möchten Sie eine Nachricht hinterlassen?
[møçtn zi ˀaɪnə ˈna:xɪçt hɪntɐˈlasn]

Would you tell him/her that I called?
Würden Sie ihm/ihr bitte sagen, ich hätte angerufen?
[ˈvʏɐdn zi ˀi:m/ˀiɐ ˈbɪtə ˈza:gŋ ˀɪç ˈhɛtə ˈˀangəʀu:fn]

"The number you have dialled has not been recognized."
„Kein Anschluss unter dieser Nummer."
[kaɪn ˈˀanʃlʊs ˈˀʊntɐ di:zɐ ˈnʊmɐ]

to answer the phone	abnehmen [ˈʔapneːmm]
answering machine	der Anrufbeantworter [dɐ ˈʔanfuːfbəˌʔantvɔɐtɐ]
area code	die Vorwahlnummer [di ˈfoɐvaːlˌnʊmɐ]
booking	die Voranmeldung [di ˈfoɐʔanmɛldʊŋ]
busy	besetzt [bəˈzɛtst]
call	der Anruf [dɐ ˈʔanʀuːf]
to call	anrufen [ˈʔanʀuːfn]
cellular phone	das Handy [das ˈhɛndi]
charge	die Gebühr [di gəˈbyɐ]
connection	die Verbindung [di fɐˈbɪndʊŋ]
conversation	das Gespräch [das gəˈʃpʀɛːç]
to dial	wählen [vɛːln]
directory enquiries/assistance	die Auskunft [di ˈʔaʊskʊnft]
engaged	besetzt [bəˈzɛtst]
international call	das Auslandsgespräch [das ˈʔaʊslantsgəˌʃpʀɛːç]
line	die Verbindung [di fɐˈbɪndʊŋ]
local call	das Ortsgespräch [das ˈʔɔɐtsgəʃpʀɛːç]
long-distance call	das Ferngespräch [das ˈfɛɐngəʃpʀɛːç]
mobile (phone)	das Handy [das ˈhɛndi], das Mobiltelefon [das moˈbiːltelәˌfoːn]
national code	die Vorwahlnummer [di ˈfoɐvaːlˌnʊmɐ]
to phone	anrufen [ˈʔanʀuːfn]
phone call	der Anruf [dɐ ˈʔanʀuːf]
phone box/booth	die Telefonzelle [di teləˈfoːntsɛlə]
phone number	die Telefonnummer [di teləˈfoːnnʊmɐ]
phonecard	die Telefonkarte [di teləˈfoːnkaːtə]
receiver	der Hörer [dɐ ˈhøːʀɐ]
reverse charge call	das R-Gespräch [das ˈʔɛɐgəˌʃpʀɛːç]
telephone	das Telefon [das ˈteːləfoːn]
telephone directory	das Telefonbuch [das teləˈfoːnbuːx]

Handy

A SIM card, please.
Bitte eine SIM-Karte. [ˈbɪtə ˌʔaɪnə ˈzɪm-kaːtə]

An international telephone card, please.
Bitte eine internationale Telefonkarte.
[ˈbɪtə ˌʔaɪnə ˌʔɪntɐnatsjoˈnaːlə teləˈfoːnkaːtə]

How much call time do I get with a card for ...?
Wie viele Minuten kann ich mit einer Karte für ... sprechen?
[ˈviː fiːlə mɪˈnuːtn kan ɪç mɪt ˌaɪnɐ ˈkaːtə fyɐ ... ˈʃpʁɛçn]

For what area is this SIM card valid?
Für welches Gebiet gilt diese SIM-Karte?
[fyɐ ˈvɛlçəs gəˈbiːt gɪlt ˌdiːzə ˈzɪm-kaːtə]

Please give me a list of charges.
Geben Sie mir bitte eine Tarifübersicht.
[ge:bm zi miɐ ˈbɪtə ˌʔaɪnə taˈʁi:fʔy:bɐzɪçt]

Have you got prepaid cards of the mobile communications provider ...?
Haben Sie Guthabenkarten der Mobilfunkgesellschaft ...?
[ha:bm zi ˈgu:tha:bmˌka:tn dɐ moˈbi:lfʊŋkəˌzɛlʃaft ...]

Toilet and bathroom

Where is the toilet, please?
Wo ist bitte die Toilette? [vo: ʔɪst ˈbɪtə di toˈlɛtə]

May I use your toilet?
Dürfte ich Ihre Toilette benutzen? [ˈdʏɐftə ʔɪç ˈʔi:ʀə toˈlɛtə bəˈnʊtsn]

Would you give me the key for the toilet, please?
Würden Sie mir bitte den Schlüssel für die Toiletten geben? [ˈvʏɐdn zi miɐ ˈbɪtə den ˈʃlʏsl fyɐ di toˈlɛtə ge:bm]

clean	sauber [ˈzaʊbɐ]
cubicle	die Kabine [di kaˈbi:nə]
dirty	schmutzig [ˈʃmʊtsɪç]
flush the toilet	(die Toilette) spülen [(di toˈlɛtə) ʃpy:ln]
Gents	Herren [ˈhɛʀən]
Ladies	Damen [da:mm]
Men's Room	die Herrentoilette [di ˈhɛʀəntoˌlɛtə]
sanitary towels	die Damenbinden *f pl* [di ˈda:mmbɪndn]
soap	die Seife [di ˈzaɪfə]
tampons	die Tampons *m pl* [di ˈtampɔŋs]
toilet-paper	das Toilettenpapier [das toˈlɛtnpaˌpiɐ]
towel	das Handtuch [das ˈhan(t)tu:x]
washbasin	das Waschbecken [das ˈvaʃbɛkŋ]
Women's Room	die Damentoilette [di ˈda:mmtoˌlɛtə]

Articles

The article indicates the gender of a noun. There are three genders in German: masculine, feminine and neuter, as well as four cases: nominative, accusative, genitive and dative.

	definite article				**indefinite article**			
	m	f	n	pl	m	f	n	pl
nom.	der	die	das	die	ein	eine	ein	*no article*
acc.	den	die	das	die	einen	eine	ein	*used with*
gen.	des	der	des	der	eines	einer	eines	*plural nouns*
dat.	dem	der	dem	den	einem	einer	einem	

Nouns

All German nouns are written with a capital letter.
There are three declensions: strong, weak and mixed. (These terms classify nouns according to their endings in the genitive case.)
Nouns which end in *'s,' 'sch', 'ß/ss' and 'z '* always have an *'-es'* in the genitive case.
Some nouns are declined like adjectives.

1. Strong masculine and neuter nouns

	nom. plural: +e	**nom. plural: umlaut+e**	**nom. plural: +er**	**nom. plural: umlaut+er**
singular				
nom.	der Tag (the day)	der Traum (the dream)	das Kind (the child)	das Dach (the roof)
acc.	den Tag	den Traum	das Kind	das Dach
gen.	des Tag(e)s	des Traum(e)s	des Kind(e)s	des Dach(e)s
dat.	dem Tag(e)	dem Traum(e)	dem Kind(e)	dem Dach(e)
plural				
nom.	die Tage	die Träume	die Kinder	die Dächer
acc.	die Tage	die Träume	die Kinder	die Dächer
gen.	der Tage	der Träume	der Kinder	der Dächer
dat.	den Tagen	den Träumen	den Kindern	den Dächern

	nom. plural: +s	nom. plural: umlaut only	nom. plural: no change	nom. plural: no change
singular				
nom.	das Auto (the car)	der Vogel (the bird)	der Tischler (the carpenter)	der Lappen (the cloth)
acc.	das Auto	den Vogel	den Tischler	den Lappen
gen.	des Autos	des Vogels	des Tischlers	des Lappens
dat.	dem Auto	dem Vogel	dem Tischler	dem Lappen
plural				
nom.	die Autos	die Vögel	die Tischler	die Lappen
acc.	die Autos	die Vögel	die Tischler	die Lappen
gen.	der Autos	der Vögel	der Tischler	der Lappen
dat.	den Autos	den Vögeln	den Tischlern	den Lappen

2. Strong feminine nouns

	nom. plural: umlaut+e	nom. plural: umlaut only	nom. plural: +s
singular			
nom.	die Wand (the wall)	die Mutter (the mother)	die Bar (the bar)
acc.	die Wand	die Mutter	die Bar
gen.	der Wand	der Mutter	der Bar
dat.	der Wand	der Mutter	der Bar
plural			
nom.	die Wände	die Mütter	die Bars
acc.	die Wände	die Mütter	die Bars
gen.	der Wände	der Mütter	der Bars
dat.	den Wänden	den Müttern	den Bars

3. Weak masculine nouns

singular			
nom.	der Bauer (the farmer)	der Bär (the bear)	der Hase (the hare)
acc.	den Bauern	den Bären	den Hasen
gen.	des Bauern	des Bären	des Hasen
dat.	dem Bauern	dem Bären	dem Hasen
plural			
nom.	die Bauern	die Bären	die Hasen
acc.	die Bauern	die Bären	die Hasen
gen.	der Bauern	der Bären	der Hasen
dat.	den Bauern	den Bären	den Hasen

4. Weak feminine nouns

singular				
nom.	die Uhr (the clock)	die Feder (the feather)	die Gabe (the gift)	die Ärztin (the doctor)
acc.	die Uhr	die Feder	die Gabe	die Ärztin
gen.	der Uhr	der Feder	der Gabe	der Ärztin
dat.	der Uhr	der Feder	der Gabe	der Ärztin
plural				
nom.	die Uhren	die Federn	die Gaben	die Ärztinnen
acc.	die Uhren	die Federn	die Gaben	die Ärztinnen
gen.	der Uhren	der Federn	der Gaben	der Ärztinnen
dat.	den Uhren	den Federn	den Gaben	den Ärztinnen

5. Mixed masculine and neuter nouns

These are declined as strong nouns in the singular and weak nouns in the plural.

singular				
nom.	das Auge (the eye)	das Ohr (the ear)	der Name (the name)	das Herz (the heart)
acc.	das Auge	das Ohr	den Namen	das Herz
gen.	des Auges	des Ohr(e)s	des Namens	des Herzens
dat.	dem Auge	dem Ohr(e)	dem Namen	dem Herzen
plural				
nom.	die Augen	die Ohren	die Namen	die Herzen
acc.	die Augen	die Ohren	die Namen	die Herzen
gen.	der Augen	der Ohren	der Namen	der Herzen
dat.	den Augen	den Ohren	den Namen	den Herzen

6. Nouns declined as adjectives

masculine singular		
nom.	der Reisende (the traveller)	ein Reisender
acc.	den Reisenden	einen Reisenden
gen.	des Reisenden	eines Reisenden
dat.	dem Reisenden	einem Reisenden
plural		
nom.	die Reisenden	Reisende
acc.	die Reisenden	Reisende
gen.	der Reisenden	Reisender
dat.	den Reisenden	Reisenden
feminine singular		
nom.	die Reisende	eine Reisende
acc.	die Reisende	eine Reisende
gen.	der Reisenden	einer Reisenden
dat.	der Reisenden	einer Reisenden
plural		
nom.	die Reisenden	Reisende
acc.	die Reisenden	Reisende
gen.	der Reisenden	Reisender
dat.	den Reisenden	Reisenden
neuter singular		
nom.	das Neugeborene (the new born [baby])	ein Neugeborenes
acc.	das Neugeborene	ein Neugeborenes
gen.	des Neugeborenen	eines Neugeborenen
dat.	dem Neugeborenen	einem Neugeborenen
plural		
nom.	die Neugeborenen	Neugeborene
acc.	die Neugeborenen	Neugeborene
gen.	der Neugeborenen	Neugeborener
dat.	den Neugeborenen	Neugeborenen

There are three types of adjective declension: strong, weak and mixed.

The strong declension

is used when there is no article, pronoun or other word preceeding the adjective indicating the case (e.g. *manch(e)*, *mehrere* etc.). It is also used with cardinal numbers and expressions like *ein paar* and *ein bisschen.*

	m	f	n
singular			
nom.	guter Wein (good wine)	schöne Frau (beautiful woman)	liebes Kind (well-behaved child)
acc.	guten Wein	schöne Frau	liebes Kind
gen.	guten Wein(e)s	schöner Frau	lieben Kindes
dat.	gutem Wein(e)	schöner Frau	liebem Kind(e)
plural			
nom.	gute Weine	schöne Frauen	liebe Kinder
acc.	gute Weine	schöne Frauen	liebe Kinder
gen.	guter Weine	schöner Frauen	lieber Kinder
dat.	guten Weinen	schönen Frauen	lieben Kindern

The weak declension

is used with adjectives preceeded by the definite article or with any other word already clearly showing the case of the noun (e.g. *diese(r,s)*, *folgende(r,s)* etc.).

	m	f	n
singular			
nom.	der gute Wein	die schöne Frau	das liebe Kind
acc.	den guten Wein	die schöne Frau	das liebe Kind
gen.	des guten Wein(e)s	der schönen Frau	des lieben Kindes
dat.	dem guten Wein	der schönen Frau	dem lieben Kind
plural			
nom.	die guten Weine	die schönen Frauen	die lieben Kinder
acc.	die guten Weine	die schönen Frauen	die lieben Kinder
gen.	der guten Weine	der schönen Frauen	der lieben Kinder
dat.	den guten Weinen	den schönen Frauen	den lieben Kindern

The mixed declension

is used with singular masculine and neuter nouns and the indefinite articles *ein* and *kein* and with the possessive pronouns *mein, dein, sein, unser, euer, ihr.*

	m	n
singular		
nom.	ein guter Wein (a good wine)	ein liebes Kind (a well-behaved child)
acc.	einen guten Wein	ein liebes Kind
gen.	eines guten Wein(e)s	eines lieben Kindes
dat.	einem guten Wein(e)	einem lieben Kind

Adverbs

- For the adverbial use of adjectives the unchanged basic form of the adjective is used.

Verbs

Present Tense

The basic ending of German verbs is *'-en'* (*machen, sagen, essen* etc.). To form the present tense remove the *'-en'* and add the corresponding personal endings to the stem of the verb. There is no continuous form in German , e.g. *„Ich gehe um acht Uhr ins Büro."* can be translated as *'I go to the office at eight o'clock.'* (routine) or *'I'm going to the office at eight o'clock.'* (single event).

		machen (to do)	**legen** (to put)	**sagen** (to say)
I	ich	mach**e**	leg**e**	sag**e**
you	du	mach**st**	leg**st**	sag**st**
he she it	er sie es	mach**t**	leg**t**	sag**t**
we	wir	mach**en**	leg**en**	sag**en**
you	ihr	mach**t**	leg**t**	sag**t**
they	sie	mach**en**	leg**en**	sag**en**

- The vowel *'-a-'* in some verbs changes to the umlaut *'-ä-'*.

tragen ich trage, du tr**ä**gst, er/sie/es tr**ä**gt,
wir tragen, ihr tragt, sie tragen

Auxiliary verbs *haben*, *sein* and *werden*

Present tense

	sein (to be)	**haben** (to have)	**werden** (to become)
ich	bin	habe	werde
du	bist	hast	wirst
er / sie / es	ist	hat	wird
wir	sind	haben	werden
ihr	seid	habt	werdet
sie	sind	haben	werden

Past tense and past participle

	sein (to be)	**haben** (to have)	**werden** (to become)
ich	war	hatte	wurde
du	warst	hattest	wurdest
er / sie / es	war	hatte	wurde
wir	waren	hatten	wurden
ihr	wart	hattet	wurdet
sie	waren	hatten	wurden
past participle	bin gewesen	habe gehabt	bin geworden

Modal auxiliaries

Here is a list of the most important ones. Note that most are irregular.

Present tense

	können (be able to)	**dürfen** (be allowed to)	**mögen** (like)	**müssen** (have to)	**sollen** (should)	**wollen** (want to)
ich	kann	darf	mag	muss	soll	will
du	kannst	darfst	magst	musst	sollst	willst
er / sie / es	kann	darf	mag	muss	soll	will
wir	können	dürfen	mögen	müssen	sollen	wollen
ihr	könnt	dürft	mögt	müsst	sollt	wollt
sie	können	dürfen	mögen	müssen	sollen	wollen

Past Tense

There are two tenses for the past in German, the imperfect and the present perfect. Both describe events which took place in the past. There is no past continuous form.

Gestern war ich krank.	Yesterday I was ill.
Letztes Jahr sind wir in Berlin gewesen.	Last year we were in Berlin.

To form the **imperfect**, the following verb endings are added to the stem of the verb:

	machen (to do)	**begegnen** (to meet)	**wetten** (to bet)
ich	mach**te**	begegne**te**	wett**ete**
du	mach**test**	begegne**test**	wett**etest**
er / sie / es	mach**te**	begegne**te**	wett**ete**
wir	mach**ten**	begegne**ten**	wett**eten**
ihr	mach**tet**	begegne**tet**	wett**etet**
sie	mach**ten**	begegne**ten**	wett**eten**

The **present perfect** is the most common way of referring to the past and is formed with the present tense of either *haben* (to have) or *sein* (to be) followed by the past participle of the verb. The past participle of regular verbs is formed by adding the prefix *'ge-'* and the ending *'-t'* to the stem.

machen	**ge**-mach-**t**	fragen	**ge**-frag-**t**
(to do)	(done)	(to ask)	(asked)

Most verbs take *haben* to form the present perfect:

Er hat es gemacht.	He's done it./He did it.
Ich habe es gesagt.	I've said it./I said it.

sein is used with verbs of motion and verbs that indicate a transition from one state to another. Many irregular verbs form the present perfect with the prefix *'ge-'*, a vowel change and the ending *'-en'*.

Wir sind gefahren.	We drove.

Future

- The future tense is formed with auxiliary verb *werden* and the infinitive.

	fahren (to drive)	**sein** (to be)	**haben** (to have)	**können** (to be able to)
ich	werde fahren	werde sein	werde haben	werde können
du	wirst fahren	wirst sein	wirst haben	wirst können
er / sie / es	wird fahren	wird sein	wird haben	wird können
wir	werden fahren	werden sein	werden haben	werden können
ihr	werdet fahren	werdet sein	werdet haben	werdet können
sie	werden fahren	werden sein	werden haben	werden können

- Often the present tense is also used to express the future.

Questions

Simple questions are formed by changing the order of subject and verb.

Es regnet.	It's raining.
Regnet es?	Is it raining?
Der Laden macht um 9 Uhr auf.	The shop opens at 9 o'clock.
Macht der Laden um 9 Uhr auf?	Does the shop open at 9 o'clock?

Negation

To negate a sentence add **nicht** after the main verb.

Sie wohnt in Berlin.	She lives in Berlin.
Er wohnt **nicht** in Berlin	He doesn't live in Berlin.

Nicht + **ein, eine, einen** etc. becomes **kein, keine, keinen** etc.

Ich habe eine Fahrkarte	I have a ticket.
Ich habe keine Fahrkarte	I don't have a ticket.

Pronouns

Pronouns agree with the gender and case/number of the noun they refer to.

1. Personal pronouns

nominative	accusative	genitive	dative
ich (I)	mich (me)	meiner	mir
du (you)	dich (you)	deiner	dir
er (he)	ihn (him)	seiner	ihm
sie (she)	sie (her)	ihrer	ihr
es (it)	es (it)	seiner	ihm
wir (we)	uns (us)	unser	uns
ihr (you)	euch (you)	euer	euch
sie (they)	sie (them)	ihrer	ihnen
Sie (you)	Sie (you)		

- **du** is the familiar form of address when speaking to family, friends and children.
- **Sie** is the polite form of address (for both the singular and plural).
- **ihr** is the familiar form of address used when speaking to more than one person.

2. Reflexive pronouns

These are used with reflexive verbs such as *sich freuen, sich waschen, sich bedanken*.

myself	mich	ich freue mich
yourself	dich *(familiar)*	du freust dich
	sich *(polite)*	Sie freuen sich
himself/herself/itself	sich	er/sie/es freut sich
ourselves	uns	wir freuen uns
yourselves	euch *(familiar)*	ihr freut euch
	sich *(polite)*	Sie freuen sich
themselves	sich	sie freuen sich

3. Possessive pronouns

	m	f	n	pl
singular				
nom. acc. gen. dat.	mein meinen meines meinem	meine meine meiner meiner	mein mein meines meinem	meine meine meiner meinen
• *dein* (your), *sein* (his), *ihr* (her), *sein* (its) are declined like *mein* (my).				
1st person plural (our)				
nom. acc. gen. dat.	unser uns(e)ren unsern uns(e)res uns(e)rem unserm	uns(e)re uns(e)re uns(e)rer uns(e)rer	unser unser uns(e)res uns(e)rem unserm	uns(e)re unsre uns(e)rer uns(e)ren
2nd person plural (your)				
nom. acc. gen. dat.	euer euren eures eurem	eure eure eurer eurer	euer euer eures eurem	eure eure eurer euren
3rd person plural (their)				
nom. acc. gen. dat.	ihr ihren ihres ihrem	ihre ihre ihrer ihrer	ihr ihr ihres ihrem	ihre ihre ihrer ihren

A short guide to German pronunciation

Vowels

Vowel sounds in German can be **long** or **short**.

A vowel is usually **long** if it is followed by a _single_ consonant:
Schlaf, schlafen, Kino, groß
(exception: mit)

or if it is followed by a silent **h**:
mehr, mähen, hohlen

or if it is doubled:
Meer, Haar, Boot

The vowel combination **ie** is usually long:
wie viel, Ziel, ziehen

A vowel is usually **short** if it is followed by _two or more_ consonants:
nass, Hund, Tisch, immer, Koch
(exception: hoch)

or if it comes before **ck**:
Hecke, Rucksack, backen, Bäcker, Stücke

NB: if the root form of the word is long (e.g. sagen, groß) but the inflected form is followed by two consonants, the vowel remains long:
gesagt, größte

Long and short 'a'

The **long a** sound - which can be written **a, aa** or **ah** - is like the English **a** in *car, calm, father:*
Glas, Haar, wahr, kam, Kahn

The **short a** sound is somewhere between the vowel sound in *fan* and *fun,* pronounced in a short, clipped way:
Land, danke, Stadt, Kamm, kann

Long and short 'e'

The **long e** sound - which can be written **e, ee** or **eh** - is like the English **a** in *bathe* or *hay* (but without sliding away into *ee* as the English does):
hebt, Meer, mehr, geht

The **short e** sound is like the **e** in *bed, net*:
Bett, Netz, wenn, leckt

Many German words end in a single unstressed **-e** or **-el**. This should be pronounced as in the final syllable of *Tina, sister* or *bubble, trouble*:
danke, Stelle, Gabel, Stachel

German words ending in a single unstressed **-er** should be pronounced very similarly but with the addition of a gently rolled **r** at the end; contrast:

bitte - bitter; Fische - Fischer

Long and short 'i'

The **long i** sound is like the English **ee** in *feet* or the **ea** in *beach:*

Kilo, Bibel, wir

The **short i** sound is like the **i** in *bit:*

mit, mich

Long and short 'o'

The **long o** sound - which can be written **o, oo** or **oh** - is somewhere between the English **o** sound in *go* or *show* (but with the lips more rounded and the mouth more open) and the **aw** sound in *lawn*:

tot, Hose, Boot, Moos, froh, holen

The **short o** sound is like the **o** in *pot* only shorter and with a more rounded mouth:

Sonne, Gott, hoffen, kochen

Long and short 'u'

The **long u** sound - which can be written **u** or **uh** - is like the English **oo** in *hoot* or *rule* but with more rounded lips:

Fuß, gut, Ruf, Schule, Stuhl, Tuch, Uhr, zu

The **short u** sound is a shorter version of the vowel sound in *put* or *foot:*

Fluss, Hund, Mutter, Suppe, unter, putzen

Long and short 'ä'

The **long ä** sound - which can be written **ä** or **äh** - is somewhere between the vowel sounds in *day* (but without sliding away into *ee* as the English does) and *dare*:

Mädchen, wählen, täglich, spät, Lärm

The **short ä** sound is like the **e** in *get, set:*

Männer, Hände, hätte, lästig

Long and short 'ö'

The **long ö** sound - which can be written **ö** or **öh** - sounds a bit like the vowel sounds in *earth* and *learn* but said with rounded lips:

schön, böse, Flöte, Größe, Söhne, Höhle, hören, mögen

The **short ö** sound is a shorter, more clipped version of the above:

Löffel, Stöcke, Hölle, können, möchte

Long and short 'ü'

These are the hardest sounds in the German alphabet for the English speaker to master.

The **long ü** sound - which can be written **ü** or **üh** - is produced by saying an *ee* sound with very rounded lips.
Try saying *Tier* like this and with a bit of luck it should sound like *Tür*; try *spielen* too - this should come out as *'spülen'*.

früh, für, grün, müde, Schüler, Hügel, über

The **short ü** sound is a shorter, more clipped version of the above:

Stück, dünn, Küsse, hübsch, müssen

Groups of vowels

ai, ay, ei, ey sound like the **i** in *'mine:*

Mai, Main, Bayern, mein, Rhein, Speyer

au sounds like a shorter more clipped version of the **ow** in *now:*

Frau, braun, auch

äu, eu sound like the **oy** in *boy:*

Fräulein, Gebäude, neu, Freund

ie sounds like the **ee** in *deep* (but with a little more precision than in English):

die, viel, Lied, Bier, ziehen

When **ie** occurs at the end of a word, it can be pronounced in two separate ways: if the final syllable of the word is stressed, it is pronounced as the normal **ie** outlined above:

Biographie, Philosophie, Symphonie

But when it is unstressed, it is pronounced as two separate vowels:

Familie *(fa-mee-leeya)*

Consonants

b and **d** are usually pronounced as they are in English, except at the end of a word or syllable or before **s** or **t**, when the **b** sounds more like a **p** and the **d** sounds more like a **t**:

baden - Bad	Diebe - Dieb(stahl)	Handel - Hand
Hunde - Hund	leider - Leid	lieben - lieb(ster)
rauben - Raub	schreiben - Schreibtisch	wenden - Wand
gibt	siebter	Stadt

ch - has a multiplicity of regional variations but when it follows an **a, o, u** or **au** it is like the rather harsh guttural **ch** in the Scottish *Loch Ness*:

nach, lachen, Koch, Tochter, Buch, Kuchen, auch, rauchen

Otherwise it sounds a lot softer, rather like the **h** sound at the beginning of *hymn* or *humour*:

brechen, ich, lächeln, möchte, Bücher, Küche, euch, geräuchert, Milch, welche, manche, Hähnchen, München, durch, Kirche

ch at the beginning of a word indicates a word that has been imported from a foreign language; if this is French then it sounds like **sh**:
Chalet, Champagner, Chance, Chef

others sound like **k**:

Chaos, Charakter, Cholera, Chor, Christ

or like the **ch** in *mich*:

Chemie, chinesisch, Chirurg

and others are taken directly from languages like English and spoken as closely as possible to the original:

Champion, Chart, Chat, checken

chs usually sounds like the **x** in *axe*:

Lachs, sechs, wachsen, Wechsel

(exceptions: machst [harsh 'ch'] nächste [soft 'ch'])

ck sounds like the English **k** and the vowel preceding it is always short and stressed:

backen, Gepäck, Glück, lecker, Rock, zurück
[Try these problem words: glücklich, schrecklich]

g is usually pronounced like the **g** in *gold* when it comes before a vowel:

Geld, gelb

but at the end of a word or syllable or before **s** or **t**, it sounds more like a strangulated **k**:

Berge – Berg bürgen – Burg   fliegen – fliegt
schlagen – Schlag(sahne)   tagen – Tag

ig at the end of a word, is pronounced just like the German **ich**, i.e. ending in a sound rather like the **h** in *hymn* or *humour*:

fertig, Honig, hungrig, König, richtig, sonnig, zwanzig

gn, kn - both consonants are pronounced:

Gnade, Kneipe, Knie, Knopf

h is clearly pronounced at the beginning of a word or second element in a compound noun:

Haushalt, hier, holen, Buchhandlung

however, when it comes after a vowel, it is not usually sounded and the preceding vowel is lengthened:

fahren, gehen, Lehrer, stehen

j sounds like the **y** in *yes*:

ja, Jacke, jetzt, Johannes, Junge, Juni, Major

l sounds a little lighter and flatter than an English **l**, quite close to the sound in *million*:

alles, Liebe

ng always sounds like the nasal sound in *song, singer, ring,* even in the middle of a word (never like *finger)*:

singen, schwanger, Engel, England, Zunge

q - as in English, **q** is always followed by a **u** but is pronounced **kv**: Quittung, quer, Quiz

r has a multiplicity of regional variations but the basic sound when it occurs before a vowel is somewhere between a growl and a gargle made at the back of the throat:

drei, fahren, Frau, Jahre, Lehrerin, rot, Straße, trocken, warum

At the end of a word however, the **r** is hardly pronounced at all, rather as in the English words: *beer, brother, year*:

Bier, Bruder, Jahr

s sounds like the **s** in *sister*, except when it comes before a vowel, when it sounds like the **z** in *zoo*:

das, Glas, Maske, Maus, Pflaster, Reis
Masern, reisen, See, sie, Vase, Versicherung

sch sounds like the **sh** in *shoe*:

Geschichte, Schuh, Schule, schwimmen, Tisch, waschen

sp and **st** - when they occur at the beginning of a word or the beginning of the second element in a compound noun, or after unstressed *Ge* or *ge*, sound like **shp** and **sht**:

(Ball)Spiel, Sport, Sprache, (Haupt)Stadt, Stein, (Haupt)Straße, Gespräch, gesprochen, Gestank, gestohlen

Otherwise, they are pronounced as they would be in English:

Dienstag, Gast, ist, kosten, Liste, sagst

ss or **ß** is always pronounced like an English **ss**; when the preceding vowel is short it is written **ss**; when it comes after a long vowel or diphthong it is written **ß**:

besser, dass, muss, müssen, Pass, Schloss, Schlüssel, wissen
groß, Gruß, Grüße, schließen, Schoß, Spaß, Strauß, süß, weiß

th sounds like an English **t**:

Apotheke, Theater, Thema

tz is pronounced **ts**:

Blitz, Dutzend, jetzt, Metzger, Platz, plötzlich, putzen

v, f, ph sound like the English **f** in *before, father, from*:

bevor, Vater, vier, von, frei, für, Triumph, Typhus

In a few loan words from other languages however, **v** is pronounced as it is in English:

Klavier, Vase, Verb

w sounds like the English **v** in *very, video*:

Wasser, wenn, wieder, wir, Witwe, zuwinken
[Try these problem words:
Volkswagen, vorwärts, wievielte, wovon]

y – the pronunciation of the German **y** depends on the position of the letter in the word; if it occurs <u>within a word</u> it sounds like an **ü**:

Physik, Pyramide, Rhythmus, typisch

If **y** occurs at the beginning or end of a word, then it is pronounced in exactly the same way as it is in English:

Handy, Hobby, Yoga, Yucca,

z sounds like the **ts** in *cats, nuts* - even at the beginning of a word:

Herz, März, salzig, zehn, Zeit, Zimmer, zu, zwanzig

A

Aal *m* [ˀa:l] eel
ab [ˀap] from
abbestellen [ˈˀapbəʃtɛln] *(tickets etc.)* cancel
Abblendlicht *n* [ˈˀapblɛntlɪçt] dipped/dimmed headlights
abbrechen [ˈˀapbʀɛçn] to stop
Abend *m* [ˈˀa:bmt] evening, night
Abendessen *n* [ˈˀa:bmtˀɛsn] dinner
abends [ˈˀa:bms] in the evening
aber [ˈˀa:bɐ] but
abfahren (von) [ˈˀapfa: (ʀə)n fɔn] start (from), leave
Abfahrt *f* [ˈˀapfa:t] departure
Abfall *m* [ˈˀapfal] rubbish, garbage
Abfallbeutel *m* [ˈˀapfalbɔɪtl] bin liner
Abfalleimer *m* [ˈˀapfalˌˀaɪmɐ] bin
Abflug *m* [ˈˀapflu:k] departure, take-off
Abführmittel *n* [ˈˀapfyɐˌmɪtl] laxative
abgeben [ˈˀapge:bm] hand in, leave **abgelegen** [ˈˀapgəle:gŋ] isolated
abgelaufen [ˈˀapgəlaʊfn] past the sell-by date
abholen [ˈˀapho:ln] call for, pick up; **abholen lassen** [ˈˀapho:ln lasn] send for
Abkürzung *f* [ˈˀapkʰʏʀtsʊŋ] abbreviation; short-cut
ablehnen [ˈˀaple:nn] decline, refuse
abnehmen [ˈˀapne:mm] slim
abreisen (nach) [ˈˀapʀaɪzn (nax)] leave (for)
absagen [ˈˀapza:gŋ] *(appointment)* cancel
Abschied nehmen [ˈˀapʃi:t ne:mm] say goodbye
abschleppen [ˈˀapʃlɛpm] tow (away)
Abschleppseil *n* [ˈˀapʃlɛpzaɪl] towrope
Abschleppwagen *m* [ˈˀapʃlɛpva:gŋ] breakdown vehicle
abschließen [ˈˀapʃli:sn] to lock
abseits [ˈˀapzaɪts] offside
Absender/in *m/f* [ˈˀapzɛndɐ/-dəʀɪn] sender
Abstand *m* [ˈˀapʃtant] distance
abstellen [ˈˀapʃtɛln] to park
Abszess *m* [ˀapsˈɛs] abscess
Abtei *f* [ˀapˈtaɪ] abbey
Abteil *n* [ˀapˈtaɪl] compartment
Achtung [ˈˀaxtʊŋ] attention; **Achtung!** [ˈˀaxtʊŋ] look out!
Actionfilm *m* [ˈˀɛktʃnfɪlm] action film
Adapter *m* [ˀaˈdaptɐ] adapter
Adresse *f* [ˀaˈdʀɛsə] address
adressieren [ˀadʀɛˈsi:ʀən/-ˈsiɐn] to address
Aerobic *n* [ˀɛˈʀɔbɪk] aerobics
Agentur *f* [ˀagɛnˈtʰuɐ] agency
ähnlich [ˈˀɛ:nlɪç] similar
Ahnung *f* [ˈˀa:nʊŋ] idea
Akku *m* [ˈˀaku] rechargeable battery
Akt *m* [ˀakt] *(play)* act; *(painting)* nude
Akupunktur *f* [ˀakupʊŋ(k)ˈtuɐ] acupuncture
Alarmanlage *f* [ˀaˈla:manla:gə] alarm system
alkoholfrei [ˀalkoˈho:lfʀaɪ] non-alcoholic
alle [ˈˀalə] all
allein [ˀaˈlaɪn] alone
Allergie *f* [ˀal(ɛ)ɐˈgi:] allergy
alles [ˈˀaləs] everything
als [ˀals] when; *(comparison)* than
also [ˈˀalzo:] so, thus
alt [ˀalt] old
Altar *m* [ˀalˈta:] altar
Alter *n* [ˈˀaltʰɐ] age
Alufolie *f* [ˈˀalufo:ljə] tin foil
Amerika [ˀaˈme:ʀɪkʰa:] America
Amerikaner/in *m/f* [ˀameʀɪˈka:nɐ/-ˈka:nəʀɪn] American
Ampel *f* [ˀampl] traffic light
amputiert [ampuˈtiɐt] amputated
Amt *n* [ˀamt] office, department
amtlich [ˈˀamtlɪç] official
Ananas *f* [ˈˀananas] pineapple
anbieten [ˈˀanbi:tn] to offer
anders [ˈˀandɐs] different(ly)
anderswo [ˈˀandɐsvo:] elsewhere
Anfall *m* [ˈˀanfal] attack, fit
Anfang *m* [ˈˀanfaŋ] beginning
anfangen [ˈˀanfaŋŋ] begin
Angabe *f* [ˈˀanga:bə] statement
Angel *f* [ˀaŋl] fishing rod
Angelegenheit *f* [ˈˀangəle:gŋhaɪt] matter
angeln [ˈˀaŋln] go fishing
Angelschein *m* [ˈˀaŋlʃaɪn] fishing licence
angenehm [ˈˀangəne:m] agreeable, pleasant
Angina *f* [ˀaŋˈgi:na] angina
Angst *f* [ˀaŋst] fear
anhalten [ˈˀanhaltn] to stop
Anhänger *m* [ˈˀanhɛŋɐ] pendant
Ankunft *f* [ˈˀankʊnft] arrival
Ankunftszeit *f* [ˀankʊnfˌtsaɪt] time of arrival
Anlage *f* [ˈˀanla:gə] *(letter)* enclosure; park
Anlass *m* [ˈˀanlas] cause, reason

Anlasser *m* [ˈˀanlasɐ] starter (motor)
anlegen in [ˈˀanle:gŋ ˀɪn] dock at, land at
anmelden [ˈˀanmɛldn] announce; **sich anmelden** [zɪç ˈˀanmɛldn] register
Anmeldung *f* [ˈˀanmɛldʊŋ] registration
annehmen [ˈˀane:mm] accept
Anorak *m* [ˈˀanoʀak] anorak
Anreisetag *m* [ˈˀanʀaɪzəˌta:k] day of arrival
Anruf *m* [ˈˀanʀu:f] (phone) call
Anrufbeantworter *m* [ˈˀanfu:fbəˌˀantvɔɐtɐ] answering machine
anrufen [ˈˀanʀu:fn] to call, to phone
anschauen [ˈˀanʃaʊn] look at
Anschluss *m* [ˈˀanʃlʊs] connection
Anschrift *f* [ˈˀanʃʀɪft] address
ansehen [ˈˀanze:n] look at
Ansicht *f* [ˈˀanzɪçt] opinion, view
Ansichtskarte *f* [ˈˀanzɪçtska:tə] picture postcard
anstatt [ˀanˈʃtat] instead of
ansteckend [ˈˀanʃtɛkŋt] contagious
anstrengend [ˈˀanʃtʀɛŋŋt] strenuous
antik [ˀanˈti:k] ancient
Antiquitätengeschäft *n* [ˀantɪkvɪˈtɛ:tngəʃɛft] antique shop
Antwort *f* [ˈˀantvɔɐt] answer
antworten [ˈˀantvɔɐtn] to answer, to reply
anwenden [ˈˀanvɛndn] to use
Anwendung *f* [ˈˀanvɛndʊŋ] use
anwesend [ˈˀanve:znt] present
anzeigen [ˈˀantsaɪgŋ] to report
anziehen [ˈˀantsi:n] put on; **sich anziehen** [zɪç ˈˀantsi:n] dress, get dressed
Anzug *m* [ˈˀantsu:k] *(for men)* suit
anzünden [ˈˀantsʏndn] to light
Äpfel *m pl* [ˀɛpfl] apples
Apfelsinen *f pl* [ˀapflˈzi:nn] oranges
Apotheke *f* [ˀapoˈte:kə] chemist's
Apparat *m* [ˀapʰaˈʀa:t] gadget; *(Foto~)* camera; *(Fernseh~)* television set
Appetit *m* [ˀapəˈtɪt] appetite
Aprikosen *f pl* [ˀapʀɪˈko:zn] apricots
April [ˀaˈpʀɪl] April
Aqua-Jogging *n* [ˈˀakvaˌdʒɔgɪŋ] aqua jogging
Aquarell *n* [ˀakvaˈʀɛl] water-colour (picture)
Arbeit *f* [ˈˀa:baɪt] work; job
arbeiten [ˈˀa:baɪtn] to work
arbeitslos [ˈˀa:baɪtslo:s] unemployed
Archäologie *f* [ˀa:çeoloˈgi:] archaeology
Architekt/Architektin [ˀa:çɪˈtɛkt/ ˀa:çɪˈtɛkt ɪn] architect
Architektur *f* [ˀa:çitɛkˈtuɐ] architecture
ärgerlich [ˈˀɛɐgɐlɪç] *(adj)* cross
arm [ˀa:m] poor

Armband *n* [ˈˀa:mbant] bracelet
Armbanduhr *f* [ˈˀa:mbantˌˀuɐ] wrist-watch
Ärmel *m* [ˀɛɐml] sleeve
Aromabad *n* [ˀaˈʀo:maba:t] aroma bath
Art *f* [ˀa:t] kind, sort
Artischocken *f pl* [ˀa:tɪˈʃɔkŋ] artichokes
Aschenbecher *m* [ˈˀaʃnbɛçɐ] ashtray
Aspirin *n* [ˀaspiˈʀi:n] aspirin
Asthma *n* [ˈˀastma] asthma
Atembeschwerden *f pl* [ˈˀa:tmbəʃveɐdn] difficulty in breathing
Atlantik *m* [ˀatˈlantʰɪk] Atlantic
atmen [ˈˀa:tmən] breathe
Attest *n* [ˀaˈtɛst] certificate
Auberginen *f pl* [ˀobɐˈʒi:nn] aubergines
auch [ˀaʊx] also; too; **auch nicht** [ˀaʊx nɪç(t)] nor, neither
auf [ˀaʊf] on
aufbrechen [ˈˀaʊfbʀɛçn] break into/ open
Aufenthalt *m* [ˈˀaʊfntʰalt] stay; *(train)* stop
Aufenthaltsraum *m* [ˈˀaʊfntaltsˌʀaʊm] lounge
auffordern [ˈˀaʊfɔɐdɐn] ask, invite
aufgeben [ˈˀaʊfge:bm] *(luggage)* register
aufhalten, sich ~ [zɪç ˈˀaʊfhaltn] to stay
aufhören [ˈˀaʊfhøɐn] to stop
aufladen [ˈˀaʊfla:dn] put on, load
aufmachen [ˈˀaʊfmaxn] to open
aufpassen [ˈˀaʊfpasn] pay attention (to)
aufrufen [ˈˀaʊfʀu:fn] call (out)
aufschieben [ˈˀaʊfʃi:bm] postpone, put off
Aufschnitt *m* [ˈˀaʊfʃnɪt] cold cuts, lunch meat
aufschreiben [ˈˀaʊfʃʀaɪbm] write down
aufstehen [ˈˀaʊfʃte:n] get up
aufwachen [ˈˀaʊfvaxn] wake up
aufwärts [ˈˀaʊfvɛɐts] up(wards)
Aufzug *m* [ˈˀaʊftsu:k] elevator, lift
Auge *n* [ˈˀaʊgə] eye
Augenbrauen zupfen [ˈˀaʊgŋbʀaʊn ˈtsʊpfn] pluck (your) eyebrows
Augentropfen *m pl* [ˈˀaʊgŋtʀɔpfn] eye-drops
August [ˀaʊˈgʊst] August
aus [ˀaʊs] from; out of
Ausbildung *f* [ˈˀaʊsbɪldʊŋ] education, training
Ausdruck *m* [ˈˀaʊsdʀʊk] expression
ausdrücklich [ˈˀaʊsdʀʏklɪç] explicit(ly)
Ausflug *m* [ˈˀaʊsflu:k] excursion, trip
ausfüllen [ˈˀaʊsfʏln] fill in
Ausgang *m* [ˈˀaʊsgaŋ] exit, way out
ausgeben [ˈˀaʊsge:bm] spend
ausgehen [ˈˀaʊsge:n] go out

ausgeschlossen [ˈʔaʊsgəˌʃlɔsn] impossible
ausgezeichnet [ˈʔaʊsgəˌtsaɪçnət] excellent
Ausgrabungen *f pl* [ˈʔaʊsgʀa:bʊŋŋ] excavations
Auskunft *f* [ˈʔaʊskʰʊnft] information; *(Telefon~)* telephone operator
Ausland, im/ins ~ [ʔɪm/ʔɪns ˈʔaʊslant] abroad
Ausländer/in *m/f* [ˈʔaʊslɛndɐ/-lɛndəʀɪn] foreigner
ausländisch [ˈʔaʊslɛndɪʃ] foreign
Auslandsflug *m* [ˈʔaʊslantsflu:k] international flight
Auslandsgespräch *n* [ˈʔaʊslantsgəˌʃpʀɛ:ç] international call
ausleihen [ˈʔaʊslaɪn] borrow
Auslöser *m* [ˈʔaʊslø:zɐ] *(camera)* shutter release
ausmachen [ˈʔaʊsmaxn] *(light)* turn off, *(fire)* put out; agree
Auspuff *m* [ˈʔaʊspʊf] exhaust (pipe)
ausrichten [ˈʔaʊsʀɪçtn] tell
ausruhen, sich ~ [zɪç ˈʔaʊsʀu:n] to rest
Aussage *f* [ˈʔaʊsza:gə] statement
aussagen [ˈʔaʊsza:gŋ] to state
Ausschlag *m* [ˈʔaʊʃla:k] rash
aussehen [ˈʔaʊse:n] to look
außen [ˈʔaʊsn] outside
außer [ˈʔaʊsɐ] except
außerdem [ˈʔaʊsɐde:m] besides
außergewöhnlich [ˌʔaʊsɐgəˈvø:nlɪç] extraordinary
außerhalb [ˈʔaʊsɐhalp] outside
Aussicht *f* [ˈʔaʊszɪçt] view
Aussichtspunkt *m* [ˈʔaʊsɪçtspʊŋt] vantage point
aussprechen [ˈʔaʊ (s)ʃpʀɛçn] pronounce
Ausstellung *f* [ˈʔaʊʃtɛluŋ] exhibition, show
aussuchen [ˈʔaʊsu:xn] pick out
Austausch *m* [ˈʔaʊstaʊʃ] exchange
austauschen [ˈʔaʊstʰaʊʃn] to exchange
Austern *f pl* [ˈʔaʊstɐn] oysters
ausüben [ˈʔaʊsʔy:bm] *(profession)* practise
Ausverkauf *m* [ˈʔaʊsfɐkʰaʊf] (clearance) sale
Auswahl *f* [ˈʔaʊsva:l] choice
auszahlen [ˈʔaʊstsa:ln] pay out
Auto *n* [ˈʔaʊtʰo:] car; Auto fahren [ˈʔaʊtʰo fa:n] drive a car
Autobahn *f* [ˈʔaʊtoba:n] freeway, motorway
Autobahnausfahrt *f* [ˈʔaʊtoba:nˌʔaʊsfa:t] (motorway) exit
Autobahngebühren *f* [ˈʔaʊtoba:ngəˌby:ʀən] motorway toll
Automat *m* [ʔaʊtʰoˈma:t] vending machine
Automatikgetriebe *n* [ʔaʊtoˈma:tɪkgəˌtʀi:bə] automatic (transmission)
automatisch [ʔaʊtʰoˈma:tʰɪʃ] automatic
Autoradio *n* [ˈʔaʊtoˌʀa:djo] car radio
Avocado *f* [ʔavoˈka:do] avocado
Ayurveda [ʔajʊˈve:da] Ayurveda

B

Baby *n* [ˈbe:bi:] baby
Babyfon *n* [ˈbe:bifo:n] baby intercom
Babylift [ˈbe:bilɪft] baby lift
Babyschale *f* [ˈbe:biʃa:lə] baby seat
Babysitter *m* [ˈbe:bisɪtɐ] babysitter
Bäckerei *f* [bɛkəˈʀaɪ] baker's
Backofen *m* [ˈbakʔo:fn] oven
Badeanzug *m* [ˈba:dəˌʔantsu:k] swimsuit
Badehose *f* [ˈba:dəho:zə] swimming trunks
Bademantel *m* [ˈba:dəmantl] bathrobe
Bademeister/in *m/f* [ˈba:dəmaɪstɐ/-təʀɪn] lifeguard
baden [ba:dn] to swim
Badeort *m* [ˈba:dəʔɔɐt] seaside resort, beach resort
Badeschuhe *m pl* [ˈba:dəʃuə] bathing shoes
Badewanne *f* [ˈba:dəvanə] bath
Badezimmer *n* [ˈba:dətsɪmɐ] bathroom
Badminton *n* [ˈbɛtmɪntn] badminton
Bahnhof *m* [ˈba:nho:f] station
bald [balt] soon
Balkon *m* [balˈkɔŋ] balcony
Ball *m* [bal] ball; *(event)* ball, dance
Ballett *n* [baˈlɛt] ballet
Bananen *f pl* [baˈna:nn] bananas
Band *f* [bɛ(:)nt] band
Bänderriss *m* [ˈbɛndɐʀɪs] torn ligament
Bank *f* [baŋk] bank; bench
Bar *f* [ba:] bar
bar zahlen [ˈba: tsa:ln] pay (in) cash
Bargeld *n* [ˈba:gɛlt] cash
barock [baˈʀɔk] baroque
Barsch *m* [ba:ʃ] *(fish)* perch
Bart *m* [ba:t] beard
Basilikum *n* [baˈzi:lɪkʊm] basil
Basketball *m* [ˈba:skətbal] basketball
Batterie *f* [batəˈʀi:] battery
Bauch *m* [baʊx] stomach
Bauernhof *m* [ˈbaʊɐnho:f] farm
Baum *m* [baʊm] tree
Baumwolle *f* [ˈbaʊmvɔlə] cotton
beachten [bəˈʔaxtn] pay attention to
beantworten [bəˈʔantvɔɐtn] to reply, to answer

Bearbeitungsgebühr *f* [bəˈʔa:baɪtʊŋsgəˌbyɐ] service charge
bedauern [bəˈdaʊɐn] to regret
bedeutend [bəˈdɔɪtnt] important
Bedeutung *f* [bəˈdɔɪtʰʊŋ] meaning; importance
bedienen [bəˈdi:nn] serve
Bedienung *f* [bəˈdi:nʊŋ] service; waitress
beeilen, sich ~ [zɪç bəˈʔaɪln] to hurry
beeindruckend [bəˈʔaɪndʀʊkŋt] impressive
befahrbar [bəˈfa:ba:] passable
befinden, sich ~ [zɪç bəˈfɪndn] be
befreundet sein [bəˈfʀɔɪndət zaɪn] be friends
befriedigt [bəˈfʀi:dɪçt] satisfied
befürchten [bəˈfʏɐçtn] to fear, be afraid (of)
begegnen [bəˈge:kn (ə)n] meet
begeistert (von) [bəˈgaɪstɐt fɔn] enthusiastic (about)
Beginn *m* [bəˈgɪn] beginning
beginnen [bəˈgɪnn] begin
begleiten [bəˈglaɪtn] accompany
Begleitperson *f* [bəˈglaɪtp(ɛ)ɐˌzo:n] accompanying person
begrüßen [bəˈgʀy:sn] greet, welcome
behalten [bəˈhaltn] keep
Behälter *m* [bəˈhɛltʰɐ] container
behandeln [bəˈhandln] to treat
Behandlung *f* [bəˈhandlʊŋ] treatment
behaupten [bəˈhaʊptn] maintain; insist
Behinderte *m/f* [bəˈhɪndɐtə] disabled person
behindertengerecht [bəˈhɪndɐtngəˌʀɛçt] suitable for the disabled
Behindertentoilette *f* [bəˈhɪndɐtntoˌlɛtə] toilet for the disabled
Behinderung *f* [bəˈhɪndəʀʊŋ] disability, handicap
Behörde *f* [bəˈhøɐdə] authorities
beide [ˈbaɪdə] both
Beifall *m* [ˈbaɪfal] applause
beige [be:ʃ] beige
Bein *n* [baɪn] leg
beinahe [ˈbaɪna:] almost, nearly
Beispiel *n* [ˈbaɪʃpi:l] example; **zum Beispiel** [tsʊm ˈbaɪʃpi:l] for example
beißen [baɪsn] to bite
bekannt [bəˈkʰant] well-known; **bekannt machen** [bəˈkʰant maxn] introduce
Bekannte *m/f* [bəˈkantə] acquaintance, friend
Bekanntschaft *f* [bəˈkʰantʃaft] acquaintance
bekommen [bəˈkʰɔmm] get, receive
belästigen [bəˈlɛstɪgŋ] bother, harrass (sexually)
belegte Brötchen [bəˈle:ktə bʀø:tçn] filled rolls
beleidigen [bəˈlaɪdɪgŋ] to insult
Beleidigung *f* [bəˈlaɪdɪgŋ] insult
Belgien [ˈbɛlgɪən] Belgium
Belichtungsmesser *m* [bəˈlɪçtʊŋsˌmɛsɐ] light meter
Beliebige, jeder ~ [ˌje:dɐ bəˈli:bɪgə] any
belohnen [bəlo:nn] to reward
Belohnung *f* [bəˈlo:nʊŋ] reward
bemerken [bəˈmɛɐkŋ] to notice; *(say)* to remark
bemühen, sich ~ [zɪç bəˈmy:n] try hard
benachrichtigen [bəˈna:xʀɪçtɪgŋ] inform
benötigen [bəˈnø:tʰɪgŋ] need
benutzen [bəˈnʊtsn] to use; *(means of transport)* to take
Benzinkanister *m* [bɛnˈtsi:nkaˌnɪstɐ] petrol can
Benzinpumpe *f* [bɛnˈtsi:npʊmpə] petrol pump
beobachten [bəˈʔo:baxtn] observe, watch
bequem [bəˈkve:m] comfortable
berechnen [bəˈʀɛçn (ə)n] calculate
bereit [bəˈʀaɪt] ready
bereits [bəˈʀaɪts] already
Berg *m* [bɛɐk] mountain
Bergdorf *n* [ˈbɛɐkdoɐf] mountain village
Bergstation *f* [ˈbɛɐkʃtaˌtsjo:n] summit station, top station
Bergsteigen *n* [ˈbɛɐkʃtaɪgŋ] mountaineering/mountain climbing
Beruf *m* [bəˈʀu:f] job, profession
beruhigen, sich ~ [zɪç bəˈʀʊɪgŋ] calm down
Beruhigungsmittel *n* [bəˈʀʊɪgʊŋsmɪtl] sedative, tranquilliser
berühmt [bəˈʀy:mt] famous
berühren [bəˈʀy:ʀən /-ˈʀyɐn] to touch
Berührung *f* [bəˈʀy:ʀʊŋ] contact
beschädigen [bəˈʃɛ:dɪgŋ] to damage
Beschädigung *f* [bəˈʃɛ:dɪgʊŋ] damage
Bescheid wissen [bəˈʃaɪt vɪsn] know
bescheinigen [bəˈʃaɪnɪgŋ] certify
Bescheinigung *f* [bəˈʃaɪnɪgʊŋ] statement
beschließen [bəˈʃli:sn] decide; make up one's mind
beschreiben [bəˈʃʀaɪbm] describe
Besen *m* [be:zn] broom
besetzt [bəˈzɛtst] *(seat)* occupied, taken; full; *(telephone)* engaged, busy
besichtigen [bəˈzɪçtɪgŋ] to visit
Besichtigung *f* [bəˈzɪçtɪgʊŋ] tour
besitzen [bəˈzɪtsn] to own

Besitzer/in *m/f* [bəˈzɪtsɐ/-ˈzɪtsəʀɪn] owner
besonders [bəˈzɔndɐs] particularly, especially
besorgen [bəˈzɔɐgŋ] get
besser [ˈbɛsɐ] better
bestätigen [bəˈʃtɛːtʰɪgŋ] confirm
beste(r, s) [ˈbɛstə (-tɐ, -təs)] best
bestechen [bəˈʃtɛçn] to bribe, to corrupt
bestechlich [bəˈʃtɛçlɪç] corrupt
Besteck *n* [bəˈʃtɛk] cutlery
bestehen auf [bəˈʃteːn ˀaʊf] insist on; bestehen aus [ˈbəˈʃteːn ˀaʊs] consist of
bestellen [bəˈʃtɛln] to order
Bestellung *f* [bəˈʃtɛlʊŋ] order
bestimmt [bəˈʃtɪmt] certain(ly)
Besuch *m* [bəˈzuːx] visit
besuchen, jdn ~ [ˌjemandn bəˈzuːxn] visit s. o., call on s. o.
Besuchszeit *f* [bəˈzuːxstsaɪt] visiting hours
beten [beːtn] pray
betrachten [bəˈtʀaxtn] look at
Betrag *m* [bəˈtʀaːk] amount
betragen [bəˈtʀaːgŋ] be, come/amount to
Betreuung *f* [bəˈtʀɔɪʊŋ] care
Betrug *m* [bəˈtʀuːk] swindle; fraud
betrügerisch [bəˈtʀyːgəʀɪʃ] deceitful
betrunken [bəˈtʀʊŋkŋ] drunk
Bett *n* [bɛt] bed; **ins Bett gehen** [ˀɪns ˈbɛt geːn] go to bed
Bettdecke *f* [ˈbɛtdɛkə] blanket
Bettwäsche *f* [ˈbɛtvɛʃə] bed linen
beunruhigen, sich ~ [zɪç bəˈˀʊnʀʊɪgŋ] to worry
bevor [bəˈfoɐ] before
Bewohner/in *m/f* [bəˈvoːnɐ/ -ˈvoːnəʀɪn] inhabitant
bewölkt [bəˈvœlkt] *(weather)* cloudy
bewusst [bəˈvʊst] aware
bewusstlos [bəˈvʊstloːs] unconscious
bezahlen [bəˈtsaːln] to pay
bezaubernd [bəˈtsaʊbɐnt] charming
Biene *f* [ˈbiːnə] bee
Bier *n* [biɐ] beer
bieten [biːtn] to offer
Bikini *m* [biˈkiːni] bikini
Bild *n* [bɪlt] picture; illustration; painting
bilden [bɪldn] to form
Bildhauer/in *m/f* [ˈbɪlthaʊɐ/ ˈbɪlthaʊəʀɪn] sculptor
billig [ˈbɪlɪç] cheap
Bindehautentzündung *f* [ˈbɪndəhaʊtɛnˌtsʏndʊŋ] conjunctivitis
Bioladen *m* [ˈbiolaːdn] organic food shop
Birnen *f pl* [bɪɐnn] pears
bis [bɪs] to; *(time)* til(l), until; **bis jetzt** [bɪs ˈjɛtst] til(l) now
Bitte *f* [ˈbɪtʰə] request
bitten, jdn um etw. ~ [ˌjemandn ʊm ˌˀɛtvas ˈbɪtn] ask s.o. for s.th.
bitter [ˈbɪtʰɐ] bitter
Blähungen *f pl* [ˈblɛːʊŋŋ] *(med)* wind
Blase *f* [ˈblaːzə] bladder; blister
blau [blaʊ] blue
Blazer *m* [ˈbleːzɐ] blazer
bleiben [blaɪbm] remain, stay
Blick *m* [blɪk] look; view
blind [blɪnt] blind
Blinddarmentzündung *f* [ˈblɪntdaːmɛnˌtsʏndʊŋ] appendicitis
Blinde *m/f* [ˈblɪnde] blind person
Blindenhund *m* [ˈblɪndnhʊnt] guide dog
Blindenschrift *f* [ˈblɪndnʃʀɪft] braille
Blinklicht *n* [ˈblɪŋklɪçt] indicator
Blitz *m* [blɪts] lightning
Blitzgerät *n* [ˈblɪtsgəʀɛːt] *(camera)* flash
Block *m* [blɔk] writing pad
blöd(e) [bløːt/ˈbløːdə] silly, stupid
blond [blɔnt] blond(e)
Blues *m* [bluːs] blues
Blume *f* [ˈbluːmə] flower
Blumengeschäft *n* [ˈbluːmmgəʃɛft] florist's
Blumenkohl *m* [ˈbluːmmkoːl] cauliflower
Blumenstrauß *m* [ˈbluːmmʃtʀaʊs] bunch of flowers
Bluse *f* [ˈbluːzə] blouse
Blut *n* [bluːt] blood
bluten [bluːtn] bleed
Blutgruppe *f* [ˈbluːtgʀʊpə] blood group
Bluthochdruck *m* [ˈbluːthoːxdrʊk] high blood pressure
Blutung *f* [ˈbluːtʊŋ] bleeding
Blutvergiftung *f* [ˈbluːtfɐgɪftʊŋ] blood-poisoning
Bö *f* [bøː] gust of wind
Boden *m* [boːdn] ground; floor
Bogen *m* [ˈboːgŋ] arch
Bohnen *f pl* [boːnn] beans
Bordkarte *f* [ˈbɔɐtkaːtə] boarding card
Borreliose *f* [bɔʁɛlˈjoːzə] borreliosis
böse [ˈbøːzə] evil; naughty; angry
botanischer Garten *m* [boˈtanɪʃə ˈgaːtn] botanic garden
Botschaft *f* [ˈboːtʃaft] embassy
Boutique *f* [buˈtiːk] boutique
Brand *m* [bʀant] fire
Bratensoße *f* [ˈbʀaːtnzoːsə] gravy
Bräter *m* [ˈbʀɛːtɐ] roasting tray
brauchen [bʀaʊxn] need, want; *(time)* take
braun [bʀaʊn] brown

Brechreiz *m* [ˈbʀɛçʀaɪts] nausea
breit [bʀaɪt] broad, wide
Breite *f* [ˈbʀaɪtə] width
Bremse *f* [ˈbʀɛmzə] brake; horsefly
Bremsflüssigkeit *f* [ˈbʀɛmsflʏsɪçkaɪt] brake fluid
Bremslichter *f* [ˈbʀɛmslɪçtɐ] brake lights
brennen [bʀɛnn] to burn; to sting
Brennholz *n* [ˈbʀɛnhɔlts] firewood
Brennspiritus *m* [ˈbʀɛnˌʃpiʀitʊs] methylated spirits
Brief *m* [bʀi:f] letter
Briefmarke *f* [ˈbʀi:fˌma:kə] *(postage)* stamp
Briefmarkenautomat *m* [ˈbʀi:fma:kŋʔaʊtoˌma:t] stamp machine
Briefpapier *n* [ˈbʀi:fpapiɐ] writing paper
Brieftasche *f* [ˈbʀi:ftʰaʃə] wallet, billfold
Briefumschlag *m* [ˈbʀi:fʊmʃla:k] envelope
bringen [(ˈheɐ)bʀɪŋŋ] bring
Brombeeren *f pl* [ˈbʀɔmbe:ʀən] blackberries
Bronchien *f pl* [ˈbʀɔnçɪən] bronchial tubes
Bronchitis *f* [bʀɔnˈçi:tɪs] bronchitis
Bronze *f* [ˈbʀɔŋsə] bronze
Brosche *f* [ˈbʀɔʃə] brooch
Brot *n* [bʀo:t] bread
Brötchen *n pl* [bʀø:tçn] rolls
Brücke *f* [ˈbʀʏkə] bridge
Bruder *m* [ˈbʀu:dɐ] brother
Brunnen *m* [(ˈbʀʊnn] fountain, well
Brust *f* [bʀʊst] chest
Buch *n* [bu:x] book
buchen [bu:xn] *(seat)* to book
Buchhandlung *f* [ˈbu:xhantlʊŋ] book shop
Büchse *f* [ˈbʏksə] can, tin
buchstabieren [buxʃtaˈbi:ʀən/ -ˈbiɐn] to spell
Bucht *f* [bʊxt] bay
Buchung *f* [ˈbu:xʊŋ] booking
Bügeleisen *n* [ˈby:glʔaɪzn] iron
bügeln [by:gln] to iron
Bummel *m* [bʊml] stroll
Bungalow *m* [ˈbʊŋgalo:] bungalow
Burg *f* [bʊɐk] *(fortress)* castle
Bürgschaft *f* [ˈbʏɐkʃaft] security
Büro *n* [byˈʀo:] office
Bürste *f* [ˈbʏɐstə] brush
Bus *m* [bʊs] bus
Busbahnhof *m* [ˈbʊsˌba:nho:f] bus station
Busch *m* [bʊʃ] bush
Butter *f* [ˈbʊtɐ] butter
Buttermilch *f* [ˈbʊtɐmɪlç] buttermilk
Bypass *m* [ˈbaɪpa:s] bypass

C

Café *n* [kʰaˈfe:] café
Camcorder *m* [ˈkamkhɔɐdɐ] camcorder
Camping *n* [ˈkɛmpɪŋ] camping
Campingführer *m* [ˈkɛmpɪŋfy:ʀɐ] camping guide
Campingplatz *m* [ˈkɛmpɪŋplats] camping site
CD *f* [tseˈde:] CD
CD-Spieler *m* [tseˈde:ʃpi:lɐ] CD player
Champagner *m* [ʃamˈpanjɐ] champagne
Chauffeur *m* [ʃɔˈføɐ] chauffeur, driver
Chef/Chefin *m/f* [ʃɛf/ʃɛfɪn] boss, head
chemisch reinigen [ˈçe:mɪʃ ˈʀaɪnɪgŋ] dry-clean
Chipkarte *f* [ˈtʃɪpka:tə] chip card
Chirurg/Chirurgin *m/f* [çɪˈʀʊɐk/ çɪˈʀʊɐgɪn] surgeon
Chor *m* [koɐ] choir
Christentum *n* [ˈkʀɪstntu:m] Christianity
Clubhaus *n* [ˈklʊphaʊs] clubhouse
Computerfachgeschäft *n* [kɔmˈpju:tɐˌfaxgəʃɛft] computer shop
Cousin/e*m/f* [kʰʊˈzɛŋ /kʰʊˈzi:nə] cousin
Creme *f* [kʀɛ:m] cream
Curling *n* [ˈkə:lɪŋ] curling

D

da [da:] *(place)* there; *(time)* then; *(reason)* as, because; **da sein** [ˈda:zaɪn] be present, be there
Dach *n* [dax] roof
dagegen sein [daˈge:gŋ zaɪn] be against s. th.
daheim [daˈhaɪm] at home
daher [ˈda:heɐ] therefore
damals [ˈda:ma (:)ls] then, at that time
Damen [da:mɪn] Ladies
Damenbinden *f pl* [ˈda:mmbɪndn] sanitary towels
Damenslip *m* [ˈda:mənslɪp] panties
danach [daˈna:x] afterwards
danken [ˈdaŋkŋ] thank
dann [dan] then
Darm *m* [da:m] intestines
dass [das] that
dasselbe [dasˈzɛlbə] the same
Datum *n* [ˈda:tʰʊm] date
dauern [ˈdaʊɐn] to last
Dauerwelle *f* [ˈdaʊɐvɛlə] perm
Deck *n* [dɛk] deck
Decke *f* [ˈdɛkə] ceiling
Defekt *m* [deˈfɛkt] fault
dein [daɪn] your

Delle *f* [ˈdɛlə] dent
denken (an) [ˈdɛŋkŋ ˀan] think (of)
Denkmal *n* [ˈdɛŋkma:l] monument
denn [dɛn] for; because
Deo *n* [ˈdeo] deodorant
derselbe [dɐˈzɛlbə] the same
deshalb [ˈdɛshalp] therefore
Desinfektionsmittel *n* [dezɪnfɛkˈtsjo:nsmɪtl] disinfectant
desinfizieren [dezɪnfɪˈtsi:ʀən] disinfect
deutlich [ˈdɔɪtlɪç] distinct(ly), clear(ly)
deutsch [dɔɪtʃ] German
Deutsche *m/f* [ˈdɔɪtʃə] German
Deutschland [ˈdɔɪtʃlant] Germany
Dezember [deˈtsɛmbɐ] December
Dia *n* [ˈdia] slide
Diabetes *m* [diaˈbe:təs] diabetes
Diabetiker/in *m/f* [diaˈbe:tɪkɐ/-kəʀɪn] *(person)* diabetic
diabetisch [diaˈbe:tɪʃ] diabetic
Diagnose *f* [diaˈgno:zə] diagnosis
Diät *f* [diˈɛ:t] diet
dich [dɪç] you
dicht [dɪçt] *(crowd, fog etc.)* thick
dick [dɪk] thick, swollen; *(person)* stout, fat
Dieb/Diebin *m/f* [di:p/ˈdi:bɪn] thief
Diebstahl *m* [ˈdi:pʃta:l] theft
dienen [di:nn] to serve
Dienst *m* [di:nst] service
Dienstag [ˈdi:nsta:k] Tuesday
diese [ˈdi:zə] these, those
diese(r, s) [ˈdi:zə/ˈdi:zɐ/ˈdi:zəs] that, this
Digitalkamera *f* [digiˈta:lˌkaməʀa] digital camera
Ding *n* [dɪŋ] thing
Diphtherie *f* [dɪftəˈʀi:] diphtheria
dir [diɐ] to/for you
direkt [diˈʀɛkt] direct
Dirigent/Dirigentin *m/f* [diʀiˈgɛnt/ diʀiˈgɛntɪn] conductor
Diskothek *f* [dɪskoˈte:k] discotheque
doch [dɔx] yet, however
Dokumentarfilm *m* [dɔkumɛnˈta:fɪlm] documentary
Donnerstag [ˈdɔnɐsta:k] Thursday
Doppel *n* [dɔpl] doubles
doppelt [dɔplt] *(adj)* double; *(adv)* twice
Dorf *n* [doɐf] village
dort [dɔɐt] there
dorthin [ˈdɔɐthɪn] *(location)* there
Dose *f* [ˈdo:zə] tin, can
Dosenöffner *m* [ˈdo:znˀœfnɐ] tin opener
Drachenfliegen *n* [ˈdʀaxnfli:gŋ] hang-gliding
Drama *n* [ˈdʀa:ma] drama
draußen [ˈdʀaʊsn] outside
Dressing *f* [ˈdʀɛsɪŋ] *(food)* dressing
drin [dʀɪn] inside
dringend [dʀɪŋŋt] urgent
drinnen [dʀɪnn] indoors
dritte(r, s) [ˈdʀɪtə (-tɐ, -təs)] third
Drucker *m* [ˈdʁʊkɐ] printer
du [du:] you
dumm [dʊm] stupid
dunkel [dʊŋkl] dark
dunkelblau [dʊŋklˈblaʊ] dark blue
dünn [dʏn] thin; slim, slender
durch [dʊɐç] through; *(quer ~)* across; by (means of)
durchaus nicht [dʊɐçˈˀaʊs nɪç(t)] not at all
Durchfall *m* [ˈdʊɐçfal] diarrhoea
durchgebraten [ˈdʊɐçgəbʀa:tn] well-done
Durchreise, auf der ~ [ˀaʊf dɐ ˈdʊɐçʀaɪzə] passing through
durchschnittlich [ˈdʊɐçʃnɪtlɪç] average
dürfen [dʏɐfn] be allowed
dürftig [ˈdʏɐftɪç] *(sparse)* thin
Dusche *f* [ˈdu:ʃə] shower
Duschgel *n* [ˈdu:ʃge:l] shower gel
Duschsitz *m* [ˈdu:ʃzɪts] shower seat
DVD *f* [defaʊˈde:] DVD
Dynastie *f* [dʏnasˈti:] dynasty

E

Ebbe *f* [ˀɛbə] low tide
eben [ˀe:bm] flat; smooth; *(time)* just now
Ebene *f* [ˀe:bənə] plain
ebenerdig [ˈˀe:bmˀeɐdɪç] at ground level
echt [ˀɛçt] genuine
Ecke *f* [ˈˀɛkʰə] corner
Ehefrau *f* [ˈˀe:əfʀaʊ] wife
Ehemann *m* [ˈˀe:əman] husband
Ehepaar *n* [ˈˀe:əpa:] couple
eher [ˀeɐ] rather
Eier *n pl* [ˈˀaɪɐ] eggs; **Eierbecher** *m* [ˈˀaɪɐˌbɛçɐ] egg cup
eigen [ˀaɪgŋ] own; peculiar, strange, odd, weird
Eigenschaft *f* [ˈˀaɪgŋʃaft] quality, characteristic
eigentlich [ˈˀaɪgŋtlɪç] actual(ly)
Eigentümer/in *m/f* [ˈˀaɪgŋty:mɐ/-məʀɪn] owner
eilig [ˈˀaɪlɪç] urgent; **es eilig haben** [ˀəs ˈˀaɪlɪç ha:bm] be in a hurry
Eimer *m* [ˈˀaɪmɐ] bucket
ein(e) [ˀɐn /ˈˀɐɪnə] a, one
einchecken [ˈˀaɪntʃɛkŋ] check in
einfach [ˈˀaɪnfax] simple
Einfahrt *f* [ˈˀaɪnfa:t] entrance
einfarbig [ˀaɪnfaʀbɪç] plain

Eingang *m* [ˈʔaɪngaŋ] entrance
einheimisch [ˈʔaɪnhaɪmɪʃ] native, local
einig sein [ˈʔaɪnɪç zaɪn] agree
einige [ˈʔaɪnɪgə] some
einigen, sich ~ [zɪç ˈʔaɪnɪgŋ] agree
einkaufen [ˈʔaɪnkʰaʊfn] buy, go shopping
einladen [ˈʔaɪnla:dn] invite
einmal [ˈʔɐɪ (n)ma:l] once
einpacken [ˈʔaɪnpʰakŋ] wrap, pack
eins [ʔaɪns] one
einsam [ˈʔaɪnza:m] lonely; secluded, isolated
Einschreibebrief *m* [ˈʔaɪnʃʀaɪbəbʀi:f] registered letter
einsteigen [ˈʔaɪnʃtaɪgŋ] get in/on
eintreffen [ˈʔaɪntʀɛfn] arrive (at)
Eintritt *m* [ˈʔaɪntʀɪt] entrance, admission
Eintrittskarte *f* [ˈʔaɪntʀɪtsˌkʰa:tʰə] (admission) ticket
Eintrittspreis *m* [ˈʔaɪntʀɪtspʀaɪs] admission charge
Einwohner/in *m/f* [ˈʔaɪnvo:nɐ/-nəʀɪn] inhabitant
Einzel *n* [ˈʔaɪntsəl] singles
einzelne, jeder ~ [ˌje:dɐ ˈʔaɪntslnə] each
einzig [ˈʔaɪntsɪç] only
Eis *n* [ʔaɪs] ice
Eisbahn *f* [ˈʔaɪsba:n] ice rink
Eishockey *n* [ˈʔaɪshɔke:] ice hockey
Eiter *m* [ˈʔaɪtɐ] pus
Elastikbinde *f* [ʔeˈlastɪkbɪndə] elastic bandage
elektrisch [ʔeˈlɛktʀɪʃ] electric
Eltern *pl* [ˈʔɛltʰɐn] parents
empfangen [ʔɛmpˈfaŋŋ] receive; greet, welcome
Empfänger *m* [ʔɛmpˈfɛŋɐ] addressee
empfehlen [ʔɛmpˈfe:ln] recommend
Ende *n* [ˈʔɛndə] end
endgültig [ˈʔɛntgʏltʰɪç] definite; definitely
endlich [ˈʔɛntlɪç] finally
Endstation *f* [ˈʔɛntʃtatsjo:n] terminus
eng [ʔɛŋ] narrow; *(clothes)* tight
England [ˈʔɛŋlant] England
Engländer/in *m/f* [ˈʔɛŋlɛndɐ/-dəʀɪn] Englishman/-woman
englisch [ˈʔɛŋlɪʃ] English
entdecken [ʔɛntˈdɛkŋ] discover
Entfernung *f* [ʔɛntˈfɛɐnʊŋ] distance
entgegengesetzt [ʔɛntˈge:gŋgəˌzɛtst] opposite
entscheiden [ʔɛntˈʃaɪdn] decide
entschuldigen [ʔɛntˈʃʊldɪgŋ] to excuse; sich ~ [zɪç ʔɛntˈʃʊldɪgŋ] apologize

Entschuldigung *f* [ʔɛntˈʃʊldɪgʊŋ] apology; excuse; **Entschuldigung!** sorry!; **Ich bitte um Entschuldigung!** [ʔɪç ˈbɪtə ʔʊm ɛntˈʃʊldɪgʊŋ] I beg your pardon!; **Entschuldigung, ...** excuse me, ...
enttäuscht [ʔɛnˈtʰɔɪʃt] disappointed
entweder ... oder [ˈʔɛntve:dɐ ... ˈʔo:dɐ] either ... or
entwickeln [ʔɛntˈvɪkln] develop
entzückend [ʔɛnˈtsʏkŋt] charming, delightful
Entzündung *f* [ʔɛnˈtsʏndʊŋ] inflammation
Epilepsie *f* [epilɛpˈsi] epilepsy
Epoche *f* [ʔeˈpɔxə] epoch
er [ʔeɐ] he
Erbsen *f pl* [ʔɛɐpsn] peas
Erdbeeren *f pl* [ˈʔeɐtbe:ʀən] strawberries
Erde *f* [ˈʔeɐdə] earth
Erdgeschoss *n* [ˈʔeɐtgəʃɔs] ground floor, *(US)* first floor
Ereignis *n* [ʔɐˈʔaɪknɪs] event
erfahren [ʔɐˈfa: (ʀə)n] learn, hear, experience; *(adj)* experienced
Erfolg *m* [ʔɐˈfɔlk] success
erfreut (über) [ʔɐˈfʀɔɪt (ˈʔy:bɐ)] pleased (with), glad (of)
erhalten [ʔɐˈhaltn] receive, get
erholen, sich ~ [zɪç ʔɐˈho:ln] recover
Erholung *f* [ʔɐˈho:lʊŋ] rest
erinnern, sich ~ [zɪç ɐˈʔɪnɐn] remember
Erkältung *f* [ʔɐˈkɛltʊŋ] cold
Ermäßigung *f* [ʔɐˈmɛ:sɪgʊŋ] reduction
ernst [ʔɛɐnst] serious
E-Rollstuhl *m* [ˈʔe:ˌʀɔlʃtu:l] electric wheelchair
erreichen [ʔɐˈʀaɪçn] to reach
Ersatz *m* [ʔɐˈzats] replacement; compensation
Ersatzreifen *m* [ʔɐˈzatsʀaɪfn] spare tyre
erschöpft [ʔɐˈʃœpft] exhausted
erschrecken [ʔɐˈʃʀɛkŋ] frighten, startle; be alarmed
erschrocken [ʔɐˈʃʀɔkŋ] afraid, alarmed
ersetzen [ʔɐˈzɛtsn] replace
erst [eɐst] first of all; *(not later than)* only
erste(r, s) [ˈʔeɐstə (-tɐ, -təs)] first
ertragen [ʔɐˈtʀa:gŋ] to bear, to stand
Erwachsene(r) *m/f* [ʔɐˈvaks (ə)nə/ʔɐˈvaks(ə)nɐ] adult
erwarten [ʔɐˈva:tn] expect, wait for
erwidern [ʔɐˈvi:dɐn] to reply
erzählen [ʔɐˈtsɛ:ln] tell
Erzeugnis *n* [ʔɐˈtsɔɪknɪs] product
Erziehung *f* [ʔɐˈtsiʊŋ] education
essbar [ˈʔɛsba:] edible
essen [ʔɛsn] eat
Essen *n* [ˈʔɛsn] meal; food

Essig *m* [ˈʔɛsɪç] vinegar
Esszimmer *n* [ˈʔɛstsɪmɐ] (private) dining room
Etagenbett *n* [ʔeˈtaːʒnbɛt] bunk bed
etwa [ˈʔɛtvaː] about
etwas [ˈʔɛtvas] something; anything; a little
EU-Bürger/in [ʔeˈʔuː bʏʀgɐ/-gəʀɪn] EU citizen
euch [ʔɔɪç] you
euer [ˈʔɔɪɐ] your
Euro *m* [ˈʔɔɪʀo] euro
Europa [ʔɔɪˈʀoːpʰaː] Europe
Europäer/in *m/f* [ʔɔɪʀoˈpɛːɐ/-pɛːəʀɪn] European
europäisch [ʔɔɪʀoˈpʰɛːɪʃ] European
eventuell [ʔevɛntuˈ(ʔ)ɛl] perhaps, possible
Exponat *n* [ʔɛkspoˈnaːt] exhibit
Expressionismus *m* [ʔɛkspʀɛsjoˈnɪsmus] expressionism
extra [ˈʔɛkstʀaː] extra, special

F

Fabrik *f* [faˈbʀi (ː)k] factory
Facharzt/-ärztin *m/f* [ˈfaxaːtst/ˈfaxʔɛɐtstɪn] specialist
Faden *m* [faːdn] thread
Fähre *f* [ˈfɛːʀə] ferry
fahren [faː (ʀə)n] go (by train, car etc.); drive
Fahrer/in *m/f* [ˈfaːʀɐ/ˈfaːʀəʀɪn] driver
Fahrgast *m* [ˈfaːgast] passenger
Fahrkartenautomat *m* [ˈfaːkaːtnʔaʊtoˌmaːt] ticket machine
Fahrkartenschalter *m* [ˈfaːkaːtnˌʃaltɐ] ticket office
Fahrplan *m* [ˈfaːplaːn] timetable
Fahrpreis *m* [ˈfaːpʀaɪs] fare
Fahrrad *n* [ˈfaːʀat] bicycle, bike
Fahrradweg *m* [ˈfaːʀatveːk] cycle path
Fahrstuhl *m* [ˈfaːʃtuːl] lift, elevator
Fahrt *f* [faːt] journey, trip, voyage; *(car)* drive
fair [fɛɐ] fair
fallen [faln] to fall
falls [fals] in case, if
Fallschirmspringen *n* [ˈfalʃɪɐmʃpʀɪŋŋ] parachuting
falsch [falʃ] wrong; deceitful
Faltrollstuhl *m* [ˈfaltˌʀɔlʃtuːl] folding wheelchair
Familie *f* [faˈmiːljə] family
fangen [faŋŋ] to catch
Fango *m* [ˈfaŋgo] fango
färben [fɛɐbm] to dye
farbig [ˈfaʀbɪç] coloured
Farbstift *m* [ˈfaːpʃtɪft] coloured pencil
Fassade *f* [faˈsaːdə] façade, front
fast [fast] almost, nearly
faul [faʊl] lazy; *(fruit)* rotten
Februar [ˈfeːbʀuaː] February
Federball *m* [ˈfeːdɐbal] shuttlecock; badminton
fehlen [feːln] be missing
Fehler *m* [ˈfeːlɐ] mistake; fault
Fehlgeburt *f* [ˈfeːlgəbuɐt] miscarriage
fein [faɪn] fine; delicate; distinguished
Feinkostgeschäft *n* [ˈfaɪnkɔstgəˌʃɛft] delicatessen
Feld *n* [fɛlt] field
Fell *n* [fɛl] fur, fleece
Fels *m* [fɛls] rock; cliff
Fenchel *m* [fɛnçl] fennel
Fenster *n* [ˈfɛnstɐ] window
Fensterplatz *m* [ˈfɛnstɐplats] window seat
Ferien *pl* [ˈfeːʀɪən (ˈfeɐjən)] holidays, vacation
Ferienanlage *f* [ˈfeːʀiənʔanlaːgə] holiday camp
Ferienhaus *n* [ˈfeːʀiənhaʊs] holiday home
Ferngespräch *n* [ˈfɛɐngəʃpʀɛːç] long-distance call
Fernlicht *n* [ˈfɛɐnlɪçt] full beam, high beam
Fernsehapparat *m* [ˈfɛɐnzeʔapaˌʀaːt] (TV) set
Fernsehraum *m* [ˈfɛɐnzeːˌʀaʊm] television lounge
fertig [ˈfɛɐtʰɪç] ready; finished
fest [fɛst] firm, solid, rigid
Fest *n* [fɛst] celebration(s), party
Festival *n* [ˈfɛstɪval] festival
feststellen [ˈfɛ(st)ʃtɛln] to state
Festung *f* [ˈfɛstʊŋ] fortress
fett [fɛt] fat; greasy
fettarm [ˈfɛtʔaːm] low-fat;
~e Milch [ˈfɛtʔaːmə mɪlç] low-fat milk
feucht [fɔɪçt] moist, damp
Feuer *n* [ˈfɔɪɐ] fire
feuergefährlich [ˈfɔɪɐgəˌfeɐlɪç] (in)flammable
Feuerlöscher *m* [ˈfɔɪɐlœʃɐ] fire extinguisher
Feuermelder *m* [ˈfɔɪɐmɛldɐ] fire alarm
Feuerwerk *n* [ˈfɔɪɐvɛɐk] fireworks display
Feuerzeug *n* [ˈfɔɪɐtsɔɪk] lighter
Fieber *n* [ˈfiːbɐ] fever
Fieberthermometer *n* [ˈfiːbɐtɛɐmoˌmeːtɐ] thermometer
Film *m* [fɪlm] film
Filmempfindlichkeit *f* [ˈfɪlmɛmpfɪntlɪçkaɪt] film speed
Filmschauspieler/-in *m/f* [ˈfɪlmʃaʊʃpiːlɐ/-ləʀɪn] film/movie actor/actress

finden [fɪndn] to find
Finger *m* [ˈfɪŋɐ] finger
finster [ˈfɪnstɐ] dark
Firma *f* [ˈfɪʁma:] firm, company
Fischerhafen *m* [ˈfɪʃɐha:fn] fishing port
Fischgeschäft *n* [ˈfɪʃgəʃɛft] fishmonger's
fit [fɪt] fit
Fitnesscenter *n* [ˈfɪtnəsˌtsɛntɐ] fitness centre
FKK-Strand *m* [ˀɛfkaˈka:ʃtʀant] nudist beach
flach [flax] flat; level
Fläschchenwärmer *m* [ˈflɛʃçənvɛɐmɐ] bottle warmer
Flasche *f* [ˈflaʃə] bottle
Flaschenöffner *m* [ˈflaʃnˀœfnɐ] bottle opener
Fleck *m* [flɛk] stain
Fleisch *n* [flaɪʃ] meat
Flickzeug *n* [ˈflɪktsɔɪk] repair kit
Fliege *f* [ˈfli:gə] fly
fliegen [fli:gŋ] to fly
Flipflops *f* [ˈflɪpflɔps] flip-flops
Flohmarkt *m* [ˈflo:ma:kt] flea market
Flug *m* [flu:k] flight
Flügel *m* [fly:gl] wing
Fluggesellschaft *f* [ˈflu:kgəˌzɛlʃaft] airline
Flughafen *m* [ˈflu:kha:fn] airport
Flughafenbus *m* [ˈflu:kha:fnˌbʊs] airport bus
Flughafengebühr *f* [ˈflu:kha:fngəˌbyɐ] airport tax
Flugsteig *m* [ˈflu:kʃtaɪg] *(airport)* gate
Fluss *m* [flʊs] river
flüssig [ˈflʏsɪç] liquid
Flut *f* [flu:t] high tide
Föhn *m* [fø:n] hair dryer
föhnen [fø:nn] to blow-dry
fordern [ˈfɔɐdɐn] ask
Form *f* [fɔɐm] form, shape
Format *n* [fɔˈma:t] *(paper)* size
Formular *n* [fɔmʊˈla:] *(paper)* form
fort [fɔɐt] away
Foto *n* [ˈfoto] photo
Fotografie *f* [fotogʀaˈfi:] photography
fotografieren [ˌfotogʀaˈfi:ʀən] to photograph
Frage *f* [ˈfʀa:gə] question
fragen [fʀa:gŋ] ask
frankieren [fʀaŋˈkiɐn] to stamp
französisch [fʀanˈtsø:zɪʃ] French
Frau *f* [fʀaʊ] woman; wife; Madam; Ms, Mrs
Fräulein *n* [ˈfʀɔ (ɪ)laɪn] young lady; Miss
frei [fʀaɪ] free; exempt; **im Freien** [ˀɪm ˈfʀaɪn] in the open air, outdoors
Freiberufler *m* [ˈfʁaɪbəʁu:flɐ] freelancer, self-employe
Freilichtkino *n* [ˈfʀaɪlɪçtki:no] drive-in cinema
Freitag [ˈfʀaɪta:k] Friday
Freizeitpark *m* [ˈfʀaɪtsaɪtˌpa:k] amusement park
fremd [fʀɛmt] strange; foreign; unknown
Fremde *m/f* [ˈfʀɛmdə] stranger; foreigner
Fremdenführer/in *m/f* [ˈfʀɛmdnfy:ʀɐ/-fy:ʀəʀɪn] guide
Freude *f* [ˈfʀɔɪdə] joy, pleasure
freuen, sich ~ (über) [zɪç ˈfʀɔɪn (ˌy:bɐ)] be pleased (with/about); **sich ~ auf** [zɪç ˈfʀɔɪn ˀaʊf] look forward to
Freund/in *m/f* [fʀɔɪnt/ˈfʀɔɪndɪn] friend; boyfriend/girlfriend
freundlich [ˈfʀɔɪntlɪç] friendly, kind
Friedhof *m* [ˈfʀi:to:f] cemetery, graveyard
frieren [ˈfʀi:ʀən /fʀiɐn] be cold, freeze
frisch [fʀɪʃ] fresh; *(clothing)* clean
Frischhaltefolie *f* [ˈfʀɪʃhaltəˌfo:ljə] cling film
Friseur *m* [fʀɪˈzøɐ] hairdresser's
Frisur *f* [fʀɪˈzuɐ] hairstyle
froh [fʀo:] glad; happy; merry
Frost *m* [fʀɔst] frost
Frostschutzmittel *n* [ˈfʀɔstʃʊtsmɪtl] anti-freeze
Frühling *m* [ˈfʀy:lɪŋ] *(season)* spring
Frühstück *n* [ˈfʀy:ʃtʏk] breakfast
frühstücken [ˈfʀy:ʃtʏkŋ] have breakfast
Frühstücksbüfett *n* [ˈfʀy:ʃtʏksbʏˌfe:] buffet breakfast
Frühstücksraum *m* [ˈfʀy:ʃtʏksʀaʊm] breakfast room
fühlen [fy:ln] to feel
Führerschein *m* [ˈfy:ʀɐʃaɪn] driving licence
Führung *f* [ˈfy:ʀʊŋ] guided tour
funktionieren [fʊŋktsjoˈni:ʀən/-ˈniɐn] to work, to function
für [fyɐ] for
Furcht *f* [fʊɐçt] fear
fürchten [fʏɐçtn] to fear; **sich ~ (vor)** [zɪç ˈfʏɐçtn foɐ] be afraid (of)
fürchterlich [ˈfʏɐçtɐlɪç] terrible, dreadful, horrible
Fuß *m* [fu:s] foot
Fußball *m* [ˈfu:sbal] football
Fußballspiel *n* [ˈfu:sbalˌʃpi:l] football match
Fußgänger/in *m/f* [ˈfu:sgɛŋɐ/-gɛŋəʀɪn] pedestrian
Fußgängerzone *f* [ˈfu:sgɛŋɐˌtso:nə] pedestrian precinct/zone

Fuß(reflexzonen)massage *f* [ˈfu:s(ʁeˈflɛkstso:nn)maˌsa:ʒə] reflexology (foot) massage

G

Gabel *f* [ˈga:bl] fork
Galerie *f* [galəˈʀi:] gallery
Gallenblase *f* [ˈgalnbla:zə] gall-bladder
Gang *m* [gaŋ] *(meal)* course; corridor; *(engine)* gear
ganz [gants] *(adj)* whole; entire, complete; *(adv)* quite
Ganzkörpermassage *f* [ˈgantsˌkœɐpɐmaˌsa:ʒə] full body massage
gar [ga:] cooked, done
gar nicht [ˈga: nɪç(t)] not at all
Garage *f* [gaˈʀa:ʒə] garage
Garantie *f* [gaʀanˈtʰi:] guarantee
Garderobe *f* [gaˈdʀo:bə] cloakroom
Garnelen *f pl* [gaˈne:ln] prawns
Garten *m* [ga:tn] garden
Gasflasche *f* [ga:sflaʃə] gas canister
Gasherd *m* [ˈga:sheɐt] gas cooker
Gaskartusche *f* [ˈga:skaˌtʊʃə] gas cartridge
Gaspedal *n* [ˈga:speda:l] accelerator, gas pedal
Gasse *f* [ˈgasə] alley, lane
Gast *m* [gast] guest
Gastfreundschaft *f* [ˈgastfʀɔɪntʃaft] hospitality
Gastgeber/in [ˈgastge:bɐ / -bəʀɪn] host/hostess
gebacken [gəˈbakŋ] baked
Gebäude *n* [gəˈbɔɪdə] building
geben [ge:bm] give
Gebirge *n* [gəˈbɪɐgə] mountains
geboren [gəˈbo:ʀən /gəˈboɐn] born
gebraten [gəˈbʀa:tn] roasted
Gebrauch *m* [gəˈbʀaʊx] use
gebrauchen [gəˈbʀaʊx] to use
gebräuchlich [gəˈbʀɔɪçlɪç] common
gebrochen [gəˈbʀɔxn] broken
Gebühren *f pl* [gəˈby:ʀən /-ˈbyɐn] fees
Geburtsdatum *n* [gəˈbʊɐtsda:tʊm] date of birth
Geburtsname *m* [gəˈbʊɐtsna:mə] maiden name
Geburtsort *m* [gəˈbʊɐtsˀɔɐt] place of birth
Geburtstag *m* [gəˈbʊɐtstʰa:k] birthday
gedämpft [gəˈdɛmpft] steamed
Gedenkstätte *f* [gəˈdɛŋkʃtɛtə] memorial
Geduld *f* [gəˈdʊlt] patience
gedünstet [gəˈdʏnstət] steamed
Gefahr *f* [gəˈfa:] danger
gefährlich [gəˈfeɐlɪç] dangerous
gefallen [gəˈfaln] to please
Gefallen *m* [gəˈfaln] favour
Gefängnis *n* [gəˈfɛŋnɪs] prison
Gefäß *n* [gəˈfɛ:s] container
Gefühl *n* [gəˈfy:l] feeling
gefüllt [gəˈfʏlt] stuffed
gegen [ge:gŋ] against; *(sport)* versus; towards; *(time)* about
Gegend *f* [ˈge:gŋt] region, area, district
Gegenstand *m* [ˈge:gŋʃtant] object
Gegenteil *n* [ˈge:gŋtʰaɪl] opposite, contrary
gegenüber [gegŋˈˀy:bɐ] opposite
Geheimzahl *f* [gəˈhaɪmtsa:l] Personal Identification Number (PIN)
gehen [ge:n] to go; to walk
Gehirn *n* [gəˈhɪɐn] brain
Gehirnerschütterung *f* [gəˈhɪɐnɐˌʃʏtəʀʊŋ] concussion
Gehör *n* [gəˈhøɐ] hearing
gehören [gəˈhø:ʀən /-ˈhøɐn] belong to
gehörlos [gəˈhøɐlo:s] deaf
Gehörlose *m/f* [gəˈhøɐlo:zə] deaf person
geistig behindert [ˈgaɪstɪç bəˈhɪndɐt] mentally handicapped
gekocht [gəˈkɔxt] boiled, cooked
Gelände *n* [geˈlɛndə] ground; grounds
gelb [gɛlp] yellow
Geld *n* [gɛlt] money
Geldautomat *m* [ˈgɛltaʊtoˌma:t] automated teller machine, cashpoint
Geldbeutel *m* [ˈgɛltbɔɪtl] purse
Geldbörse *f* [ˈgɛltbœɐzə] purse
Geldschein *m* [ˈgɛltʃaɪn] banknote
Geldstrafe *f* [ˈgɛltʃtʀa:fə] *(monetary)* fine
gelegentlich [gələ:gŋtlɪç] occasional(ly)
Gelenk *n* [gəˈlɛŋk] joint
Gemälde *n* [gəˈmɛ:ldə] painting
gemeinsam [gəˈmaɪnza (:)m] common; together
Gemüse *n* [gəˈmy:zə] vegetables
gemütlich [gəˈmy:tlɪç] comfortable, cosy
genau [gəˈnaʊ] exact(ly)
genauso ... wie [gəˈnaʊzo ... vi] just as ... as
genießen [gəˈni:sn] enjoy
genug [gəˈnu:k] enough, sufficient
geöffnet [gəˈˀœfnət] open
Gepäck *n* [geˈpɛk] baggage, luggage
Gepäckaufbewahrung *f* [gəˈpɛkˌˀaʊfbəva:ʀʊŋ] baggage deposit, left-luggage office
Gepäckausgabe *f* [gəˈpɛkˀaʊsga:bə] baggage/luggage reclaim
Gepäckschalter *m* [gəˈpɛkʃaltɐ] baggage/luggage counter

Gepäckwagen *m* [gəˈpɛkva:gŋ] baggage/luggage car
gerade [g (ə)ˈʀa:də] straight; *(time)* just
geradeaus [gʀa:dəˈˀaʊs] straight on/straight ahead
geräuchert [gəˈʀɔɪçɐt] smoked
Geräusch *n* [gəˈʀɔɪʃ] noise
gerecht [gəˈʀɛçt] just, fair
Gericht *n* [gəˈʀɪçt] *(food)* dish; (law) court
gering [gəˈʀɪŋ] little, small
gern [gɛɐn] gladly; **nicht gern** [nɪç(t) gɛɐn] reluctantly
Geruch *m* [gəˈʀu (:)x] smell
Geschäft *n* [gəˈʃɛft] shop, store
Geschenk *n* [gəˈʃɛŋk] present, gift
Geschichte *f* [gəˈʃɪçtə] history; story
Geschirr *n* [gəˈʃɪɐ] crockery
Geschirrspülbecken *n* [gəˈʃɪɐspy:lbɛkŋ] sink
Geschirrspülmaschine *f* [gəˈʃɪɐʃpy:lmaˌʃɪnə] dishwasher
Geschirrtuch *n* [gəˈʃɪɐtu:x] tea towel
geschlossen [gəˈʃlɔsn] shut, closed
Geschmack *m* [gəˈʃmak] taste
geschmort [gəˈʃmoɐt] braised
Geschwindigkeit *f* [gəˈʃvɪndɪçkʰaɪt] speed
geschwollen [gəˈʃvɔln] swollen
Geschwulst *f* [gəˈʃvʊlst] tumour, growth
Geschwür *n* [gəˈʃvyɐ] ulcer
Gesellschaft *f* [gəˈzɛlʃaft] company
Gesichtsbehandlung *f* [gəˈzɪçtsbəˌhandlʊŋ] face treatment
Gespräch *n* [gəˈʃpʀɛ:ç] conversation, talk
gestern [ˈgɛstɐn] yesterday
gesund [gəˈzʊnt] healthy
Getränk *n* [gəˈtʀɛŋk] drink
Getriebe *n* [gəˈtʀi:bə] gearbox, transmission
Gewicht *n* [gəˈvɪçt] weight
Gewinn *m* [gəˈvɪn] profit
gewinnen [gəˈvɪnn] to win
gewiss [gəˈvɪs] certain(ly), sure(ly)
gewöhnlich [gəˈvø:nlɪç] usual, ordinary
gewohnt [gəˈvo:nt] usual
gewöhnt sein [ˌˀɛtvas gəˈvø:nt zaɪn] be used to
Gewölbe *n* [gəˈvœlbə] vault(s)
Gewürz *n* [gəˈvʏɐts] spice, seasoning
Giebel *m* [gi:bl] gable
Gift *n* [gɪft] poison
giftig [ˈgɪftɪç] poisonous
glänzend [glɛntsnt] splendid, glorious
Glas *n* [gla:s] glass
Glasmalerei *f* [ˈgla:sma:ləˌʀaɪ] glass painting
glauben [glaʊbm] believe
gleich [glaɪç] same; immediately, at once
gleichfalls [ˈglaɪçfals] also; likewise
gleichzeitig [ˈglaɪçtsaɪtʰɪç] simultaneous(ly)
Gleis *n* [glaɪs] platform
Glück *n* [glʏk] luck; success
glücklich [ˈglʏklɪç] happy; lucky
Glückwunsch *m* [ˈglʏkvʊnʃ] congratulations
Glühbirne *f* [ˈgly:bɪɐnə] light bulb
Gold *n* [ˈgɔlt] gold
Goldschmiedekunst *f* [ˈgɔltʃmi:dəˌkʊnst] gold work
Golf *n* [gɔlf] golf
Golfclub *m* [ˈgɔlfklʊp] *(establishment)* golf club
Golfschläger *m* [ˈgɔlfʃlɛ:gɐ] *(implement)* golf club
Gotik *f* [ˈgo:tik] Gothic
Gott *m* [gɔt] God
Grab *n* [gʀa:p] grave, tomb
Grabmal *n* [ˈgʀa:bma:l] *(tomb)* monument
Grafik *f* [ˈgʀa:fɪk] graphic arts
Gramm *n* [gʀam] gram(s)
Gras *n* [gʀa:s] grass
Gräte *f* [ˈgʀɛ:tə] fishbone
gratis [ˈgʀa:tɪs] free
gratulieren [gʀatʰʊˈli:ʀən /-ˈliɐn] congratulate
grau [gʀaʊ] grey
Grenze *f* [ˈgʀɛntsə] border
Grieche/Griechin *m/f* [ˈgʀi:çə/ˈgʀi:çɪn] Greek
griechisch *adj* [ˈgʀi:çɪʃ] Greek
Grill *m* [gʀɪl] grill; **vom Grill** [fɔm ˈgʀɪl] grilled
Grillkohle *f* [ˈgʀɪlko:lə] charcoal
Grippe *f* [ˈgʀɪpə] flu, influenza
groß [gʀo:s] big, large; tall; great
großartig [ˈgʀo:s(ˀ)a:tɪç] great
Größe *f* [ˈgʀø:sə] size; height
Großmutter *f* [ˈgʀo:smʊtʰɐ] grandmother
Großvater *m* [ˈgʀo:sfa:tʰɐ] grandfather
grün [gʀy:n] green
Grund *m* [gʀʊnt] reason, cause
grüne Bohnen [ˌgʀy:nə ˈbo:nn] green beans
grüne Versicherungskarte *f* [ˈgry:nə fɐˈzɪçəʀʊŋska:tə] green card
Gruppe *f* [ˈgʀʊpʰə] group
grüßen [ˈgʀy:sn] greet
gültig [ˈgʏltʰɪç] valid
Gummistiefel *m pl* [ˈgʊmiʃti:fl] rubber boots, wellingtons
Gurke *f* [ˈgʊɐkə] cucumber
Gürtel *m* [gʏɐtl] belt
gut [gu:t] *(adj)* good; *(adv)* well

Gutschein *m* ['gu:tʃaɪn] voucher
Gymnastik *f* [gʏm'nastɪk] gymnastics

H

Haar *n* [ha:] hair
Haargel *n* ['ha:ge:l] hair gel
Haarklammern *f pl* ['ha:klamɐn] hairpins
haben ['ha:bm] have
Hackfleisch *n* ['hakflaɪʃ] mince(d meat)
Hafen *m* ['ha:fn] port
Hähnchen *n* [hɛ:nçn] chicken
Haken *m* [ha:kŋ] hook
halb [halp] *(adj/adv)* half
Hälfte *f* ['hɛlftə] half
Halle *f* ['halə] hall
Hals *m* [hals] neck, throat
Halsschmerzen *m pl* ['halʃmɛɐtsn] sore throat
Halstabletten *f pl* ['halsta,blɛtn] throat lozenges
Halstuch *n* ['halstu:x] *(decorative)* scarf
halt! [halt] halt!, stop!
haltbar ['haltba:] durable; ~ **bis** use by
Haltbarkeit *f* ['haltba(:)kaɪt] best before, sell-by date
Haltegriff *m* ['haltəgʀɪf] handle
halten [haltn] hold; keep; last; stop
Haltestelle *f* ['haltəʃtɛlə] stop
Hand *f* [hant] hand
Handball *m* ['hantbal] handball
Handbike *n* ['hɛntbaɪk] hand-operated bike
Handbremse *f* ['hantbʀɛmzə] hand brake
Handgas *n* ['hantga:s] hand throttle
handgemacht ['hantgəmaxt] handmade
Handlauf *m* ['hantlaʊf] handrail
Handschuhe *m pl* ['hantʃu:ə] gloves
Handtasche *f* ['han(t)taʃə] handbag
Handtuch *n* ['han(t)tu:x] towel
Handy *n* ['hɛndi] mobile (phone)
Handygeschäft *n* ['hɛndigə,ʃɛft] mobile communications centre
hart [ha:t] hard, solid
hässlich ['hɛslɪç] ugly
häufig ['hɔɪfɪç] frequent(ly)
Hauptbahnhof *m* ['haʊptba:nho:f ('haʊpba:nof)] main station
Hauptpostamt *n* ['haʊpt,pɔstˀamt] main post office
Hauptquartier *n* ['haʊptkva,tiɐ] headquarters
Hauptrolle *f* ['haʊptʀɔlə] leading role
hauptsächlich ['haʊptzɛçlɪç] especially; mainly
Hauptsaison *f* ['haʊptzɛ,zɔŋ] high season
Hauptspeise *f* ['haʊptʃpaɪzə] main course
Hauptstadt *f* ['haʊptʃtat] capital
Hauptstraße *f* ['haʊptʃtʀa:sə] main street
Haus *n* [haʊs] house; **im Haus** [ˀɪm haʊs] indoors
Hausbesitzer/in *m/f* ['haʊsbəzɪtsɐ/-bəzɪtsəʀɪn] landlord/landlady
Hausboot *n* ['haʊsbo:t] houseboat
hausgemacht ['haʊsgəmaxt] homemade
Hausnummer *f* ['haʊsnʊmɐ] house number
Haustiere *n pl* ['haʊsti:ʀə] pets
Haut *f* [haʊt] skin
heben [e:bm] to lift
Heilbad *n* ['haɪlba:t] therapeutic bath
Heilfasten *n* ['haɪlfastn] fasting cure
heilig ['haɪlɪç] holy
Heiligabend [,haɪlɪç 'ˀa:bmt] Christmas Eve
Heiliger Abend ['haɪlɪgɐ 'ˀa:bmt] Christmas Eve
Heilmittel *n* ['haɪlmɪtl] remedy
Heimat *f* ['haɪma:t] home, native country
Heimreise *f* ['haɪmʀaɪzə] return journey, trip home
heiraten ['haɪʀa:tn] marry
heiser ['haɪzɐ] hoarse
heiß [haɪs] hot
heißen [haɪsn] be called
heiter ['haɪtɐ] *(weather)* clear
heizen [haɪtsn] to heat
Heizung *f* ['haɪtsʊŋ] heating
hellblau [hɛl'blaʊ] light blue
Hemd *n* [hɛmt] shirt
herb [hɛɐp] *(wine)* dry
Herbst *m* ['hɛɐpst] autumn, *(US)* fall
Herd *m* [heɐt] cooker, stove
herein! [hɐ'ʀaɪn] come in!
Hering *m* ['he:ʀɪŋ] herring
Herpes *m* ['hɛɐpəs] herpes
Herr *m* [hɛɐ] gentleman; Mr
Herrenfriseur *m* ['hɛʀənfʀɪ'zøɐ] barber's
Herrenslip *m* ['hɛʀənslɪp] briefs
Herrentoilette *f* ['hɛʀənto,lɛtə] Gents, Men's Room
herrlich ['hɛɐlɪç] glorious, splendid, terrific
herum [hɐ'ʀʊm] around
Herz *n* [hɛɐts] heart
Herzbeschwerden *f pl* ['hɛɐtsbəʃveɐdn] heart trouble
Herzinfarkt *m* ['hɛɐtsɪnfa:kt] cardiac infarction, heart attack

herzlich [ˈhɛɐtslɪç] warm, sincere
Herzschrittmacher *m* [ˈhɛɐt(s)ʃʀɪtmaxɐ] pacemaker
Heu-Bad *n* [ˈhɔɪba:t] hay bath
Heuschnupfen *m* [ˈhɔɪʃnʊpfn] hay fever
heute [ˈhɔɪtə] today; **heute Morgen** [hɔɪtə ˈmɔɐgŋ] this morning; **heute Abend** [hɔɪtə ˈʔa:bmt] this evening; **heute Nacht** [hɔɪtʰ(ə) ˈnaxt] tonight
Hexenschuss *m* [ˈhɛksnʃʊs] lumbago
hier [hiɐ] here
Hilfe *f* [ˈhɪlfə] help, aid; **erste Hilfe** [ˌʔeɐstə ˈhɪlfə] first aid
Himmel *m* [hɪml] sky; heaven
hinausgehen [hɪˈnaʊsge:n] go out, leave
hindern [ˈhɪndɐn] prevent, hinder
hinlegen [ˈhɪnle:gŋ] put down; **sich ~** [zɪç ˈhɪnle:gŋ] lie down
hinter [ˈhɪntʰɐ] behind
hinterlassen [hɪntɐˈlasn] to leave
hinterlegen [hɪntʰɐˈle:gŋ] to deposit
hinzufügen [hɪnˈtsu:fy:gŋ] add
Hirnhautentzündung *f* [ˈhɪʀnhaʊtɛnˌtsʏndʊŋ] meningitis
Hitze *f* [ˈhɪtsə] heat
HIV-positiv [haʔiˌfaʊ-ˈpo:zɪti:f] HIV positive
hoch [ho:x] high
höchstens [hø:çstns/hø:kstns] at the most, at best
Hochzeit *f* [ˈhɔxtsaɪt] wedding
Hof *m* [ho:f] (court)yard
höflich [ˈhø:flɪç] polite
Höhe *f* [ˈhøə] height
Höhepunkt *m* [ˈhøəpʰʊŋkt] highlight; *(career)* peak, height; *(film, play)* climax
Höhle *f* [ˈhø:lə] cave
holen [ho:ln] fetch, get
Holz *n* [hɔlts] wood
Holzschnitt *m* [ˈhɔltʃnɪt] woodcut
Honig *m* [ˈho:nɪç] honey
hören [ˈhø:ʀən/høɐn] hear
Hörer *m* [ˈhø:ʀɐ] receiver
Hose *f* [ˈho:zə] trousers, *(US)* pants
hübsch [hʏpʃ] pretty, cute
Hüfte *f* [ˈhʏftə] hip
Hügel *m* [hy:gl] hill
Hund *m* [hʊnt] dog
hungrig [ˈhʊŋʀɪç] hungry
Hupe *f* [ˈhu:pə] *(car)* horn
Husten *m* [hu:stn] cough
Hustensaft *m* [ˈhu:stnzaft] cough mixture/syrup
Hut *m* [hu:t] hat
Hütte *f* [ˈhʏtʰə] hut, cabin

I

ich [ʔɪç] I
Idee *f* [ʔiˈde:] idea
Ihnen [ʔi:nn] *(polite)* to/for you
ihr [ʔiɐ] her, their
Illustrierte *f* [ɪlʊˈstʀiɐtə] *(glossy)* magazine
Imbiss *m* [ˈʔɪmbɪs] snack
immer [ˈʔɪmɐ] always
Impfpass *m* [ˈʔɪm(p)fpas] vaccination card
Impfung *f* [ˈʔɪmpfʊŋ] vaccination
Impressionismus *m* [ʔɪmpʀɛsjoˈnɪsmʊs] impressionism
in [ʔɪn] in
inbegriffen [ˈʔɪnbəgʀɪfn] included
Infektion *f* [ʔɪnfɛkˈtsjo:n] infection
informieren [ʔɪnfɔˈmi:ʀən/-ˈmiɐn] inform
Infusion *f* [ʔɪnfʊˈzjo:n] infusion
Inhalt *m* [ˈʔɪnhalt] contents
Inlandsflug *m* [ˈʔɪnlantsflu:k] domestic flight
innen [ʔɪnn] inside
Innenhof *m* [ˈʔɪnnho:f] inner courtyard
Innenstadt *f* [ˈʔɪnnʃtat] town centre
Inschrift *f* [ˈʔɪnʃʀɪft] inscription
Insekt *n* [ʔɪnˈzɛkt] insect
Insel *f* [ʔɪnzl] island
Insulin *n* [ʔɪnzʊˈli:n] insulin
Inszenierung *f* [ʔɪntsəˈni:ʀʊŋ] *(stage)* production
interessant [ʔɪntʀəˈsant] interesting
interessieren, sich ~ (für) [zɪç ʔɪntʀəˈsi:ʀən /-ˈsiɐn fyɐ] be interested (in)
iPod *m* [ˈʔaɪpɔt] iPod
irisch [ˈʔi:ʀɪʃ] Irish
Irland [ˈʔɪɐlant] Ireland, Eire
irren, sich ~ [zɪç ˈʔɪʀən/ˈʔɪɐn] be mistaken
Irrtum *m* [ˈʔɪɐtʰu:m] mistake
Ischias *m* [ˈʔɪʃias] sciatica

J

Jacke *f* [ˈjakə] jacket
Jahr *n* [ja:] year
Jahreszeit *f* [ˈja:ʀəstsaɪt] season
Jahrhundert *n* [jaˈhʊndɐt] century
jährlich [ˈjɛɐlɪç] annual(ly)
Jahrmarkt *m* [ˈja:ma:kt] funfair
Jänner [ˈjɛnɐ] *(Austria)* January
Januar [ˈjanʊa:] January
Jazz *m* [ˈdʒɛs] jazz
Jazzgymnastik *f* [ˈdʒɛsgʏmˌnastɪk] jazz aerobics
Jeans *f* [ˈdʒi:ns] jeans
jede(r, s) [ˈje:də(-dɐ, -dəs)] every, each
jedermann [ˈje:dɐman] everybody
jedoch [jeˈdɔx] however
jemand [ˈje:mant] somebody; anybody

jene(r,s) [ˈjeːnə (-nɐ, -nəs)] that, *(pl)* those
jetzt [jɛtst] now
Jodtinktur *f* [ˈjoːtɪŋktuɐ] tincture of iodine
joggen [ˈdʒɔgŋ] to jog
Joghurt *m* [ˈjoːgʊɐt] yoghurt
Jugendstil *m* [ˈjuːgŋtstiːl] art nouveau
Juli [ˈjuːli] July
jung [jʊŋ] young
Junge *m* [ˈjʊŋə] boy
Junggeselle *m* [ˈjʊŋgəzɛlə] bachelor
Juni [ˈjuːni] June
Juwelier *m* [juveˈliɐ] jeweller's

K

Kabarett *n* [kabaˈʀeː] cabaret
Kabine *f* [kaˈbiːnə] cabin; cubicle
Kaffee *m* [ˈkafeː/kaˈfeː] coffee
Kaffeefilter *m* [ˈkafefɪltɐ/kaˈfeːfɪltɐ)] coffee filter
Kaffeelöffel *m* [ˈkafelœfl/kaˈfeːlœfl] coffee spoon
Kaffeemaschine *f* [ˈkafemaʃiːnə] coffee machine
Kai *m* [kaɪ] quay
Kalbfleisch *n* [ˈkalpflaɪʃ] veal
kalorienarm [kaloˈʁiːnˀaːm] low-calorie
kalt [kʰalt] cold
Kamera *f* [ˈkaməʀaː] camera
Kamillentee *m* [kaˈmɪl(ə)nteː] camomile tea
Kamm *m* [kam] comb
kämmen [kɛmm] to comb
Kanal *m* [kʰaˈnaːl] canal; channel
Kaninchen *n* [kaˈniːnçn] rabbit
Kanu *n* [ˈkaːnu] canoe
Kapelle *f* [kaˈpɛlə] chapel
Kapitän *m* [kapiˈtɛːn] captain
kaputt [kʰaˈpʰʊt] broken, out of order
Karfreitag [kaːˈfʀaɪtaːk] Good Friday
Karotten *f pl* [kaˈʀɔtn] carrots
Karte *f* [ˈkaːtə] ticket
Kartoffeln *f pl* [kaˈtɔfln] potatoes
Käse *m* [ˈkɛːzə] cheese
Kasse *f* [ˈkʰasə] cash-desk; box-office, ticket-office
Kassette *f* [kaˈsɛtə] cassette
Kathedrale *f* [kateˈdʀaːlə] cathedral
Katze *f* [ˈkʰatsə] cat
kaufen [kʰaʊfn] to buy
Kaufhaus *n* [ˈkaʊfhaʊs] department store
kaum [kʰaʊm] hardly, scarcely, barely
Kaution *f* [kʰaʊˈtsjoːn] security, down payment
Kehle *f* [keːlə] throat
Kehrschaufel *f* [ˈkeɐʃaʊfl] dustpan
kein [kʰaɪn] no
keiner [ˈkʰaɪnɐ] nobody
Kellner/in *m/f* [ˈkɛlnɐ/ˈkɛlnəʀɪn] waiter/waitress
kennen [kʰɛnn] to know; **kennen lernen** [ˈkʰɛnnlɛɐnn] to meet
Keramik *f* [keˈʀaːmɪk] ceramics
Kerzen *f pl* [kɛɐtsn] candles
Ketschup *n* [ˈkɛtʃap] ketchup
Kette *f* [ˈkɛtə] chain; necklace
Keuchhusten *m* [ˈkɔɪçhuːstn] whooping-cough
Kfz-Schein *m* [kaˀefˈtsɛtʃaɪn] car registration documents
Kiefer *m* [ˈkiːfɐ] jaw; pine
Kilo *n* [ˈkiːlo] kilogram(s)
Kilometer *m* [ˌkiloˈmeːtɐ] kilometre
Kind *n* [kʰɪnt] child
Kinder *n pl* [ˈkɪndɐ] children **Kinderbecken** *n* [ˈkɪndɐbɛkŋ] children's pool
Kinderbetreuung *f* [ˈkɪndɐbətʀɔjʊŋ] babysitting service
Kinderbett *n* [ˈkɪndɐbɛt] cot
Kinderermäßigung *f* [ˈkɪndɐˀɐˈmɛːsɪgʊŋ] child reduction
Kinderkleidung *f* [ˈkɪndɐklaɪdʊŋ] children's clothing
Kinderkrankheit *f* [ˈkɪndɐˌkʀaŋkhaɪt] children's illness
Kinderlähmung *f* [ˈkɪndɐlɛːmʊŋ] polio
Kindernahrung *f* [ˈkɪndɐnaːʀʊŋ] baby food
Kindersitz *m* [ˈkɪndɐzɪts] child seat
Kinderspielplatz *m* [ˈkɪndɐʃpiːlplats] children's playground
Kinderteller *m* [ˈkɪndɐtɛlɐ] children's portion
Kino *n* [ˈkiːno] cinema, movie theater
Kirche *f* [ˈkɪɐçə] church
Kirchturm *m* [ˈkɪɐçtʊɐm] steeple
Kirmes *f* [ˈkɪɐməs] fair, fête
Kirschen *f pl* [kɪɐʃn] cherries
Kiste *f* [ˈkʰɪstə] box, chest
Kiwi *f* [ˈkiːvi] kiwi fruit
Klang *m* [klaŋ] sound
klar [klaː] clear
Klasse *f* [ˈklasə] class
Klassik *f* [ˈklasɪk] classical
Klassiker *m* [ˈklasɪkɐ] classic film
Klassizismus *m* [klasɪˈtsɪsmʊs] classicism
Kleid *f* [klaɪt] dress
Kleiderbügel *m* [ˈklaɪdɐbyːgl] coat hanger
Kleiderhaken *m* [ˈklaɪdɐhaːkŋ] peg
Kleidung *f* [ˈklaɪdʊŋ] clothing
klein [klaɪn] little, small
Klima *n* [ˈkliːmaː] climate
Klimaanlage *f* [ˈkliːmɐˀanˌlaːgə] air-conditioning
Klingel *f* [klɪŋl] bell

Klippe *f* [ˈklɪpə] cliff
Kloster *n* [ˈklo:stɐ] monastery; convent
klug [klu:k] clever, intelligent
Kneipe *f* [ˈknaɪpə] pub
Kneipp-Anwendung *f* [ˈknaɪpanˌvɛndʊŋ] kneipism
Knie *n* [kni:] knee
Knoblauch *m* [ˈkno:blaʊx] garlic
Knöchel *m* [knœçl] ankle
Knochen *m* [knɔxn] bone
Knochenbruch *m* [ˈknɔxnbʀʊx] fracture
Knopf *m* [knɔpf] button
Koch *m* [kɔx] cook
Kochbuch *n* [ˈkɔxbu:x] cookbook
kochen [kʰɔxn] to cook; *(coffee, tea)* make; *(water)* boil
Kocher *m* [ˈkɔxɐ] cooker
Köchin *f* [ˈkʰœxɪn] cook
Kochnische *f* [ˈkɔxni:ʃə] kitchenette
Koffer *m* [ˈkʰɔfɐ] suitcase
Kofferraum *m* [ˈkɔfɐʀaʊm] boot, *(US)* trunk
Kohl *m* [ko:l] cabbage
Kokosnuss *f* [ˈko:kosnʊs] coconut
Kolik *f* [ˈko:lɪk] colic
Kollege/Kollegin*m/f* [kʰoˈle:gə / kʰoˈle:gɪn] colleague
kommen [kʰɔmm] come
Komödie *f* [koˈmø:diə] comedy
Kompass *m* [ˈkʰɔmpʰas] compass
Komponist/in *m/f* [kɔmpoˈnɪst/ -ɪn] composer
Konditorei *f* [kɔnditoˈʀaɪ] cake shop
Kondom *n* [kɔnˈdo:m] condom
König *m* [ˈkø:niç] king
Königin *f* [ˈkø:nɪgɪn] queen
können [ˈkʰœnn] be able to, can
Konsulat *n* [kʰɔnzʊˈla:t] consulate
Kontakt *m* [kʰɔnˈtʰakt] contact
Konto *n* [ˈkɔnto] account
Kontrolleur/in *m/f* [kɔntʀoˈløɐ/ -ˈløʀɪn] inspector
kontrollieren [kʰɔntʀoˈli:ʀən/ -ˈliɐn] to control; to check
Konzert *n* [kɔnˈtsɛɐt] concert
Kopf *m* [kɔpf] head
Kopfhörer *m* [ˈkɔpfhø:ʀɐ] headphones
Kopfkissen *n* [ˈkɔpfkɪsn] pillow
Kopfsalat *m* [ˈkɔpfsaˌla:t] lettuce
Kopfschmerzen *m pl* [ˈkɔpfʃmɛɐtsn] headache
Kopfschmerztabletten *f pl* [ˈkɔpfʃmɛɐtstaˌblɛtn] headache tablets
Kopie *f* [koˈpi:] copy
Korb *m* [kɔɐp] basket
Korkenzieher *m* [ˈkɔɐkŋtsi:ɐ] corkscrew
Körper *m* [ˈkœɐpʰɐ] body
kosten [kʰɔstn] to cost
kostenlos [ˈkʰɔstnlo:s] free (of charge)
kostspielig [ˈkɔs(t)ʃpi:lɪç] expensive
Kostüm *n* [kɔsˈty:m] *(women's)* suit
Kotelett *n* [ˈkɔtlɛt] chop, cutlet
Krabben *f pl* [kʀabm] shrimps
kräftig [ˈkʀɛftɪç] strong
Krafttraining *n* [ˈkʀaftʀɛ:nɪŋ] weight training
Krampf *m* [kʀampf] cramp
krank [kʀaŋk] ill, sick; **krank werden** [ˈkʀaŋk veɐdn] be taken ill, get sick
Krankenhaus *n* [ˈkʀaŋkŋhaʊs] hospital
Krankenkasse *f* [ˈkʀaŋkŋkasə] health insurance scheme/company
Krankenschwester *f* [ˈkʀaŋkŋʃvɛstɐ] nurse
Krankenwagen *m* [ˈkʀaŋkŋva:gŋ] ambulance
Krankheit *f* [ˈkʀaŋkhaɪt] illness
Kratzer *m* [ˈkʁatsɐ] scratch
Kräuter *n pl* [ˈkʀɔɪtɐ] herbs
Krawatte *f* [kʀaˈvatə] tie
kreativ [kʀeaˈti:f] creative
Krebs *m* [kʀe:ps] cancer; crab
Kreditkarte *f* [kʀedi:tka:tə] credit card
Kreislaufmittel *n* [ˈkʀaɪslaʊfˌmɪtl] cardiac stimulant
Kreislaufstörung *f* [ˈkʀaɪslaʊfˌʃtø:ʀʊŋ] circulatory disorder
Kreuz *n* [kʀɔɪts] cross
Kreuzgang *m* [ˈkʀɔɪtsgaŋ] cloister
Kreuzung *f* [ˈkʀɔɪtsʊŋ] intersection, junction
kriegen [kʀi:gŋ] catch, get
Kriminalroman *m* [kʀɪmiˈna:lʀoma:n] thriller
Kristall *m* [kʀɪsˈtal] crystal
Krone *f* [ˈkʀo:nə] crown
Krücke *f* [ˈkʀʏkə] crutch
Küche *f* [ˈkʰʏçə] kitchen
Küchensieb *n* [ˈkʏçnzi:p] sieve
Kuchen *m* [kʊ:xn] cake
Kugelschreiber *m* [ˈku:glʃʀaɪbɐ] ballpoint pen
kühl [kʰy:l] cool
Kühlelement *n* [ˈky:lɛləˌmɛnt] ice pack
Kühler *m* [ˈky:lɐ] *(car)* radiator
Kühlschrank *m* [ˈky:lʃʀaŋk] fridge, refrigerator
Kühlwasser *n* [ˈky:lvasɐ] cooling water
Kuli *m* [ˈku:li] biro
Kultur *f* [kʰʊlˈtʰuɐ] culture
Kümmel *m* [kʏml] caraway seed(s)
Kunde/Kundin*m/f* [ˈkʰʊndə /ˈkʰʊndɪn] customer
Kunst *f* [kʊnst] art
Kunstgewerbe *n* [ˈkʊnstgəvɛɐbə] arts and crafts
Kunsthändler/in *m/f* [ˈkʊnstˌhɛntlɐ/-ˌhɛntləʀɪn] art dealer
Kuppel *f* [kʊpl] dome

Kupplung *f* ['kʊplʊŋ] *(car)* clutch
Kürbis *m* ['kʏɐbɪs] pumpkin
Kurs *m* [kʊɐs] course
Kurtaxe *f* ['kuɐtaksə] visitor's tax
Kurve *f* ['kʊɐvə] bend, curve
kurz [kʰʊɐts] short
kurze Hose *f* ['kʊɐtsə 'ho:zə] shorts
Kurzfilm *m* [kʊɐtsfɪlm] short film
kurzfristig ['kʰʊɐtsfʀɪstɪç] at short notice
kürzlich ['kʏɐtslɪç] recently
Kurzschluss *m* ['kʊɐtʃlʊs] short-circuit
Kuss *m* [kʰʊs] kiss
küssen [kʰʏsn] to kiss
Küste *f* ['kʰʏstə] coast

L

lachen [laxn] to laugh
lächerlich ['lɛçɐlɪç] ridiculous
Ladegerät *n* ['la:dəgəʀɛ:t] battery charger
Ladekabel *(Handy)* *n* ['la:dəka:bl ('hɛndi)] battery charger lead *(mobile phone)*
Laden *m* ['la:dn] shop, store
Lage *f* ['la:gə] situation; position, location
Lähmung *f* ['lɛ:mʊŋ] paralysis
Lammfleisch *n* ['lamflaɪʃ] *(meat)* lamb
Lampe *f* ['lampə] lamp
Land *n* [lant] country; land
Landgut *n* ['lantgu:t] estate
Landkarte *f* ['lantkʰa:tʰə] map
Landschaft *f* ['lantʃaft] scenery
Landsmann *m* ['lantsman] fellow countryman
Landstraße *f* ['lantʃtʀa:sə] country road
Landung *f* ['landʊŋ] landing
lang [laŋ] long
langsam ['laŋza:m] slow(ly)
langweilig ['laŋvaɪlɪç] boring
Laptop *m* ['lɛptɔp] laptop
Lärm *m* [lɛɐm] noise
lassen [lasn] to let; to leave
lästig ['lɛstɪç] annoying
laufen [laʊfn] to run; to go; to walk
Läuse *f pl f* ['lɔɪzə] lice
laut [laʊt] loud; noisy
Lautsprecher *m* ['laʊtʃpʀɛçɐ] speaker
leben [le:bm] to live
Leben *n* [le:bm] life
Lebensmittel *n* ['le:bmsmɪtl] food
Lebensmittelgeschäft *n* ['le:bmsmɪtlgəˌʃɛft] food store, grocery store
Lebensmittelvergiftung *f* ['le:bmsmɪtlfeˌgɪftʊŋ] food poisoning
Leber *f* ['le:bɐ] liver
lebhaft ['le:phaft] lively
lecker ['lɛkɐ] tasty
Lederjacke *f* ['le:dɐjakə] leather jacket
ledig ['le:dɪç] single
leer [leɐ] empty
Leerlauf *m* ['leɐlaʊf] *(gear)* neutral
Leerung *f* ['le:ʀʊŋ] collection (of mail)
legen [le:gŋ] put
Leggings *f* ['lɛgɪŋs] leggings
lehren ['le:ʀən/leɐn] teach
leicht [laɪçt] easy; slight; *(weight)* light
Leichtathletik *f* ['laɪçtˀatˌle:tɪk] athletics
leider ['laɪdɐ] unfortunately
leihen [laɪn] lend; borrow
Leinen *n* [laɪnn] linen
leise ['laɪzə] quiet(ly)
Leistenbruch *m* ['laɪstnbʀʊx] hernia, rupture
Leiter/in *m/f* ['laɪtɐ/'laɪtəʀɪn] head, manager, boss
Leitung *f* ['laɪtʊŋ] *(telephone)* line
lernen [lɛɐnn] learn
lesen [le:zn] read
letzte(r, s) ['lɛtstʰə (-tʰɐ' -tʰəs)] last
Leute *pl* ['lɔɪtʰə] people
Licht *n* [lɪçt] light
Lichtmaschine *f* ['lɪçtmaʃi:nə] dynamo, generator
Lichtschutzfaktor *m* ['lɪçtʃʊtsˌfaktoɐ] protection factor
lieb [li:p] nice; **jdn lieb haben** [ˌjemandn 'li:p ha:bm] be fond of s.o.; Liebe(r) ['li:bə/'li:bɐ] Dear
Liebe *f* ['li:bə] love
lieben [li:bm] to love
liebenswürdig ['li:bmsvʏɐdɪç] kind
lieber ['li:bɐ] *(adv)* rather
Liebling *m* ['li:plɪŋ] darling; favourite
Lied *n* [li:t] song
liegen [li:gŋ] to lie
Liegewiese *f* ['li:gəvi:zə] sunbathing area
Lift *m* [lɪft] elevator, lift
lila ['li:la] purple
Limonade *f* [lɪmo'na:də] lemonade
Linie *f* ['li:njə] line
linke(r, s) ['lɪŋkʰə (-kʰɐ' -kʰəs)] left(-hand)
links [lɪŋks] on the left, to the left
Linsen *f pl* [lɪnzn] lentils
Lippe *f* ['lɪpə] lip
Lippenstift *m* ['lɪpmʃtɪft] lipstick
Liter *m* ['li:tɐ] litre
Loch *n* [lɔx] hole, puncture
Locken *f pl* [lɔkŋ] curls
Lockenwickler *m pl* ['lɔkŋvɪklɐ] curlers
Löffel *m* [lœfl] spoon
Loge *f* ['lo:ʒə] box
Lorbeerblätter *n pl* ['lɔɐbeɐˌblɛtɐ] bayleaves

Luft *f* [lʊft] air
lüften [ˈlʏftn] to air
Luftkissenboot *n* [ˈlʊftkɪsnboːt] hovercraft
Luftpumpe *f* [ˈlʊftpʊmpə] pump
Lüge *f* [ˈlyːgə] lie
lügen [lyːgŋ] to (tell a) lie
Lunge *f* [ˈlʊŋə] lungs
Lungenentzündung *f* [ˈlʊŋənˀɛnˌtsʏndʊŋ] pneumonia
Lust *f* [lʊst] pleasure, joy; desire; lust
lustig [ˈlʊstɪç] merry, in a good mood; funny
luxuriös [lʊksʊʀiˈøːs] luxurious
Lymphdrainage *f* [ˈlʏmfdʁɛˌnaːʒə] lymphatic drainage

M

machen [ˈmaxn] do; make
Mädchen *n* [ˈmɛːtçn] girl
Magen *m* [maːgŋ] stomach
Magenschmerzen *m pl* [ˈmaːgŋʃmɛɐtsn] stomach-ache
mager [ˈmaːgɐ] lean, thin
Mahlzeit *f* [ˈmaːltsaɪt] meal
Mai [maɪ] May
Makrele *f* [maˈkʀeːlə] mackerel
Mal *n* [maːl] time
Malbuch *n* [ˈmaːlbuːx] colouring book
malen [maːln] to paint
Maler/in *m/f* [ˈmaːlɐ/ˈmaːləʀɪn] painter
Malerei *f* [maːləˈʀaɪ] *(type of art)* painting
manchmal [ˈmançmaːl] sometimes
Mandarinen *f pl* [mandaˈʀiːnn] mandarins
Mandelentzündung *f* [ˈmandlˀɛnˌtsʏndʊŋ] tonsilitis
Mandeln *f pl* [ˈmandln] almonds; tonsils
Mangel *m* [maŋl] defect, fault; lack, shortage
Mango *f* [ˈmaŋgo] mango
Mann *m* [man] man; husband
Männer *f* [m] men
Mannschaft *f* [ˈmanʃaft] team; crew
Mantel *m* [mantl] coat
Margarine *f* [magaˈʀiːnə] margarine
Marke *f* [ˈmaːkə] *(postage)* stamp
Markt *m* [maːkt] market
Marmelade *f* [maməˈlaːdə] jam, marmalade
März [mɛɐts] March
Maschine *f* [maˈʃiːnə] machine
Masern *f pl* [ˈmaːzɐn] measles
Massage *f* [maˈsaːʒə] massage
Material *n* [matʰ (ə)ʀiˈaːl] material
Matratze *f* [maˈtʀatsə] mattress
Mauer *f* [ˈmaʊɐ] *(external)* wall

Medikament *n* [medɪkaˈmɛnt] medicine
Meditation *f* [ˌmeditaˈtsjoːn] meditation
Meer *n* [meɐ] sea
Mehl *n* [meːl] flour
mehr [meɐ] more; **mehr als** [ˈmeɐ ˀals] more than
mein [maɪn] my
meinen [maɪnn] to mean; think
meinetwegen [ˈmaɪnətˌveːgŋ] I don't mind
Meinung *f* [ˈmaɪnʊŋ] opinion, view
melden [mɛldn] announce; inform
Melone *f* [meˈloːnə] melon
Memorystick *m* [ˈmɛmoʁistɪk] memory stick
Mensch *m* [mɛnʃ] person, man/woman; man
Menstruation *f* [mɛnstʀuaˈtsjon] menstruation
Menü *n* [meˈnyː] set meal
merken [mɛɐkŋ] be aware of; **sich etw.** ~ [zɪç ˈˀɛtvas ˈmɛɐkŋ] remember s. th.
Messe *f* [ˈmɛsə] *(rel.)* mass; fair, exhibition
Messer *n* [ˈmɛsɐ] knife
Meter *m* [ˈmeːtɐ] metre
Metzgerei *f* [mɛtsgəˈʀaɪ] butcher's
mich [mɪç] me
Miete *f* [ˈmiːtə] rent
mieten [ˈmiːtn] to rent, to hire
Migräne *f* [miˈgʀɛːnə] migraine
Mikrowelle *f* [ˈmiːkʀovɛlə] microwave
Milch *f* [mɪlç] milk
mild [mɪlt] mild
Millimeter *m* [ˈmɪliˌmeːtɐ] millimetre
mindestens [ˈmɪndəstns] at least
Minigolf *n* [ˈmɪnigɔlf] crazy golf
Minute *f* [miˈnuːtʰə] minute
mir [miɐ] (to) me
Missverständnis *n* [ˈmɪsfɐʃtɛntnɪs] misunderstanding
mit [mɪt] with
mitbringen [ˈmɪtbʀɪŋŋ] bring
Mittag *m* [ˈmɪtʰaːk] noon, midday
Mittagessen *n* [ˈmɪtakˌˀɛsn] lunch
Mitte *f* [ˈmɪtʰə] middle
mitteilen [ˈmɪtaɪln] inform
Mitteilung *f* [ˈmɪtʰaɪlʊŋ] announcement; memo
Mittel *n* [ˈmɪtl] means; remedy
Mittelalter *n* [ˈmɪtlˀaltɐ] Middle Ages
Mittelohrentzündung *f* [ˈmɪtlˀoɐˀɛnˌtsʏndʊŋ] inflammation of the middle ear
Mittwoch [ˈmɪtvɔx] Wednesday
Mixer *m* [ˈmɪksɐ] blender
Möbel *n* [møːbl] furniture
Mobiltelefon *n* [moˈbiːltelәˌfoːn] mobile phone

Mode *f* [ˈmo:də] fashion
Modell *n* [moˈdɛl] model
modern [moˈdɛɐn] modern, up to date
Modeschmuck *m* [ˈmo:dəʃmʊk] costume jewellery
mögen [ˈmø:gŋ] to like; to want
möglich [ˈmø:klɪç] possible
Monat *m* [ˈmo:na:t] month
monatlich [ˈmo:natlɪç] monthly
Mond *m* [mo:nt] moon
Montag [ˈmo:nta:k] Monday
Morgen *m* [mɔɐgŋ] morning
morgen früh/morgen Abend [mɔɐgŋ ˈfʀy:/mɔɐgŋ ˈˀa:bmt] tomorrow morning/tomorrow evening
morgens [ˈmɔɐgŋs] in the morning
Mosaik *n* [mozaˈˀi:k] mosaic
Motel *n* [moˈtɛl] motel
Motor *m* [ˈmo:toɐ] engine, motor
Motorboot *n* [ˈmo:tɔbo:t] motorboat
Motorhaube *f* [ˈmo:tɔˌhaʊbə] bonnet, *(US)* hood
Mountainbike *n* [ˈmaʊntnbaɪk] mountain bike
Möwe *f* [ˈmø:və] seagull
Mücke *f* [ˈmʏkʰə] gnat, midge, mosquito
Mückenschutz *m* [ˈmʏkŋʃʊts] insect repellant
müde [ˈmy:də] tired
Müll *m* [mʏl] rubbish, garbage
Mullbinde *f* [ˈmʊlbɪndə] gauze bandage
Mülltonne *f* [ˈmʏltʰɔnə] dustbin, trashcan
Mülltrennung *f* [ˈmʏltʁɛnʊŋ] separation of rubbish
Mumps *m* [mʊmps] mumps
Mund *m* [mʊnt] mouth
Mündung *f* [ˈmʏndʊŋ] *(river)* mouth
Münze *f* [ˈmʏntsə] coin
Muscheln *f pl* [mʊʃln] mussels
Museum *n* [muˈze:ʊm] museum
Musical *n* [ˈmju:zɪkl] musical
Musik *f* [muˈzi:k] music; **Musik hören** [mʊˈzi:k ˈhø:ʀən] listen to music
musizieren [mʊzɪˈtsi:ʀən] make music
Muskatnuss *f* [mʊsˈka:tnʊs] nutmeg
Muskel *m* [ˈmʊskl] muscle
Müsli *n* [ˈmy:sli] muesli
müssen [mʏsn] have to, must
Mutter *f* [mʊtʰɐ] mother
Mütze *f* [ˈmʏtsə] cap

N

nach [na:x] after; to
nach oben [nax ˈˀo:bm] up
nachher [ˈna:x(h)eɐ] afterwards
Nachmittag *m* [ˈna:xmɪtʰa:k] afternoon
nachmittags [ˈnaxmɪta:ks] in the afternoon
nachprüfen [ˈna:xpʀy:fn] to check
Nachricht *f* [ˈna:xʀɪçt] message; news
Nachsaison *f* [ˈna:xzeˌzɔŋ] low season, off-season
nachsehen [ˈna:xze:n] to check
nachsenden [ˈna:xzɛndn] send on
nächste(r, s) [ˈnɛ:çstə/ˈnɛ:kstə (-stɐ, -stəs)] next
Nacht *f* [naxt] night
Nachtisch *m* [ˈna:xtɪʃ] dessert, sweet
Nachtklub *m* [ˈnaxtklʊp] night club
nachts [naxts] at night
Nachttisch *m* [ˈnaxttɪʃ] bedside table
nackt [nakt] naked, nude
Nadel *f* [na:dl] needle
Nagellack *m* [ˈna:gllak] nail varnish/polish
Nagellackentferner *m* [ˈna:gllakɛntˌfɛɐnɐ] nail varnish/polish remover
Nagelschere *f* [ˈna:glʃe:ʀə] nail scissors
nahe [ˈna: (ə)] near, close; **nahe bei** [na: baɪ] close to
Nähe, in der ~ von [ˀɪn dɐ ˈnɛə fɔn] near
nähen [nɛ:n] sew, stitch (up)
nähere Angaben [ˈnɛəʀə ˈˀanga:bm] particulars
Nahrung *f* [ˈna:ʀʊŋ] food
Nahverkehrszug *m* [ˈna:feˌkeɐstsu:k] local train
Name *m* [na:mə] name
Narbe *f* [ˈna:bə] scar
Nase *f* [ˈna:zə] nose
Nasenbluten *n* [ˈna:znblu:tn] nosebleed
nass [nas] wet
Nationalitätskennzeichen *n* [natsjonalɪˈtɛ:tskɛntsaɪçn] international car index mark
Nationalpark *m* [natsjoˈna:lpa:k] national park
Natur *f* [naˈtʰuɐ] nature
natürlich [naˈtʰyɐlɪç] natural(ly); of course
Naturschutzgebiet *n* [naˈtuɐʃʊtsgəbi:t] nature reserve
Nebel *m* [ˈne:bl] fog
neben [ˈne:bm] next to, beside
Nebenkosten *f* [ˈne:bmkɔstn] additional costs
nehmen [ne:mm] to take
nein [naɪn] no
Nelken *f pl* [nɛlkŋ] cloves
nennen [nɛnn] to name, to call
Neoprenanzug *m* [neoˈpʀe:nˌˀantsu:k] wetsuit
Nerv *m* [nɛɐf] nerve

nervös [nɐˈvøːs] nervous
nett [nɛt] nice
neu [nɔɪ] new
neugierig [ˈnɔɪgiːʀɪç] curious
Neujahr [nɔɪˈjaː] New Year's Day
nicht [nɪçt] not; **noch nicht** [nɔx ˈnɪç(t)] not yet
Nichtraucherabteil *n* [ˈnɪçtʀaʊxɐˀapˌtaɪl] no-smoking compartment
nichts [nɪçts/nɪks] nothing
nie [niː] never
niemand [ˈniːmant] nobody
Niere *f* [ˈniːʀə] kidney
Nierenstein *m* [ˈniːʀənʃtaɪn] kidney stone
nirgends [ˈnɪɐgŋ (t)s] nowhere
noch [nɔx] still
Norden *m* [nɔɐdn] north
Nordirland [nɔatˈˀɪɐlant] Northern Ireland
Nordsee *f* [di ˈnɔɐtzeː] North Sea
normal [nɔˈmaːl] normal; standard
normalerweise [nɔˈmaːlɐvaɪzə] normally, usually
Notausgang *m* [ˈnoːtˀaʊsgaŋ] emergency exit
Notfall [ˈnoːtfal] emergency
nötig [ˈnøːtɪç] necessary
Notizblock *m* [noˈtiːtsblɔk] notepad
Notrufsäule *f* [ˈnoːtʀufzɔɪlə] emergency telephone
notwendig [ˈnoːtvɛndɪç] necessary
November [noˈvɛmbɐ] November
nüchtern [ˈnʏçtɐn] sober
Nudeln *f pl* [nuːdln] noodles, pasta
Nummer *f* [ˈnʊmɐ] number
nummerieren [nʊməˈʀiːʀən/-ˈʀiɐn] to number
Nummernschild *n* [ˈnʊmɐnʃɪlt] number plate, *(US)* license plate,
nun [nuːn] now; well
nur [nuɐ] only
Nüsse *f pl* [ˈnʏsə] nuts

O

ob [ˀɔp] whether
oben [ˀoːbm] up
Objektiv *n* [ˀɔbjɛkˈtiːf] lens
Obst *n* [ˀoːpst] fruit
Obst- und Gemüsehändler *m* [ˀoːpst ʊnt gəˈmyːzəˌhɛndlɐ] greengrocer('s)
obwohl [ˀɔpˈvoːl] although
oder [ˈˀoːdɐ] or
offen [ˀɔfn] open
öffentlich [ˈˀœfntlɪç] public
offiziell [ˀɔfɪˈtsjɛl] official
öffnen [ˈˀœfn (ə)n] to open
Öffnungszeiten *f pl* [ˈˀœfnʊŋstsaɪtn] opening hours, hours of business
oft [ˀɔft] often
ohne [ˈˀoːnə] without
ohne Kohlensäure [ˈˀoːnə ˈkoːl(ə)nzɔɪʀə] still, uncarbonated
in Ohnmacht fallen [ˀɪn ˈˀoːnmaxt faln] to faint
Ohr *n* [ˀoɐ] ear
Ohrentropfen *m pl* [ˈˀoːʀəntʀɔpfn] eardrops
Ohrringe *m pl* [ˈˀoːʀɪŋə] earrings
Oktober [ˀɔkˈtoːbɐ] October
Öl *n* [ˀøːl] oil
Ölgemälde *n* [ˈˀøːlgəˌmɛːldə] *(picture)* oil painting
Oliven *f pl* [ˀoˈliːvn] olives
Olivenöl *n* [ˀoˈliːvnˀøːl] olive oil
Ölmalerei *f* [ˈˀøːlmaːləˌʀaɪ] *(activity)* oil painting
Ölquelle *f* [ˈˀøːlˈkvɛlə] oil well
Ölwechsel *m* [ˈˀøːlvɛksl] oil change
Oper *f* [ˈˀoːpɐ] opera
Operation *f* [ˀɔpəʀaˈtsjoːn] operation; surgery
Operette *f* [ˀopəˈʀɛtə] operetta
Optiker *m* [ˈˀɔptɪkɐ] optician's
Orangensaft *m* [ˀoˈʀaŋʒnzaft] orange juice
Orchester *n* [ˀɔɐˈkɛstɐ] orchestra
Orden *m* [ˀɔɐdn] *(rel.)* order
ordinär [ˀɔdiˈnɛːɐ] vulgar
Ordnung *f* [ˈˀɔɐtnʊŋ] order
Original *n* [ˀɔʀɪgiˈnaːl] original
Originalfassung *f* [ˀoʀɪgɪˈnaːlfasʊŋ] original version
Ort *m* [ˀɔɐt] place; spot
Ortschaft *f* [ˈˀɔɐtʃaft] village, town
Ortsgespräch *n* [ˈˀɔɐtsgəʃpʀɛːç] local call
Osten *m* [ˀɔstn] east
Ostermontag [ˌˀoːstɐˈmoːntaːk] Easter Monday
Österreich [ˈˀøːstəʀaɪç] Austria
Österreicher/in *m/f* [ˈˀøːstəʀaɪçɐ/-ʀaɪçəʀɪn] Austrian

P

Paar [ˈpʰaː] pair; couple
paar, ein ~ [(ˀaɪ)n ˈpʰaː] a few
Päckchen *n* [pɛkçn] small packet
packen [pakŋ] to pack
Packung *f* [ˈpakʊŋ] box, pack
Paket *n* [paˈkeːt] parcel
Palast *m* [paˈlast] palace
Panne *f* [ˈpanə] breakdown, puncture
Pannendienst *m* [ˈpanndiːnst] breakdown service

Papier *n* [pa'piɐ] paper; **Papiere** *n pl* [pa'pi:ʀə] documents, papers
Papierservietten *f pl* [pa'piɐzɐˌvjɛtn] paper napkins/ serviettes
Papiertaschentücher *n pl* [pa'piɐˌtaʃnty:çɐ] paper handkerchiefs
Paprika *m* ['papʀɪka] paprika
Paprikaschoten *f pl* ['papʀɪkaˌʃo:tn] peppers
Parfüm *n* [pa'fy:m] perfume, scent
Parfümerie *f* [pafʏmə'ʀi:] perfumery
Park *m* [pʰa:k] park
parken ['pʰa:kŋ] to park
Parkett *n* [pa'kɛt] stalls
Pass *m* [pas] *(mountain)* pass
Passagier *m* [pasa'ʒiɐ] passenger
passen [pʰasn] to fit; to suit
Pauschalpreis *m* [paʊ'ʃa:lpʀaɪs] flat rate
Pelz *m* [pɛlts] fur
Perle *f* ['pɛɐlə] pearl
Person *f* [pʰɐ'zo:n] person
Personalausweis *m* [p(ɛ)ɐzo'na:lˌˀaʊsvaɪs] identity card
Personalien *pl* [pʰɐzo'na:ljən] particulars, personal data
persönlich [pʰɐ'zø:nlɪç] personal
Petersilie *f* [pe:tɐ'zi:ljə] parsley
Petroleum *n* [pe'tʀo:leʊm] paraffin
Pfad *m* [(p)fa:t] path
Pfand *n* [(p)fant] deposit; security
Pfanne *f* ['(p)fanə] pan
Pfeffer *m* ['pfɛfɐ] pepper
Pfeiler *m* ['pfaɪlɐ] pillar
Pferd *n* [pfeɐt] horse
Pfirsiche *m pl* ['pfɪɐzɪçə] peaches
Pflanze *f* [' (p)flantsə] plant
Pflaster *n* ['pflastɐ] plaster
pflegebedürftig ['pfle:gəbədʏɐftɪç] in need of care
Pfund *n* [(p)fʊnt] pound(s)
Pilot *m* [pi'lo:t] pilot
Pilz *m* [pɪlts] mushroom; **Pilzinfektion** *f* ['pɪltsɪnfɛkˌtsjo:n] fungal infection
Pkw *m* ['pe:kave:] car
Plakat *n* [pla'kʰa:t] poster
Planschbecken *n* ['planʃbɛkn] paddling pool
Plastikbeutel *m* ['plastɪkbɔɪtl] plastic bag
Plattenladen *m* ['platnla:dn] music shop
Platz *m* [plats] place; seat
Platzreservierung *f* ['platsʀezɐˌvi:ʀʊŋ] seat reservation
Plombe *f* ['plɔmbə] *(tooth)* filling
plötzlich ['plœtslɪç] suddenly
Polizei *f* [pɔlɪ'tsaɪ] police
Polizeiwagen *m* [pɔlɪ'tsaɪva:gŋ] police car
Polizist/Polizistin *m/f* [pɔlɪ'tsɪst/ pɔlɪ'tsɪstɪn] policeman/policewoman
Pony *m* ['pɔni] fringe
Portal *n* [pɔ(ɐ)'ta:l] portal
Portier *m* [pɔɐ'tje:] porter
Portion *f* [pɔ'tsjo:n] portion
Porto *n* ['pɔɐto] postage
Porträt *n* [pɔ(ɐ)'tʀɛ:] portrait
Porzellan *n* [pɔ(ɐ)tsə'la:n] porcelain, china
Postamt *n* ['pɔstamt] post office
Postkarte *f* ['pɔstka:tə] postcard
postlagernd ['pɔstla:gɐnt] poste restante
Postleitzahl *f* ['pɔstlaɪtsa:l] post code
Postsparbuch *n* ['pɔstʃpa:bu:x] post office savings book
praktisch ['pʀaktʰɪʃ] practical(ly)
Preis *m* [pʀaɪs] price; prize
Prellung *f* ['pʀɛlʊŋ] bruise
Premiere *f* [pʀəm'je:ʀə] premiere
Priester *m* ['pʀi:stɐ] priest
prima ['pʀi:ma:] great
privat [pʀɪ'va:t] private
Probe *f* ['pʀo:bə] experiment, test, trial
Problem *n* [pʀo'ble:m] problem
Produkt *n* [pʀo'dʊkt] product
Programmheft *n* [pʀo'gʀamhɛft] *(booklet)* programme
Promillegrenze *f* [pʀo'mɪləˌgʀɛntsə] legal alcohol limit
Prospekt *m* [pʀos'pɛkt] prospectus, leaflet, brochure
Prothese *f* [pʀo'te:zə] artificial limb
provisorisch [pʀovɪ'zo:ʀɪʃ] provisional, temporary
Prozent *n* [pʀo'tsɛnt] percent
Prozession *f* [pʀotsɛs'jo:n] procession
Prüfung *f* ['pʀy:fʊŋ] examination, test
Publikum *n* ['pʰʊblɪkʰʊm] public; audience
Puder *m* ['pu:dɐ] powder
Pullover *m* [pʊ'lo:vɐ] jumper, pullover, sweater
Puls *m* [pʊls] pulse
pünktlich ['pʰʏŋktlɪç] punctual(ly); on time
putzen [pʰʊtsn] to clean
Putzmittel *n* ['pʊtsmɪtl] cleaning agent

Q

Qualität *f* [kvalɪ'tʰɛ:t] quality
Qualle *f* ['kvalə] jellyfish
Quelle *f* ['kvɛlə] source; spring
quer durch [kveɐ dʊɐç] straight across/through
Quetschung *f* ['kvɛtʃʊŋ] bruise

Quittung *f* [ˈkvɪtʰʊŋ] receipt

R

Rabatt *m* [ʀaˈbat] discount
Rad *n* [ʀaːt] wheel
Rad fahren [ˈʀaːt ˈfaːʀən] to cycle
Radarkontrolle *f* [ʀaˈdaːkɔnˌtʀɔlə] radar check
Radierung *f* [ʀaˈdiːʀʊŋ] etching
Radio *n* [ˈʀaːdjoː] radio
Radsport *m* [ˈʀaːtʃpɔɐt] cycling
Radtour *f* [ˈʀaːttuɐ] cycle tour
Rampe *f* [ˈʀampə] ramp
rasch [ʀaʃ] quick
Rasen *m* [ʀaːzn] lawn, grass
Rasierapparat *m* [ʀaˈziɐˀapaˌʀaːt] shaver
Rasierklinge *f* [ʀaˈziɐklɪŋə] razor blade
Rasierpinsel *m* [ʀaˈziɐpɪnzl] shaving brush
Rasierschaum *m* [ʀaˈziɐʃaʊm] shaving foam
Rasierwasser *n* [ʀaˈziɐvasɐ] aftershave lotion
Rathaus *n* [ˈʀaːthaʊs] town hall
Rauch *m* [ʀaʊx] smoke
rauchen [ʀaʊxn] to smoke
Raucher/in *m/f* [ˈʀaʊxɐ/ˈʀaʊxəʀɪn] smoker
Raucherabteil *n* [ˈʀaʊxɐˀapˌtaɪl] smoking compartment
Raum *m* [ʀaʊm] space; room
rechnen [ˈʀɛçn(ə)n] calculate
Rechnung *f* [ˈʀɛçnʊŋ] bill, invoice
Recht *n* [ʀɛçt] right
rechte(r, s) [ˈʀɛçtə (-tɐ, -təs)] right(-hand)
rechts [ʀɛçts] on the right, to the right
Rechtsanwalt/-anwältin *m/f* [ˈʀɛçtsanvalt/-anvɛltɪn] lawyer
rechtzeitig [ˈʀɛçtsaɪtʰɪç] in time
reden [ʀeːdn] to talk
Reformhaus *n* [ʀeˈfɔɐmhaʊs] health food shop
regelmäßig [ˈʀeːglmɛːsɪç] regular(ly)
Regen *m* [ˈʀeːgŋ] rain
Regenmantel *m* [ˈʀeːgŋmantl] raincoat
Regenschauer *m* [ˈʀeːgŋʃaʊɐ] shower
Regie *f* [ʀəˈʒiː] *(film)* direction; directed by
Regierung *f* [ʀeˈgiːʀʊŋ] government
regnerisch [ˈʀeːknəʀɪʃ] rainy
Reibe *f* [ˈʁaɪbə] grater
reich [ʀaɪç] rich
reichen [ʀaɪçn] be sufficient; hand over, pass
reif [ʀaɪf] ripe
Reifen *m* [ˈʀaɪfn] tyre
Reifenpanne [ˈʀaɪfnˌpanə] flat tyre
reinigen [ˈʀaɪnɪgŋ] to clean
Reinigung *f* [ˈʀaɪnɪgʊŋ] dry-cleaner's
Reis *m* [ʀaɪs] rice
Reise *f* [ˈʀaɪzə] journey, trip
Reisebüro *n* [ˈʀaɪzəbyˌʀoː] travel agency
Reiseführer *m* [ˈʀaɪzəˌfyːʀɐ] guidebook
Reiseführer/in *m/f* [ˈʀaɪzəˌfyːʀɐ/-ˌfyːʀəʀɪn] guide, courier
Reisegesellschaft *f* [ˈʀaɪzəgəˌzɛlʃaft] party of tourists
reisen [ʀaɪzn] to travel
Reisende *m/f* [ˈʀaɪzndə] tourist
Reisepass *m* [ˈʀaɪzəpas] passport
Reisescheck *m* [ˈʀaɪzəʃɛk] traveller's cheque
Reisetasche *f* [ˈʀaɪzətaʃə] travelling bag
reißen [ʀaɪsn] to tear; to pull
reiten [ˈʀaɪtn] to ride
Reitschule *f* [ˈʀaɪtʃuːlə] riding school
Religion *f* [ʀelɪˈgjoːn] religion
Renaissance *f* [ʀənɛˈsa):s] Renaissance
rennen [ʀɛnn] to run
Rennrad *n* [ˈʀɛnʀaːt] racing bike
Reparatur *f* [ʀɛpaʀaˈtuɐ] repair
reparieren [ʀɛpʰaˈʀiːʀən /-ˈʀiɐn] to repair
reservieren [ʀɛzɐˈviːʀən /-ˈviɐn] to reserve
Reservierung *f* [ʀezɐˈviːʀʊŋ] reservation
Rest *m* [ʀɛst] *(remainder)* rest
Restaurant *n* [ʁɛstoˈʁɑ̃/ʁɛstoˈʁaŋ] restaurant
Rettungsboot *n* [ˈʀɛtʊŋsboːt] lifeboat
Rettungsring *m* [ˈʀɛtʊŋsʀɪŋ] life belt, *(US)* life preserver
Revue *f* [ʀeˈvyː] show
Rezept *n* [ʀeˈtsɛpt] prescription
Rezeption *f* [ʀetsɛpˈtsjoːn] reception
R-Gespräch *n* [ˈˀɛɐgəˌʃpʀɛːç] reverse charge call
Rheuma *n* [ˈʀɔɪma] rheumatism
Richter/in *m/f* [ˈʀɪçtɐ/ˈʀɪçtəʀɪn] judge
richtig [ˈʀɪçtɪç] right; proper
Richtung *f* [ˈʀɪçtʊŋ] direction
riechen [ʀiːçn] to smell
Rindfleisch *n* [ˈʀɪntflaɪʃ] beef
Rock *m* [ʀɔk] skirt
roh [ʀoː] raw; **roher Schinken** [ʀoːɐ ʃɪŋkŋ] smoked ham
Rohling *m* [ˈʁoːlɪŋ] blank
Rollschuhe *m pl* [ˈʀɔlʃuːə] roller skates
Rollstuhl *m* [ˈʀɔlʃtuːl] wheelchair
Rollstuhlfahrer/in *m/f* [ˈʀɔlʃtuːlˌfaːʀɐ/-ˌfaːʀəʀɪn] wheelchair user
Rollstuhlkabine *f* [ˈʀɔlʃtuːlkaˌbiːnə] wheelchair cabin
Roman *m* [ʀoˈmaːn] novel

röntgen [ˈʀœnçn] to X-ray
Röntgenaufnahme *f* [ˈʀœnçnˀaʊfnaːmə] X-ray
rosa [ˈʀoːza] pink
Rosmarin *m* [ˈʀoːsmaʀiːn] rosemary
rot [ʀoːt] red
Röteln *f pl* [ʀøːtln] German measles
Rotwein [ˈʀoːtvaɪn] red wine
Route *f* [ˈʀuːtʰə] route
Rücken *m* [ʀʏkŋ] back
Rückenschmerzen *m pl* [ˈʀʏkŋʃmɛɐtsn] backache
Rückfahrkarte *f* [ˈʀʏkfaːˌkaːtə] return ticket
Rückfahrt *f* [ˈʀʏkfaːt] return journey, trip back
Rückholservice *m* [ˈʀʏkhoːlœsœɐvɪs] pick-up service
Rückkehr *f* [ˈʀʏkʰeɐ] return
Rücklicht *n* [ˈʀʏklɪçt] rear light, tail light
Rucksack *m* [ˈʀʊkzak] rucksack, backpack
Rückspiegel *m* [ˈʀʏkʃpiːgl] rear-view mirror
rückwärts [ˈʀʏkvɛɐts] backwards
Rückwärtsgang *m* [ˈʀʏkvɛɐtsgaŋ] reverse gear
Ruderboot *n* [ˈʀuːdɐboːt] rowing boat
rudern [ˈʀuːdɐn] to row
rufen [ʀuːfn] to call
Ruhe *f* [ʀuə] rest; calm; silence
ruhen [ʀuːn] to rest
ruhig [ʀuɪç] silent, quiet, calm
Rührlöffel *m* [ˈʁyɐlœfl] stir spoon
Ruine *f* [ʀuˈʔiːnə] ruin
rund [ʀʊnt] *(adj)* round
Runde *f* [ˈʀʊndə] round
Rundfahrt *f* [ˈʀʊntfaːt] round trip, tour

S

Saal *m* [zaːl] room; hall
Sache *f* [ˈzaxə] thing; matter, affair
Sack *m* [zak] sack; bag
Safaripark *m* [zaˈfaːʀipaːk] safari park
Safe *m* [sɛɪf/seːf] safe
Safran *m* [ˈzafraːn] saffron
saftig [ˈzaftɪç] juicy
sagen [zaːgŋ] say; tell
Sahne *f* [ˈzaːnə] cream
Saison *f* [zɛˈzɔŋ] season
Salami *f* [zaˈlaːmi] salami
Salat *m* [zaˈlaːt] salad
Salatbüfett *n* [zaˈlaːtbʏˈfeː] salad bar
Salbe *f* [ˈzalbə] ointment
Salbei *m* [ˈzalbaɪ] sage
Salmonellen *pl f* [zalmoˈnɛln] salmonella
Salz *n* [zalts] salt
sammeln [zamln] collect
Samstag [ˈzamstaːk] Saturday
Sandalen *f pl* [zanˈdaːln] sandals
Sandburg *f* [ˈzantbuɐk] sand-castle
Sandkasten *m* [ˈzantkastn] sand pit
Sänger/in *m/f* [ˈzɛŋɐ/ˈzɛŋəʀɪn] singer
Satz *m* [zats] sentence
sauber [ˈzaʊbɐ] clean
sauer [ˈzaʊɐ] sour
Sauger *m* [ˈzaʊgɐ] teat
Saugflasche *f* [ˈzaʊkflaʃə] feeding bottle
Säule *f* [ˈzɔɪlə] column, pillar
Sauna *f* [ˈzaʊna] sauna
saure Sahne *f* [zaʊʀə ˈzaːnə] sour cream
Scanner *m* [ˈskɛnɐ] scanner
Schachtel *f* [ʃaxtl] box
schade, wie ~! [vi ˈʃaːdə] what a pity/shame!
Schaden *m* [ʃaːdn] damage
Schadenersatz *m* [ˈʃaːdnˀɐˌzats] compensation
schaffen [ʃafn] make, create; manage; work
Schafsfell *n* [ˈʃaːfsfɛl] fleece
Schal *m* [ʃaːl] scarf
Schalter *m* [ˈʃaltɐ] switch
Schampoo *n* [ˈʃampo/ˈʃampu] shampoo
scharf [ʃaːf] *(spicy)* hot
Schatten *m* [ʃatn] shade, shadow
schätzen [ʃɛtsn] *(person)* to like; to estimate *(amount etc.)*
schauen [ˈʃaʊn] to look
Schaufenster *n* [ˈʃaʊfɛnstɐ] shop window
Schauspiel *n* [ˈʃaʊʃpiːl] play
Schauspieler/in [ˈʃaʊʃpiːlɐ/-ʃpiːləʀɪn] actor/actress
Scheck *m* [ʃɛk] cheque; *(US)* check
Scheibe *f* [ˈʃaɪbə] slice
Scheibenwischer *m* [ˈʃaɪbmvɪʃɐ] windscreen wiper
Scheinwerfer *m* [ˈʃaɪnvɛɐfɐ] headlight
Scheitel *m* [ʃaɪtl] parting
schenken [ʃɛŋkŋ] give (as a present)
Scherz *m* [ʃɛɐts] joke
schicken [ʃɪkŋ] send
Schiebedach *n* [ˈʃiːbədax] sunroof
Schienbein *n* [ˈʃiːnbaɪn] shin
Schiene *f* [ˈʃiːnə] splint
Schild *n* [ʃɪlt] sign
Schinken *m* [ʃɪŋkŋ] ham
Schirm *m* [ʃɪɐm] umbrella
Schlaf *m* [ʃlaːf] sleep
Schlafcouch *f* [ˈʃlaːfkaʊtʃ] studio couch
schlafen [ʃlaːfn] to sleep
Schlaflosigkeit *f* [ˈʃlaːflozɪçkaɪt] insomnia, sleeplessness
Schlaftabletten *f pl* [ˈʃlaːftaˌblɛtn] sleeping pills

Schlafzimmer *n* [ˈʃla:ftsɪmɐ] bedroom
Schlaganfall *m* [ˈʃla:kanfal] stroke
Schläger *m* [ˈʃlɛ:gɐ] racquet
Schlagsahne *f* [ˈʃla:kza:nə] whipping cream
Schlange *f* [ˈʃlaŋə] snake
schlank [ʃlaŋk] slim, slender
schlau [ʃlaʊ] clever
Schlauchboot *n* [ˈʃlaʊxbo:t] rubber dinghy
schlecht [ʃlɛçt] bad; badly
schließen [ʃli:sn] to shut, to close
schlimm [ʃlɪm] bad
Schlitten *m* [ʃlɪtn] sledge, toboggan
Schlittschuh laufen [ˈʃlɪtʃu: laʊfn] go ice skating
Schlittschuhe *m pl* [ˈʃlɪtʃu:ə] ice skates
Schloss *n* [ʃlɔs] castle; *(door)* lock
Schlucht *f* [ˈʃlʊxt] ravine
Schluss *m* [ʃlʊs] end
Schlüssel *m* [ˈʃlʏsl] key
Schlüsselbein *n* [ˈʃlʏslbaɪn] collarbone
schmal [ʃma:l] narrow; slim, thin
schmerzen [ʃmɛɐtsn] to hurt
schmerzhaft [ˈʃmɛɐtshaft] painful
Schmerztabletten *f pl* [ˈʃmɛɐtstaˌblɛtn] pain-killing tablets
Schmuck *m* [ʃmʊk] jewellery
Schmuggel *m* [ʃmʊgl] smuggle
schmuggeln [ʃmʊgln] to smuggle
schmutzig [ˈʃmʊtsɪç] dirty
Schnappschuss *m* [ˈʃnapʃʊs] snapshot
schnarchen [ʃna:çn] to snore
Schnee *m* [ʃne:] snow
Schneebesen *m* [ˈʃne:be:zn] whisk
Schneidebrett *n* [ˈʃnaɪdəbʁɛt] chopping board
schneiden [ʃnaɪdn] to cut
Schneider/in *m/f* [ˈʃnaɪdɐ/ˈʃnaɪdərɪn] dressmaker, tailor
schnell [ʃnɛl] quick(ly), fast
Schnittwunde *f* [ˈʃnɪtvʊndə] cut
Schnitzerei *f* [ʃnɪtsəˈraɪ] wood-carving
Schnorchel *m* [ʃnɔɐçl] snorkel
schnorcheln [ʃnɔɐçln] go snorkelling
Schnuller *m* [ˈʃnʊlɐ] *(baby's)* dummy, *(US) pacifier*
Schnupfen *m* [ʃnʊpfn] cold
Schnurrbart *m* [ˈʃnʊɐba:t] moustache
Schokolade *f* [ʃokoˈla:də] chocolate
Schokoriegel *m* [ˈʃo:kori:gl] chocolate bar
schon [ʃo:n] already
schön [ʃø:n] beautiful(ly)
Schonkost *f* [ˈʃo:nkɔst] diet
Schonzeit *f* [ˈʃo:ntsaɪt] off-season
Schöpfkelle *f* [ˈʃœpfkɛlə] dipper *(US)*, ladle *(GB)*
schottisch [ˈʃɔtʰɪʃ] Scottish
Schottland [ˈʃɔtlant] Scotland
Schraube *f* [ˈʃraʊbə] screw
schrecklich [ˈʃrɛklɪç] terrible, terribly, awful(ly), dreadful(ly)
schreiben [ʃraɪbm] write
Schreibtelefon *n* [ˈʃraɪptelәfo:n] keyboard telephone
Schreibwarengeschäft *n* [ˈʃraɪpva:rəngəˌʃɛft] stationer's
schreien [ˈʃraɪn] to shout; to scream
schriftlich [ˈʃrɪftlɪç] in writing
schüchtern [ˈʃʏçtɐn] shy
Schuh *m* [ʃu:] shoe
Schuhbürste *f* [ˈʃu:bʏɐstə] shoe brush
Schuhcreme *f* [ˈʃu:krɛ:m] shoe cream
Schuhgeschäft *n* [ˈʃu:gəʃɛft] shoe shop
Schuhmacher *m* [ˈʃu:maxɐ] cobbler, shoemaker's
Schuld *f* [ʃʊlt] guilt
Schule *f* [ˈʃu:lə] school
Schulter *f* [ˈʃʊltɐ] shoulder
Schuppen *f pl* [ʃʊpm] dandruff
Schüssel *f* [ʃʏsl] bowl
Schutz *m* [ʃʊts] security
schwach [ʃvax] weak, feeble
Schwager *m* [ˈʃva:gɐ] brother-in-law
Schwägerin *f* [ˈʃvɛ:gərɪn] sister-in-law
Schwangerschaft *f* [ˈʃvaŋɐʃaft] pregnancy
schwarz [ʃva:ts] black
Schwarzbrot *n* [ˈʃva:tsbro:t] brown rye bread
Schwarzweiß-Film *m* [ʃva:tsˈvaɪsfɪlm] black-and-white film
schweigen [ʃvaɪgŋ] be silent, keep quiet
Schweinefleisch *n* [ˈʃvaɪnəflaɪʃ] pork
Schweiz *f* [ʃvaɪts] Switzerland
Schweizer Franken *m pl* [ˌʃvaɪtsɐ ˈfraŋkŋ] Swiss francs
Schweizer/in *m/f* [ˈʃvaɪtsɐ/ˈʃvaɪtsərɪn] Swiss (man/woman)
Schwellung *f* [ˈʃvɛlʊŋ] swelling
schwer [ʃveɐ] heavy; *(illness)* serious; difficult
Schwerbehinderte *m/f* [ˈʃveɐbəhɪndɐtə] severely handicapped person
schwerhörig [ˈʃveɐhø:rɪç] hard of hearing
Schwertfisch *m* [ˈʃveɐtfɪʃ] swordfish
Schwester *f* [ˈʃvɛstɐ] sister
schwierig [ˈʃvi:rɪç] difficult
Schwimmbad *n* [ˈʃvɪmba:t] swimming pool
schwimmen [ʃvɪmm] to swim
Schwimmer/in *m/f* [ˈʃvɪmɐ/ˈʃvɪmərɪn] swimmer
Schwimmflügel *m pl* [ˈʃvɪmfly:gl] water wings
Schwimmkurs *m* [ˈʃvɪmkʊɐs] swimming lessons

Schwimmring *m* ['ʃvɪmʀɪŋ] rubber ring
Schwimmweste *f* ['ʃvɪmvɛstə] life jacket
Schwindelgefühl *n* ['ʃvɪndlgəfy:l] dizziness
schwitzen ['ʃvɪtsn] perspire, sweat
schwül [ʃvy:l] humid
See *f* [di ze:] sea
Seefahrt *f* ['ze:fa:t] voyage
seekrank ['ze:kʀaŋk] seasick
Seereise *f* ['ze:ʀaɪzə] voyage
Seezunge *f* ['ze:tsʊŋə] *(fish)* sole
Segelboot *n* ['ze:glbo:t] sailing boat
Segelfliegen *n* ['ze:glfli:gŋ] gliding
segeln ['ze:gln] to sail
Segeltörn *m* ['ze:gltœɐn] sailing cruise
sehbehindert ['se:bəhɪndɐt] partially sighted
sehen ['ze:n] see
Sehenswürdigkeiten *f pl* ['ze:nsvʏɐdɪçkaɪtn] sights
sehr [zeɐ] very; very much
Seide *f* ['zaɪdə] silk
Seidenmalerei *f* ['zaɪdnma:lə,ʀaɪ] silk painting
Seife *f* ['zaɪfə] soap
Seil *n* [zaɪl] rope
Seilbahn *f* ['zaɪlba:n] cable railway, funicular
sein [zaɪn] *(vb)* to be
sein [zaɪn] *(poss. pron.)* his; its
seit [zaɪt] since; for
Seite *f* ['zaɪtʰə] side; page
Sekunde *f* [ze'kʰʊndə] second
Selbstauslöser *m* ['zɛlpstaʊslø:zɐ] self-timer
Selbstbedienung *f* ['zɛlps (t)bədi:nʊŋ] self-service
selbstverständlich [zɛlp(st)fɐ'ʃtɛntlɪç] of course
Sellerie *m* ['zɛləʀi:] celeriac
selten [zɛltn] rare; seldom
senden ['zɛndn] send
Senf *m* [zɛnf (zɛmf)] mustard
September [zɛp'tɛmbɐ] September
servieren [zɐ'vi:ʀən /-'viɐn] serve
Serviette *f* [zɐ'vjɛtə] napkin, serviette
setzen [zɛtsn] put
sexuelle Belästigung *f* [sɛksu'ɛlə bə'lɛstɪgʊŋ] sexual harassment
Show *f* [ʃo:] show
sicher ['zɪçɐ] safe; sure, certain(ly)
Sicherheit *f* ['zɪçɐhaɪt] safety; security
Sicherheitsgebühr *f* ['zɪçɐhaɪtsgə,byɐ] security charge
Sicherheitsgurt *m* ['zɪçɐhaɪtsgʊɐt] seat belt
Sicherheitskontrolle *f* ['zɪçɐhaɪtskɔn,tʀɔlə] security control
Sicherung *f* ['zɪçəʀʊŋ] fuse
Sicht *f* [zɪçt] visibility; view
sie [zi:] she, her; they, them
Sie [zi:] you
Silber *n* ['zɪlbɐ] silver
Silvester [sɪl'vɛstɐ] New Year's Eve
Sinfoniekonzert *n* [zɪmfo'ni:kɔn,tsɛɐt] symphony concert
singen [zɪŋŋ] sing
Sitz *m* [zɪts] seat; (place of) residence; headquarters
sitzen [zɪtsn] sit
Sitzplatz *m* ['zɪtsplats] seat
Skateboard *n* ['skɛɪtbɔɐt] skateboard; Skateboard fahren ['skɛɪtbɔɐt 'fa:ʀən] to skateboard
Ski *m* [ʃi:] ski
Skibindungen *f pl* ['ʃi:bɪndʊŋŋ] ski bindings
Skibrille *f* ['ʃi:bʀɪlə] ski goggles
Skikurs *m* ['ʃi:kʊɐs] skiing course
Skilehrer/in *m/f* ['ʃi:le:ʀɐ/-le:ʀəʀɪn] ski instructor
Skistiefel *m pl* ['ʃi:ʃti:fl] ski boots
Skistöcke *m pl* ['ʃi:'ʃtœkə] ski poles
Skulptur *f* [skʊlp'tuɐ] sculpture
Slipeinlagen *f pl* ['slɪpaɪnla:gŋ] panty liners
so [zo:] so, thus
Socken *f pl* ['zɔkŋ] socks
Sodbrennen *n* ['zo:tbʀɛnn] heartburn
sofort [zo'fɔɐt] at once
Sofortbildkamera *f* [zo'fɔɐtbɪlt,kaməʀa] Polaroid® camera
Sohle *f* ['zo:lə] *(shoe)* sole
Sohn *m* [zo:n] son
Solarium *n* [zo'la:ʀɪʊm] solarium
Solist/Solistin *m/f* [zo'lɪst/zo'lɪstɪn] soloist
sollen [zɔln] shall, should
Sommer *m* ['zɔmɐ] summer
Sondermarke *f* ['zɔndɐma:kə] special issue stamp
sondern ['zɔndɐn] but
Sonnabend ['zɔna:bmt] Saturday
Sonne *f* ['zɔnə] sun
Sonnenbrand *m* ['zɔnnbʀant] sunburn
Sonnencreme *f* ['zɔnnkʀɛ:m] sun cream
Sonnenhut *m* ['zɔnnhu:t] sun hat
Sonnenmilch *f* ['zɔnnmɪlç] suntan lotion
Sonnenöl *n* ['zɔnnˀø:l] suntan oil
Sonnenstich *m* ['zɔnnʃtɪç] sunstroke
sonnig ['zɔnɪç] sunny
Sonntag ['zɔnta:k] Sunday
Sorge *f* ['zɔɐgə] worry
sorgen, sich ~ um [zɪç 'zɔɐgŋ ˀʊm] be worried about
sorgfältig ['zɔɐkfɛltɪç] careful
Sorte *f* ['zɔɐtə] kind, sort

Soße *f* ['zo:sə] gravy, sauce
Souvenir *n* [zʊvə'niɐ] souvenir
Souvenirladen *m* [zʊvə'niɐla:dn] souvenir shop
Spargel *m* [ʃpa:gl] asparagus
spärlich ['ʃpɛ:ɐlɪç] *(sparse)* thin
Spaß *m* [ʃpa:s] joke; fun
spät [ʃpɛ:t] late
spazieren gehen [ʃpa'tsi:Rənge:n/-'tsiɐnge:n] go for a walk
Spaziergang *m* [ʃpa'tsiɐgaŋ] walk, stroll; einen Spaziergang machen [(ˀaɪn)n ʃpa'tsiɐgaŋ maxn] go for a walk
Speicherkarte *f* ['ʃpaɪçɐˌka:tə] memory card
Speisekarte *f* ['ʃpaɪzəka:tə] menu
Speiseröhre *f* ['ʃpaɪzəRø:Rə] gullet
Speisesaal *m* ['ʃpaɪzəza:l] dining room
Speisewagen *m* ['ʃpaɪzəva:gŋ] restaurant car
Spezialität *f* [ʃpetsjali'tɛ:t] speciality
speziell [ʃpɛ'tsjɛl] special
Spiegel *m* [ʃpi:gl] mirror
Spiel *n* [ʃpi:l] game, match
spielen [ʃpi:ln] to play
Spielkamerad/in *m/f* ['ʃpi:lkaməˌRa:t/-kaməˌRa:dɪn] playmate
Spielkasino *n* ['ʃpi:lkaˌzi:no] casino
Spielsachen *f pl* ['ʃpi:l za:xn] toys
Spielwarengeschäft *n* ['ʃpi:lva:Rəngə'ʃɛft] toy shop
Spinat *m* [ʃpɪ'na:t] spinach
Spirituosengeschäft *n* [ʃpiRitu'o:zngəʃɛft] off-licence
Spitzen schneiden ['ʃpɪtsn 'ʃnaɪdn] cut the ends
Sport *m* [ʃpɔɐt] sport
Sportgeschäft *n* ['ʃpɔɐtgəʃɛft] sports shop
Sportler/in *m/f* ['ʃpɔɐtlɐ/'ʃpɔɐtləRɪn] athlete
Sportplatz *m* ['ʃpɔɐtplats] sports ground, athletics field
Sprache *f* ['ʃpRa:xə] language
sprechen [ʃpRɛçn] speak
Sprechstunde *f* ['ʃpRɛçʃtʊndə] *(hours)* surgery
Springbrunnen *m* ['ʃpRɪŋbRʊnn] fountain
Spritze *f* ['ʃpRɪtsə] injection
Spülbürste *f* ['ʃpy:lbʏɐstə] washing-up brush
Spülmittel *n* ['ʃpy:lmɪtl] detergent, washing-up liquid
Spültuch *n* ['ʃpy:ltu:x] dishcloth
Staat *m* [ʃta:t] state, country
Staatsangehörigkeit *f* ['ʃta:tsˌˀangehø:Rɪçkaɪt] nationality
Stadion *n* ['ʃta:djon] stadium
Stadt *f* [ʃtat] town, city
Stadtmauern *f pl* ['ʃtatmaʊɐn] town/city walls
Stadtplan *m* ['ʃtatpla:n] town plan, city map
Stadtrundfahrt *f* ['ʃtatRʊntfa:t] sightseeing tour of the town/city
Stadtteil *m* ['ʃtatʰaɪl] district
Stadtzentrum *n* ['ʃtattsɛntRʊm] city centre
stammen aus [ʃtamm] come from
im Stande sein [ˀɪm'ʃtandə zaɪn] be able to
Standlicht *n* ['ʃtantlɪçt] sidelights
stark [ʃta:k] strong; *(pain)* severe
Starthilfekabel *n* ['ʃta:thɪlfəka:bl] jump leads
Station *f* [ʃta'tsjo:n] station, stop; ward
Stativ *n* [ʃta'ti:f] tripod
statt [ʃtat] instead of
stattfinden ['ʃtatfɪndn] take place
Statue *f* ['ʃta:tuə] statue
Stau *m* [ʃtaʊ] traffic jam
Staub *m* [ʃtaʊp] dust
Staubsauger *m* ['ʃtaʊpzaʊgɐ] vacuum cleaner
stechen [ʃtɛçn] to sting, to bite
Steckdose *f* ['ʃtɛkdo:zə] power point, socket
Stecker *m* ['ʃtɛkɐ] plug
stehen [ʃte:n] to stand
stehen bleiben ['ʃte:nblaɪbm] to stop, stand still
stehlen [ʃte:ln] to steal
steil [ʃtaɪl] steep
Stein *m* [ʃtaɪn] stone
steinig ['ʃtaɪnɪç] stony
Stelle *f* ['ʃtɛlə] spot, place; job
stellen [ʃtɛln] put
Stellung *f* ['ʃtɛlʊŋ] job, position
Stempel *m* [ʃtɛmpl] stamp
Stern *m* [ʃtɛɐn] star
Sternwarte *f* ['ʃtɛɐnva:tə] observatory
stets [ʃte:ts] always
Steward/Stewardess *m/f* ['stjua:t/'stjuadɛs] flight attendant, steward/stewardess
Stich *m* [ʃtɪç] sting, bite
Stiefel *m pl* [ʃti:fl] boots
Stil *m* [sti:l (ʃti:l)] style
still [ʃtɪl] quiet, silent; still, calm
Stillleben *n* ['ʃtɪle:bm] still life
Stimme *f* ['ʃtɪmə] voice; vote
stinken [ʃtɪŋkŋ] to smell, to stink
Stirnhöhlenentzündung *f* ['ʃtɪɐnhø:lnˀɛnˌtsʏndʊŋ] sinusitis
Stock *m* [ʃtɔk] stick
Stockwerk *n* ['ʃtɔkvɛɐk] floor, storey
Stoff *m* [ʃtɔf] material
stören [ʃtøɐn] disturb, bother

stornieren [ʃtɔˈniɐn] cancel
Stoßstange *f* [ˈʃto:ʃtaŋə] bumper
Strafe *f* [ˈʃtʀa:fə] punishment; fine
Strafraum *m* [ˈʃtʀa:fʀaʊm] penalty box
Strähnchen *n pl* [ˈʃtʀɛ:nçn] highlights
Strähne *f* [ˈʃtʀɛ:nə] highlight
Strand *m* [ʃtʀant] beach
Strandschuhe *m pl* [ˈʃtʀantʃuə] beach shoes
Straße *f* [ˈʃtʀa:sə] street; road
Straßenbahn *f* [ˈʃtʀa:snba:n] streetcar, tram
Straßenkarte *f* [ˈʃtʀa:snka:tə] road map
Strecke *f* [ˈʃtʀɛkʰə] distance; *(railway)* line; road, route
Streichhölzer *n pl* [ˈʃtʀaɪçhœltsɐ] matches
streng [ʃtʀɛŋ] severe; strict
Strickjacke *f* [ˈʃtʀɪkjakə] cardigan
Strohhalm *m* [ˈʃtʀo:halm] straw
Strom *m* [ʃtʀo:m] (large) river; *(electricity)* current
Strompauschale *f* [ˈʃtʀo:mpaʊˌʃa:lə] flat rate for electricity
Stromspannung *f* [ˈʃtʀo:mˌʃpanʊŋ] voltage
Strömung *f* [ˈʃtʀø:mʊŋ] *(water)* current
Strümpfe *m pl* [ˈʃtʀʏmpfə] stockings
Strumpfhose *f* [ˈʃtʀʊmpfho:zə] tights
Stück *n* [ʃtʏk] piece; play
studieren [ʃtʊˈdi:ʀən /-ˈdiɐn] to study
Stufe *f* [ˈʃtu:fə] step
Stufen *f* [ˈʃtu:fn] layers
Stufenschnitt *m* [ˈʃtu:fnʃnɪt] layered cut
Stuhl *m* [ʃtu:l] chair
Stuhlgang *m* [ˈʃtu:lgaŋ] bowel movement
stumm [ʃtʊm] mute
Stunde *f* [ˈʃtʊndə] hour; lesson; **eine halbe Stunde** [(ˌʔaɪ)nə ˌhalbə ˈʃtʊndə] half an hour
stündlich [ˈʃtʏntlɪç] every hour, hourly
Sturm *m* [ʃtʊɐm] gale, storm
Sturz *m* [ʃtʊɐts] fall
stürzen [ʃtʏɐtsn] to fall
Sturzhelm *m* [ˈʃtʊɐtshɛlm] crash helmet
suchen [zu:xn] look for
Sucher *m* [ˈzu:xɐ] viewfinder
Süden *m* [zy:dn] south
südlich von [ˈzy:tlɪç fɔn] south of
Summe *f* [ˈzʊmə] sum; amount
Supermarkt *m* [ˈzu:pɐma:kt] supermarket
Suppe *f* [ˈzʊpə] soup
Suppenteller *m* [ˈzʊpmtɛlɐ] soup plate
Surfbrett *n* [ˈsœɐfbʀɛt] surfboard
surfen [ˈsœɐfn] to surf
süß [zy:s] sweet
Süßigkeiten *f pl* [ˈzy:siçkaɪtn] sweets
Süßstoff *m* [ˈzy:ʃtɔf] sweetener
Süßwarengeschäft *n* [ˈzy:sva:ʀəngəˌʃɛft] sweet shop
Swimmingpool *m* [ˈsvɪmɪŋpu:l] *(private)* swimming pool
sympathisch [sʏmˈpʰa:tʰɪʃ] nice, pleasant

T

Tabak *m* [ˈtʰabak] tobacco
Tabakladen *m* [ˈtabakla:dn] tobacconist's
Tablette *f* [taˈblɛtə] pill, tablet
Tacho(meter) *m* [ˌtaxo(ˈme:tɐ)] speedometer
Tag *m* [tʰa:k] day; **jeden ~** [je:dn ta:k] every day
Tagesausflug *m* [ˈta:gəsˌʔaʊsflu:k] day trip
Tagesgericht *n* [ˈta:gəsgəʀɪçt] dish of the day
Tageskarte *f* [ˈta:gəska:tə] day ticket
Tagesmenü *n* [ˈta:gəsmeˌny:] special (of the day)
Tagespass *m* [ˈta:gəspas] day pass
täglich [tɛ:klɪç] daily
tagsüber [ˈta:ksˀy:bɐ] during the day
Tal *n* [ta:l] valley
Tampons *m pl* [ˈtampɔŋs] tampons
Tank *m* [taŋk] (petrol) tank
tanken [tʰaŋkŋ] fill up
Tanz *m* [tʰants] dance
tanzen [tantsn] to dance
Tänzer/in *m/f* [təntsɐ/təntsəˈʀɪn] dancer
Tanzkapelle *f* [ˈtantskaˌpɛlə] dance band
Tanztheater *n* [ˈtantsteˌʔa:tɐ] dance theatre
Tasche *f* [ˈtʰaʃə] pocket; bag
Taschenbuch *n* [ˈtaʃnbu:x] paperback
Taschendieb/in *m/f* [ˈtaʃndi:p/-ˌdi:bɪn] pickpocket
Taschenmesser *n* [ˈtaʃnmɛsɐ] pocket knife
Taschenrechner *m* [ˈtaʃnʀɛçnɐ] pocket calculator
Tasse *f* [ˈtasə] cup
Taststock *m* [ˈtastʃtɔk] cane
Tätigkeit *f* [ˈtɛ:tɪçkaɪt] *(job)* work
taubstumm [ˈtaʊpʃtʊm] deaf-mute
tauchen [taʊxn] to dive
Taucherausrüstung *f* [ˈtaʊxɐˀaʊsʀʏstʊŋ] diving equipment
Taucherbrille *f* [ˈtaʊxɐbʀɪlə] diving goggles
tauschen [tʰaʊʃn] to exchange, to swap; *(money)* to change

täuschen, sich ~ [zɪç ˈtʰɔɪʃn] be mistaken, be wrong
Taxifahrer/in *m/f* [ˈtaksifa:ʀɐ/-fa:ʀəʀɪn] taxi driver
Taxistand *m* [ˈtaksiˈʃtant] taxi rank/stand
Tee *m* [te:] tea
Teebeutel *m* [ˈte:bɔɪtl] tea bag
Teelöffel *m* [ˈte:lœfl] teaspoon
Teil *m* [tʰaɪl] part
teilnehmen (an) [ˈtʰaɪlne:mm (ˀan)] take part (in)
Telefon *n* [ˈte:ləfo:n] telephone
Telefonbuch *n* [teləˈfo:nbu:x] telephone directory
telefonieren [tʰeləfoˈni:ʀən/-ˈniɐn] make a phone call, to phone
Telefonkarte *f* [teləˈfo:nka:tə] phonecard
Telefonnummer *f* [teləˈfo:nnʊmɐ] phone number
Telefonzelle *f* [teləˈfo:ntsɛlə] phone box/booth
telegrafische Überweisung *f* [teləˈgʀa:fɪʃə ˀy:bɐˈvaɪzʊŋ] telegraphic transfer
Teleobjektiv *n* [ˈte:ləˀɔbjɛkˌti:f] telephoto lens
Telex *n* [ˈte:lɛks] telex
Teller *m* [ˈtɛlɐ] plate
Tempel *m* [tɛmpl] temple
Temperatur *f* [ˌtɛmpəʀaˈtuɐ] temperature
Tennis *n* [ˈtɛnɪs] tennis
Tennisschläger *m* [ˈtɛnɪʃlɛ:gɐ] tennis racquet
Termin *m* [tʰɐˈmi:n] appointment; deadline
Terminal *n* [ˈtə:mɪnəl] terminal
Terrakotta *f* [tɛʀaˈkɔta] terracotta
Terrasse *f* [teˈʀasə] terrace
Tetanus *m* [ˈtɛtanʊs] tetanus
teuer [ˈtʰɔɪɐ] dear, expensive
Theater *n* [teˈˀa:tɐ] theatre
Theaterkasse *f* [teˈˀa:tɐˌkasə] box-office
Therapie *f* [teʁaˈpi:] therapy
Thermalbad *n* [tɛɐˈma:lba:t] thermal baths
Thriller *m* [ˈθʀɪlɐ] thriller
Thunfisch *m* [ˈtu:nfɪʃ] tuna
Thymian *m* [ˈty:mia:n] thyme
tief [tʰi:f] deep; low
Tier *n* [tʰiɐ] animal
Tintenfisch *m* [ˈtɪntnfɪʃ] squid
Tipp *m* [tʰɪp] *(information)* tip
Tisch *m* [tʰɪʃ] table
Tischtennis *n* [ˈtiʃtɛnɪs] table tennis
Tischtuch *n* [ˈtɪʃtu:x] tablecloth
Toast *m* [to:st] toast
Toaster *m* [ˈto:stɐ] toaster
Tochter *f* [ˈtʰɔxtʰɐ] daughter
Toilette *f* [toˈlɛtə] lavatory, toilet
Toilettenpapier *n* [toˈlɛtnpaˌpiɐ] toilet paper
toll [tɔl] wonderful
Tomaten *f pl* [toˈma:tn] tomatoes
Ton *m* [to:n] sound, tone; *(colour)* shade
tönen [tø:nn] to tint
Topf *m* [tɔpf] pot
Töpferei *f* [tœpfəˈʀaɪ] *(place)* pottery
Töpfern [ˈtœpfɐn] *(activity)* pottery
Töpferwaren *f pl* [ˈtœpfɐva:ʀən] *(product)* pottery
Tor *n* [toɐ] gate; *(sport)* goal
Torwart/in *m/f* [ˈtoɐva:t/ˈtoɐva:tin] goalkeeper
Tour *f* [tʰuɐ] tour, excursion, trip
Tourist/in *m/f* [tuˈʀɪst/tuˈʀɪstɪn] tourist
tragen [tʀa:gŋ] carry; wear
Tragödie *f* [tʀaˈgø:diə] tragedy
trampen [tʀɛmpm] hitchhike
Traum *m* [tʀaʊm] dream
träumen [tʀɔɪmm] to dream
traurig [ˈtʀaʊʀɪç] sad
treffen [tʀɛfn] meet
Trekkingrad *n* [ˈtʀɛkɪŋʀa:t] trekking bike
Treppe *f* [ˈtʀɛpʰə] stairs, staircase; steps
trinken [tʀɪŋkŋ] to drink
Trinkflasche *f* [ˈtʀɪŋkflaʃə] baby's bottle
Trinkgeld *n* [ˈtʀɪŋkgɛlt] *(gratuity)* tip
Trinkwasser *n* [ˈtʀɪŋkvasɐ] drinking water
trocken [ˈtʀɔkŋ] dry
Trockner *m* [ˈtʁɔknɐ] drier
Trödelladen *m* [ˈtʀø:dlla:dn] second-hand shop
Trommelfell *n* [ˈtʀɔmlfɛl] eardrum
tropfen [tʀɔpfn] to drip; *(nose)* to run
Tropfen *m pl* [ˈtʀɔpfn] drops
Tropfsteinhöhle *f* [ˈtʀɔpfʃtaɪnˌhø:lə] dripstone cave
trotzdem [ˈtʀɔtsde:m] nevertheless
trüb [tʀy:p] *(liquid)* cloudy; *(weather)* overcast, cloudy
Tuch *n* [tʰu:x] cloth
tun [tʰu:n] do
Tunnel *m* [tʰʊnl] tunnel
Tür *f* [tʰyɐ] door
Türbreite *f* [ˈtyɐbʀaɪtə] door width
Türcode *m* [ˈtyɐko:t] door code
türkisfarben [tʏɐˈki:sfa:bm] turquoise
Turm *m* [tʊɐm] tower
Türöffner *m* [ˈtyɐˀœfnɐ] door opener
Türschwelle *f* [ˈtyɐʃvɛlə] doorstep
Tüte *f* [ˈtʰy:tʰə] bag; *(ice cream)* cone

Typhus *m* [ˈtyːfʊs] typhoid
typisch [ˈtʰyːpʰɪʃ] typical

U

U-Bahn *f* [ˈʔuːbaːn] underground, *(US)* subway
üben [ʔyːbm] practise
über [ˈʔyːbɐ] over
überall [ʔybɐˈʔal] everywhere
überbacken [ʔybɐˈbakŋ] au gratin
Überfall *m* [ˈʔyːbɐfal] mugging
Übergang *m* [ˈʔyːbɐgaŋ] crossing; transition
überholen [ʔybɐˈhoːln] overtake, pass
übermorgen [ˈʔyːbɐmɔɐgŋ] the day after tomorrow
übernachten [ʔybɐˈnaxtn] stay (overnight), spend the night
überqueren [ʔybɐˈkveːʀən/-ˈkveɐn] to cross
Überreste *m pl* [ˈʔyːbɐʀɛstə] remains
überschreiten [ʔybɐˈʃʀaɪtn] to cross
übersetzen [ʔybɐˈzɛtsn] translate
Überweisung *f* [ʔybɐˈvaɪzʊŋ] remittance, transfer
üblich [ˈʔyːplɪç] usual
Ufer *n* [ˈʔuːfɐ] *(river)* bank; shore
Uhrmacher *m* [ˈʔuɐmaxɐ] watchmaker('s)
um [ʔʊm] around; *(time)* at, about
umbuchen [ˈʔʊmbuːxn] change the booking
Umgebung [ʔʊmˈgeːbʊŋ] surroundings
umgekehrt [ˈʔʊmgəkʰeɐt] reverse
Umhängetasche *f* [ˈʔʊmhɛŋəˌtaʃə] shoulder bag
umkehren [ˈʔʊmkʰeːʀən/-kʰeɐn] turn back
umsonst [ʔʊmˈzɔnst] free (of charge); in vain
umsteigen [ˈʔʊmʃtaɪgŋ] to change *(trains etc.)*
umtauschen [ˈʔʊmtʰaʊʃn] to change, to exchange
Umweg *m* [ˈʔʊmveːk] detour
Umwelt *f* [ˈʔʊmvɛlt] environment
umziehen, sich ~ [zɪç ˈʔʊmtsiːn] to change (clothes)
unangenehm [ˈʔʊnangəneːm] unpleasant
unbedingt [ˈʔʊnbədɪŋt] really
und [ʔʊnt] and
unentschieden [ˈʔʊnɛntˌʃiːdn] *(sport)* draw
unerfreulich [ˈʔʊnɐfʀɔɪlɪç] unpleasant
unerträglich [ˈʔʊnɐˌtʀɛːklɪç] intolerable, unbearable
Unfall *m* [ˈʔʊnfal] accident
ungeeignet [ˈʔʊngəʔaɪknət] unfit, unsuited
ungefähr [ˈʔʊngəˌfeɐ] about
ungern [ˈʔʊngɛɐn] reluctantly
ungewöhnlich [ˈʔʊngəvøːnlɪç] unusual
unglaublich [ʔʊnˈglaʊplɪç] incredible
Unglück *n* [ˈʔʊnglʏkʰ] accident; misfortune
unglücklicherweise [ˌʔʊnglʏklɪçɐˈvaɪzə] unfortunately
Universität *f* [ʔunivɛɐziˈtʰɛːt] university
unmöglich [ˈʔʊnˌmøːglɪç] impossible
Unrecht haben [ˈʔʊnʀɛçt haːbm] be wrong
uns [ʔʊns] us
unser(e) [ˈʔʊnzɐ (-ʀə)] our
unten [ʔʊntn] below
unter [ˈʔʊntʰɐ] under; among
unterbrechen [ʔʊntʰɐˈbʀɛçn] interrupt
Unterführung *f* [ʔʊntʰɐˈfyːʀʊŋ] subway, underpass
unterhalb [ˈʔʊntʰɐhalp] below
unterhalten [ʔʊntɐˈhaltn] *(feed)* keep, maintain, support; entertain; **sich ~** [zɪç ʔʊntʰɐˈhaltn] to talk; to amuse oneself
Unterhaltung *f* [ʔʊntʰɐˈhaltʰʊŋ] conversation; entertainment
Unterhemd *n* [ˈʊntɐhɛmt] vest
Unterhose *f* [ˈʊntɐhoːzə] pants
Unterkunft *f* [ˈʔʊntʰɐkʰʊnft] accommodation
Unternehmen *n* [ʔʊntɐˈneːmm] firm
unterrichten [ʔʊntʰɐˈʀɪçtn] inform; teach
Unterrichtsstunde *f* [ˈʔʊntɐʀɪçtˌʃtʊndə] lesson
unterschreiben [ʔʊntʰɐˈʃʀaɪbm] to sign
Unterschrift *f* [ˈʔʊntʰɐʃʀɪft] signature
Untersuchung *f* [ʔʊntɐˈzuːxʊŋ] examination
Untersuchungshaft *f* [ʔʊntɐˈzuːxʊŋshaft] police custody
Untertasse *f* [ˈʔʊntɐtasə] saucer
Untertitel *m* [ˈʔʊntɐtɪtl] subtitles
Unterwäsche *f* [ˈʔʊntɐvɛʃə] underwear
Unterwasserkamera *f* [ʔʊntɐˈvasɐˌkaməʁa] underwater camera
unverschämt [ˈʔʊnfɐʃɛːmt] impertinent, cheeky, rude
unwahrscheinlich [ˈʔʊnvaʃaɪnlɪç] unlikely, improbable
unwichtig [ˈʔʊnvɪçtɪç] unimportant
Urin *m* [ʔuˈʀiːn] urine
Urlaub *m* [ˈʔuɐlaʊp] holidays, vacation
Ursache *f* [ˈʔuɐzaxə] cause, reason
Urteil *n* [ˈʔʊɐtaɪl] judgement; opinion

V

Varietee *n* [vaʀiə'te:] music hall, variety theatre
Vase *f* ['va:zə] vase
Vater *m* ['fa:tʰɐ] father
Vaterland *n* ['fa:tɐlant] native country
Vegetarier/in [vegə'ta:ʀiɐ/ vegə'ta:ʀiəʀin] *(person)* vegetarian
vegetarisch [vegə'ta:ʀiʃ] vegetarian
Ventilator *m* [vɛnti'la:toɐ] fan
Verabredung *f* [fɐ'ˀapʀe:dʊŋ] appointment; date
verabschieden, sich ~ [zɪç fɐ'ˀapʃi:dn] say goodbye
verändern [fɐ'ˀɛndɐn] to change, alter
Veränderung *f* [fɐ'ˀɛndəʀʊŋ] change
Veranstaltung *f* [fɐ'ˀanʃtaltʰʊŋ] event
verantwortlich [fɐ'ˀantvɔɐtlɪç] responsible
Verband *m* [fɐ'bant] bandage, dressing
Verbandskasten *m* [fɐ'bantskastn] first-aid kit
verbinden [fɐ'bɪndn] join, connect; *(med.)* to dress
Verbindung *f* [fɐ'bɪndʊŋ] connection
verboten [fɐ'bo:tn] forbidden, prohibited
Verbrechen *n* [fɐ'bʀɛçn] crime
verbrennen [fɐ'bʀɛnn] to burn
Verbrennung *f* [fɐ'bʀɛnʊŋ] burn
verbringen [fɐ'bʀɪŋŋ] spend *(time)*
Verdauung *f* [fɐ'daʊʊŋ] digestion
Verdauungsstörung *f* [fɐ'daʊʊŋʃtø:ʀʊŋ] indigestion
verdorben [fɐ'dɔɐbm] spoiled; rotten; corrupt
Verein *m* [fɐ'ˀaɪn] association, club
vereinbaren [fɐ'ˀaɪnba: (ʀə)n] agree on
verfehlen [fɐ'fe:ln] *(not attain)* to miss
Vergangenheit *f* [fɐ'gaŋŋhaɪt] past
vergehen [fɐ'ge:n] *(time)* to pass
vergessen [fɐ'gɛsn] forget
Vergewaltigung *f* [fɐgə'valtɪgʊŋ] rape
Vergiftung *f* [vɐ'gɪftʊŋ] poisoning
Vergnügen *n* [fɐ'gny:gŋ] pleasure
verhaften [fɐ'haftn] to arrest
Verhandlung *f* [fɐ'handlʊŋ] *(court)* trial
verheiratet [fɐ'haɪʀa:tət] married
verhindern [fɐ'hɪndɐn] prevent
verirren, sich ~ [zɪç fɐ'ˀɪʀən/ -'ˀɪɐn] lose one's way, get lost
Verkauf *m* [fɐ'kʰaʊf] sale
verkaufen [fɐ'kʰaʊfn] to sell
Verkehr *m* [fɐ'kʰeɐ] traffic
verkehren [fɐ'ke:ʀən/-'keɐn] *(bus etc.)* to run
Verkehrsbüro *n* [fɐ'keɐsbyˌʀo:] tourist information office
verlängern [fɐ'lɛŋɐn] extend
Verlängerungsschnur *f* [fɐ'lɛŋəʀʊŋˌʃnuɐ] extension lead
verlassen [fɐ'lasn] to leave
verletzen [fɐ'lɛtsn] injure
Verletzte *m/f* [fɐ'lɛtstə] injured person
Verletzung *f* [fɐ'lɛtsʊŋ] injury
verlieren [fɐ'li:ʀən /-'liɐn] lose
Verlobte *m/f* [fɐ'lo:ptə] fiancé/fiancée
vermieten [fɐ'mi:tn] let (out), rent (out)
verpacken [fɐ'pakŋ] pack, wrap
Verpackung *f* [fɐ'pʰakʰʊŋ] packing, wrapping
verpassen [fɐ'pʰasn] to miss *(bus, opportunity)*
Verpflegung *f* [fɐ' (p)fle:gʊŋ] food; board
verrechnen, sich ~ [zɪç fɐ'ʀɛçn (ə)n] miscalculate, make a mistake
verreisen [fɐ'ʀaɪzn] go on a journey
verrückt [fɐ'ʀʏkt] mad, crazy
verschieben [fɐ'ʃi:bm] put off, postpone
verschieden [fɐ'ʃi:dn] different(ly)
verschließen [fɐ'ʃli:sn] to lock
Verschluss *m* [fɐ'ʃlʊs] *(door)* lock
verschreiben [fɐ'ʃʀaɪbm] prescribe
Versicherung *f* [fɐ'zɪçəʀʊŋ] insurance
Verspätung *f* [fɐ'ʃpɛ:tʊŋ] delay
Verstand *m* [fɐ'ʃtant] *(mind)* reason
verstaucht [fɐ'ʃtaʊxt] sprained
verstehen [fɐ'ʃte:n] understand
Verstopfung *f* [fɐ'ʃtɔpfʊŋ] constipation
Versuch *m* [fɐ'zu:x] attempt, try; experiment, test
versuchen [fɐ'zu:xn] to try; to taste
vertauschen [fɐ'taʊʃn] mistake for
Vertrag *m* [fɐ'tʀa:k] contract
Vertrauen *n* [fɐ'tʀaʊn] confidence
verunglücken [fɐ'ˀʊnglʏkŋ] have an accident
verursachen [fɐ'ˀuɐzaxn] to cause
Verwaltung *f* [fɐ'valtʰʊŋ] administration
verwandt [fɐ'vant] related
verwechseln [fɐ'vɛksln] confuse, mix up
verwenden [fɐ'vɛndn] to employ, to use
Verwendung *f* [fɐ'vɛndʊŋ] use
verwitwet [fɐ'vɪtvət] widowed
verzögern [fɐ'tsø:gɐn] to delay
Videofilm *m* ['vi:deofɪlm] video film
Videokamera *f* ['vi:deoˌkaməʀa] video camera
Videokassette *f* ['vi:deokaˌsɛtə] video cassette
Videorekorder *m* ['vi:deoʀeˌkɔɐdɐ] video recorder
viel [fi:l] a lot of; much

vielleicht [fɪˈlaɪçt] perhaps, maybe
vielmehr [ˈfiːlmeɐ] rather
Viertelstunde *f* [fɪɐtlˈʃtʊndə] quarter of an hour
Virus *n* [ˈviːʀʊs] virus
Visum *n* [ˈviːzʊm] visa
Vogel *m* [foːgl] bird
Vogelschutzgebiet *n* [ˈfoːglʃʊtsgəbiːt] bird reserve
Volk *n* [fɔlk] people
voll [fɔl] full; crowded
vollenden [fɔlˈʔɛndn] to complete
Volleyball *m* [ˈvɔlɪbal] volleyball
völlig [ˈfœlɪç] complete(ly)
Vollkasko *f* [ˈfɔlkasko] fully comprehensive insurance
Vollkornbrot *n* [ˈfɔlkɔɐnbʁoːt] wholemeal bread
von [fɔn] from; of; by
vor [foɐ] in front of; before
Voranmeldung *f* [ˈfoɐʔanmɛldʊŋ] booking
im Voraus [ʔɪm ˈfoːʀaʊs] in advance
vorbei [fɔˈbaɪ] over, past
vorbeigehen [fɔˈbaɪgeːn] go by/past; pass
vorbereiten [ˈfoɐbəʀaɪtn] prepare
vorbestellen [ˈfoɐbəʃtɛln] to book
Vorfall *m* [ˈfoɐfal] incident
vorgestern [ˈfɔɐgɛstɐn] the day before yesterday
vorher [ˈfoɐheɐ] before
vorläufig [ˈfoɐlɔɪfɪç] temporary
Vormittag *m* [ˈfoɐmɪtʰaːk] morning
vormittags [ˈfɔɐmɪtaːks] in/during the morning
vorn [fɔɐn] in front
Vorname *m* [ˈfoɐnaːmə] Christian name, first name
vornehm [ˈfoɐneːm] distinguished, posh, noble
Vorort [ˈfoɐʔɔɐtˈ ˈfoɐʃtat] suburb
Vorrat *m* [ˈfoːʀaːt] stock, store, provisions
Vorsaison *f* [ˈfoɐzeˌzɔŋ] low season, off-season
Vorschlag *m* [ˈfoɐʃlaːk] suggestion
Vorschrift *f* [ˈfoɐʃʀɪft] rule
Vorsicht *f* [ˈfoɐzɪçt] caution
vorsichtig [ˈfoɐzɪçtɪç] careful, cautious
Vorspeise *f* [ˈfoɐʃpaɪzə] hors d'œuvre, starter
Vorstadt *f* [ˈfoɐʃtat] suburb
vorstellen [ˈfoɐʃtɛln] introduce
Vorstellung *f* [ˈfoɐʃtɛlʊŋ] introduction; notion, idea; *(theatre)* performance
Vorteil *m* [ˈfɔɐtʰaɪl] advantage
vorüber [foˈʀyːbɐ] past, over; gone
vorübergehen [foˈʀyːbɐgeːn] *(time)* to pass
vorübergehend [foˈʀyːbɐgeːnt] temporary
Vorverkauf *m* [ˈfoɐfɐkaʊf] advance booking
Vorwahlnummer *f* [ˈfoɐvaːlˌnʊmɐ] area code
vorwärts [ˈfɔɐvɛɐts] forward(s)
vorzeigen [ˈfoɐtsaɪgŋ] to show
Vorzug *m* [ˈfoɐtsuːk] advantage

W

wach [vax] awake
wagen [vaːgŋ] to dare
Wagenheber *m* [ˈvaːgŋheːbɐ] jack
Wagennummer *f* [ˈvaːgŋnʊmɐ] coach number
Wahl *f* [vaːl] choice
wählen [ˈvɛːln] to choose; to vote; *(telephone)* to dial
wahr [vaː] true
während [ˈvɛːʀənt (veɐnt)] during; while
wahrscheinlich [vaˈʃaɪnlɪç] probable; probably
Währung *f* [ˈvɛːʀʊŋ] currency
Wahrzeichen *n* [ˈvaːtsaɪçn] emblem, symbol; landmark
Wald *m* [valt] forest, woods
Wales [wɛɪls (vɛɪls)] Wales
Waliser/in *m/f* [vaˈliːzɐ/vaˈliːzəʀɪn] Welshman/Welshwoman
walisisch [vaˈliːzɪʃ] Welsh
Wallfahrtsort *m* [ˈvalfaːtsˌʔɔɐt] place of pilgrimage
Wand *f* [vant] wall
Wanderkarte *f* [ˈvandɐkaːtə] hiking map
wandern [ˈvandɐn] to hike, to ramble
Wanderung [ˈvandəʀʊŋ] hike
Wander-/Trekkingschuh *m* [ˈvandɐ-/ˈtʁɛkɪŋ-ʃuː] hiking boots
Ware *f* [ˈvaːʀə] product
warm [vaːm] warm; **warmes Wasser** [ˈkaltəs ˈvasɐ] hot water
Wärme *f* [ˈvɛɐmə] heat
wärmen [vɛɐmm] to heat, to warm
Warnblinkanlage *f* [ˈvaːnblɪŋkʔanlaːgə] hazard warning lights
Warndreieck *n* [ˈvaːndʀaɪɛk] warning triangle
warten (auf) [vaːtn (ʔaʊf)] wait (for)
Wartesaal *m* [ˈvaːtəzaːl] waiting room
Wartezimmer *n* [ˈvaːtətsɪmɐ] waiting room
was [vas] what
Waschbecken *n* [ˈvaʃbɛkŋ] washbasin
Wäscheklammern *f pl* [ˈvɛʃəklamɐn] clothes pegs
Wäscheleine *f* [ˈvɛʃəlaɪnə] clothes line

waschen [vaʃn] to wash
Wäscherei *f* [vɛʃəˈʀaɪ] laundry
Waschlappen *m* [ˈvaʃlapm] flannel
Waschmittel *n* [ˈvaʃmɪtl] *(clothes)* detergent
Waschraum *m* [ˈvaʃʀaʊm] washroom
Waschsalon *m* [ˈvaʃzaˌlɔŋ] launderette
Wasser *n* [ˈvasɐ] water
wasserdicht [ˈvasɐdɪçt] waterproof
Wasserfall *m* [ˈvasɐfal] waterfall
Wasserglas *n* [ˈvasɐglaːs] tumbler
Wasserhahn *m* [ˈvasɐhaːn] *(water)* tap
Wasserkanister *m* [ˈvasɐkanˌɪstɐ] water canister
Wasserkocher *m* [ˈvasɐˌkɔxɐ] kettle
Wasserski fahren [ˈvasɐʃiː ˈfaːʀən] go water-skiing
Wasserverbrauch *m* [ˈvasɐfɐbʀaʊx] water consumption
Watte *f* [ˈvatə] cotton wool
Wattestäbchen *n* [ˈvatəʃtɛːpçn] cotton bud
Wechsel *m* [vɛksl] change; exchange
Wechselgeld *n* [ˈvɛkslgɛlt] *(money)* change
wechselhaft [ˈvɛkslhaft] changeable
Wechselkurs *m* [ˈvɛkslkʊɐs] exchange rate
wechseln [(gɛlt) vɛksln] to change *(money)*
wecken [vɛkŋ] wake
Wecker *m* [ˈvɛkɐ] alarm clock
weg [vɛk] away; gone
Weg *m* [veːk] way; path; road
wegen [veːgŋ] because of
weggehen [ˈvɛkgeːn] go away, leave
Wegweiser *m* [ˈveːkvaɪzɐ] *(directions)* sign
wehtun [ˈveːtuːn] to hurt
weich [vaɪç] soft
weigern, sich ~ [zɪç ˈvaɪgɐn] to refuse
Weihnachten [ˈvaɪnaxtn] Christmas
weil [vaɪl] because, since
Wein *m* [vaɪn] wine
Weinberg *m* [ˈvaɪnbɛɐk] vineyard
weinen [vaɪnn] to cry
Weinglas *n* [ˈvaɪnglaːs] wineglass
Weinhandlung *f* [ˈvaɪnhantlʊŋ] wine merchant's
Weintrauben *f pl* [ˈvaɪntʀaʊbm] grapes
Weise *f* [ˈvaɪzə] way
Weisheitszahn *m* [ˈvaɪshaɪtsaːn] wisdom tooth
weiß [vaɪs] white
Weißbrot *n* [ˈvaɪsbʀoːt] white bread
Weißwein [ˈvaɪsvaɪn] white wine
weit [vaɪt] wide; *(distance)* long; far
Wellenbad *n* [ˈvɛlnbaːt] wave pool
Welt *f* [vɛlt] world
wenig [ˈveːnɪç] little, few
wenigstens [ˈve (ː)nɪkstns] at least
wenn [vɛn] if; when
werden [veɐdn] become
Werkstatt *f* [ˈvɛɐkʃtat] *(repairs)* garage
werktags [ˈvɛɐktʰaːks] on weekdays
Werkzeug *n* [ˈvɛɐktsɔɪk] tools
Wertangabe *f* [ˈveɐtangaːbə] declaration of value
wertlos [ˈveɐtloːs] worthless
Wertsachen *f pl* [ˈveɐtzaxn] valuables
Wespe *f* [ˈvɛspə] wasp
Weste *f* [ˈvɛstə] waistcoat; *(US)* vest
Westen *m* [vɛstn] west
Western *m* [ˈvɛstɐn] *(film)* western
Wettervorhersage *f* [ˈvɛtɐfoˌheɐzaːgə] weather forecast
Wettkampf *m* [ˈvɛtkamf] competition, contest
wichtig [ˈvɪçtɪç] important
Wickeltisch *m* [ˈvɪkltɪʃ] baby's changing table
wie [viː] how; *(comparison)* like; **wie schade!** [vi ˈʃaːdə] what a pity/shame!
wieder [ˈviːdɐ] again
wiedergeben [ˈviːdɐgeːbm] give back, return
wiederholen [vidɐˈhoːln] to repeat
wiederkommen [ˈviːdɐkʰɔmm] come back, return
Wiedersehen, auf ~ [ˀaʊf ˈvi(ː)dɐzeːn] goodbye
Wiese *f* [ˈviːzə] meadow
wild [vɪlt] wild(ly)
Willkommen*n* [vɪlˈkʰɔmm] welcome
willkommen [vɪlˈkʰɔmm] *(adj)* welcome; willkommen heißen [vɪlˈkʰɔmm haɪsn] to welcome
Wimperntusche *f* [ˈvɪmpɐntʊʃə] mascara
Wind *m* [vɪnt] wind
Windeln *f pl* [vɪndln] nappies, *(US)* diapers
Windpocken *f pl* [ˈvɪntpɔkŋ] chickenpox
Windschutzscheibe *f* [ˈvɪntʃʊtʃaɪbə] windscreen, *(US)* windshield
Windstärke *f* [ˈvɪntʃtɛɐkə] wind-force
Windsurfen *n* [ˈvɪntsœɐfn] windsurfing
Winkel *m* [ˈvɪŋkl] corner
Winter *m* [ˈvɪntɐ] winter
Winterreifen *m* [ˈvɪntɐʀaɪfn] winter tyres
wir [viɐ/vɐ] we
Wirbelsäule *f* [ˈvɪɐblzɔɪlə] spine
wirklich [ˈvɪɐklɪç] real; true; really, truly
Wischmopp *m* [ˈvɪʃmɔp] mop
wissen [vɪsn] know
Witz *m* [vɪts] joke
Woche *f* [ˈvɔxə] week

Wochenende *n* [ˈvɔxnˀɛndə] weekend
Wochenendpauschale *f* [ˈvɔxnˀɛntpaʊʃa:lə] weekend rate
wochentags [ˈvɔxntʰa:ks] on weekdays
wöchentlich [ˈvœçntlɪç] weekly; once a week
wohl [vo:l] *(comfortable)* well
wohlwollend [ˈvo:lvɔlnt] kind
wohnen [vo:nn] to live, to stay
Wohnort *m* [ˈvo:nˀɔɐt] place of residence
Wohnung *f* [ˈvo:nʊŋ] flat, apartment
Wohnzimmer *n* [ˈvo:ntsɪmɐ] living room
Wolke *f* [ˈvɔlkə] cloud
Wolle *f* [ˈvɔlə] wool
wollen [vɔln] to want, to wish
Wort *n* [vɔɐt] word
Wunde *f* [ˈvʊndə] wound
wunderbar [ˈvʊndɐba:] wonderful, marvellous
wundern, sich ~ (über) [zɪç ˈvʊndɐn (ˌˀybɐ)] be surprised (at/about)
Wunsch *m* [vʊnʃ] request
wünschen [vʏnʃn] to want; to wish for
Wurm *m* [vʊɐm] worm
Wurst *f* [vʊɐst] sausage
würzen [vʏɐtsn] to season
wütend [vy:tnt] furious

Y

Yoga *n* [ˈjo:ga] yoga

Z

zäh [tsɛ:] tough
Zahl *f* [tsa:l] number, figure
zahlen [ˈtsa:ln] to pay
zählen [tsɛ:ln] to count
Zahlung *f* [ˈtsa:lʊŋ] payment
Zahn *m* [tsa:n] tooth
Zahnbürste *f* [ˈtsa:nbʏɐstə] toothbrush
Zahnfleisch *n* [ˈtsa:nflaɪʃ] gums
Zahnpasta *f* [ˈtsa:npasta] toothpaste
Zahnschmerzen *m pl* [ˈtsa:nʃmɛɐtsn] toothache
Zahnstocher *m* [ˈtsa:nʃtɔxɐ] toothpick
Zäpfchen *n* [ˈtsɛpfçn] suppository
zart [tsa:t] *(soft)* tender
zärtlich [ˈtsɛɐtlɪç] tender, gentle
Zecke *f* [ˈtsɛkə] tick
Zehe *f* [ˈtseə] toe
Zeichen *n* [ˈtsaɪçn] sign
Zeichensprache *f* [ˈtsaɪçnʃpʀa:xə] sign language
Zeichentrickfilm *m* [ˈtsaɪçnˌtʀɪkfɪlm] cartoon
zeichnen [ˈtsaɪçn (ə)n] to draw
Zeichnung *f* [ˈtsaɪçnʊŋ] drawing
zeigen [ˈtsaɪgŋ] to show
Zeit *f* [tsaɪt] time
Zeitschrift *f* [ˈtsaɪtʃʀɪft] *(news)* magazine
Zeitung *f* [ˈtsaɪtʰʊŋ] newspaper
Zeitungshändler *m* [ˈtsaɪtʊŋshɛntlɐ] newsagent's
Zelt *n* [tsɛlt] tent
zelten [ˈtsɛltn] to camp
Zentimeter *m* [ˌtsɛntiˈme:tɐ] centimetre
zentral [tsɛnˈtʀa:l] central
Zerrung *f* [ˈtsɛʀʊŋ] pulled muscle
ziehen [tsi:n] to pull
Ziel *n* [tsi:l] aim; target; goal; destination
ziemlich [ˈtsi:mlɪç] fairly, rather, pretty, quite
Zigarette *f* [tsɪgaˈʀɛtə] cigarette
Zigarillo *n* [tsɪgaˈʀɪlo] cigarillo
Zigarre *f* [tsɪˈgaʀə] cigar
Zimmer *n* [ˈtsɪmɐ] room
Zimmermädchen *n* [ˈtsɪmɐmɛ:tçn] maid
Zimmertelefon *n* [ˈtsɪmɐteləˌfo:n] in-room telephone
Zirkus *m* [ˈtsɪɐkʊs] circus
Zitronen *f pl* [tsɪˈtʀo:nn] lemons
Zoll *m* [ˈtsɔl] customs
Zollerklärung *f* [ˈtsɔlɐklɛ:ʀʊŋ] customs declaration
zollfrei [ˈtsɔlfʀaɪ] duty-free
Zollgebühren *f pl* [ˈtsɔlgəby:ʀən] customs duty
zollpflichtig [ˈtsɔl(p)flɪçtɪç] liable to duty
Zoo *m* [tso:] zoo
zornig [ˈtsɔɐnɪç] angry
zu [tsu (:)] to; shut, closed; too; **zu viel** [tsʊˈfi:l] too much
zubereiten [ˈtsu:bəʀaɪtn] prepare, cook; mix *(drinks)*
Zucchini *f* [tsʊˈki:ni] courgette *(GB)*, zucchini *(US)*
Zucker *m* [ˈtsʊkɐ] sugar
zuerst [tsʊˈˀeɐst] (at) first
zufällig [ˈtsu:fɛlɪç] by chance
zufrieden [tsʊˈfʀi:dn] satisfied
Zug *m* [tsu:k] train
Zugang *m* [ˈtsu:gaŋ] access, entrance
zugänglich [ˈtsu:gɛŋlɪç] accessible
Zukunft *f* [ˈtsu:kʰʊnft] future
zukünftig [ˈtsu:kʰʏnftɪç] *(adj)* future
zulassen [ˈtsu:lasn] to register *(car)*
zulässig [ˈtsu:lɛsɪç] permitted, allowed
zuletzt [tsʊˈlɛtst] finally; last
zumachen [ˈtsu:maxn] to close, to shut
zunächst [tsʊˈnɛ:çst/-ˈnɛ:kst] first (of all)
Zündkerze *f* [ˈtsʏntkɛɐtsə] spark plug

Zündschlüssel *m* [ˈtsʏntʃlʏsl] ignition key
Zündung *f* [ˈtsʏndʊŋ] ignition
Zunge *f* [ˈtsʊŋə] tongue
zurück [tsʊˈʀʏk] back
zurückbringen [tsʊˈʀʏkbʀɪŋŋ] bring back
zurückfahren [tsʊˈʀʏkfa: (ʀə)n] drive back, return
zurückgeben [tsʊˈʀʏkge:bm] give back
zurückkehren [tsʊˈʀʏkʰe:ʀən/-kʰeɐn] come back, return
zurückweisen [tsʊˈʀʏkvaɪzn] to refuse
zurzeit [tsʊɐˈtsaɪt] at the moment
zusagen [ˈtsu:za:gŋ] accept *(invitation)*
zusammen [tsʊˈzamm] together
zusammenschlagen [tsʊˈzammʃla:gŋ] beat up
Zusammenstoß *m* [tsʊˈzammʃto:s] collision, crash
zusätzlich [ˈtsu:zɛtslɪç] additional; in addition
zuschauen [ˈtsu:ʃaʊn] to watch
Zuschauer/in *m/f* [ˈtsu:ʃaʊɐ/ˈtsu:ʃaʊəʀɪn] viewer, spectator
Zustand *m* [ˈtsu:ʃtant] state, condition
zuständig [ˈtsu:ʃtɛndɪç] responsible
zweimal [ˈtsvaɪma:l] twice
zweite(r, s) [ˈtsvaɪtə (-tɐ/-təs)] second
zweitens [tsvaɪtns] second(ly)
Zwiebeln *f pl* [tsvi:bln] onions
zwischen [tsvɪʃn] between; among
Zwischenfall *m* [ˈtsvɪʃnfal] incident
Zwischenlandung *f* [ˈtsvɪʃnˌlandʊŋ] stopover
Zwischenstecker *m* [ˈtsvɪʃnʃtɛkɐ] adapter
Zyste *f* [ˈtsʏstə] cyst

A

abbey die Abtei [di ˀapˈtaɪ]
abbreviation die Abkürzung [di ˈˀapkʏɐtsʊŋ]
able, be ~ to im Stande sein [ˀɪmˈʃtandə zaɪn], können [kœnn]
about ungefähr [ˀʊngəˈfeɐ], etwa [ˈˀɛtva:]; *(time)* gegen [ge:gŋ]
about noon gegen Mittag [ˈge:gŋ ˈmɪta:k]
abroad im/ins Ausland [ˀɪm/ˀɪns ˈˀaʊslant]
abscess der Abszess [dɐ ˀapsˈɛs]
accelerator das Gaspedal [das ˈga:speda:l]
accept annehmen [ˈˀane:mm]; *(invitation)* zusagen [ˈtsu:za:gŋ]
access der Zugang [dɐ ˈtsu:gaŋ]
accessible zugänglich [ˈtsu:gɛŋlɪç]
accident der Unfall [dɐ ˈˀʊnfal]; **have an accident** verunglücken [fɐˈˀʊnglʏkŋ]
accommodation die Unterkunft [di ˈˀʊntɐkʊnft]
accompany begleiten [bəˈglaɪtn]
accompanying person die Begleitperson [di bəˈglaɪtp(ɛ)ɐˌzo:n]
account das Konto [das ˈkɔnto]
acquaintance die Bekanntschaft [di bəˈkantʃaft]; *(person)* der/die Bekannte [dɐ/di bəˈkantə]
across quer durch [kveɐ dʊɐç]
act der Akt [dɐ ˀakt]
action film der Actionfilm [dɐ ˈˀɛktʃnfɪlm]
actor/actress der Schauspieler/die Schauspielerin [dɐ ˈʃaʊʃpi:lɐ/di ˈʃaʊʃpi:lərɪn]
actual(ly) eigentlich [ˈˀaɪgŋtlɪç]
acupuncture die Akupunktur [ˀakupʊŋ(k)ˈtuɐ]
adapter der Adapter [dɐ ˀaˈdaptɐ], der Zwischenstecker [dɐ ˈtsvɪʃnʃtɛkɐ]
add hinzufügen [hɪnˈtsu:fy:gŋ]; **in addition** zusätzlich [ˈtsu:zɛtslɪç]; **additional** zusätzlich [ˈtsu:zɛtslɪç]
additional costs die Nebenkosten [di ˈne:bmkɔstn]
address die Anschrift [di ˈˀanʃrɪft], die Adresse [di ˀaˈdrɛsə]; *(vb)* adressieren [ˀadrɛˈsi:rən/-ˈsiɐn]
addressee der Empfänger [dɐ ˀɛmpˈfɛŋɐ]
administration die Verwaltung [di fɐˈvaltʊŋ]
admission charge der Eintrittspreis [dɐ ˈˀaɪntrɪtspraɪs]
admission ticket die Eintrittskarte [di ˈˀaɪntrɪtsˌka:tə]
adult der/die Erwachsene [dɐ/di ˀɐˈvaks(ə)nə]
advance booking der Vorverkauf [dɐ ˈfoɐfɐkaʊf]
advance, in ~ im Voraus [ˀɪm ˈfo:raʊs]
advantage der Vorzug [dɐ ˈfoɐtsu:k]; der Vorteil [dɐ ˈfɔɐtaɪl]
aerobics das Aerobic [das ˀɛˈrɔbɪk]
afraid erschrocken [ˀɐˈʃrɔkŋ]; **be afraid (of)** sich fürchten (vor) [zɪç ˈfʏɐçtn foɐ]; befürchten [bəˈfʏɐçtn]
after nach [na:x]
afternoon der Nachmittag [dɐ ˈna:xmɪta:k]; **in the afternoon** nachmittags [ˈnaxmɪta:ks]
after-shave lotion das Rasierwasser [das raˈziɐvasɐ]
afterwards nachher [ˈna:x(h)eɐ], danach [daˈna:x]
again wieder [ˈvi:dɐ]
against gegen [ge:gŋ]; **be against it** dagegen sein [daˈge:gŋ zaɪn]
age das Alter [das ˈˀaltɐ]
agency die Agentur [di ˀagɛnˈtuɐ]
agree sich einigen [zɪç ˈˀaɪnɪgŋ]; einig sein [ˈˀaɪnɪç zaɪn]; *(on a date, time etc.)* ausmachen [ˈˀaʊsmaxn]; **agree on** vereinbaren [fɐˈˀaɪnba:(rə)n]
agreeable angenehm [ˈˀangəne:m]
aid die Hilfe [di ˈhɪlfə]; **first aid** erste Hilfe [ˌˀeɐstə ˈhɪlfə]
aim das Ziel [das tsi:l]
air die Luft [di lʊft]; lüften [ˈlʏftn]
air-conditioning die Klimaanlage [di ˈkli:mɐˀanˌla:gə]
airline die Fluggesellschaft [di ˈflu:kgəˌzɛlʃaft]
airport der Flughafen [dɐ ˈflu:kha:fn]
airport bus der Flughafenbus [dɐ ˈflu:kha:fnˌbʊs]
airport tax die Flughafengebühr [di ˈflu:kha:fngəˌbyɐ]
alarm clock der Wecker [dɐ ˈvɛkɐ]
alarm system die Alarmanlage [di ˀaˈla:manla:gə]
alarmed erschrocken [ˀɐˈʃrɔkŋ]
all alle [ˈˀalə]; ganz [gants]
allergy die Allergie [di ˀal(ɛ)ɐˈgi:]

alley die Gasse [di ˈgasə]
allowed zulässig [ˈtsuːlɛsɪç]; **be allowed** dürfen [dʏɐfn]
almonds die Mandeln *f pl* [di ˈmandln]
almost fast [fast], beinahe [ˈbaɪnaː]
alone allein [ˀaˈlaɪn]
already bereits [bəˈʀaɪts], schon [ʃoːn]
also auch [ˀaʊx], gleichfalls [ˈglaɪçfals]
altar der Altar [dɐ ˀalˈtaː]
although obwohl [ˀɔpˈvoːl]
always immer [ˈˀɪmɐ], stets [ʃteːts]
ambulance der Krankenwagen [dɐ ˈkʀaŋkŋvaːgŋ]
America Amerika [ˀaˈmeːʀɪkaː]
American der Amerikaner/die Amerikanerin [dɐ ˀameʀɪˈkaːnɐ/di ˀameʀɪˈkaːnəʀɪn]
among zwischen [ˈtsvɪʃn]
amount der Betrag [dɐ bəˈtʀaːk]
amputated amputiert [ampuˈtiɐt]
amusement park der Freizeitpark [dɐ ˈfʀaɪtsaɪtˌpaːk]
ancient antik [ˀanˈtiːk]
and und [ˀʊnt]
angina die Angina [di ˀaŋˈgiːna]
angry zornig [ˈtsɔɐnɪç]; böse [ˈbøːzə]
animal das Tier [das tiɐ]
ankle der Knöchel [dɐ knœçl]
announce melden [mɛldn], anmelden [ˈˀanmɛldn]
announcement die Mitteilung [di ˈmɪtaɪlʊŋ]
annoying lästig [ˈlɛstɪç]
annual(ly) jährlich [ˈjɛɐlɪç]
anorak der Anorak [dɐ ˈˀanoʀak]
answer die Antwort [di ˈˀantvɔɐt]; *(vb)* antworten [ˈˀantvɔɐtn], beantworten [bəˈˀantvɔɐtn]
answering machine der Anrufbeantworter [dɐ ˈˀanfuːfbəˌˀantvɔɐtɐ]
anti-freeze das Frostschutzmittel [das ˈfʀɔstʃʊtsmɪtl]
antique shop das Antiquitätengeschäft [das ˀantɪkvɪˈtɛːtngəʃɛft]
any jeder Beliebige [ˌjeːdɐ bəˈliːbɪgə]; *(in questions)* einige [ˈˀaɪnɪgə]
anybody *(in questions)* jemand [ˈjeːmant]
anything *(in questions)* etwas [ˈˀɛtvas]
apartment die Wohnung [di ˈvoːnʊŋ]
apologize sich entschuldigen [zɪç ˀɛntˈʃʊldɪgŋ]
appendicitis die Blinddarmentzündung [di ˈblɪntdaːmɛnˌtsʏndʊŋ]
appetite der Appetit [dɐ ˀapəˈtɪt]
applause der Beifall [dɐ ˈbaɪfal]
apples die Äpfel *m pl* [di ˀɛpfl]
appointment der Termin [dɐ tɐˈmiːn]; *(meeting)* die Verabredung [di fɐˈˀapʀeːdʊŋ]
apricots die Aprikosen *f pl* [di ˀapʀɪˈkoːzn]
April April [ˀaˈpʀɪl]
aqua jogging das Aqua-Jogging [das ˈˀakvaˌdʒɔgɪŋ]
arch der Bogen [dɐ ˈboːgŋ]
archaeology die Archäologie [di ˀaːçeoloˈgiː]
architect Architekt/Architektin [ˀaːçɪˈtɛkt/ˀaːçɪˈtɛkt ɪn]
architecture die Architektur [di ˀaːçitɛkˈtuɐ]
area die Gegend [di ˈgeːgŋt]
area code die Vorwahlnummer [di ˈfoɐvaːlˌnʊmɐ]
arm der Arm [dɐ ˀaːm]
aroma bath das Aromabad [das ˀaˈʁoːmabaːt]
around herum [hɐˈʀʊm]
arrest verhaften [fɐˈhaftn]
arrival die Ankunft [di ˈˀankʊnft]
arrive (at) eintreffen [ˈˀaɪntʀɛfn]
art die Kunst [di kʊnst]
art dealer der Kunsthändler [dɐ ˈkʊnstˌhɛntlɐ]
art nouveau der Jugendstil [dɐ ˈjuːgŋtstiːl]
artichokes die Artischocken *f pl* [di ˀaːtɪˈʃɔkŋ]
artificial limb die Prothese [di pʀoˈteːzə]
arts and crafts das Kunstgewerbe [das ˈkʊnstgəvɛɐbə]
as *(reason)* da [daː]
ashtray der Aschenbecher [dɐ ˈˀaʃnbɛçɐ]
ask fragen [fʀaːgŋ], fordern [ˈfɔɐdɐn], auffordern [ˈˀaʊfɔɐdɐn]; **ask s.o. for s.th.** jdn um etw. bitten [ˌjemandn ʊm ˌˀɛtvas ˈbɪtn]
asparagus der Spargel [ʃpaːgl]
aspirin das Aspirin [das ˀaspiˈʀiːn]
association der Verein [dɐ fɐˈˀaɪn]
asthma das Asthma [das ˈˀastma]
at *(time)* um [ˀʊm]
athlete der Sportler/die Sportlerin [dɐ ˈʃpɔɐtlɐ/di ˈʃpɔɐtləʀɪn]
athletics die Leichtathletik [di ˈlaɪçtˀatˌleːtɪk]
Atlantic der Atlantik [dɐ ˀatˈlantɪk]
attack der Anfall [dɐ ˈˀanfal]
attention die Achtung [di ˈˀaxtʊŋ]; **pay attention (to)** aufpassen [ˈˀaʊfpasn], beachten [bəˈˀaxtn]
au gratin überbacken [ˀybɐˈbakŋ]
aubergines die Auberginen *f pl* [di ˀobɐˈʒiːnn]

August August [ˀaʊˈgʊst]
Austria Österreich [das ˈˀøːstəʀaɪç]
Austrian der Österreicher/die Österreicherin [dɐ ˈˀøːstəʀaɪçɐ/ di ˈˀøːstəʀaɪçəʀɪn]
authorities die Behörde [di bəˈhøɐdə]
automated teller machine der Geldautomat [dɐ ˈgɛltaʊtoˌmaːt]
automatic automatisch [ˀaʊtoˈmaːtɪʃ]
automatic (transmission) das Automatikgetriebe [das ˀaʊtoˈmaːtɪkgəˌtʀiːbə]
autumn der Herbst [dɐ ˈhɛɐpst]
average durchschnittlich [ˈdʊɐçʃnɪtlɪç]
avocado die Avocado [di ˀavoˈkaːdo]
awake wach [vax]
aware bewusst [bəˈvʊst]; **be aware of** merken [mɛɐkŋ]
away weg [vɛk], fort [fɔɐt]
awful schrecklich [ˈʃʀɛklɪç]
Ayurveda Ayurveda [ˀajʊˈveːda]

B

baby das Baby [das ˈbeːbiː]
baby food die Kindernahrung [di ˈkɪndɐnaːʀʊŋ]
baby intercom das Babyfon [das ˈbeːbifoːn]
baby lift Babylift [ˈbeːbilɪft]
baby seat die Babyschale [di ˈbeːbiʃaːlə]
baby's bottle die Trinkflasche [di ˈtʀɪŋkflaʃə]
baby's changing table der Wickeltisch [dɐ ˈvɪkltɪʃ]
babysitter der Babysitter [dɐ ˈbeːbisɪtɐ]
babysitting service die Kinderbetreuung [di ˈkɪndɐbətʀɔjʊŋ]
bachelor der Junggeselle [dɐ ˈjʊŋgəzɛlə]
back der Rücken [dɐ ʀʏkŋ]; *(adv)* zurück [tsʊˈʀʏk]
backache die Rückenschmerzen *m pl* [di ˈʀʏkŋʃmɛɐtsn]
backwards rückwärts [ˈʀʏkvɛɐts]
bad schlimm [ʃlɪm], schlecht [ʃlɛçt]
badly schlecht [ʃlɛçt]
badminton das Badminton [das ˈbɛtmɪntn]
bag der Sack [dɐ zak], die Tüte [di ˈtyːtə], die Handtasche [di ˈhan(t)taʃə]
baggage das Gepäck [das geˈpɛk]
baggage car der Gepäckwagen [dɐ gəˈpɛkvaːgŋ]
baggage deposit die Gepäckaufbewahrung [di gəˈpɛkˌˀaʊfbəvaːʀʊŋ]
baggage reclaim die Gepäckausgabe [di gəˈpɛkˀaʊsgaːbə]
baked gebacken [gəˈbakŋ]
baker's die Bäckerei [di bɛkəˈʀaɪ]
balcony der Balkon [dɐ balˈkɔŋ]
ball der Ball [dɐ bal]; *(festivity)* der Ball [dɐ bal]
ballet das Ballett [das baˈlɛt]
ball-point pen der Kugelschreiber [dɐ ˈkuːglʃʀaɪbɐ]
bananas die Bananen *f pl* [di baˈnaːnn]
band die Band [di bɛ(ː)nt]
bandage der Verband [dɐ fɐˈbant]
bank die Bank [di baŋk]; *(river)* das Ufer [das ˈˀuːfɐ]
banknote der Geldschein [dɐ ˈgɛltʃaɪn]
bar die Bar [di baː]
barber's der (Herren)Friseur [dɐ(ˈhɛʀən)fʀɪˈzøɐ]
baroque barock [baˈʀɔk]
basil das Basilikum [das baˈziːlɪkʊm]
basket der Korb [dɐ kɔɐp]
basketball der Basketball [dɐ ˈbaːskətbal]
bath die Badewanne [di ˈbaːdəvanə]
bathing shoes die Badeschuhe *m pl* [di ˈbaːdəʃuə]
bathrobe der Bademantel [dɐ ˈbaːdəmantl]
bathroom das Badezimmer [das ˈbaːdətsɪmɐ]
battery die Batterie [di batəˈʀiː]
battery charger das Ladegerät [das ˈlaːdəgəʀɛːt]
battery charger lead *(mobile phone)* das Ladekabel (Handy) [das ˈlaːdəkaːbl (ˈhɛndi)]
bay die Bucht [di bʊxt]
bay-leaves die Lorbeerblätter *n pl* [di ˈlɔɐbeɐˌblɛtɐ]
be sein [zaɪn], sich befinden [zɪç bəˈfɪndn]
beach der Strand [dɐ ʃtʀant]
beach shoes die Strandschuhe *m pl* [di ˈʃtʀantʃuə]
beans die Bohnen *f pl* [di boːnn]
beard der Bart [dɐ baːt]
beat up zusammenschlagen [tsʊˈzammʃlaːgŋ]
beautiful schön [ʃøːn]
because weil [vaɪl]; da [daː]; **because of** wegen [veːgŋ]
become werden [veɐdn]
bed das Bett [das bɛt]; **go to bed** ins Bett gehen [ˀɪns ˈbɛt geːn]
bed linen die Bettwäsche [di ˈbɛtvɛʃə]

bedroom das Schlafzimmer [das ˈʃla:ftsɪmɐ]
bedside table der Nachttisch [dɐ ˈnaxttɪʃ]
bee die Biene [di ˈbi:nə]
beef das Rindfleisch [ˈʀɪntflaɪʃ]
beer das Bier [das biɐ]
before vor [foɐ]; *(conj)* bevor [bəˈfoɐ]; *(previously)* vorher [ˈfoɐheɐ]
begin anfangen [ˈʔanfaŋŋ], beginnen [bəˈgɪnn]
beginning der Anfang [dɐ ˈʔanfaŋ], der Beginn [dɐ bəˈgɪn]
behind hinter [ˈhɪntɐ]
beige beige [be:ʃ]
Belgian der Belgier/die Belgierin [dɐ ˈbɛlgɪɐ/di ˈbɛlgɪəʀɪn]
Belgium Belgien [ˈbɛlgɪən]
believe glauben [glaʊbm]
bell die Klingel [di klɪŋl]
belong to gehören [gəˈhø:ʀən/-ˈhøɐn]
below unterhalb [ˈʔʊntɐhalp], unten [ˈʔʊntn]
belt der Gürtel [dɐ gʏɐtl]
bench die (Sitz)Bank [di (ˈzɪts)baŋk]
bend die Kurve [di ˈkʊɐvə]
beside neben [ˈne:bm]
besides außerdem [ˈʔaʊsɐde:m]
best beste(r, s) [ˈbɛstə (-tɐ, -təs)]; at best höchstens [ˈhø:çstns/ˈhø:kstns]
best before die Haltbarkeit [ˈhaltba(:)kaɪt]
better besser [ˈbɛsɐ]
between zwischen [ˈtsvɪʃn]
bicycle das Fahrrad [das ˈfa:ʀat]
big groß [gʀo:s]
bike das Fahrrad [das ˈfa:ʀat]
bikini der Bikini [dɐ biˈki:ni]
bill die Rechnung [di ˈʀɛçnʊŋ]
bin der Abfalleimer [dɐ ˈʔapfalˌʔaɪmɐ]
bin liner der Abfallbeutel [dɐ ˈʔapfalbɔɪtl]
bird der Vogel [dɐ fo:gl]
bird reserve das Vogelschutzgebiet [das ˈfo:glʃʊtsgəbi:t]
biro der Kuli [dɐ ˈku:li]
birthday der Geburtstag [dɐ gəˈbʊɐtsta:k]
bite *(vb)* beißen [baɪsn]
bitter bitter [ˈbɪtɐ]
black schwarz [ʃva:ts]
black-and-white film der Schwarz-weiß-Film [dɐ ʃva:tsˈvaɪsfɪlm]
blackberries die Brombeeren *f pl* [di ˈbʀɔmbe:ʀən]
bladder die Blase [di ˈbla:zə]
blank der Rohling [dɐ ˈʁo:lɪŋ]
blanket die Bettdecke [di ˈbɛtdɛkə]
blazer der Blazer [dɐ ˈble:zɐ]
bleed bluten [blu:tn]
bleeding die Blutung [di ˈblu:tʊŋ]
blender der Mixer [dɐ ˈmɪksɐ]
blind blind [blɪnt]
blind person der/die Blinde [dɐ/di ˈblɪnde]
blond(e) blond [blɔnt]
blood das Blut [das blu:t]
blood group die Blutgruppe [di ˈblu:tgʀʊpə]
blood-poisoning die Blutvergiftung [di ˈblu:tfɐgɪftʊŋ]
blouse die Bluse [di ˈblu:zə]
blow dry föhnen [fø:nn]
blue blau [blaʊ]
blues der Blues [dɐ blu:s]
boarding card die Bordkarte [di ˈbɔɐtka:tə]
body der Körper [dɐ ˈkœɐpɐ]
boil kochen [kɔxn]
boiled gekocht [gəˈkɔxt]
bone der Knochen [dɐ knɔxn]
bonnet die Motorhaube [di ˈmo:tɔˌhaʊbə]
book das Buch [das bu:x]; *(vb)* buchen [bu:xn], vorbestellen [ˈfoɐbəʃtɛln]
book shop die Buchhandlung [di ˈbu:xhantlʊŋ]
booking die Buchung [di ˈbu:xʊŋ], die Voranmeldung [di ˈfoɐʔanmɛldʊŋ]
boot der Kofferraum [dɐ ˈkɔfɐʀaʊm]
boots die Stiefel *m pl* [di ʃti:fl]
border die Grenze [di ˈgʀɛntsə]
boring langweilig [ˈlaŋvaɪlɪç]
born geboren [gəˈbo:ʀən (gəˈboɐn)]
borreliosis die Borreliose [di bɔʁɛlˈjo:zə]
borrow (aus)leihen [(ˈʔaʊs)laɪn]
boss der Leiter/die Leiterin [dɐ ˈlaɪtɐ/di ˈlaɪtəʀɪn], der Chef/die Chefin [dɐ ʃɛf/di ʃɛfɪn]
botanic gardens der botanische Garten [dɐ boˈtanɪʃə ˈga:tn]
both beide [ˈbaɪdə]
bother belästigen [bəˈlɛstɪgŋ], stören [ʃtøɐn]
bottle die Flasche [di ˈflaʃə]
bottle opener der Flaschenöffner [dɐ ˈflaʃnʔœfnɐ]
bottle warmer der Fläschchenwärmer [dɐ ˈflɛʃçənvɛɐmɐ]
boutique die Boutique [di buˈti:k]
bowel movement der Stuhlgang [dɐ ˈʃtu:lgaŋ]
bowl die Schüssel [di ʃʏsl]
box die Kiste [di ˈkɪstə], die Schachtel [di ʃaxtl], die Packung [di ˈpakʊŋ]; *(theatre)* die Loge [di ˈlo:ʒə]

box office die (Theater)Kasse [di (te'ʔa:tɐ)ˌkasə]
boy der Junge [dɐ 'jʊŋə]
bracelet das Armband [das 'ʔa:mbant]
braille die Blindenschrift [di 'blɪndnʃʀɪft]
brain das Gehirn [das gə'hɪɐn]
braised geschmort [gə'ʃmoɐt]
brake die Bremse [di 'bʀɛmzə]
brake fluid die Bremsflüssigkeit [di 'bʀɛmsflʏsɪçkaɪt]
brake lights die Bremslichter [di 'bʀɛmslɪçtɐ]
bread das Brot [das bʀo:t]
break into/open aufbrechen ['ʔaʊfbʀɛçn]
breakdown die Panne [di 'panə]
breakdown service der Pannendienst [dɐ 'panndi:nst]
breakdown vehicle der Abschleppwagen [dɐ 'ʔapʃlɛpva:gŋ]
breakfast das Frühstück [das 'fʀy:ʃtʏk]; **have breakfast** frühstücken ['fʀy:ʃtʏkŋ]
breakfast room der Frühstücksraum [dɐ 'fʀy:ʃtʏksʀaʊm]
breathe atmen ['ʔa:tmən]
bridge die Brücke [di 'bʀʏkə]
briefs der (Herren)Slip [dɐ ('hɛʀən) slɪp]
bring mitbringen ['mɪtbʀɪŋŋ]; *(her-)* bringen [('hɛɐ)bʀɪŋŋ]; **bring back** zurückbringen [tsʊ'ʀʏkbʀɪŋŋ]
broad breit [bʀaɪt]
brochure der Prospekt [dɐ pʀos'pɛkt]
broken kaputt [ka'pʊt]; *(bone)* gebrochen [gə'bʀɔxn]
bronchial tubes die Bronchien *f pl* [di 'bʀɔnçɪən]
bronchitis die Bronchitis [di bʀɔn'çi:tɪs]
bronze die Bronze [di 'bʀɔŋsə]
brooch die Brosche [di 'bʀɔʃə]
broom der Besen [dɐ be:zn]
brother der Bruder [dɐ 'bʀu:dɐ]
brother-in-law der Schwager [dɐ 'ʃva:gɐ]
brown braun [bʀaʊn]
brown (rye) bread das Schwarzbrot [das 'ʃva:tsbʀo:t]
bruise *(caused by hitting)* die Prellung [di 'pʀɛlʊŋ]; *(caused by pinching)* die Quetschung [di 'kvɛtʃʊŋ]
brush die Bürste [di 'bʏɐstə]
bucket der Eimer [dɐ 'ʔaɪmɐ]
buffet breakfast das Frühstücksbüfett [das 'fʀy:ʃtʏksbʏˌfe:]
building das Gebäude [das gə'bɔɪdə]
bumper die Stoßstange [di 'ʃto:ʃtaŋə]
bunch of flowers der Blumenstrauß [dɐ 'blu:mmʃtʀaʊs]
bungalow der Bungalow [dɐ 'bʊŋgalo:]
bunk bed das Etagenbett [das ʔe'ta:ʒnbɛt]
burn die Verbrennung [di fɐ'bʀɛnʊŋ]; *(vb)* brennen [bʀɛnn]; verbrennen [fɐ'bʀɛnn]
bus der Bus [dɐ bʊs]
bus station der Busbahnhof [dɐ 'bʊsˌba:nho:f]
bush der Busch [dɐ bʊʃ]
but aber ['ʔa:bɐ]; sondern ['zɔndɐn]
butcher's die Metzgerei [di mɛtsgə'ʀaɪ]
butter die Butter [di 'bʊtɐ]
buttermilk die Buttermilch [di 'bʊtɐmɪlç]
button der Knopf [dɐ knɔpf]
buy kaufen [kaʊfn], einkaufen ['ʔaɪnkaʊfn]
by von [fɔn]; **by (means of)** durch [dʊɐç]
bypass der Bypass [dɐ 'baɪpa:s]

C

cabaret das Kabarett [das kaba'ʀe:]
cabbage der Kohl [dɐ ko:l]
cabin die Kabine [di ka'bi:nə]
cable railway die (Stand)Seilbahn [di ('ʃtant)ˌzaɪlba:n]
café das Café [das ka'fe:]
cake der Kuchen [dɐ ku:xn]
cake shop die Konditorei [di kɔndito'ʀaɪ]
calculate rechnen ['ʀɛçn(ə)n], berechnen [bə'ʀɛçn(ə)n]
call der Anruf [dɐ 'ʔanʀu:f]; *(vb, phone)* anrufen ['ʔanʀu:fn]; *(shout)* rufen [ʀu:fn]; *(call out)* aufrufen ['ʔaʊfʀu:fn]; *(name)* nennen [nɛnn]; **be called** heißen [haɪsn]; **call for** *(pick up)* abholen ['ʔapho:ln]; **call on s.o.** jdn besuchen [ˌjemandn bə'zu:xn]; **be called** heißen [haɪsn]
calm die Ruhe [di 'ʀuə]; *(adj)* ruhig [ʀʊɪç], still [ʃtɪl]; **calm down** sich beruhigen [zɪç bə'ʀʊɪgŋ]
camcorder der Camcorder [dɐ 'kamkhɔɐdɐ]
camera die Kamera [di 'kaməʀa:]
camomile tea der Kamillentee [dɐ ka'mɪl(ə)nte:]
camp *(vb)* zelten ['tsɛltn]
camping das Camping [das 'kɛmpɪŋ]
camping guide der Campingführer [dɐ 'kɛmpɪŋfy:ʀɐ]

camping site der Campingplatz [dɐ ˈkɛmpɪŋplats]
can die Büchse [di ˈbʏksə], die Dose [di ˈdo:zə]
canal der Kanal [dɐ kaˈna:l]
cancel *(tickets etc.)* abbestellen [ˈˀapbəʃtɛln]; *(appointment)* absagen [ˈˀapza:gŋ]; *(flight)* stornieren [ʃtɔˈniɐn]
cancer der Krebs [dɐ kʀe:ps]
candles die Kerzen *f pl* [di kɛɐtsn]
cane der Taststock [dɐ ˈtastʃtɔk]
canoe das Kanu [das ˈka:nu]
cap die Mütze [di ˈmʏtsə]
capital die Hauptstadt [di ˈhaʊptʃtat]
captain der Kapitän [dɐ kapiˈtɛ:n]
car das Auto [das ˈˀaʊto:], der Wagen [dɐ ˈva:gŋ], der Pkw [dɐ ˈpe:kave:]
car radio das Autoradio [das ˈˀaʊtoˌʀa:djo]
car registration documents der Kfz-Schein [dɐ kaˀefˈtsɛtʃaɪn]
caraway seed(s) der Kümmel [dɐ kʏml]
cardiac infarction der Herzinfarkt [dɐ ˈhɛɐtsɪnfa:kt]
cardiac stimulant das Kreislaufmittel [das ˈkʀaɪslaʊfˌmɪtl]
cardigan die Strickjacke [di ˈʃtʀɪkjakə]
care die Betreuung [di bəˈtʀɔɪʊŋ]; **in need of care** pflegebedürftig [ˈpfle:gəbədʏɐftɪç]
careful vorsichtig [ˈfoɐzɪçtɪç], sorgfältig [ˈzɔɐkfɛltɪç]
carrots die Karotten *f pl* [di kaˈʀɔtn]
carry tragen [tʀa:gŋ]
cartoon der Zeichentrickfilm [dɐ ˈtsaɪçnˌtʀɪkfɪlm]
in case falls [fals]
cash das Bargeld [das ˈba:gɛlt]
cash: to pay (in) ~ bar zahlen [ˈba: tsa:ln]
cashpoint der Geldautomat [dɐ ˈgɛltaʊtoˌma:t]
casino das Spielkasino [das ˈʃpi:lkaˌzi:no]
cassette die Kassette [di kaˈsɛtə]
castle *(fortress)* die Burg [di bʊɐk]; *(palace)* das Schloss [das ʃlɔs]
cat die Katze [di ˈkatsə]
catch fangen [faŋŋ]; *(train)* kriegen [kʀi:gŋ]
cathedral die Kathedrale [di kateˈdʀa:lə]
cauliflower der Blumenkohl [ˈblu:mmko:l]
cause die Ursache [di ˈˀuɐzaxə], der Anlass [dɐ ˈˀanlas], der Grund [dɐ gʀʊnt]; *(vb)* verursachen [fɐˈˀuɐzaxn]
caution die Vorsicht [di ˈfoɐzɪçt]
cautious vorsichtig [ˈfoɐzɪçtɪç]
cave die Höhle [di ˈhø:lə]
CD die CD [di tseˈde:]
CD player der CD-Spieler [dɐ tseˈde:ʃpi:lɐ]
ceiling die Decke [di ˈdɛkə]
celebration(s) das Fest [das fɛst]
celeriac der Sellerie [dɐ ˈzɛləʀi:]
cemetery der Friedhof [dɐ ˈfʀi:to:f]
centimetre der Zentimeter [dɐ ˌtsɛntiˈme:tɐ]
central zentral [tsɛnˈtʀa:l]
century das Jahrhundert [das jaˈhʊndɐt]
ceramics die Keramik [di keˈʀa:mɪk]
certain *(adj)* gewiss [gəˈvɪs], bestimmt [bəˈʃtɪmt], sicher [ˈzɪçɐ]; **certainly** *(adv)* gewiss [gəˈvɪs], unbedingt [ˈˀʊnbəˈdɪŋt]
certificate das Attest [das ˀaˈtɛst]
certify bescheinigen [bəˈʃaɪnɪgŋ]
chair der Stuhl [dɐ ʃtu:l]
champagne der Champagner [dɐ ʃamˈpanjɐ]
chance, by ~ zufällig [ˈtsu:fɛlɪç]
change der Wechsel [dɐ vɛksl], die Veränderung [di fɐˈˀɛndəʀʊŋ]; *(money)* das Wechselgeld [das ˈvɛkslgɛlt]; *(vb)* verändern [fɐˈˀɛndɐn]; *(money)* wechseln [(gɛlt) vɛksln], umtauschen [ˈˀʊmtaʊʃn]; *(trains)* umsteigen [ˈˀʊmʃtaɪgŋ]; *(clothes)* sich umziehen [zɪç ˈˀʊmtsi:n]; **change the booking** umbuchen [ˈˀʊmbu:xn]
changeable wechselhaft [ˈvɛkslhaft]
channel der Kanal [dɐ kaˈna:l]
chapel die Kapelle [di kaˈpɛlə]
charcoal die Grillkohle [di ˈgʀɪlko:lə]
charming entzückend [ˀɛnˈtsʏkŋt], bezaubernd [bəˈtsaɪçnʊŋ]
cheap billig [ˈbɪlɪç]
check *(US)* der Scheck [dɐ ʃɛk]; *(vb)* kontrollieren [kɔntʀoˈli:ʀən/-ˈliɐn], nachprüfen [ˈna:xpʀy:fn], nachsehen [ˈna:xze:n]; **check in** einchecken [ˈˀaɪntʃɛkŋ]
cheeky unverschämt [ˈˀʊnfɐʃɛ:mt]
cheese der Käse [dɐ ˈkɛ:zə]
chemist's die Apotheke [di ˀapoˈte:kə]
cherries die Kirschen *f pl* [di kɪɐʃn]
chest die Brust [di bʀʊst]; *(box)* die Kiste [di ˈkɪstə]
chicken das Hähnchen [das hɛ:nçn]
chickenpox die Windpocken *f pl* [di ˈvɪntpɔkŋ]
child das Kind [das kɪnt]; **children** *(pl)* die Kinder *n pl* [di ˈkɪndɐ]
child reduction die Kinderermäßigung [di ˈkɪndɐˀɐˈmɛ:sɪgʊŋ]

child seat der Kindersitz [dɐ ˈkɪndɐzɪts]
children's clothing die Kinderkleidung [di ˈkɪndɐklaɪdʊŋ]
children's illness die Kinderkrankheit [di ˈkɪndɐˌkʀaŋkhaɪt]
children's playground der Kinderspielplatz [dɐ ˈkɪndɐʃpi:lplats]
children's pool das Kinderbecken [das ˈkɪndɐbɛkŋ]
children's portion der Kinderteller [dɐ ˈkɪndɐtɛlɐ]
china das Porzellan [das pɔɐtsəˈla:n]
chip card die Chipkarte [di ˈtʃɪpka:tə]
chocolate die Schokolade [di ʃokoˈla:də]
chocolate bar der Schokoriegel [dɐ ˈʃo:koʀi:gl]
choice die Auswahl [di ˈʔaʊsva:l], die Wahl [di va:l]
choir der Chor [dɐ koɐ]
choose wählen [ˈvɛ:ln]
chop das Kotelett [ˈkɔtlɛt]
chopping board das Schneidebrett [das ˈʃnaɪdəbʀɛt]
Christian name der Vorname [dɐ ˈfoɐna:mə]
Christianity das Christentum [das ˈkʀɪstntu:m]
Christmas Weihnachten [ˈvaɪnaxtn]
Christmas Eve Heiliger Abend [ˈhaɪlɪgɐ ˈʔa:bmt], Heiligabend [ˌhaɪlɪç ˈʔa:bmt]
church die Kirche [di ˈkɪɐçə]
cigar die Zigarre [di tsɪˈgaʀə]
cigarette die Zigarette [di tsɪgaˈʀɛtə]
cigarillo das Zigarillo [das tsɪgaˈʀɪlo]
cinema das Kino [das ˈki:no]
circulatory disorder die Kreislaufstörung [di ˈkʀaɪslaufˌʃtø:ʀʊŋ]
circus der Zirkus [dɐ ˈtsɪɐkʊs]
city centre das Stadtzentrum [das ˈʃtattsɛntʀʊm]
city map der Stadtplan [dɐ ˈʃtatpla:n]
class die Klasse [di ˈklasə]
classic film der Klassiker [dɐ ˈklasɪkɐ]
classical die Klassik [di ˈklasɪk]
classicism der Klassizismus [dɐ klasɪˈtsɪsmʊs]
clean sauber [ˈzaʊbɐ]; *(washing)* frisch [fʀɪʃ]; *(vb)* putzen [pʊtsn], reinigen [ˈʀaɪnɪgŋ]
cleaning agent das Putzmittel [das ˈpʊtsmɪtl]
clear klar [kla:]; *(weather)* heiter [ˈhaɪtɐ]
clearance sale der Ausverkauf [dɐ ˈʔaʊsfɐkaʊf]
clever klug [klu:k], schlau [ʃlaʊ]
cliff die Klippe [di ˈklɪpə]
climate das Klima [das ˈkli:ma:]
cling film die Frischhaltefolie [di ˈfʀɪʃhaltəˌfo:ljə]
cloakroom die Garderobe [di gaˈdʀo:bə]
cloister der Kreuzgang [dɐ ˈkʀɔɪtsgaŋ]
close *(vb)* schließen [ʃli:sn], zumachen [ˈtsu:maxn]
close (to) *(adj)* nahe (bei) [ˈna:(ə) baɪ]
closed geschlossen [gəˈʃlɔsn]
cloth das Tuch [das tu:x]
clothes line die Wäscheleine [di ˈvɛʃəlaɪnə]
clothes pegs die Wäscheklammern *f pl* [di ˈvɛʃəklamɐn]
clothing die Kleidung [di ˈklaɪdʊŋ]
cloud die Wolke [di ˈvɔlkə]
cloudy *(liquid)* trüb [tʀy:p]; *(weather)* bewölkt [bəˈvœlkt]
cloves die Nelken *f pl* [di nɛlkŋ]
club der Verein [dɐ fɐˈʔaɪn]
clubhouse das Clubhaus [das ˈklʊphaʊs]
clutch die Kupplung [di ˈkʊplʊŋ]
coach number die Wagennummer [di ˈva:gŋnʊmɐ]
coast die Küste [di ˈkʏstə]
coat der Mantel [dɐ mantl]
coat hanger der Kleiderbügel [dɐ ˈklaɪdɐby:gl]
cobbler der Schuhmacher [dɐ ˈʃu:maxɐ]
coconut die Kokosnuss [di ˈko:kosnʊs]
coffee der Kaffee [dɐ ˈkafe:/kaˈfe:]
coffee filter der Kaffeefilter [dɐ ˈkafefɪltɐ/dɐ kaˈfe:fɪltɐ)]
coffee machine die Kaffeemaschine [di ˈkafemaʃi:nə]
coffee spoon der Kaffeelöffel [dɐ ˈkafelœfl/dɐ kaˈfe:lœfl]
coin die Münze [di ˈmʏntsə]
cold die Erkältung [di ʔɐˈkɛltʊŋ] , der Schnupfen [dɐ ʃnʊpfn]; *(adj)* kalt [kalt]; **be cold** frieren [ˈfʀi:ʀən/fʀi:ɐn]
cold cuts der Aufschnitt [dɐ ˈʔaʊfʃnɪt]
cold water kaltes Wasser [ˈva:məs ˈvasɐ]
colic die Kolik [di ˈko:lɪk]
collarbone das Schlüsselbein [das ˈʃlʏslbaɪn]
colleague der Kollege/die Kollegin [dɐ koˈle:gə/di koˈle:gɪn]
collect sammeln [zamln]
collection (of mail) die Leerung [di ˈle:ʀʊŋ]
collision der Zusammenstoß [dɐ tsʊˈzammʃto:s]
coloured farbig [ˈfaʀbɪç]
coloured pencil der Farbstift [dɐ ˈfa:pʃtɪft]

colouring book das Malbuch [das ˈmaːlbuːx]
column die Säule [di ˈzɔɪlə]
comb der Kamm [dɐ kam]; *(vb)* kämmen [kɛmm]
come kommen [kɔmm]; **come back** zurückkehren [tsʊˈʀʏkeːʀən/-keɐn], wiederkommen [ˈviːdɐkɔmm]; **come from** stammen aus [ʃtamm ˀaʊs]; **come in!** herein! [hɐˈʀaɪn]
comedy die Komödie [di koˈmøːdiə]
comfortable bequem [bəˈkveːm], gemütlich [gəˈmyːtlɪç]
common *(adj)* gemeinsam [gəˈmaɪnza(ː)m]; gebräuchlich [gəˈbʀɔɪçlɪç], gewöhnlich [gəˈvøːnlɪç]
company die Firma [di ˈfɪɐmaː]; *(people)* die Gesellschaft [di gəˈzɛlʃaft]
compartment das Abteil [das ˀapˈtaɪl]
compass der Kompass [dɐ ˈkɔmpas]
compensation der Ersatz [dɐ ˀɐˈzats]; der Schadenersatz [dɐ ˈʃaːdnˀɐˌzats]
complete ganz [gants]; *(vb)* vollenden [fɔlˈˀɛndn]
composer der Komponist/die Komponistin [dɐ kɔmpoˈnɪst/di kɔmpoˈnɪstɪn]
computer shop das Computerfachgeschäft [das kɔmˈpjuːtɐˌfaxgəʃɛft]
concert das Konzert [das kɔnˈtsɛɐt]
concussion die Gehirnerschütterung [di gəˈhɪɐnɐˌʃʏtəʀʊŋ]
condom das Kondom [das kɔnˈdoːm]
conductor der Dirigent/die Dirigentin [dɐ diʀiˈgɛnt/di diʀiˈgɛntɪn]
confidence das Vertrauen [das fɐˈtʀaʊn]
confirm bestätigen [bəˈʃtɛːtɪgŋ]
congratulate gratulieren [gʀatʊˈliːʀən/-ˈliɐn]
congratulations der Glückwunsch [dɐ ˈglʏkvʊnʃ]
conjunctivitis die Bindehautentzündung [di ˈbɪndəhaʊtɛnˌtsʏndʊŋ]
connection der Anschluss [dɐ ˈˀanʃlʊs], die Verbindung [di fɐˈbɪndʊŋ]
consist of bestehen aus [ˈbəˈʃteːn ˀaʊs]
constipation die Verstopfung [di fɐˈʃtɔpfʊŋ]
consulate das Konsulat [das kɔnzʊˈlaːt]
contact der Kontakt [dɐ kɔnˈtakt], die Berührung [di bəˈʀyːʀʊŋ]
contagious ansteckend [ˈˀanʃtɛkŋt]
container der Behälter [dɐ bəˈhɛltɐ], das Gefäß [das gəˈfɛːs]
contents der Inhalt [dɐ ˈˀɪnhalt]
contest der Wettkampf [dɐ ˈvɛtkamf]
contract der Vertrag [dɐ fɐˈtʀaːk]
contrary das Gegenteil [das ˈgeːgŋtaɪl]
control *(vb)* kontrollieren [kɔntʀoˈliːʀən/-ˈliɐn]
convent das (Nonnen)Kloster [das (ˈnɔnn)ˌkloːstɐ]
conversation das Gespräch [das gəˈʃpʀɛːç], die Unterhaltung [di ˀʊntɐˈhaltʊŋ]
cook der Koch/die Köchin [dɐ kɔx/di ˈkʰœxɪn]; *(vb)* kochen [kɔxn]; zubereiten [ˈtsuːbəʀaɪtn]
cookbook das Kochbuch [das ˈkɔxbuːx]
cooked gar [gaː]
cooked ham gekochter Schinken [gəˈkɔxtɐ ʃɪŋkŋ]
cooker der Herd [dɐ heɐt]; der Kocher [dɐ ˈkɔxɐ]
cool frisch [fʀɪʃ], kühl [kyːl]
cooling water das Kühlwasser [das ˈkyːlvasɐ]
copy die Kopie [di koˈpiː]
corkscrew der Korkenzieher [dɐ ˈkɔɐkŋtsiːɐ]
corner die Ecke [di ˈˀɛkə], der Winkel [dɐ ˈvɪŋkl]
corridor der Gang [dɐ gaŋ]
corrupt verdorben [fɐˈdɔɐbm], bestechlich [bəˈʃtɛçlɪç]
cost die Kosten *pl* [di kɔstn]; *(vb)* kosten [kɔstn]
costume jewellery der Modeschmuck [dɐ ˈmoːdəʃmʊk]
cosy gemütlich [gəˈmyːtlɪç]
cot das Kinderbett [das ˈkɪndɐbɛt]
cottage die Hütte [di ˈhʏtə]
cotton die Baumwolle [di ˈbaʊmvɔlə]
cotton swabs das Wattestäbchen [das ˈvatəʃtɛːpçn]
cotton wool die Watte [di ˈvatə]
cough der Husten [dɐ huːstn]
cough mixture/syrup der Hustensaft [dɐ ˈhuːstnzaft]
count *(vb)* zählen [tsɛːln]
country das Land [das lant]; **native country** das Vaterland [das ˈfaːtɐlant]; **fellow countryman** der Landsmann [dɐ ˈlantsman]
country road die Landstraße [di ˈlantʃtʀaːsə]
couple das Paar [das paː]; *(married)* das Ehepaar [das ˈˀeːəpaː]
courgette *(GB)* die Zucchini [di tsʊˈkiːni]
course der Kurs [dɐ kʊɐs]; *(meal)* der Gang [dɐ gaŋ]; **of course** selbstverständlich [zɛlp(st)fɐˈʃtɛntlɪç]; natürlich [naˈtyɐlɪç]
cousin der Cousin/die Cousine [dɐ kuˈzɛŋ/di kuˈziːnə]
crab der Krebs [dɐ kreːps]
cramp der Krampf [dɐ kʀampf]

crash der Zusammenstoß [dɐ tsʊˈzammʃto:s]
crash helmet der Sturzhelm [dɐ ˈʃtʊɐtshɛlm]
crazy verrückt [fɐˈʀʏkt]
crazy golf das Minigolf [das ˈmɪnigɔlf]
cream die Creme [di kʀɛ:m]; *(cook)* die Sahne [di ˈza:nə]
creative kreativ [kʀeaˈti:f]
credit card die Kreditkarte [di kʀedi:tka:tə]
crew die Mannschaft [di ˈmanʃaft]
crime das Verbrechen [das fɐˈbʀɛçn]
crockery das Geschirr [das gəˈʃɪɐ]
cross das Kreuz [das kʀɔɪts]; *(adj)* ärgerlich [ˈʔɛɐgɐlɪç]; *(vb)* überqueren [ʔybɐˈkve:ʀən/-ˈkveɐn], überschreiten [ʔybɐˈʃʀaɪtn]
crossing der Übergang [dɐ ˈʔy:bɐgaŋ]
crowded voll [fɔl]
crown die Krone [di ˈkʀo:nə]
crutch die Krücke [di ˈkʀʏkə]
cry *(vb)* weinen [vaɪnn]
crystal der Kristall [dɐ kʀɪsˈtal]
cubicle die Kabine [di kaˈbi:nə]
cucumber die Gurke [di ˈgʊɐkə]
culture die Kultur [di kʊlˈtuɐ]
cup die Tasse [di ˈtasə]
curious neugierig [ˈnɔɪgi:ʀɪç]
curlers die Lockenwickler *m pl* [di ˈlɔkŋvɪklɐ]
curling das Curling [das ˈkə:lɪŋ]
curls die Locken *f pl* [di lɔkŋ]
currency die Währung [di ˈvɛ:ʀʊŋ]
current *(electricity)* der Strom [dɐ ʃtʀo:m]; *(water)* die Strömung [di ˈʃtʀø:mʊŋ]
curve die Kurve [di ˈkʊɐvə]
customer der Kunde/die Kundin [dɐ ˈkʊndə/di ˈkʊndɪn]
customs der Zoll [dɐ ˈtsɔl]
customs declaration die Zollerklärung [di ˈtsɔlɐklɛ:ʀʊŋ]
cut die Schnittwunde [di ˈʃnɪtvʊndə]; *(vb)* schneiden [ʃnaɪdn]; **cut the ends** Spitzen schneiden [ˈʃpɪtsn ˈʃnaɪdn]
cutlery das Besteck [das bəˈʃtɛk]
cutlet das Kotelett [das ˈkɔtlɛt]
cycle *(vb)* Rad fahren [ˈʀa:t ˈfa:ʀən]
cycle path der Fahrradweg [dɐ ˈfa:ʀatve:k]
cycle tour die Radtour [di ˈʀa:ttuɐ]
cycling der Radsport [dɐ ˈʀa:tʃpɔɐt]
cyst die Zyste [di ˈtsʏstə]

D

daily täglich [tɛ:klɪç]
damage die Beschädigung [di bəˈʃɛ:dɪgʊŋ], der Schaden [dɐ ʃa:dn]; *(vb)* beschädigen [bəˈʃɛ:dɪgŋ], schaden [ʃa:dn]
damp feucht [fɔɪçt]
dance der Tanz [dɐ tants]; *(vb)* tanzen [tantsn]
dance band die Tanzkapelle [di ˈtantskaˌpɛlə]
dance theatre das Tanztheater [das ˈtantsteˌʔa:tɐ]
dancer der Tänzer/die Tänzerin [dɐ təntsɐ/di təntsəˈʀɪn]
dandruff die Schuppen *f pl* [di ʃʊpm]
danger die Gefahr [di gəˈfa:]
dangerous gefährlich [gəˈfeɐlɪç]
dark dunkel [dʊŋkl], finster [ˈfɪnstɐ]
dark blue dunkelblau [dʊŋklˈblaʊ]
darling der Liebling [dɐ ˈli:plɪŋ]
date das Datum [das ˈda:tʊm]; *(meeting)* die Verabredung [di fɐˈʔapʀe:dʊŋ]; **up to date** modern [moˈdɛɐn]
date of birth das Geburtsdatum [das gəˈbʊɐtsda:tʊm]
daughter die Tochter [di ˈtɔxtɐ]
day der Tag [dɐ ta:k]
day of arrival der Anreisetag [dɐ ˈʔanʀaɪzəˌta:k]
day pass der Tagespass [dɐ ˈta:gəspas]
day ticket die Tageskarte [di ˈta:gəska:tə]
day trip der Tagesausflug [dɐ ˈta:gəsˌʔaʊsflu:k]
deadline der Termin [dɐ tɐˈmi:n]
deaf gehörlos [gəˈhøɐlo:s], taub [taʊp]
deaf person der/die Gehörlose [dɐ/di gəˈhøɐlo:zə]
deaf-mute *(adj)* taubstumm [ˈtaʊpʃtʊm]
debt die Schuld [di ʃʊlt]
deceitful betrügerisch [bəˈtʀy:gəʀɪʃ]
December Dezember [deˈtsɛmbɐ]
decide entscheiden [ʔɛntˈʃaɪdn], beschließen [bəˈʃli:sn]
deck das Deck [das dɛk]
declaration of value die Wertangabe [di ˈveɐtanga:bə]
decline *(vb)* ablehnen [ˈʔaple:nn]
deep tief [ti:f]
definite(ly) endgültig [ˈʔɛntgʏltɪç]
delay die Verspätung [di fɐˈʃpɛ:tʊŋ]; *(vb)* verzögern [fɐˈtsø:gɐn]
delicatessen das Feinkostgeschäft [das ˈfaɪnkɔstgəˌʃɛft]
delightful entzückend [ʔɛnˈtsʏkŋt]

Dictionary English - German

dent die Delle [di ˈdɛlə]
deodorant das Deo [das ˈdeo]
department store das Kaufhaus [das ˈkaʊfhaʊs]
departure die Abfahrt [di ˈʔapfa:t], *(flight)* der Abflug [dɐ ˈʔapflu:k]
deposit die Kaution [di kaʊˈtsjo:n], *(on bottle)* das Pfand [das (p)fant]; *(vb)* (Geld) hinterlegen [(gɛlt) hɪntɐˈle:gŋ]
describe beschreiben [bəˈʃʀaɪbm]
dessert der Nachtisch [dɐ ˈna:xtɪʃ]
destination das (Reise)Ziel [das (ˈʀaɪzə-)tsi:l]
detergent *(clothes)* das Waschmittel [das ˈvaʃmɪtl]; *(dishes)* das Spülmittel [das ˈʃpy:lmɪtl]
detour der Umweg [dɐ ˈʔʊmve:k]
develop entwickeln [ʔɛntˈvɪkln]
diabetes der Diabetes [dɐ diaˈbe:təs]
diabetic *(person)* der Diabetiker/die Diabetikerin [dɐ diaˈbe:tɪkɐ/di diaˈbe:tɪkəʀɪn]; *(adj)* diabetisch [diaˈbe:tɪʃ]
diagnosis die Diagnose [di diaˈgno:zə]
dial *(vb)* wählen [ˈvɛ:ln]
diarrhoea der Durchfall [dɐ ˈdʊɐçfal]
diet die Diät [di diˈɛ:t], *(food)* die Schonkost [di ˈʃo:nkɔst]
different(ly) verschieden [fɐˈʃi:dn], anders [ˈʔandɐs]
difficult schwierig [ˈʃvi:ʀɪç], schwer [ʃveɐ]
difficulty in breathing die Atembeschwerden *f pl* [di ˈʔa:tmbəʃveɐdn]
digestion die Verdauung [di fɐˈdaʊʊŋ]
digital camera die Digitalkamera [di digiˈta:lˌkaməʀa]
dining room *(hotel)* der Speisesaal [dɐ ˈʃpaɪzəza:l]; *(private)* das Esszimmer [das ˈʔɛstsɪmɐ]
dinner das Abendessen [das ˈʔa:bmtʔɛsn]
diphtheria die Diphtherie [di dɪftəˈʀi:]
dipped headlights das Abblendlicht [das ˈʔablɛntlɪçt]
dipper *(US)* die Schöpfkelle [di ˈʃœpfkɛlə]
direct direkt [diˈʀɛkt]
directed by die Regie [di ʀəˈʒi:]
direction *(way)* die Richtung [di ˈʀɪçtʊŋ]
dirty schmutzig [ˈʃmʊtsɪç]
disability die Behinderung [di bəˈhɪndəʀʊŋ]
disabled person der/die Behinderte [dɐ/di bəˈhɪndɐtə]
disappointed enttäuscht [ʔɛnˈtɔɪʃt]
discotheque die Diskothek [di dɪskoˈte:k]
discount der Rabatt [dɐ ʀaˈbat]
discover entdecken [ʔɛntˈdɛkŋ]
dish *(meal)* das Gericht [das gəˈʀɪçt]
dish of the day das Tagesgericht [das ˈta:gəsgəʀɪçt]
dishcloth das Spültuch [das ˈʃpy:ltu:x]
dishwasher die Geschirrspülmaschine [di gəˈʃɪɐʃpy:lmaˌʃɪnə]
disinfect desinfizieren [dezɪnfɪˈtsi:ʀən]
disinfectant das Desinfektionsmittel [das dezɪnfɛkˈtsjo:nsmɪtl]
distance der Abstand [dɐ ˈʔapʃtant], die Entfernung [di ʔɛntˈfɛɐnʊŋ], die Strecke [di ˈʃtʀɛkə]
distinct deutlich [ˈdɔɪtlɪç]
distinguished fein [faɪn], vornehm [ˈfoɐne:m]
district die Gegend [di ˈge:gŋt], der Stadtteil [dɐ ˈʃtataɪl]
disturb stören [ʃtøɐn]
dive tauchen [taʊxn]
diving equipment die Taucherausrüstung [di ˈtaʊxɐʔaʊsʀʏstʊŋ]
diving goggles die Taucherbrille [di ˈtaʊxɐbʀɪlə]
dizziness das Schwindelgefühl [das ˈʃvɪndlgəfy:l]
do tun [tu:n], machen [ˈmaxn]
dock at anlegen in [ˈʔanle:gŋ ʔɪn]
documentary der Dokumentarfilm [dɐ dɔkʊmɛnˈta:fɪlm]
documents die Papiere *n pl* [di paˈpi:ʀə]
dog der Hund [dɐ hʊnt]
dome die Kuppel [di kʊpl]
domestic flight der Inlandsflug [dɐ ˈʔɪnlantsflu:k]
done *(cooked)* gar [ga:]
door die Tür [di tyɐ]
door code der Türcode [dɐ ˈtyɐko:t]
door opener der Türöffner [dɐ ˈtyɐʔœfnɐ]
door width die Türbreite [di ˈtyɐbʀaɪtə]
doorstep die Türschwelle [di ˈtyɐʃvɛlə]
double doppelt [dɔplt]
doubles das Doppel [das dɔpl]
drama das Drama [das ˈdʀa:ma]
draw zeichnen [ˈtsaɪçnn]; *(sport)* unentschieden spielen [ˈʔʊnɛntˌʃi:dn ʃpi:ln]
drawing die Zeichnung [di ˈtsaɪçnʊŋ]
dreadful schrecklich [ˈʃʀɛklɪç], fürchterlich [ˈfʏɐçtɐlɪç]
dream der Traum [dɐ tʀaʊm]; *(vb)* träumen [tʀɔɪmm]
dress das Kleid [das klaɪt]; *(vb)* sich anziehen [zɪç ˈʔantsi:n]; *(med.)* verbinden [fɐˈbɪndn]
dressing *(med)* der Verband [dɐ fɐˈbant]; *(cook)* das Dressing [das ˈdʀɛsɪŋ]

dressmaker der Schneider/die Schneiderin [dɐ ˈʃnaɪdɐ/di ˈʃnaɪdəʀɪn]
drier der Trockner [dɐ ˈtʀɔknɐ]
drink das Getränk [das gəˈtʀɛŋk]; *(vb)* trinken [tʀɪŋkŋ]
drinking water das Trinkwasser [das ˈtʀɪŋkvasɐ]
dripstone cave die Tropfsteinhöhle [di ˈtʀɔpfʃtaɪnˌhøːlə]
drive die Fahrt [di faːt]; *(vb)* fahren [faː(ʀə)n]; **drive a car** Auto fahren [ˈʔaʊto faːn]; **drive back** zurückfahren [tsʊˈʀʏkfaː(ʀə)n]
drive-in cinema das Freilichtkino [das ˈfʀaɪlɪçtkiːno]
driver der Chauffeur [dɐ ʃɔˈføɐ], der Fahrer/die Fahrerin [dɐ ˈfaːʀɐ/di ˈfaːʀəʀɪn]
driving licence der Führerschein [dɐ ˈfyːʀɐʃaɪn]
drops die Tropfen *m pl* [di ˈtʀɔpfn]
drunk betrunken [bəˈtʀʊŋkŋ]
dry trocken [ˈtʀɔkŋ]; *(wine)* herb [hɛɐp], trocken [ˈtʀɔkŋ]
dry-clean chemisch reinigen [ˈçeːmɪʃ ˈʀaɪnɪgŋ]
drycleaner's die Reinigung [di ˈʀaɪnɪgʊŋ]
dummy der Schnuller [dɐ ˈʃnʊlɐ]
durable haltbar [ˈhaltbaː]
during während [ˈveːʀənt]
during the day tagsüber [ˈtaːksʔyːbɐ]
during the morning vormittags [ˈfɔɐmɪtaːks]
dust der Staub [dɐ ʃtaʊp]
dustbin die Mülltonne [di ˈmʏltɔnə]
dustpan die Kehrschaufel [di ˈkeɐʃaʊfl]
duty die Zollgebühren *f pl* [di ˈtsɔlgəbyːʀən]
duty-free zollfrei [ˈtsɔlfʀaɪ]
duty-free shop zollfreier Laden [ˈtsɔlfʀaɪɐ laːdn]
DVD die DVD [di defaʊˈdeː]
dye *(vb)* färben [fɛɐbm]
dynamo die Lichtmaschine [di ˈlɪçtmaʃiːnə]
dynasty die Dynastie [di dʏnasˈtiː]

E

each jede(r, s) [ˈjeːdə(-dɐ, -dəs)]
ear das Ohr [das ʔoɐ]
ear-drops die Ohrentropfen *m pl* [di ˈʔoːʀəntʀɔpfn]
eardrum das Trommelfell [das ˈtʀɔmlfɛl]
earrings die Ohrringe *m pl* [di ˈʔoːʀɪŋə]
earth die Erde [di ˈʔeɐdə]
east der Osten [dɐ ʔɔstn]
Easter Monday Ostermontag [ˌʔoːstɐˈmoːntaːk]
easy leicht [laɪçt]
eat essen [ʔɛsn]
edible essbar [ˈʔɛsbaː]
education die Erziehung [di ʔɐˈtsiːʊŋ], die Ausbildung [di ˈʔaʊsbɪldʊŋ]
eel der Aal [dɐ ʔaːl]
eggs die Eier *n pl* [di ˈʔaɪɐ]; **egg cup** der Eierbecher [dɐ ˈʔaɪɐˌbɛçɐ]
Eire Irland [ˈʔɪɐlant]
either ... or entweder ... oder [ˈʔɛntveːdɐ ... ˈʔoːdɐ]
elastic bandage die Elastikbinde [di ʔeˈlastɪkbɪndə]
electric elektrisch [ʔeˈlɛktʀɪʃ]
electric wheelchair der E-Rollstuhl [dɐ ˈʔeːˌʀɔlʃtuːl]
elevator *(US)* der Fahrstuhl [dɐ ˈfaːʃtuːl], der Aufzug [dɐ ˈʔaʊftsuːk], der Lift [dɐ lɪft]
elsewhere anderswo [ˈʔandɐsvoː]
embassy die Botschaft [di ˈboːtʃaft]
emblem das Wahrzeichen [das ˈvaːtsaɪçn]
emergency der Notfall [dɐ ˈnoːtfal]
emergency brake die Handbremse [di ˈhantbʀɛmzə]
emergency exit der Notausgang [dɐ ˈnoːtʔaʊsgaŋ]
emergency telephone die Notrufsäule [di ˈnoːtʀufzɔɪlə]
empty leer [leɐ]
enclosure *(letter)* die Anlage [di ˈʔanlaːgə]
end das Ende [das ˈʔɛndə], der Schluss [dɐ ʃlʊs]
engaged *(telephone)* besetzt [bəˈzɛtst]
engine der Motor [dɐ ˈmoːtoɐ]
England England [ˈʔɛŋlant]
English englisch [ˈʔɛŋlɪʃ]; **Englishman/-woman** der Engländer/die Engländerin [dɐ ˈʔɛŋlɛndɐ/di ˈʔɛŋlɛndəʀɪn]
enjoy genießen [gəˈniːsn]
enough genug [gəˈnuːk]
entertainment die Unterhaltung [di ʔʊntɐˈhaltʊŋ]
enthusiastic (about) begeistert (von) [bəˈgaɪstɐt fɔn]
entire ganz [gants]
entrance die Einfahrt [di ˈʔaɪnfaːt], der Eingang [dɐ ˈʔaɪngaŋ]; der Zugang [dɐ ˈtsuːgaŋ], *(fee)* der Eintritt [dɐ ˈʔaɪntʀɪt]
envelope der Briefumschlag [dɐ ˈbʀiːfʊmʃlaːk]
environment die Umwelt [di ˈʔʊmvɛlt]
epilepsy die Epilepsie [di epilɛpˈsi]
epoch die Epoche [di ʔeˈpɔxə]
especially hauptsächlich [ˈhaʊptzɛçlɪç], besonders [bəˈzɔndɐs]
estate das Landgut [das ˈlantguːt]

Dictionary English – German

etching die Radierung [di ʀaˈdiːʀʊŋ]
EU citizen EU-Bürger/EU-Bürgerin [ˀeˈˀuː bʏʀgɐ/ˀeˈˀuː bʏʀgəʀɪn]
euro der Euro [dɐ ˈˀɔɪʀo]
Europe Europa [ˀɔɪˈʀoːpaː]
European der Europäer/ die Europäerin [dɐ ˀɔɪʀoˈpɛːɐ/ di ˀɔɪʀoˈpɛːəʀɪn]; europäisch [ˀɔɪʀoˈpɛːɪʃ]
evening der Abend [dɐ ˈˀaːbmt]; **in the evening** abends [ˈˀaːbms]
event das Ereignis [das ˀɐˈˀaɪknɪs], die Veranstaltung [di fɐˈˀanʃtaltʊŋ]
every jede(r, s) [ˈjeːdə(-dɐ, -dəs)]
every day jeden Tag [jeːdn taːk]
every hour stündlich [ˈʃtʏntlɪç]
everybody jedermann [ˈjeːdɐman]
everything alles [ˈˀaləs]
everywhere überall [ˀybɐˈˀal]
evil böse [ˈbøːzə]
exact(ly) genau [gəˈnaʊ]
examination die Untersuchung [di ˀʊntɐˈzuːxʊŋ]
example das Beispiel [das ˈbaɪʃpiːl]; **for example** zum Beispiel [tsʊm ˈbaɪʃpiːl]
excavations die Ausgrabungen *f pl* [di ˈˀaʊsgʀaːbʊŋŋ]
excellent ausgezeichnet [ˀaʊsgəˈtsaɪçnət]
except außer [ˈˀaʊsɐ]
exchange der Austausch [dɐ ˈˀaʊstaʊʃ], der Wechsel [dɐ vɛksl]; *(vb)* tauschen [taʊʃn], austauschen [ˈˀaʊstaʊʃn]
exchange rate der Wechselkurs [dɐ ˈvɛkslkʊɐs]
excursion der Ausflug [dɐ ˈˀaʊsfluːk], die Tour [di tuɐ]
excuse die Entschuldigung [di ˀɛntˈʃʊldɪgʊŋ]; *(vb)* entschuldigen [ˀɛntˈʃʊldɪgŋ]
exhaust der Auspuff [dɐ ˈˀaʊspʊf]
exhausted erschöpft [ˀɐˈʃœpft]
exhibit das Exponat [das ˀɛkspoˈnaːt]
exhibition die Ausstellung [di ˈˀaʊʃtɛlʊŋ]
exit der Ausgang [dɐ ˈˀaʊsgaŋ]; *(motorway)* die (Autobahn)Ausfahrt [di (ˈˀaʊtobaːn-) ˌˀaʊsfaːt]
expect erwarten [ˀɐˈvaːtn]
expensive kostspielig [ˈkɔs(t)ʃpiːlɪç], teuer [ˈtɔɪɐ]
experienced erfahren [ˀɐˈfaː(ʀə)n]
explicit(ly) ausdrücklich [ˈˀaʊsdʀʏklɪç]
expression der Ausdruck [dɐ ˈˀaʊsdʀʊk]
expressionism der Expressionismus [dɐ ˀɛkspʀɛsjoˈnɪsmus]
extend verlängern [fɐˈlɛŋɐn]
extension lead/cord die Verlängerungsschnur [di fɐˈlɛŋəʀʊŋˌʃnuɐ]
extra extra [ˈˀɛkstʀaː]
extraordinary außergewöhnlich [ˌˀaʊsɐgəˈvøːnlɪç]
eye das Auge [das ˈˀaʊgə]
eye-drops die Augentropfen *m pl* [di ˈˀaʊgŋtʀɔpfn]

F

façade die Fassade [di faˈsaːdə]
face treatment die Gesichtsbehandlung [di gəˈzɪçtsbəˌhandlʊŋ]
factory die Fabrik [di faˈbʀi(ː)k]
faint *(vb)* in Ohnmacht fallen [ˀɪn ˈˀoːnmaxt faln]
fair *(fête)* die Kirmes [di ˈkɪɐməs]; *(exhibition)* die Messe [di ˈmɛsə]; *(adj)* gerecht [gəˈʀɛçt], fair [feɐ]; *(weather)* schön [ʃøːn]
fairly ziemlich [ˈtsiːmlɪç]
fall der Sturz [dɐ ʃtʊɐts]; *(US)* der Herbst [dɐ ˈhɛɐpst]; *(vb)* stürzen [ʃtʏɐtsn], fallen [faln]
family die Familie [di faˈmiːljə]
famous berühmt [bəˈʀyːmt]
fan der Ventilator [dɐ ventiˈlaːtoɐ]
fango der Fango [dɐ ˈfaŋgo]
far weit [vaɪt]
fare der Fahrpreis [dɐ ˈfaːpʀaɪs]
farm der Bauernhof [dɐ ˈbaʊɐnhoːf]
fashion die Mode [di ˈmoːdə]
fast schnell [ʃnɛl]
fasting cure das Heilfasten [das ˈhaɪlfastn]
fat fett [fɛt]; *(person)* dick [dɪk]
father der Vater [dɐ ˈfaːtɐ]
fault der Fehler [dɐ ˈfeːlɐ], der Mangel [dɐ maŋl], der Defekt [dɐ deˈfɛkt]
fear die Angst [di ˀaŋst], die Furcht [di fʊɐçt]; *(vb)* fürchten [fʏɐçtn], befürchten [bəˈfʏɐçtn]
February Februar [ˈfeːbʀuaː]
feeble schwach [ʃvax]
feeding bottle die Saugflasche [di ˈzaʊkflaʃə]
feel fühlen [fyːln]
feeling das Gefühl [das gəˈfyːl]
fees die Gebühren *f pl* [di gəˈbyːʀən/-ˈbyːn]
fennel der Fenchel [dɐ fɛnçl]
ferry die Fähre [di ˈfɛːʀə]
festival das Festival [das ˈfɛstɪval]
fever das Fieber [das ˈfiːbɐ]
few wenig [ˈveːnɪç]; **a few** ein paar [(ˀaɪ)n ˈpaː]
fiancé/fiancée der/die Verlobte [dɐ/di fɐˈloːptə]
field das Feld [das fɛlt]

figure die Nummer [di ˈnʊmɐ], die Zahl [di tsa:l]
fill in ausfüllen [ˈʔaʊsfʏln]
fill up tanken [taŋkŋ]
filled rolls belegte Brötchen [bəˈle:ktə bʀø:tçn]
filling *(med.)* die Plombe [di ˈplɔmbə]
film der Film [dɐ fɪlm]
film actor/actress der Filmschauspieler/die Filmschauspielerin [dɐ ˈfɪlmʃaʊʃpi:lɐ/di ˈfɪlmʃaʊʃpi:ləʀɪn]
film speed die Filmempfindlichkeit [di ˈfɪlmɛmpfɪntlɪçkaɪt]
finally zuletzt [tsʊˈlɛtst], endlich [ˈʔɛntlɪç]
find finden [fɪndn]
fine *(punishment)* die Strafe [di ˈʃtʀa:fə], die Geldstrafe [di ˈgɛltʃtʀa:fə]; *(thin)* fein [faɪn]
finger der Finger [dɐ ˈfɪŋɐ]
fire das Feuer [das ˈfɔɪɐ], der Brand [dɐ bʀant]
fire alarm der Feuermelder [dɐ ˈfɔɪɐmɛldɐ]
fire extinguisher der Feuerlöscher [dɐ ˈfɔɪɐlˌʃɐ]
firewood das Brennholz [das ˈbʀɛnhɔlts]
fireworks display das Feuerwerk [das ˈfɔɪɐvɛɐk]
firm die Firma [di ˈfɪɐma:], das Unternehmen [das ˀʊntɐˈne:mm]; *(adj)* fest [fɛst]
first erste(r, -s) [ˈʔeɐstə (-tɐ, -təs)]; **first (of all)** zunächst [tsʊˈnɛ:çst/-ˈnɛ:kst]; **(at) first** zuerst [tsʊˈʔeɐst]
first-aid kit der Verbandskasten [dɐ fɐˈbantskastn]
first name der Vorname [dɐ ˈfoɐna:mə]
fishbone die Gräte [di ˈgʀɛ:tə]
go fishing angeln [ˈʔaŋln]
fishing licence der Angelschein [dɐ ˈʔaŋlʃaɪn]
fishing port der Fischerhafen [dɐ ˈfɪʃɐha:fn]
fishing rod die Angel [di ˀaŋl]
fishmonger's das Fischgeschäft [das ˈfɪʃgəʃɛft]
fit der Anfall [dɐ ˈʔanfal]; *(adj)* fit [fɪt]; *(vb)* passen [pasn]
fitness centre das Fitnesscenter [das ˈfɪtnəsˌtsɛntɐ]
flannel der Waschlappen [dɐ ˈvaʃlapm]
flash das Blitzgerät [das ˈblɪtsgəʀɛ:t]
flat *(apartment)* die Wohnung [di ˈvo:nʊŋ]; *(flat tyre)* (Reifen)Panne [(ˈʀaɪfn)ˌpanə]; *(adj)* eben [ˀe:bm]
flat rate der Pauschalpreis [dɐ paʊˈʃa:lpʀaɪs]
flat rate for electricity die Strompauschale [di ˈʃtʀo:mpaʊˌʃa:lə]
flea market der Flohmarkt [dɐ ˈflo:ma:kt]
fleece das (Schafs)Fell [das (ˈʃa:fs-)fɛl]
flight der Flug [dɐ flu:k]
flight attendant der Steward/die Stewardess [dɐ ˈstjua:t/di: ˈstjuadɛs]
flip-flops die Flipflops [di ˈflɪpflɔps]
floor der Boden [dɐ bo:dn]; *(storey)* das Stockwerk [das ˈʃtɔkvɛɐk]
florist's das Blumengeschäft [das ˈblu:mmgəʃɛft]
flour das Mehl [das me:l]
flower die Blume [di ˈblu:mə]
flu die Grippe [di ˈgʀɪpə]
fly die Fliege [di ˈfli:gə]; *(vb)* fliegen [fli:gŋ]
fog der Nebel [dɐ ˈne:bl]
folding wheelchair der Faltrollstuhl [dɐ ˈfaltˌʀɔlʃtu:l]
fond, be ~ of s.o. jdn lieb haben [ˌjemandn ˈli:p ha:bm]
food das Essen [das ˈʔɛsn], das Lebensmittel [das ˈle:bmsmɪtl]
food poisoning die Lebensmittelvergiftung [di ˈle:bmsmɪtlfɐˌgɪftʊŋ]
food store das Lebensmittelgeschäft [das ˈle:bmsmɪtlgəˌʃɛft]
foot der Fuß [dɐ fu:s]
football der Fußball [dɐ ˈfu:sbal]
football match das Fußballspiel [das ˈfu:sbalˌʃpi:l]
for für [fyɐ]; *(time)* seit [zaɪt]; *(reason)* denn [dɛn]
foreign fremd [fʀɛmt], ausländisch [ˈʔaʊslɛndɪʃ]
foreigner der Ausländer/die Ausländerin [dɐ ˈʔaʊslɛndɐ/di ˈʔaʊslɛndəʀɪn]; der/die Fremde [dɐ/di ˈfʀɛmdə]
forest der Wald [dɐ valt]
forget vergessen [fɐˈgɛsn]
fork die Gabel [di ˈga:bl]
form die Form [di fɔɐm]; *(paper)* das Formular [das fɔmʊˈla:]; *(vb)* bilden [bɪldn]
fortress die Festung [di ˈfɛstʊŋ]
forward(s) vorwärts [ˈfɔɐvɛɐts]; **look forward to** sich freuen auf [zɪç ˈfʀɔɪn ˀaʊf]
fountain der (Spring)Brunnen [dɐ (ˈʃpʀɪŋ)bʀʊnn]
fracture der Knochenbruch [dɐ ˈknɔxnbʀʊx]
fraud der Betrug [dɐ bəˈtʀu:k]

free gratis [ˈɡʀaːtɪs], frei [fʀaɪ], kostenlos [ˈkɔstnloːs], umsonst [ʔʊmˈzɔnst]
freelancer der Freiberufler [dɐ ˈfʀaɪbəʀuːflɐ]
freeway die Autobahn [di ˈʔaʊtobaːn]
freeze *(vb)* frieren [ˈfʀiːʀən/fʀiɐn]
French französisch [fʀanˈtsøːzɪʃ]
frequently häufig [ˈhɔɪfɪç]
fresh frisch [fʀɪʃ]
Friday Freitag [ˈfʀaɪtaːk]
fridge der Kühlschrank [dɐ ˈkyːlʃʀaŋk]
friend der Freund/die Freundin [dɐ fʀɔɪnt/ˈdi fʀɔɪndɪn], der/die Bekannte [dɐ/di bəˈkantə]; **be friends** befreundet sein [bəˈfʀɔɪndət zaɪn]
friendly freundlich [ˈfʀɔɪntlɪç]
frighten erschrecken [ʔɐˈʃʀɛkŋ]
fringe *(hair)* der Pony [dɐ ˈpɔni]
from ab [ʔap]; von [fɔn], aus [ʔaʊs]
front, in ~ vorn [fɔɐn]; **in front of** vor [foɐ]
frost der Frost [dɐ fʀɔst]
fruit das Obst [das ʔoːpst]
fruit and vegetable store der Obst- und Gemüsehändler [dɐ ʔoːpst ʔʊnt ɡəˈmyːzəhɛntlɐ]
full voll [fɔl]
full beam das Fernlicht [das ˈfɛɐnlɪçt]
full body massage die Ganzkörpermassage [di ˈɡantsˌkœɐpɐmaˌsaːʒə]
fully comprehensive insurance die Vollkasko [di ˈfɔlkasko]
fun der Spaß [dɐ ʃpaːs]
funfair der Jahrmarkt [dɐ ˈjaːmaːkt]
fungal infection die Pilzinfektion [di ˈpɪltsɪnfɛkˌtsjoːn]
funicular die (Stand)Seilbahn [di (ˈʃtant)ˌzaɪlbaːn]
funny lustig [ˈlʊstɪç]
fur das Fell [das fɛl], der Pelz [dɐ pɛlts]
furious wütend [vyːtnt]
furniture die Möbel *n pl* [di møːbl]
fuse *(electricity)* die Sicherung [di ˈzɪçəʀʊŋ]
future die Zukunft [di ˈtsuːkʊnft]; *(adj)* zukünftig [ˈtsuːkʏnftɪç]

G

gable der Giebel [dɐ ɡiːbl]
gadget der Apparat [dɐ ʔapaˈʀaːt]
gale der Sturm [dɐ ʃtʊɐm]
gall-bladder die Gallenblase [di ˈɡalnblaːzə]
gallery die Galerie [di ɡaləˈʀiː]
game das Spiel [das ʃpiːl]
garage die Garage [di ɡaˈʀaːʒə]; *(for repairs)* die Werkstatt [di ˈvɛɐkʃtat]
garbage der Müll [dɐ mʏl]
garden der Garten [dɐ ɡaːtn]
garlic der Knoblauch [dɐ ˈknoːblaʊx]
gas canister die Gasflasche [di ɡaːsflaʃə]
gas cartridge die Gaskartusche [di ˈɡaːskaˌtʊʃə]
gas cooker der Gasherd [dɐ ˈɡaːsheɐt]
gas pedal das Gaspedal [das ˈɡaːspedaːl]
gas pump *(US)* die Benzinpumpe [di bɛnˈtsiːnpʊmpə]
gas tank *(US)* der Tank [dɐ taŋk]
gate das Tor [das toɐ]; *(airport)* der Flugsteig [dɐ ˈfluːkʃtaɪɡ]
gauze bandage die Mullbinde [di ˈmʊlbɪndə]
gear der Gang [dɐ ɡaŋ]
gearbox das Getriebe [das ɡəˈtʀiːbə]
generator die Lichtmaschine [di ˈlɪçtmaʃiːnə]
gentleman der Herr [dɐ hɛɐ]
Gents Herren [ˈhɛʀən]
genuine echt [ʔɛçt]
German der/die Deutsche [dɐ/di ˈdɔɪtʃə]; *(adj)* deutsch [dɔɪtʃ]
German measles die Röteln *f pl* [di ʀøːtln]
Germany Deutschland [ˈdɔɪtʃlant]
get *(receive)* bekommen [bəˈkɔmm], kriegen [kʀiːɡŋ]; *(obtain)* besorgen [bəˈzɔɐɡŋ]; *(fetch)* holen [hoːln]; **get in/on** einsteigen [ˈʔaɪnʃtaɪɡŋ]; **get up** aufstehen [ˈʔaʊfʃteːn]
gift das Geschenk [das ɡəˈʃɛŋk]
girl das Mädchen [das ˈmɛːtçn]
give geben [ɡeːbm]; **give back** wiedergeben [ˈviːdɐɡeːbm], zurückgeben [tsʊˈʀʏkɡeːbm]
glad froh [fʀoː]; **glad (of)** erfreut (über) [ʔɐˈfʀɔɪt (ˈʔyːbɐ)]
gladly gern [ɡɛɐn]
glass das Glas [das ɡlaːs]
glass painting die Glasmalerei [di ˈɡlaːsmaːləˌʀaɪ]
gliding das Segelfliegen [das ˈzeːɡlfliːɡŋ]
glorious herrlich [ˈhɛɐlɪç]
gloves die Handschuhe *m pl* [di ˈhantʃuːə]
gnat die Mücke [di ˈmʏkə]
go gehen [ɡeːn], fahren [faː(ʀə)n], reisen [ʀaɪzn]; **go away** weggehen [ˈvɛk(ɡ)eːn]; **go out** hinausgehen [hɪˈnaʊsɡeːn]; *(in the evening)* ausgehen [ˈʔaʊsɡeːn]
goal das Tor [das toɐ]
goalkeeper der Torwart [dɐ ˈtoɐvaːt]
God der Gott [dɐ ɡɔt]
gold das Gold [das ˈɡɔlt]

gold work die Goldschmiedekunst [di ˈgɔltʃmi:dəˌkʊnst]
golf das Golf [das gɔlf]
golf club *(implement)* der Golfschläger [dɐ ˈgɔlfʃlɛ:gɐ]; *(establishment)* der Golfclub [ˈgɔlfklʊp]
good gut [gu:t]
Good Friday Karfreitag [ka:ˈfʀaɪta:k]
goodbye auf Wiedersehen [ˀaʊf ˈvi(:)dɐze:n]; **say goodbye** Abschied nehmen [ˈˀapʃi:t ne:mm], sich verabschieden [zɪç fɐˈˀapʃi:dn]
Gothic die Gotik [di ˈgo:tik]
government die Regierung [di ʀeˈgi:ʀʊŋ]
gram(s) das Gramm [das gʀam]
grandfather der Großvater [dɐ ˈgʀo:sfa:tɐ]
grandmother die Großmutter [di ˈgʀo:smʊtɐ]
grapes die Weintrauben *f pl* [di ˈvaɪntʀaʊbm]
graphic arts die Grafik [di ˈgʀa:fɪk]
grass das Gras [das gʀa:s]; *(lawn)* der Rasen [dɐ ʀa:zn]
grater die Reibe [di ˈʁaɪbə]
grave das Grab [das gʀa:p]
graveyard der Friedhof [dɐ ˈfʀi:to:f]
gravy die (Braten)Soße [di (ˈbʀa:tn) zo:sə]
great großartig [ˈgʀo:s(ˀ)a:tɪç], prima [ˈpʀi:ma:]; *(important)* groß [gʀo:s]
Greek der Grieche/die Griechin [ˈgʀi:çə/ˈgʀi:çɪn]; *(adj)* griechisch [ˈgʀi:çɪʃ]
green grün [gʀy:n]
green beans grüne Bohnen [ˌgʀy:nə ˈbo:nn]
green card die grüne Versicherungskarte [di ˈgry:nə fɐˈzɪçəʀʊŋska:tə]
greengrocer('s) der Obst- und Gemüsehändler [dɐ ˀo:pst ʊnt gəˈmy:zəˌhɛndlɐ]
greet begrüßen [bəˈgʀy:sn], grüßen [ˈgʀy:sn]
grey grau [gʀaʊ]
grill der Grill [dɐ gʀɪl]
grilled vom Grill [fɔm ˈgʀɪl]
grocery store das Lebensmittelgeschäft [das ˈle:bmsmɪtlgəˌʃɛft]
ground der Boden [dɐ bo:dn], das Gelände [das geˈlɛndə]
ground-floor das Erdgeschoss [das ˈˀeɐdgəʃɔs]
group die Gruppe [di ˈgʀʊpə]
growth die Geschwulst [di gəˈʃvʊlst]
guarantee die Garantie [di gaʀanˈti:]
guest der Gast [dɐ gast]
guide der Fremdenführer/die Fremdenführerin [dɐ ˈfʀɛmdnfy:ʀɐ/di ˈfʀɛmdnfy:ʀəʀɪn], *(book)* der Reiseführer [dɐ ˈʀaɪzəˌfy:ʀɐ]
guide dog der Blindenhund [dɐ ˈblɪndnhʊnt]
guided tour die Führung [di ˈfy:ʀʊŋ]
guilt die Schuld [di ʃʊlt]
gullet die Speiseröhre [di ˈʃpaɪzəʀø:ʀə]
gums das Zahnfleisch [das ˈtsa:nflaɪʃ]
gust of wind die Bö [di bø:]
gymnastics die Gymnastik [di gʏmˈnastɪk]

H

hair das Haar [das ha:]
hair dryer der Föhn [dɐ fø:n]
hair gel das Haargel [das ˈha:ge:l]
hairdresser's der Friseur [dɐ fʀɪˈzøɐ]
hairpins die Haarklammern *f pl* [di ˈha:klamɐn]
hairstyle die Frisur [di fʀɪˈzuɐ]
half die Hälfte [di ˈhɛlftə]; *(adj)* halb [halp]
hall die Halle [di ˈhalə]; der Saal [dɐ za:l]
ham der Schinken [dɐ ʃɪŋkŋ]
hand die Hand [di hant]; *(vb)* reichen [ʀaɪçn]; **hand in** abgeben [ˈˀapge:bm]
hand brake die Handbremse [di ˈhantbʀɛmzə]
hand throttle *(car)* das Handgas [das ˈhantga:s]
handbag die Handtasche [di ˈhan(t)taʃə]
handball der Handball [ˈhantbal]
handicap die Behinderung [di bəˈhɪndəʀʊŋ]
handle der Haltegriff [dɐ ˈhaltəgʀɪf]
hand-made handgemacht [ˈhantgəmaxt]
hand-operated bike das Handbike [das ˈhɛntbaɪk]
handrail der Handlauf [dɐ ˈhantlaʊf]
hang-gliding das Drachenfliegen [das ˈdʀaxnfli:gŋ]
happy froh [fʀo:], glücklich [ˈglʏklɪç]
hard hart [ha:t]
hard of hearing schwerhörig [ˈʃveɐhø:ʀɪç]
hardly kaum [kaʊm]
hat der Hut [dɐ hu:t]
have haben [ˈha:bm]; **have to** müssen [mʏsn]
hay bath das Heu-Bad [das ˈhɔɪba:t]
hay fever der Heuschnupfen [dɐ ˈhɔɪʃnʊpfn]
hazard warning lights die Warnblinkanlage [di ˈva:nblɪŋkˀanla:gə]
he er [ˀeɐ]

head der Kopf [dɐ kɔpf]; *(boss)* der Leiter/die Leiterin [dɐ ˈlaɪtɐ/di ˈlaɪtərɪn], der Chef/die Chefin [dɐ ʃɛf/di ʃɛfɪn]
headache die Kopfschmerzen *m pl* [di ˈkɔpfʃmɛɐtsn]
headache tablets die Kopfschmerztabletten *f pl* [di ˈkɔpfʃmɛɐtstaˌblɛtn]
headlight der Scheinwerfer [dɐ ˈʃaɪnvɛɐfɐ]
headphones der Kopfhörer [dɐ ˈkɔpfhøːʀɐ]
headquarters der Sitz [dɐ zɪts], das Hauptquartier [das ˈhaʊptkvaˌtiɐ]
health food shop das Reformhaus [das ʀeˈfɔɐmhaʊs]
healthy gesund [gəˈzʊnt]
hear hören [ˈhøːʀən/høɐn]
hearing das Gehör [das gəˈhøɐ]
heart das Herz [das hɛɐts]
heart attack der Herzinfarkt [dɐ ˈhɛɐtsɪnfaːkt]
heart trouble die Herzbeschwerden *f pl* [ˈhɛɐtsbəʃveɐdn]
heartburn das Sodbrennen [das ˈzoːtbʀɛnn]
heat die Wärme [di ˈvɛɐmə], die Hitze [di ˈhɪtsə]; *(vb)* wärmen [vɛɐmm], heizen [haɪtsn]
heating die Heizung [di ˈhaɪtsʊŋ]
heaven *(rel)* der Himmel [dɐ hɪml]
heavy schwer [ʃveɐ]
height die Größe [di ˈgʀøːsə], die Höhe [di ˈhøə]; *(of career)* der Höhepunkt [dɐ ˈhøəpʊŋkt]
help die Hilfe [di ˈhɪlfə]
her *(pronoun)* sie [ziː], ihr [ˈʔiɐ]; *(possessive pronoun)* ihr [ˈʔiɐ]
herbs die Kräuter *n pl* [di ˈkʀɔɪtɐ]
here hier [hiɐ]
hernia der Leistenbruch [dɐ ˈlaɪstnbʀʊx]
herpes der Herpes [dɐ ˈhɛɐpəs]
herring der Hering [dɐ ˈheːʀɪŋ]
high hoch [hoːx]
high beam das Fernlicht [das ˈfɛɐnlɪçt]
high blood pressure der Bluthochdruck [dɐ ˈbluːthoːxdrʊk]
high season die Hauptsaison [di ˈhaʊptzɛˌzɔŋ]
high tide die Flut [di fluːt]
highlight der Höhepunkt [dɐ ˈhøəpʊŋkt]; die Strähne [di ˈʃtʁɛːnə]
highlights die Strähnchen *n pl* [di ˈʃtʀɛːnçn]
hike die Wanderung [di ˈvandəʀʊŋ]; *(vb)* wandern [ˈvandɐn]
hiking boots der Wander-/der Trekkingschuh [dɐ ˈvandɐ-/dɐ ˈtʁɛkɪŋ-ʃuː]
hiking map die Wanderkarte [di ˈvandɐkaːtə]
hill der Hügel [dɐ hyːgl]
hinder hindern [ˈhɪndɐn]
hip die Hüfte [di ˈhʏftə]
hire mieten [ˈmiːtn]
his sein [zaɪn]
history die Geschichte [di gəˈʃɪçtə]
hitchhike trampen [tʀɛmpm]
HIV positive HIV-positiv [haˀiˌfaʊ-ˈpoːzɪtiːf]
hoarse heiser [ˈhaɪzɐ]
hole das Loch [das lɔx]
holiday camp die Ferienanlage [di ˈfeːʀiənˀanlaːgə]
holiday home das Ferienhaus [das ˈfeːʀiənhaʊs]
holy heilig [ˈhaɪlɪç]
home das Heim [das haɪm], das Haus [das haʊs]; *(country)* die Heimat [di ˈhaɪmaːt]; **at home** daheim [daˈhaɪm]
home-made hausgemacht [ˈhaʊsgəmaxt]
honey der Honig [dɐ ˈhoːnɪç]
hook der Haken [dɐ haːkŋ]
horn die Hupe [di ˈhuːpə]
hors d' œuvre die Vorspeise [di ˈfoɐʃpaɪzə]
horse das Pferd [das pfeɐt]
hospital das Krankenhaus [das ˈkʀaŋkŋhaʊs]
hospitality die Gastfreundschaft [di ˈgastfʀɔɪntʃaft]
host/hostess der Gastgeber/die Gastgeberin [dɐ ˈgastgeːbɐ/di ˈgastgeːbəʀɪn]
hot *(temperature)* heiß [haɪs]; *(spicy)* scharf [ʃaːf]
hot water warmes Wasser [ˈkaltəs ˈvasɐ]
hour die Stunde [di ˈʃtʊndə]; **a quarter of an hour** eine Viertelstunde [(ˌˀaɪ)nə fɪɐtlˈʃtʊndə]; **half an hour** eine halbe Stunde [(ˌˀaɪ)nə ˌhalbə ˈʃtʊndə]; ; **hours of business** die Öffnungszeiten *f pl* [di ˈˀœfnʊŋstsaɪtn]
hourly stündlich [ˈʃtʏntlɪç]
house das Haus [das haʊs]
house number die Hausnummer [di ˈhaʊsnʊmɐ]
houseboat das Hausboot [das ˈhaʊsboːt]
hovercraft das Luftkissenboot [das ˈlʊftkɪsnboːt]
how wie [viː]; **how many** wie viele [viː fiːlə]; **how much** wie viel [viː fiːl]
however jedoch [jeˈdɔx], doch [dɔx]
humid schwül [ʃvyːl]
hungry hungrig [ˈhʊŋrɪç]

hurry sich beeilen [zɪç bəˈˀaɪln]; **be in a hurry** es eilig haben [ˀəs ˈˀaɪlɪç ha:bm]
hurt schmerzen [ʃmɛɐtsn], wehtun [ˈve:tu:n]
husband der Ehemann [dɐ ˈˀe:əman]
hut die Hütte [di ˈhʏtə]

I

I ich [ˀɪç]
ice das Eis [das ˀaɪs]
ice hockey das Eishockey [das ˈˀaɪshɔke:]
ice pack das Kühlelement [das ˈky:lɛləˌmɛnt]
ice rink die Eisbahn [di ˈˀaɪsba:n]
ice skates die Schlittschuhe *m pl* [di ˈʃlɪtʃu:ə]
go ice skating Schlittschuh laufen [ˈʃlɪtʃu: laʊfn]
idea die Idee [di ˀiˈde:]; **no idea!** keine Ahnung! [ˈkaɪnə ˈˀa:nʊŋ]
identity card der Personalausweis [dɐ p(ɛ)ɐzoˈna:lˌˀaʊsvaɪs]
if wenn [vɛn], falls [fals]
ignition die Zündung [di ˈtsʏndʊŋ]
ignition key der Zündschlüssel [dɐ ˈtsʏntʃlʏsl]
ill krank [kʀaŋk]; **be taken ill** krank werden [ˈkʀaŋk veɐdn]
illness die Krankheit [di ˈkʀaŋkhaɪt]
illustration das Bild [das bɪlt]
impertinent unverschämt [ˈˀʊnfɐˌʃɛ:mt]
important bedeutend [bəˈdɔɪtnt], wichtig [ˈvɪçtɪç]
impossible ausgeschlossen [ˈˀaʊsgəˌʃlɔsn], unmöglich [ˈˀʊnˌmø:glɪç]
impressionism der Impressionismus [dɐ ˀɪmpʀɛsjoˈnɪsmʊs]
impressive beeindruckend [bəˈˀaɪndʀʊkŋt]
improbable unwahrscheinlich [ˈˀʊnvaʃaɪnlɪç]
in in [ˀɪn]
incident der Vorfall [dɐ ˈfoɐfal], der Zwischenfall [dɐ ˈtsvɪʃnfal]
included inbegriffen [ˈˀɪnbəgʀɪfn]
incredible unglaublich [ˀʊnˈglaʊplɪç]
indicator *(car)* das Blinklicht [das ˈblɪŋklɪçt]
indigestion die Verdauungsstörung [di fɐˈdaʊʊŋʃtø:ʀʊŋ]
indoors drinnen [dʀɪnn], im Haus [ˀɪm haʊs]
infection die Infektion [di ˀɪnfɛkˈtsjo:n]
inflammable feuergefährlich [ˈfɔɪɐgəfeɐlɪç]
inflammation die Entzündung [di ˀɛnˈtsʏndʊŋ]
inflammation of the middle ear die Mittelohrentzündung [di ˈmɪtlˀoɐˀɛnˌtsʏndʊŋ]
influenza die Grippe [di ˈgʀɪpə]
inform benachrichtigen [bəˈna:xʀɪçtɪgŋ], informieren [ˀɪnfɔˈmi:ʀən/-ˈmiɐn], mitteilen [ˈmɪtaɪln]
information die Auskunft [di ˈˀaʊskʊnft]
infusion die Infusion [di ˀɪnfʊˈzjo:n]
inhabitant der Bewohner/die Bewohnerin [dɐ bəˈvo:nɐ/di bəˈvo:nəʀɪn], der Einwohner/die Einwohnerin [dɐ ˈˀaɪnvo:nɐ/di ˈˀaɪnvo:nəʀɪn]
injection die Spritze [di ˈʃpʀɪtsə]
injure verletzen [fɐˈlɛtsn]
injured person der/die Verletzte [dɐ/di fɐˈlɛtstə]
injury die Verletzung [di fɐˈlɛtsʊŋ]
inner courtyard der Innenhof [dɐ ˈˀɪnnho:f]
in-room telephone das Zimmertelefon [das ˈtsɪmɐteləˌfo:n]
inscription die Inschrift [di ˈˀɪnʃʀɪft]
insect das Insekt [das ˀɪnˈzɛkt]; **~ repellant** der Mückenschutz [dɐ ˈmʏkŋʃʊts]
inside innen [ˀɪnn], drin [dʀɪn]
insist behaupten [bəˈhaʊptn]; **insist on** bestehen auf [bəˈʃte:n ˀaʊf]
insomnia die Schlaflosigkeit [di ˈʃla:flozɪçkaɪt]
inspector der Kontrolleur/die Kontrolleurin [dɐ kɔntʀoˈløɐ/di kɔntʀoˈløʀɪn]
instead of statt [ʃtat], anstatt [ˀanˈʃtat]
insulin das Insulin [das ˀɪnzʊˈli:n]
insult die Beleidigung [di bəˈlaɪdɪgʊŋ]; *(vb)* beleidigen [bəˈlaɪdɪgŋ]
insurance die Versicherung [di fɐˈzɪçəʀʊŋ]
intelligent klug [klu:k]
interested, be ~ (in) sich interessieren (für) [zɪç ˀɪntʀəˈsi:ʀən/-ˈsiɐn (fyɐ)]
interesting interessant [ˀɪntʀəˈsant]
international call das Auslandsgespräch [das ˈˀaʊslantsgəˌʃpʀɛ:ç]
international car index mark das Nationalitätskennzeichen [das natsjonalɪˈtɛ:tskɛntsaɪçn]
international flight der Auslandsflug [dɐ ˈˀaʊslantsflu:k]
interrupt unterbrechen [ˀʊntɐˈbʀɛçn]
intersection die Kreuzung [di ˈkʀɔɪtsʊŋ]
intestines der Darm [dɐ da:m]
intolerable unerträglich [ˈˀʊnɐˌtʀɛ:klɪç]

introduce vorstellen ['foɐʃtɛln], bekannt machen [bə'kant maxn]
introduction die Vorstellung [di 'foɐʃtɛlʊŋ]
invite einladen ['ˀaınla:dn]
iPod der iPod [dɐ 'ˀaıpɔt]
Ireland Irland ['ˀɪɐlant]; **Northern Ireland** Nordirland [nɔat'ˀɪɐlant]
Irish irisch ['ˀi:ʀɪʃ]
iron *(metal)* das Eisen [das 'ˀaızn]; *(implement)* das Bügeleisen [das 'by:glˀaızn]; *(vb)* bügeln [by:gln]
island die Insel [di ˀɪnzl]
isolated abgelegen ['ˀapgəle:gŋ]; einsam ['ˀaınza:m]
its sein [zaın]

J

jack der Wagenheber [dɐ 'va:gŋhe:bɐ]
jacket die Jacke [di 'jakə]
jam die Marmelade [di mamə'la:də]
January Januar ['janʊa:], *(Austria)* Jänner ['jɛnɐ]
jaw der Kiefer [dɐ 'ki:fɐ]
jazz der Jazz [dɐ 'dʒɛs]
jazz aerobics die Jazzgymnastik [di 'dʒɛsgʏmˌnastɪk]
jeans die Jeans [di 'dʒi:ns]
jellyfish die Qualle [di 'kvalə]
jeweller's der Juwelier [dɐ juve'liɐ]
jewellery der Schmuck [dɐ ʃmʊk]
job die Arbeit [di 'ˀa:baıt]; *(position)* die Stellung [di 'ʃtɛlʊŋ]
jog *(vb)* joggen ['dʒɔgŋ]
joint das Gelenk [das gə'lɛŋk]
joke der Spaß [dɐ ʃpa:s], der Scherz [dɐ ʃɛɐts], der Witz [dɐ vɪts]
journey die Fahrt [di fa:t], die Reise [di 'ʀaızə]; **go on a journey** verreisen [fɐ'ʀaızn]; **return journey** die Rückfahrt [di 'ʀʏkfa:t]; **journey home** die Heimreise [di 'haımʀaızə]
judge der Richter/die Richterin [dɐ 'ʀɪçtɐ/di 'ʀɪçtəʀɪn]
juicy saftig ['zaftɪç]
July Juli ['ju:li]
jump leads das Starthilfekabel [das 'ʃta:thɪlfəka:bl]
jumper der Pullover [dɐ pʊ'lo:vɐ]
junction die Kreuzung [di 'kʀɔıtsʊŋ]
June Juni ['ju:ni]
just *(time)* gerade [g(ə)'ʀa:də]; **just as ... as** genauso ... wie [gə'naʊzo ... vi]

K

keep behalten [bə'haltn]; halten [haltn]
ketchup das Ketschup [das 'kɛtʃap]
kettle der Wasserkocher [dɐ 'vasɐˌkɔxɐ]
key der Schlüssel [dɐ 'ʃlʏsl]
keyboard telephone das Schreibtelefon [das 'ʃʀaıptelәfo:n]
kidney die Niere [di 'ni:ʀə]
kidney stone der Nierenstein [dɐ 'ni:ʀənʃtaın]
kilogram(s) das Kilo [das 'ki:lo]
kilometre der Kilometer [dɐ ˌkilo'me:tɐ]
kind die Art [di ˀa:t], die Sorte [di 'zɔɐtə]; *(adj)* freundlich ['fʀɔıntlɪç]
king der König [dɐ 'kø:nɪç]
kiss der Kuss [dɐ kʊs]; *(vb)* küssen [kʏsn]
kitchen die Küche [di 'kʏçə]
kitchenette die Kochnische [di 'kɔxni:ʃə]
kiwi fruit die Kiwi [di 'ki:vi]
knee das Knie [das kni:]
kneipism die Kneipp-Anwendung [di 'knaıpanˌvɛndʊŋ]
knife das Messer [das 'mɛsɐ]
know kennen [kɛnn], wissen [vɪsn];

L

Ladies Damen [da:mm]
ladle *(GB)* die Schöpfkelle [di 'ʃœpfkɛlə]
lady die Dame [di 'da:mə]
lake der See [dɐ ze:]
lamb das Lamm [das lam]; *(meat)* das Lammfleisch [das 'lamflaıʃ]
lamp die Lampe [di 'lampə]
land das Land [das lant]; *(vb)* landen ['landn]; **land at** *(ship)* anlegen in ['ˀanle:gŋ ˀɪn]
landing die Landung [di 'landʊŋ]
landlord/landlady der Hausbesitzer/die Hausbesitzerin [dɐ 'haʊsbəzɪtsɐ/di 'haʊsbəzɪtsəʀɪn]
lane die Gasse [di 'gasə]
language die Sprache [di 'ʃpʀa:xə]
laptop der Laptop [dɐ 'lɛptɔp]
large groß [gʀo:s]
last *(adj)* letzte(r, -s) ['lɛtstə (-tɐ, -təs)]; *(adv)* zuletzt [tsʊ'lɛtst]; *(vb)* halten [haltn], dauern ['daʊɐn]
late spät [ʃpɛ:t]
laugh *(vb)* lachen [laxn]
launderette der Waschsalon [dɐ 'vaʃzaˌlɔŋ]
laundry die Wäscherei [di vɛʃə'ʀaı]
lavatory die Toilette [di to'lɛtə]
lawn der Rasen [dɐ ʀa:zn]
lawyer der Rechtsanwalt/die Rechtsanwältin [dɐ 'ʀɛçtsanvalt/di 'ʀɛçtsanvɛltɪn]

laxative das Abführmittel [das ˈʔapfyɐˌmɪtl]
layered cut der Stufenschnitt [dɐ ˈʃtu:fnʃnɪt]
layers die Stufen [di ˈʃtu:fn]
lazy faul [faʊl]
leading role die Hauptrolle [di ˈhaʊptʀɔlə]
leaflet der Prospekt [dɐ pʀɔsˈpɛkt]
lean mager [ˈma:gɐ]
learn lernen [lɛɐnn]
least, at ~ mindestens [ˈmɪndəstns], wenigstens [ˈve(:)nɪkstns]
leather jacket die Lederjacke [di ˈle:dɐjakə]
leave abfahren (von) [ˈʔapfa:(ʀə)n fɔn], verlassen [fɐˈlasn], weggehen [ˈvɛkge:n]; *(room)* hinausgehen [hɪˈnaʊsge:n]; *(behind)* hinterlassen [hɪntɐˈlasn]; **leave (for)** abreisen (nach) [ˈʔapʀaɪzn (nax)]
left(-hand) linke(r, -s) [ˈlɪŋkə (-kɐ, -kəs)]; **on the left, to the left** links [lɪŋks]
left-luggage office die Gepäckaufbewahrung [di gəˈpɛkˌʔaʊfbəva:ʀʊŋ]
leg das Bein [das baɪn]
legal alcohol limit die Promillegrenze [di pʀoˈmɪləˌgʀɛntsə]
leggings die Leggings *pl* [di ˈlɛgɪŋs]
lemonade die Limonade [lɪmoˈna:də]
lemons die Zitronen *f pl* [di tsɪˈtʀo:nn]
lend leihen [laɪn]
lens das Objektiv [das ʔɔbjɛkˈti:f]
lentils die Linsen *f pl* [di lɪnzn]
lesson die Unterrichtsstunde [di ˈʔʊntɐʀɪçtˌʃtʊndə]
let *(permit)* lassen [lasn]; *(apartment etc.)* vermieten [fɐˈmi:tn]
letter der Brief [dɐ bʀi:f]
lettuce der Kopfsalat [dɐ ˈkɔpfsaˌla:t]
level *(adj)* flach [flax]
liable to duty zollpflichtig [ˈtsɔl(p)flɪçtɪç]
lice die Läuse *f pl* [di ˈlɔɪzə]
license plate das Nummernschild [das ˈnʊmɐnʃɪlt]
lie die Lüge [di ˈly:gə]; *(vb)* lügen [ly:gŋ]; *(in horizontal position)* liegen [li:gŋ]; **lie down** sich hinlegen [zɪç ˈhɪnle:gŋ]
life das Leben [das le:bm]
life belt/life preserver der Rettungsring [dɐ ˈʀɛtʊŋsʀɪŋ]
life jacket die Schwimmweste [di ˈʃvɪmvɛstə]
lifeboat das Rettungsboot [das ˈʀɛtʊŋsbo:t]
lifeguard der Bademeister/die Bademeisterin [dɐ ˈba:dəmaɪstɐ/ di ˈba:dəmaɪstəʀɪn]
lift der Aufzug [dɐ ˈʔaʊftsu:k], der Fahrstuhl [dɐ ˈfa:ʃtu:l]; *(ski-)* der Lift [dɐ lɪft]; *(vb)* heben [e:bm]
light das Licht [das lɪçt]; *(adj weight)* leicht [laɪçt]; *(vb)* anzünden [ˈʔantsʏndn]
light blue hellblau [hɛlˈblaʊ]
light bulb die Glühbirne [di ˈgly:bɪʀnə]
light meter der Belichtungsmesser [dɐ bəˈlɪçtʊŋsˌmɛsɐ]
lighter das Feuerzeug [das ˈfɔɪɐtsɔɪk]
lightning der Blitz [dɐ blɪts]
like *(comparison)* wie [vi:]; *(vb)* mögen [ˈmø:gŋ]
line die Linie [di ˈli:njə]; *(railway)* die Strecke [di ˈʃtʀɛkə]; *(telephone)* die Leitung [di ˈlaɪtʊŋ]
linen das Leinen [das laɪnn]
lip die Lippe [di ˈlɪpə]
lipstick der Lippenstift [dɐ ˈlɪpmʃtɪft]
liquid flüssig [ˈflʏsɪç]
listen to music Musik hören [mʊˈzi:k ˈhø:ʀən]
litre der Liter [dɐ ˈli:tɐ]
little klein [klaɪn]; *(not much)* wenig [ˈve:nɪç]
live *(vb)* leben [le:bm], wohnen [vo:nn]
lively lebhaft [ˈle:phaft]
liver die Leber [di ˈle:bɐ]
living room das Wohnzimmer [das ˈvo:ntsɪmɐ]
local einheimisch [ˈʔaɪnhaɪmɪʃ]
local call das Ortsgespräch [das ˈʔɔɐtsgəʃpʀɛ:ç]
local train der Nahverkehrszug [dɐ ˈna:fɐˌkeɐstsu:k]
lock das Schloss [das ʃlɔs]; *(vb)* verschließen [fɐˈʃli:sn], abschließen [ˈʔapʃli:sn]
lonely einsam [ˈʔaɪnza:m]
long lang [laŋ]; *(far)* weit [vaɪt]
long-distance call das Ferngespräch [das ˈfɛɐngəʃpʀɛ:ç]
look der Blick [dɐ blɪk]; *(vb)* sehen [se:n], schauen [ˈʃaʊn]; **look at** anschauen [ˈʔanʃaʊn], ansehen [ˈʔanze:n]; **look for** suchen [ˈzu:xn]; **look like** aussehen [ˈʔaʊse:n]; **look out!** Achtung! [ˈʔaxtʊŋ]
lose verlieren [fɐˈli:ʀən/-ˈliɐn]; **lose one's way** sich verirren [zɪç fɐˈʔɪʀən]
lost, get ~ sich verirren [zɪç fɐˈʔɪɐn]
loud laut [laʊt]
lounge das Wohnzimmer [das ˈvo:ntsɪmɐ]; *(hotel)* der Aufenthaltsraum [dɐ ˈʔaʊfntaltsˌʀaʊm]

love die Liebe [di 'li:bə]; *(vb)* lieben [li:bm]
low tief [ti:f]
low-calorie kalorienarm [kalo'ʁi:n'a:m]
low-fat fettarm ['fɛt'a:m]
low season die Vorsaison [di 'foɐze,zɔŋ]; die Nachsaison [di 'na:xze,zɔŋ]
low tide die Ebbe [di 'ɛbə]
low-fat milk fettarme Milch ['fɛt'a:mə mɪlç]
luck das Glück [das glʏk]
lucky glücklich ['glʏklɪç]
luggage das Gepäck [das ge'pɛk]
luggage counter der Gepäckschalter [dɐ gə'pɛkʃaltɐ]
luggage reclaim die Gepäckausgabe [di gə'pɛk'aʊsga:bə]
luggage van der Gepäckwagen [dɐ gə'pɛkva:gŋ]
lumbago der Hexenschuss [dɐ 'hɛksnʃʊs]
lunch das Mittagessen [das 'mɪtak,'ɛsn]
lunch meat der Aufschnitt [dɐ ''aʊfʃnɪt]
lungs die Lunge [di 'lʊŋə]
luxurious luxuriös [lʊksʊʀi'ø:s]
lymphatic drainage die Lymphdrainage [di 'lʏmfdʁɛ,na:ʒə]

M

machine die Maschine [di ma'ʃi:nə]
mackerel die Makrele [di ma'kʀe:lə]
mad verrückt [fɐ'ʀʏkt]
Madam Frau [fʀaʊ]
magazine *(glossy)* die Illustrierte [di ɪlʊ'stʀiɐtə]; *(news)* die Zeitschrift [di 'tsaɪtʃʀɪft]
maid das Zimmermädchen [das 'tsɪmɐmɛ:tçn]
maiden name der Geburtsname [dɐ gə'bʊɐtsna:mə]
main course die Hauptspeise [di 'haʊptʃpaɪzə]
main post office das Hauptpostamt [das 'haʊpt,pɔst'amt]
main station der Hauptbahnhof [dɐ 'haʊptba:nho:f ('haʊpba:nof)]
main street die Hauptstraße [di 'haʊptʃtʀa:sə]
maintain behaupten [bə'haʊptn]
make *(produce)* machen ['maxn], schaffen [ʃafn]; *(coffee, tea)* kochen [kɔxn]; **make good** *(damage)* ersetzen ['ɐ'zɛtsn]
man der Mann [dɐ man]; *(mankind)* der Mensch [dɐ mɛnʃ]
mandarins die Mandarinen *f pl* [di manda'ʀi:nn]
mango die Mango [di 'maŋgo]
map die Landkarte [di 'lantka:tə]
March März [mɛɐts]
margarine die Margarine [di maga'ʀi:nə]
market der Markt [dɐ ma:kt]
marmalade die Marmelade [di mamə'la:də]
married verheiratet [fɐ'haɪʀa:tət]
marry heiraten ['haɪʀa:tn]
marvellous wunderbar ['vʊndɐba:]
mascara die Wimperntusche [di 'vɪmpɐntʊʃə]
mass *(rel)* die Messe [di 'mɛsə]
massage die Massage [ma'sa:ʒə]
match das Spiel [ʃpi:l]
matches die Streichhölzer *n pl* [di 'ʃtʀaɪçhœltsɐ]
material das Material [das mat(ə)ʀi'a:l], der Stoff [dɐ ʃtɔf]
matter die Angelegenheit [di ''angəle:gŋhaɪt], die Sache [di 'zaxə]
mattress die Matratze [di ma'tʀatsə]
May Mai [maɪ]
maybe vielleicht [fɪ'laɪçt]
mayonnaise die Mayonnaise [di maɪo'ne:zə]
me mich [mɪç], mir [miɐ]
meadow die Wiese [di 'vi:zə]
meal das Essen [das ''ɛsn], die Mahlzeit [di 'ma:ltsaɪt]
meaning die Bedeutung [di bə'dɔɪtʊŋ]
means das Mittel [das 'mɪtl]
measles die Masern *f pl* ['ma:zɐn]
meat das Fleisch [das flaɪʃ]
medicine das Medikament [das medɪka'mɛnt]
meditation die Meditation [di ,medita'tsjo:n]
meet treffen [tʀɛfn], begegnen [bə'ge:kn(ə)n]; kennen lernen ['kɛnnlɛɐnn]
melon die Melone [di me'lo:nə]
memorial die Gedenkstätte [di gə'dɛŋkʃtɛtə]
memory card die Speicherkarte [di 'ʃpaɪçɐ,ka:tə]
memory stick der Memorystick [dɐ 'mɛmoʁistɪk]
men die Männer [di m]
men's für Herren [fyɐ 'hɛʀən]
Men's Room die Herrentoilette [di 'hɛʀənto,lɛtə]
meningitis die Hirnhautentzündung [di 'hɪɐnhaʊtɐn,tsʏndʊŋ]
menstruation die Menstruation [di mɛnstʀua'tsjon]

mentally handicapped geistig behindert [ˈgaɪstɪç bəˈhɪndɐt]
menu die Speisekarte [di ˈʃpaɪzəka:tə]
merry lustig [ˈlʊstɪç], froh [fʀo:]
message die Nachricht [di ˈna:xʀɪçt]
methylated spirits der Brennspiritus [dɐ ˈbʀɛnˌʃpiʀitʊs]
metre der Meter [dɐ ˈme:tɐ]
microwave die Mikrowelle [di ˈmi:kʀovɛlə]
middle die Mitte [di ˈmɪtə]
Middle Ages das Mittelalter [das ˈmɪtlˀaltɐ]
midge die Mücke [di ˈmʏkə]
migraine die Migräne [di miˈgʀɛ:nə]
mild mild [mɪlt]
milk die Milch [mɪlç]
millimetre der Millimeter [dɐ ˈmɪliˌme:tɐ]
minced meat das Hackfleisch [das ˈhakflaɪʃ]
mind, I don't ~ meinetwegen [ˈmaɪnətˌve:gŋ]
minute die Minute [di miˈnu:tə]
mirror der Spiegel [dɐ ʃpi:gl]
miscalculate sich verrechnen [zɪç fɐˈʀɛçn(ə)n]
miscarriage die Fehlgeburt [di ˈfe:lgəbʊɐt]
misfortune das Unglück [das ˈˀʊnglʏk]
Miss das Fräulein [das ˈfʀɔ(ɪ)laɪn]
miss *(vb)* verfehlen [fɐˈfe:ln]; verpassen [fɐˈpasn]; **be missing** fehlen [fe:ln]
mistake Fehler [ˈfe:lɐ], der Irrtum [dɐ ˈˀɪɐtu:m]; **mistake for** vertauschen [fɐˈtaʊʃn], verwechseln [fɐˈvɛksln]; **make a mistake** einen Fehler machen [(ˀaɪn)n ˈfe:lɐ maxn], sich verrechnen [zɪç fɐˈʀɛçn(ə)n]; **be mistaken** sich täuschen [zɪç ˈtɔɪʃn], sich irren [zɪç ˈˀɪʀən/ˈˀɪɐn]
misunderstanding das Missverständnis [das ˈmɪsfɐʃtɛntnɪs]
mobile (phone) das Handy [das ˈhɛndi], das Mobiltelefon [das moˈbi:lteləˌfo:n]
mobile communications centre das Handygeschäft [das ˈhɛndigəˌʃɛft]
model das Modell [das moˈdɛl]
modern modern [moˈdɛɐn]
moist nass [nas], feucht [fɔɪçt]
monastery das (Mönchs)Kloster [das (ˈmœnçs)ˌklo:stɐ]
Monday Montag [ˈmo:nta:k]
money das Geld [das gɛlt]
month der Monat [dɐ ˈmo:na:t]
monthly monatlich [ˈmo:natlɪç]
monument *(memorial edifice)* das Denkmal [das ˈdɛŋkma:l]; *(tomb)* das Grabmal [ˈgʀa:bma:l]
moon der Mond [dɐ mo:nt]
mop der Wischmopp [dɐ ˈvɪʃmɔp]
more mehr [meɐ]; **more than** mehr als [ˈmeɐ ˀals]
morning der Morgen [dɐ mɔɐgŋ], der Vormittag [dɐ ˈfoɐmɪta:k]; **in the morning** morgens [ˈmɔɐgŋs]
mosaic das Mosaik [das mozaˈˀi:k]
most, at the ~ höchstens [hø:çstns/hø:kstns]
motel das Motel [das moˈtɛl]
mother die Mutter [di mʊtɐ]
motive der Grund [dɐ gʀʊnt]
motor der Motor [dɐ ˈmo:toɐ]
motorboat das Motorboot [das ˈmo:tɔbo:t]
motorway die Autobahn [di ˈˀaʊtoba:n]
motorway toll die Autobahngebühren [di ˈˀaʊtoba:ngəˌby:ʀən]
mountain der Berg [dɐ bɛɐk]
mountain bike das Mountainbike [das ˈmaʊntnbaɪk]
mountain village das Bergdorf [das ˈbɛɐkdoɐf]
mountaineering/mountain climbing das Bergsteigen [das ˈbɛɐkʃtaɪgŋ]
mountains das Gebirge [das gəˈbɪɐgə]
moustache der Schnurrbart [dɐ ˈʃnʊɐba:t]
mouth der Mund [dɐ mʊnt]; *(river)* die Mündung [di ˈmʏndʊŋ]
movie actor/actress der Filmschauspieler/die Filmschauspielerin [dɐ ˈfɪlmʃaʊʃpi:lɐ/di ˈfɪlmʃaʊʃpi:ləʀɪn]
movie theater das Kino [das ˈki:no]
MP3 player der MP3Player [dɐ ˀɛmpeˈdʀaɪplɛɪɐ]
Mr Herr [hɛɐ]
Mrs Frau [fʀaʊ]
much viel [fi:l]
muesli das Müsli [das ˈmy:sli]
mugging der Überfall [dɐ ˈˀy:bɐfal]
mumps der Mumps [dɐ mʊmps]
muscle der Muskel [dɐ ˈmʊskl]
museum das Museum [das muˈze:ʊm]
music die Musik [di muˈzi:k]
music hall das Varietee [das vaʀiəˈte:]
musical das Musical [das ˈmju:zɪkl]
music shop der Plattenladen [dɐ ˈplatnla:dn]
mussels die Muscheln *f pl* [di mʊʃln]
mustard der Senf [dɐ zɛnf (zɛmf)]
mute stumm [ʃtʊm]
my mein [maɪn];
myself mich [mɪç], mir [miɐ]; **I did it myself** ich habe es selbst gemacht [ˀɪç ha:bə (ˀə)s ˈzɛlpst gəˌmaxt]

N

nail scissors die Nagelschere [di 'na:glʃe:ʀə]
nail varnish/polish der Nagellack [dɐ 'na:gllak]
nail varnish/polish remover der Nagellackentferner [dɐ 'na:gllakɛnt͵fɛɐnɐ]
naked nackt [nakt]
name der Name [dɐ na:mə]; *(vb)* nennen [nɛnn]
napkin die Serviette [di zɐ'vjɛtə]
nappies die Windeln *f pl* [di vɪndln]
narrow schmal [ʃma:l], eng [ˀɛŋ]
national park der Nationalpark [dɐ natsjo'na:lpa:k]
nationality die Staatsangehörigkeit [di 'ʃta:ts͵ˀangehø:ʀɪçkaɪt]
native einheimisch ['ˀaɪnhaɪmɪʃ]
natural natürlich [na'tyɐlɪç]
nature die Natur [di na'tuɐ]
nature reserve das Naturschutzgebiet [das na'tuɐʃʊtsgəbi:t]
naughty böse ['bø:zə]
nausea der Brechreiz [dɐ 'bʀɛçʀaɪts]
near nahe ['na:(ə)], in der Nähe von [ˀɪn dɐ 'nɛə fɔn], bei [baɪ]
nearly beinahe ['baɪna:], fast [fast]
necessary nötig ['nø:tɪç], notwendig ['no:tvɛndɪç]
neck der Hals [dɐ hals]
necklace die Kette [di 'kɛtə]
need brauchen [bʀaʊxn], benötigen [bə'nø:tɪgŋ]
needle die Nadel [di na:dl]
neither auch nicht [ˀaʊx nɪç(t)]
nerve der Nerv [dɐ nɛɐf]
nervous nervös [nɐ'vø:s]
neutral der Leerlauf [dɐ 'leɐlaʊf]
never nie [ni:]
nevertheless trotzdem ['tʀɔtsde:m]
new neu [nɔɪ], frisch [fʀɪʃ]
New Year's Day Neujahr [nɔɪ'ja:]
New Year's Eve Silvester [sɪl'vɛstɐ]
newsagent's der Zeitungshändler [dɐ 'tsaɪtʊŋshɛntlɐ]
newspaper die Zeitung [di 'tsaɪtʊŋ]
next nächste(r, s) ['nɛ:çstə/'nɛ:kstə (-stɐ, -stəs)]; **next to** neben ['ne:bm]
nice nett [nɛt], lieb [li:p], sympathisch [sʏm'pa:tɪʃ]
night die Nacht [di naxt]; der Abend [dɐ 'ˀa:bmt]; **at night** nachts [naxts]
night club der Nachtklub [dɐ 'naxtklʊp]
no nein [naɪn]; *(not any)* kein [kaɪn]
nobody keine(r, s) ['kaɪnə (-nɐ, -nəs)], niemand ['ni:mant]
noise das Geräusch [das gə'ʀɔɪʃ], der Lärm [dɐ lɛɐm]
noisy laut [laʊt]
non-alcoholic alkoholfrei [ˀalko'ho:lfʀaɪ]
noon der Mittag [dɐ 'mɪta:k]
nor auch nicht [ˀaʊx nɪçt]
normal normal [nɔ'ma:l]
normally normalerweise [nɔ'ma:lɐvaɪzə]
north der Norden [dɐ nɔɐdn]
North Sea die Nordsee [di 'nɔɐtze:]
nose die Nase [di 'na:zə]
nose bleed das Nasenbluten [das 'na:znblu:tn]
no-smoking compartment das Nichtraucherabteil [das 'nɪçtʀaʊxɐˀap͵taɪl]
not nicht [nɪçt]; **not at all** gar nicht ['ga: nɪç(t)], durchaus nicht [dʊɐç'ˀaʊs nɪç(t)]; **not yet** noch nicht [nɔx 'nɪç(t)]
notepad der Notizblock [dɐ no'ti:tsblɔk]
nothing nichts [nɪçts/nɪks]
notice das Schild [das ʃɪlt]; *(vb)* bemerken [bə'mɛɐkŋ]
notion die Vorstellung [di 'foɐʃtɛlʊŋ]
novel der Roman [dɐ ʀo'ma:n]
November November [no'vɛmbɐ]
now nun [nu:n], jetzt [jɛtst]; **till now** bis jetzt [bɪs 'jɛtst]
nowhere nirgends ['nɪɐgŋ(t)s]
nude *(adj)* nackt [nakt]; *(painting)* der Akt [dɐ ˀakt]
nudist beach der FKK-Strand [dɐ ˀɛfka'ka:ʃtʀant]
number die Nummer [di 'nʊmɐ]; *(vb)* nummerieren [nʊmə'ʀi:ʀən/ -'ʀiɐn]
number plate das Nummernschild [das 'nʊmɐnʃɪlt]
nurse die Krankenschwester [di 'kʀaŋkŋʃvɛstɐ]
nutmeg die Muskatnuss [di mʊs'ka:tnʊs]
nuts die Nüsse *f pl* [di 'nʏsə]

O

object der Gegenstand [dɐ 'ge:gŋʃtant]
observatory die Sternwarte [di 'ʃtɛɐnva:tə]
occasionally gelegentlich [gəlә:gŋtlɪç]
occupied *(seat)* besetzt [bə'zɛtst]
October Oktober [ˀɔk'to:bɐ]
of von [fɔn]; *(material)* aus [ˀaʊs]
off season die Schonzeit [di 'ʃo:ntsaɪt]
offer *(vb)* anbieten ['ˀanbi:tn], bieten [bi:tn]

office das Büro [das byˈʀoː]; *(position)* das Amt [das ˀamt]
official *(adj)* amtlich [ˈˀamtlɪç], offiziell [ˀɔfɪˈtsjɛl]
off-licence das Spirituosengeschäft [das ʃpiʀituˈoːznɡəʃɛft]
off-season die Vorsaison [di ˈfoɐzeˌzɔŋ]; die Nachsaison [di ˈnaːxzeˌzɔŋ]
offside abseits [ˈˀapzaɪts]
often oft [ˀɔft]
oil das Öl [das ˀøːl]
oil change der Ölwechsel [dɐ ˈˀøːlvɛksl]
oil painting die Ölmalerei [di ˈˀøːlmaːləˌʀaɪ]
ointment die Salbe [di ˈzalbə]
old alt [ˀalt]
olive oil das Olivenöl [das ˀoˈliːvnˀøːl]
olives die Oliven *f pl* [di ˀoˈliːvn]
on *(switch)* an [ˀan]; *(position)* auf [ˀaʊf]
once einmal [ˈˀaɪ(n)maːl]; **at once** sofort [zoˈfɔɐt], gleich [ɡlaɪç]
one *(adj)* ein(e) [ˀɐɪn/ˈˀɐɪnə], *(numeral)* eins [ˀaɪns]
onions die Zwiebeln *f pl* [di tsviːbln]
only nur [nuɐ], *(not before)* erst [eɐst]; *(adj)* einzig [ˈˀaɪntsɪç]
open offen [ˈˀɔfn], geöffnet [ɡəˈˀœfnət]; *(vb)* öffnen [ˈˀœfn(ə)n], aufmachen [ˈˀaʊfmaxn]; **in the open air** im Freien [ˀɪm ˈfʀaɪn]
opening hours die Öffnungszeiten *f pl* [di ˈˀœfnʊŋstsaɪtn]
opera die Oper [di ˈˀoːpɐ]
operation die Operation [di ˀɔpəʀaˈtsjoːn]
operetta die Operette [di ˀopəˈʀɛtə]
opinion die Meinung [di ˈmaɪnʊŋ]
opposite das Gegenteil [das ˈɡeːɡŋtaɪl]; *(adj)* entgegengesetzt [ˀɛntˈɡeːɡŋɡəzɛtst]; *(prep)* gegenüber [ɡeɡŋˈˀyːbɐ]
optician's der Optiker [dɐ ˈˀɔptɪkɐ]
or oder [ˈˀoːdɐ]
orange juice der Orangensaft [dɐ ˀoˈʀaŋʒnzaft]
oranges die Apfelsinen *f pl* [di ˀapflˈziːnn]
orchestra das Orchester [das ˀɔɐˈkɛstɐ]
order *(tidiness)* die Ordnung [di ˈˀɔɐtnʊŋ]; *(rel)* der Orden [dɐ ˀɔɐdn]; *(restaurant)* die Bestellung [di bəˈʃtɛlʊŋ]; *(vb)* bestellen [bəˈʃtɛln]; **out of order** kaputt [kaˈpʊt]
ordinary gewöhnlich [ɡəˈvøːnlɪç]
organic food shop der Bioladen [dɐ ˈbiolaːdn]
original das Original [das ˀɔʀɪɡiˈnaːl], **original version** die Originalfassung [di ˀoʀɪɡɪˈnaːlfasʊŋ]
ought to sollen [zɔln]
our unser(e) [ˈˀʊnzɐ (-ʀə)]
outside außen [ˈˀaʊsn], außerhalb [ˈˀaʊsɐhalp], draußen [ˈdʀaʊsn]
oven der Backofen [dɐ ˈbakˀoːfn]
over *(prep)* über [ˈˀyːbɐ]; *(adv at an end)* vorüber [foˈʀyːbɐ], vorbei [fɔˈbaɪ]
overtake überholen [ˀyːbɐˈhoːln]
own eigen [ˀaɪɡŋ]; *(vb)* besitzen [bəˈzɪtsn]
owner der Besitzer/die Besitzerin [dɐ bəˈzɪtsɐ/di bəˈzɪtsəʀɪn], der Eigentümer/die Eigentümerin [dɐ ˈʔaɪɡŋtyːmɐ/di ˈˀaɪɡŋtyːməʀɪn
oysters die Austern *f pl* [di ˈˀaʊstɐn]

P

pacemaker der Herzschrittmacher [dɐ ˈhɛɐt(s)ʃʀɪtmaxɐ]
pack die Packung [di ˈpakʊŋ]; *(vb)* packen [pakŋ], einpacken [ˈˀaɪnpakŋ], verpacken [fɐˈpakŋ]
packing die Verpackung [di fɐˈpakʊŋ]
paddling pool das Planschbecken [das ˈplanʃbɛkn]
page die Seite [di ˈzaɪtə]
pain die Schmerzen *m pl* [di ˈʃmɛɐtsn]
painful schmerzhaft [ˈʃmɛɐtshaft]
pain-killing tablets die Schmerztabletten *f pl* [di ˈʃmɛɐtstaˌblɛtn]
paint die Farbe [di ˈfaːbə]; *(vb)* malen [maːln]
painter der Maler/die Malerin [dɐ ˈmaːlɐ/di ˈmaːləʀɪn]
painting *(picture)* das Gemälde [das ɡəˈmɛːldə]; *(type of art)* die Malerei [di maːləˈʀaɪ]
pair das Paar [das paː]
palace der Palast [dɐ paˈlast]
pan die Pfanne [di ˈ(p)fanə]
panties der (Damen)Slip [dɐ (ˈdaːmən)slɪp]
pants *(underwear)* die Unterhose [di ˈʊntɐhoːzə]; *(US)* die Hose [di ˈhoːzə]
panty liners die Slipeinlagen *f pl* [di ˈslɪpaɪnlaːɡŋ]
paper das Papier [das paˈpiɐ]
paper handkerchiefs die Papiertaschentücher *n pl* [di paˈpiɐˌtaʃntyːçɐ]
paper napkins/serviettes die Papierservietten *f pl* [di paˈpiɐzɐˌvjɛtn]

paperback das Taschenbuch [das ˈtaʃnbuːx]
papers die Papiere *n pl* [di paˈpiːʀə]
paprika der Paprika [dɐ ˈpapʀɪka]
parachuting das Fallschirmspringen [das ˈfalʃɪʀmʃpʀɪŋŋ]
paraffin das Petroleum [das peˈtʀoːleʊm]
paralysis die Lähmung [di ˈlɛːmʊŋ]
parcel das Paket [das paˈkeːt]
pardon, I beg your ~! Ich bitte um Entschuldigung [ˀɪç ˈbɪtə ˀʊm ɛntˈʃʊldɪgʊŋ]
parents die Eltern *n pl* [di ˈˀɛltɐn]
park die Anlage [di ˈˀanlaːgə]; der Park [dɐ paːk]; *(vb)* abstellen [ˈˀapʃtɛln], parken [ˈpaːkŋ]
parsley die Petersilie [di peːtɐˈziːljə]
part der Teil [dɐ taɪl]
partially sighted sehbehindert [ˈseːbəhɪndɐt]
particularly besonders [bəˈzɔndɐs]
particulars die Personalien *f pl* [di pɐzoˈnaːljən], nähere Angaben [ˈnɛəʀə ˈˀangaːbm]
parting der Scheitel [dɐ ʃaɪtl]
party das Fest [das fɛst]
pass *(mountain)* der Pass [dɐ pas]; *(vb)* reichen [ʀaɪçn]; *(time)* vergehen [fɐˈgeːn], vorübergehen [foˈʀyːbɐgeːn], vorbeigehen [fɔˈbaɪgeːn]; *(overtake)* überholen [ˀyːbɐˈhoːln]
passable befahrbar [bəˈfaːbaː]
passenger der Fahrgast [dɐ ˈfaːgast], der Passagier [dɐ pasaˈʒiɐ]
passing through auf der Durchreise [ˀaʊf dɐ ˈdʊɐçʀaɪzə]
passport der Reisepass [dɐ ˈʀaɪzəpas]
past die Vergangenheit [di fɐˈgaŋnhaɪt]; *(adj adv)* vorüber [foˈʀyːbɐ], vorbei [fɔˈbaɪ]
past the sell-by date abgelaufen [ˀapgəlaʊfn]
pasta die Nudeln *f pl* [di nuːdln]
path der Weg [dɐ veːk], der Pfad [dɐ (p)faːt]
patience die Geduld [di gəˈdʊlt]
pay zahlen [ˈtsaːln], bezahlen [bəˈtsaːln]; **pay out** auszahlen [ˈˀaʊstsaːln]
payment die Zahlung [di ˈtsaːlʊŋ]
peaches die Pfirsiche *m pl* [di ˈpfɪɐzɪçə]
pearl die Perle [di ˈpɛɐlə]
pears die Birnen *f pl* [di bɪɐnn]
peas die Erbsen *f pl* [di ˀɛɐpsn]
pedestrian der Fußgänger/ die Fußgängerin [dɐ ˈfuːsgɛŋɐ/ di ˈfuːsgɛŋəʀɪn]
pedestrian precinct/zone die Fußgängerzone [di ˈfuːsgɛŋɐˌtsoːnə]
peg der Kleiderhaken [dɐ ˈklaɪdɐhaːkŋ]
penalty box der Strafraum [dɐ ˈʃtʀaːfʀaʊm]
pendant der Anhänger [dɐ ˈˀanhɛŋɐ]
people das Volk [das fɔlk], Leute *pl* [ˈlɔɪtə]
pepper der Pfeffer [dɐ ˈpfɛfɐ]
peppers die Paprikaschoten *f pl* [di ˈpapʀɪkaˌʃoːtn]
percent das Prozent [das pʀoˈtsɛnt]
perch der Barsch [dɐ baːʃ]
performance *(theatre)* die Vorstellung [di ˈfoɐʃtɛlʊŋ]
perfume das Parfüm [das paˈfyːm]
perfumery die Parfümerie [di pafʏməˈʀiː]
perhaps vielleicht [fɪˈlaɪçt]; eventuell [ˀevɛntʊˈ(ˀ)ɛl]
perm die Dauerwelle [di ˈdaʊɐvɛlə]
permitted zulässig [ˈtsuːlɛsɪç]
person die Person [di pɐˈzoːn]; der Mensch [dɐ mɛnʃ]
personal persönlich [pɐˈzøːnlɪç]
Personal Identification Number (PIN) die Geheimzahl [di gəˈhaɪmtsaːl]
perspire schwitzen [ˈʃvɪtsn]
petrol can der Benzinkanister [dɐ bɛnˈtsiːnkaˌnɪstɐ]
petrol pump die Benzinpumpe [di bɛnˈtsiːnpʊmpə]
petrol tank der Tank [dɐ taŋk]
pets die Haustiere *n pl* [di ˈhaʊstiːʀə]
phone das Telefon [das ˈteːləfoːn]; *(vb)* telefonieren [teləfoˈniːʀən/ -ˈniɐn], anrufen [ˈˀanʀuːfn]
phone box/booth die Telefonzelle [di teləˈfoːntsɛlə]
phone call der Anruf [dɐ ˈˀanʀuːf]; **make a phone call** telefonieren [teləfoˈniːʀən/-ˈniɐn]
phone number die Telefonnummer [di teləˈfoːnnʊmɐ]
phonecard die Telefonkarte [di teləˈfoːnkaːtə]
photograph das Foto [das ˈfoto]; *(vb)* fotografieren [ˌfotogʀaˈfiːʀən]
photography die Fotografie [di fotogʀaˈfiː]
pick out aussuchen [ˈˀaʊsuːxn]
pickpocket der Taschendieb/ die Taschendiebin [dɐ ˈtaʃndiːp/ di ˈtaʃnˌdiːbɪn]
pick-up service der Rückholservice [dɐ ˈʀʏkhoːlœsœɐvɪs]
picture das Bild [das bɪlt]
picture postcard die Ansichtskarte [di ˈˀanzɪçtskaːtə]
piece das Stück [das ʃtʏk]

pier der Pier [dɐ piɐ]
pill die Tablette [di taˈblɛtə]
pillar die Säule [di ˈzɔɪlə], der Pfeiler [dɐ ˈpfaɪlɐ]
pillow das Kopfkissen [das ˈkɔpfkɪsn]
pilot der Pilot/die Pilotin [dɐ piˈlo:t/di piˈlo:tɪn]
pineapple die Ananas [ˈʔananas]
pink rosa [ˈʀo:za]
pity, what a ~! wie schade! [vi ˈʃa:də]
place die Stelle [di ˈʃtɛlə], der Platz [dɐ plats], der Ort [dɐ ʔɔɐt]
place of birth der Geburtsort [dɐ gəˈbʊɐtsʔɔɐt]
place of pilgrimage der Wallfahrtsort [dɐ ˈvalfa:tsˌʔɔɐt]
place of residence der Wohnort [dɐ ˈvo:nʔɔɐt]
plain die Ebene [di ʔe:bənə]; *(adj)* einfarbig [ʔaɪnfaʀbɪç]
plant die Pflanze [di ˈ(p)flantsə]
plaster das Pflaster [das ˈpflastɐ]
plastic bag der Plastikbeutel [dɐ ˈplastɪkbɔɪtl]
plate der Teller [dɐ ˈtɛlɐ]
platform das Gleis [das glaɪs]
play das Schauspiel [das ˈʃaʊʃpi:l]; *(vb)* spielen [ʃpi:ln]
playmate der Spielkamerad/die Spielkameradin [dɐ ˈʃpi:lkaməˌʀa:t/di ˈʃpi:lkaməˌʀa:dɪn]
pleasant sympathisch [sʏmˈpa:tɪʃ], angenehm [ˈʔangəne:m]
please bitte [ˈbɪtə]; *(vb)* gefallen [gəˈfaln]; **be pleased (with/about)** sich freuen (über) [zɪç ˈfʀɔɪn (ˌʔybɐ)]
pleasure die Freude [di ˈfʀɔɪdə], das Vergnügen [das fɐˈgny:gŋ]
pluck (your) eyebrows Augenbrauen zupfen [ˈʔaʊgŋbʀaʊn ˈtsʊpfn]
plug der Stecker [dɐ ˈʃtɛkɐ]
pneumonia die Lungenentzündung [di ˈlʊŋənʔɛnˌtsʏndʊŋ]
pocket die Tasche [di ˈtaʃə]
pocket calculator der Taschenrechner [dɐ ˈtaʃnʀɛçnɐ]
pocket knife das Taschenmesser [das ˈtaʃnmɛsɐ]
poison das Gift [das gɪft]
poisoning die Vergiftung [di vɐˈgɪftʊŋ]
poisonous giftig [ˈgɪftɪç]
Polaroid® camera die Sofortbildkamera [di zoˈfɔɐtbɪltˌkaməʀa]
police die Polizei [di polɪˈtsaɪ]
police car der Polizeiwagen [dɐ polɪˈtsaɪva:gŋ]
police custody die Untersuchungshaft [di ʔʊntɐˈzu:xʊŋshaft]
policeman/policewoman der Polizist/die Polizistin [dɐ polɪˈtsɪst/di polɪˈtsɪstɪn]
polio die Kinderlähmung [di ˈkɪndɐlɛ:mʊŋ]
polite höflich [ˈhø:flɪç]
poor arm [ʔa:m]
porcelain das Porzellan [das pɔ(ɐ)tsəˈla:n]
pork das Schweinefleisch [ˈʃvaɪnəflaɪʃ]
port der Hafen [dɐ ˈha:fn]; *(wine)* der Portwein [der ˈpɔ(ɐ)tvaɪn]
portal das Portal [das pɔ(ɐ)ˈta:l]
porter der Portier [dɐ pɔɐˈtje:]
portion die Portion [di pɔˈtsjo:n]
portrait das Porträt [das pɔ(ɐ)ˈtʀɛ:]
posh vornehm [ˈfoɐne:m]
position *(location)* die Lage [di ˈla:gə]; *(profession)* die Stellung [di ˈʃtɛlʊŋ]
possible möglich [ˈmø:klɪç]; eventuell [ʔevɛntuˈ(ʔ)ɛl]
post code die Postleitzahl [di ˈpɔstlaɪtsa:l]
post office das Postamt [das ˈpɔstamt]
post office savings book das Postsparbuch [das ˈpɔstʃpa:bu:x]
postage das Porto [das ˈpɔɐto]
postcard die Postkarte [di ˈpɔstka:tə]
poste restante postlagernd [ˈpɔstla:gent]
poster das Plakat [das plaˈka:t]
postpone verschieben [fɐˈʃi:bm], aufschieben [ˈʔaʊfʃi:bm]
pot der Topf [dɐ tɔpf]
potatoes die Kartoffeln *f pl* [di kaˈtɔfln]
pottery *(workshop)* die Töpferei [di tœpfəˈʀaɪ]; *(products)* die Töpferwaren *f pl* [di ˈtœpfɐva:ʀən]; *(activity)* Töpfern [ˈtœpfɐn]
pound(s) das Pfund [das (p)fʊnt]
powder der Puder [dɐ ˈpu:dɐ]
power point die Steckdose [di ˈʃtɛkdo:zə]
practical praktisch [ˈpʀaktɪʃ]
practise *(vb)* üben [ʔy:bm]; *(profession)* ausüben [ˈʔaʊsʔy:bm]
prawns die Garnelen *f pl* [di gaˈne:ln]
pray beten [be:tn]
pregnancy die Schwangerschaft [di ˈʃvaŋɐʃaft]
premiere die Premiere [di pʀəmˈje:ʀə]
prepare vorbereiten [ˈfoɐbəʀaɪtn], zubereiten [ˈtsu:bəʀaɪtn]
prescribe verschreiben [fɐˈʃʀaɪbm]
prescription das Rezept [das ʀeˈtsɛpt]
present das Geschenk [das gəˈʃɛŋk]; *(adj)* anwesend [ˈʔanve:znt]; **be present** da sein [ˈda:zaɪn]

Dictionary English - German

pretty *(adj)* hübsch [hʏpʃ]; *(adv)* ziemlich [ˈtsiːmlɪç]
prevent verhindern [fɐˈhɪndɐn], hindern [ˈhɪndɐn]
price der Preis [dɐ pʀaɪs]
priest der Priester [dɐ pʀiːstɐ]
printer der Drucker [dɐ ˈdʀʊkɐ]
prison das Gefängnis [das gəˈfɛŋnɪs]
private privat [pʀɪˈvaːt]
prize der Preis [dɐ pʀaɪs]
probable wahrscheinlich [vaˈʃaɪnlɪç]
probably wahrscheinlich [vaˈʃaɪnlɪç]
problem das Problem [das pʀoˈbleːm]
procession die Prozession [di pʀotsɛsˈjoːn]
product das Erzeugnis [das ˀɐˈtsɔɪknɪs], das Produkt [das pʀoˈdʊkt], die Ware [di ˈvaːʀə]
production *(theatre)* die Inszenierung [di ˀɪntsəˈniːʀʊŋ]
profession der Beruf [dɐ bəˈʀuːf]
profit der Gewinn [dɐ gəˈvɪn]
programme *(booklet)* das Programmheft [das pʀoˈgʀamhɛft]
prohibited verboten [fɐˈboːtn]
pronounce aussprechen [ˈˀaʊ(s)ʃpʀɛçn]
proper richtig [ˈʀɪçtɪç]
prospectus der Prospekt [dɐ pʀosˈpɛkt]
protection factor der Lichtschutzfaktor [dɐ ˈlɪçtʃʊtsˌfaktoɐ]
provisional provisorisch [pʀovɪˈzoːʀɪʃ]
provisions der Vorrat [dɐ ˈfoːʀaːt]
pub die Kneipe [di ˈknaɪpə]
public das Publikum [das ˈpʊblɪkʊm]; *(adj)* öffentlich [ˈˀœfntlɪç]
pull ziehen [tsiːn]
pulled muscle die Zerrung [di ˈtsɛʀʊŋ]
pullover der Pullover [dɐ pʊˈloːvɐ]
pulse der Puls [dɐ pʊls]
pump die Luftpumpe [di ˈlʊftpʊmpə]
pumpkin der Kürbis [dɐ ˈkʏɐbɪs]
punctual pünktlich [ˈpʏŋktlɪç]
puncture das Loch [das lɔx]; *(flat tyre)* die Panne [di ˈpanə]
punishment die Strafe [di ˈʃtʀaːfə]
purple lila [ˈliːla]
purse der Geldbeutel [dɐ ˈgɛltbɔɪtl], die Geldbörse [di ˈgɛltbœɐzə]; *(handbag)* die Handtasche [di ˈhan(t)taʃə]
pus der Eiter [dɐ ˈˀaɪtɐ]
put legen [leːgŋ], stellen [ʃtɛln], setzen [zɛtsn]; **put down** hinlegen [ˈhɪnleːgŋ]; **put off** verschieben [fɐˈʃiːbm], aufschieben [ˈˀaʊfʃiːbm]; **put on** *(dress)* anziehen [ˈˀantsiːn]
quality die Qualität [di kvalɪˈtɛːt], die Eigenschaft [di ˈˀaɪgŋʃaft]
quay der Kai [dɐ kaɪ]
queen die Königin [di ˈkøːnɪgɪn]
question die Frage [di ˈfʀaːgə]
quick schnell [ʃnɛl]; rasch [ʀaʃ]
quiet leise [ˈlaɪzə], ruhig [ʀʊɪç]
quite *(entirely)* ganz [gants]; *(somewhat)* ziemlich

R

rabbit das Kaninchen [kaˈniːnçn]
race das Rennen [das ʀɛnn]
racing bike das Rennrad [das ˈʀɛnʀaːt]
racquet der Schläger [dɐ ˈʃlɛːgɐ]
radar check die Radarkontrolle [di ʀaˈdaːkɔnˌtʀɔlə]
radiator der Kühler [dɐ ˈkyːlɐ]
radio das Radio [das ˈʀaːdjo]
rain der Regen [dɐ ˈʀeːgŋ]
raincoat der Regenmantel [dɐ ˈʀeːgŋmantl]
rainy regnerisch [ˈʀeːknəʀɪʃ]
ramble wandern [ˈvandɐn]
ramp die Rampe [di ˈʀampə]
rape die Vergewaltigung [di fɐgəˈvaltɪgʊŋ]; *(vb)* vergewaltigen [fɐgəˈvaltɪgŋ]
rare selten [zɛltn]
rash der Ausschlag [dɐ ˈˀaʊʃlaːk]
rather lieber [ˈliːbɐ], vielmehr [ˈfiːlmeɐ], eher [ˀeɐ]; *(somewhat)* ziemlich [ˈtsiːmlɪç]
ravine die Schlucht [di ˈʃlʊxt]
raw roh [ʀoː]
razor blade die Rasierklinge [di ʀaˈziɐklɪŋə]
reach erreichen [ˀɐˈʀaɪçn]
read lesen [leːzn]
ready fertig [ˈfɛɐtɪç], bereit [bəˈʀaɪt]
real wirklich [ˈvɪɐklɪç]
really unbedingt [ˈˀʊnbədɪŋt]; wirklich [ˈvɪɐklɪç]
rear light das Rücklicht [das ˈʀʏklɪçt]
rear-view mirror der Rückspiegel [dɐ ˈʀʏkʃpiːgl]
reason der Anlass [dɐ ˈˀanlas], der Grund [dɐ gʀʊnt]
receipt die Quittung [di ˈkvɪtʊŋ]
receive erhalten [ˀɐˈhaltn], empfangen [ˀɛmpˈfaŋŋ]
receiver der Hörer [dɐ ˈhøːʀɐ]
recently kürzlich [ˈkʏɐtslɪç]
reception die Rezeption [di ʀetsɛpˈtsjoːn]
rechargeable battery der Akku [dɐ ˈˀaku]
recommend empfehlen [ˀɛmpˈfeːln]
recover sich erholen [zɪç ˀɐˈhoːln]
red rot [ʀoːt]
red wine Rotwein [ˈʀoːtvaɪn]
reduction die Ermäßigung [di ɐˈmɛːsɪgʊŋ]

reflexology (foot) massage die Fuß(reflexzonen)massage [di 'fu:s(ʁe'flɛkstso:nn)ma͵sa:ʒə]
refrigerator der Kühlschrank [dɐ 'ky:lʃʀaŋk]
refuse zurückweisen [tsʊ'ʀʏkvaɪzn], sich weigern [zɪç 'vaɪgɐn], ablehnen ['ʔaple:nn]
region die Gegend [di 'ge:gŋt]
register sich anmelden [zɪç 'ʔanmɛldn]; *(luggage)* aufgeben ['ʔaʊfge:bm]; *(car)* zulassen ['tsu:lasn]
registered letter der Einschreibebrief [dɐ 'ʔaɪnʃʀaɪbəbʀi:f]
registration die Anmeldung [di 'ʔanmɛldʊŋ]
regret das Bedauern [das bə'daʊɐn]; *(vb)* bedauern [bə'daʊɐn]
regular regelmäßig ['ʀe:glmɛ:sɪç]
related verwandt [fɐ'vant]
religion die Religion [di ʀelɪ'gjo:n]
reluctantly ungern ['ʔʊngɛɐn], nicht gern [nɪç(t) gɛɐn]
remain bleiben [blaɪbm]
remains die Überreste *m pl* [di 'ʔy:bɐʀɛstə]
remark *(vb)* bemerken [bə'mɛɐkŋ]
remedy das Heilmittel [das 'haɪlmɪtl]
remember sich erinnern [zɪç ɐ'ʔɪnɐn]; remember s. th. sich etw. merken [zɪç 'ʔɛtvas 'mɛɐkŋ]
remittance die Überweisung [di ʔybɐ'vaɪzʊŋ]
Renaissance die Renaissance [di ʀənɛ'sa):s]
rent die Miete [di 'mi:tə]; *(vb)* mieten ['mi:tn], vermieten [fɐ'mi:tn]
repair die Reparatur [di ʀɛpaʀa'tuɐ]; *(vb)* reparieren [ʀɛpa'ʀi:ʀən/-'ʀiɐn]
repair kit das Flickzeug [das 'flɪktsɔɪk]
repeat *(vb)* wiederholen [vidɐ'ho:ln]
replace ersetzen [ʔɐ'zɛtsn]
replacement der Ersatz [dɐ ʔɐ'zats]
reply die Antwort [di 'ʔantvɔɐt]; *(vb)* antworten ['ʔantvɔɐtn], beantworten [bə'ʔantvɔɐtn], erwidern [ʔɐ'vi:dɐn]
report der Bericht; *(vb, a crime)* anzeigen ['ʔantsaɪgŋ]
request die Bitte [di 'bɪtə]
reservation die Reservierung [di ʀezɐ'vi:ʀʊŋ]
reserve reservieren [ʀɛzɐ'vi:ʀən/-'viɐn]
responsible zuständig ['tsu:ʃtɛndɪç], verantwortlich [fɐ'ʔantvɔɐtlɪç]
rest die Ruhe [di 'ʀuə], die Erholung [di ʔɐ'ho:lʊŋ]; *(remainder)* der Rest [dɐ ʀɛst]; *(vb)* ruhen [ʀu:n], sich ausruhen [zɪç 'ʔaʊsʀu:n]
restaurant das Restaurant [das ʁɛsto'ʁɑ̃/ʁɛsto'ʁaŋ]; ~ **car** der Speisewagen [dɐ 'ʃpaɪzəva:gŋ]
return die Rückkehr [di 'ʀʏkeɐ]; *(vb)* wiederkommen ['vi:dɐkɔmm], zurückkehren [tsʊ'ʀʏke:ʀən/-keɐn]; *(give back)* wiedergeben ['vi:dɐge:bm]
return ticket die Rückfahrkarte [di 'ʀʏkfa:͵ka:tə]
reverse umgekehrt ['ʔʊmgəkeɐt]
reverse charge call das R-Gespräch [das 'ʔɛɐgə͵ʃpʀɛ:ç]
reverse gear der Rückwärtsgang [dɐ 'ʀʏkvɛɐtsgaŋ]
reward die Belohnung [di bə'lo:nʊŋ]; *(vb)* belohnen [bəlo:nn]
rheumatism das Rheuma [das 'ʀɔɪma]
rice der Reis [dɐ ʀaɪs]
rich reich [ʀaɪç]
ride *(vb)* reiten ['ʀaɪtn]
ridiculous lächerlich ['lɛçɐlɪç]
riding school die Reitschule ['ʀaɪtʃu:lə]
right das Recht [das ʀɛçt]; *(adj)* richtig ['ʀɪçtɪç]; on the right, to the right rechts [ʀɛçts]
right-hand rechte(r, s) ['ʀɛçtə (-tɐ, -təs)]
rigid fest [fɛst]
ring (up) telefonieren [teləfo'ni:ʀən/-'niɐn]
ripe reif [ʀaɪf]
river der Fluss [dɐ flʊs]
road die Straße [di 'ʃtʀa:sə]
road map die Straßenkarte [di 'ʃtʀa:snka:tə]
roasted gebraten [gə'bʀa:tn]
roasting tray der Bräter [dɐ 'bʁɛ:tɐ]
rock der Fels [dɐ fɛls]
roller skates die Rollschuhe *m pl* [di 'ʀɔlʃu:ə]
rolls die Brötchen *n pl* [di bʀø:tçn]
roof das Dach [das dax]
room das Zimmer [das 'tsɪmɐ], der Saal [dɐ za:l]; *(space)* der Raum [dɐ ʀaʊm]
rope das Seil [das zaɪl]
rosemary der Rosmarin [dɐ 'ʀo:smaʀi:n]
rotten faul [faʊl], verdorben [fɐ'dɔɐbm]
round *(drinks, sport)* die Runde [di 'ʀʊndə]; *(adj)* rund [ʀʊnt]
round trip die Rundfahrt [di 'ʀʊntfa:t]
route die Route [di 'ʀu:tə]; *(road)* die Strecke [di 'ʃtʀɛkə]
row *(vb)* rudern ['ʀu:dɐn]
rowing boat das Ruderboot [das 'ʀu:dɐbo:t]
rubber boots die Gummistiefel *m pl* [di 'gʊmiʃti:fl]

rubber dinghy das Schlauchboot [das ˈʃlaʊxboːt]
rubber ring der Schwimmring [dɐ ˈʃvɪmʀɪŋ]
rubbish der Müll [dɐ mʏl], der Abfall [dɐ ˈʔapfal]
rucksack der Rucksack [dɐ ˈʀʊkzak]
ruin die Ruine [di ʀuˈʔiːnə]
rule die Vorschrift [di ˈfoɐʃʀɪft]
run rennen [ʀɛnn], laufen [laʊfn]; *(nose)* tropfen [tʀɔpfn]; *(bus etc.)* verkehren [fɐˈkeːʀən/-ˈkeɐn]
rupture der Leistenbruch [dɐ ˈlaɪstnbʀʊx]

S

sad traurig [ˈtʀaʊʀɪç]
safari park der Safaripark [dɐ zaˈfaːʀipaːk]
safe der Safe [dɐ sɛɪf/seːf]; *(adj)* sicher [ˈzɪçɐ]
saffron der Safran [dɐ ˈzafraːn]
sage der Salbei [dɐ ˈzalbaɪ]
sail dasSegel [das ˈzeːgl]; *(vb)* segeln [ˈzeːgln]
sailing boat das Segelboot [das ˈzeːglboːt]
sailing cruise der Segeltörn [dɐ ˈzeːgltœɐn]
salad der Salat [dɐ zaˈlaːt]
salad bar das Salatbüfett [das zaˈlaːtbʏˈfeː]
salami die Salami [di zaˈlaːmi]
sale der Verkauf [dɐ fɐˈkaʊf]; **(clearance) sale** der Ausverkauf [dɐ ˈʔaʊsfɐkaʊf]
salmonella die Salmonellen *pl* [di zalmoˈnɛln]
salt das Salz [das zalts]
same gleich [glaɪç]; **the same** derselbe [dɐˈzɛlbə], dieselbe [diˈzɛlbə], dasselbe [dasˈzɛlbə]
sand pit der Sandkasten [dɐ ˈzantkastn]
sandals die Sandalen *f pl* [di zanˈdaːln]
sand-castle die Sandburg [di ˈzantbuɐk]
sanitary towels die Damenbinden *f pl* [di ˈdaːmmbɪndn]
satisfied befriedigt [bəˈfʀiːdɪçt], zufrieden [tsʊˈfʀiːdn]
Saturday *(southern Germany)* Samstag [ˈzamstaːk], *(northern Germany)* Sonnabend [ˈzɔnaːbmt]
sauce die Soße [di ˈzoːsə]
saucer die Untertasse [di ˈʔʊntɐtasə]
sauna die Sauna [di ˈzaʊna]
sausage die Wurst [di vʊɐst], das Würstchen [das ˈvʊɐstxən]

say sagen [zaːgŋ]
scanner der Scanner [dɐ ˈskɛnɐ]
scar die Narbe [di ˈnaːbə]
scarcely kaum [kaʊm]
scarf *(decorative)* das Halstuch [das ˈhalstuːx]; *(for warmth)* der Schal [dɐ ʃaːl]
scenery die Landschaft [di ˈlantʃaft]
scent das Parfüm [das paˈfyːm]
school die Schule [di ˈʃuːlə]
sciatica der Ischias [dɐ ˈʔɪʃias]
Scotland Schottland [ˈʃɔtlant]
Scottish schottisch [ˈʃɔtɪʃ]
scratch der Kratzer [dɐ ˈkʁatsɐ]
scream *(vb)* schreien [ˈʃʀaɪn]
screw die Schraube [di ˈʃʀaʊbə]
sculptor der Bildhauer/die Bildhauerin [dɐ ˈbɪlthaʊɐ/di ˈbɪlthaʊəʀɪn]
sculpture die Skulptur [di skʊlpˈtuɐ]
sea die See [di ˈzeː], das Meer [das meɐ]
seagull die Möwe [di ˈm ːvə]
seasick seekrank [ˈzeːkʀaŋk]
seaside resort der Badeort [dɐ ˈbaːdəˀɔɐt]
season die Saison [di zɛˈzɔŋ], die Jahreszeit [di ˈjaːʀəstsaɪt]; *(vb)* würzen [vʏɐtsn]
seasoning das Gewürz [das gəˈvʏɐts]
seat der Sitz [dɐ zɪts], der Sitzplatz [dɐ ˈzɪtsplats]
seat belt der Sicherheitsgurt [dɐ ˈzɪçɐhaɪtsgʊɐt]
seat reservation die Platzreservierung [di ˈplatsʀezɐˌviːʀʊŋ]
secluded einsam [ˈʔaɪnzaːm]
second die Sekunde [di zeˈkʊndə]; *(adj)* zweite(r, s) [ˈtsvaɪtə (-tɐ/-təs)]; second(ly) zweitens [tsvaɪtns]
second-hand shop der Trödelladen [dɐ ˈtʀ ːdllaːdn]
security *(safety)* die Sicherheit [di ˈzɪçɐhaɪt]; *(guarantee)* die Kaution [di kaʊˈtsjoːn], die Bürgschaft [di ˈbʏɐkʃaft]
security charge die Sicherheitsgebühr [di ˈzɪçɐhaɪtsgəˌbyɐ]
security control die Sicherheitskontrolle [di ˈzɪçɐhaɪtskɔnˌtʀɔlə]
sedative das Beruhigungsmittel [das bəˈʀʊɪgʊŋsmɪtl]
see sehen [ˈzeːn]
seldom selten [zɛltn]
self-employe der Freiberufler [dɐ ˈfʁaɪbəʁuːflɐ]
self-service die Selbstbedienung [di ˈzɛlps(t)bədiːnʊŋ]
self-timer der Selbstauslöser [dɐ ˈzɛlpstaʊsl ːzɐ]
sell verkaufen [fɐˈkaʊfn]

sell-by date die Haltbarkeit [ˈhaltba(:)kaɪt]
send senden [ˈzɛndn], schicken [ʃɪkŋ]; **send for** abholen lassen [ˈʔapho:ln lasn]; **send on** nachsenden [ˈna:xzɛndn]
sender der Absender/die Absenderin [dɐ ˈʔapzɛndɐ/di ˈʔapzɛndəʀɪn]
sentence der Satz [dɐ zats]
separation of rubbish die Mülltrennung [di ˈmʏltʁɛnʊŋ]
September September [zɛpˈtɛmbɐ]
serious ernst [ˀɛɐnst]; *(illness)* schwer [ʃveɐ]
serve servieren [zɐˈvi:ʀən/-ˈviɐn], bedienen [bəˈdi:nn], dienen [di:nn]
service der Dienst [dɐ di:nst], die Bedienung [di bəˈdi:nʊŋ]
service charge die Bearbeitungsgebühr [di bəˈʔa:baɪtʊŋsgəˌbyɐ]
serviette die Serviette [di zɐˈvjɛtə]
set *(vb)* setzen [zɛtsn], hinstellen [ˈhɪnʃtɛln], aufstellen [ˈʔaʊfʃtɛln]; *(TV)* der (Fernseh)Apparat [dɐ (ˈfɛɐnze) ˀapaˌʀa:t]
set meal das Menü [das meˈny:]
severe *(wound, accident)* schwer [ʃveɐ]; *(judgement, winter)* streng [ʃtʀɛŋ]
severely handicapped person der/die Schwerbehinderte [dɐ/di ˈʃveɐbəhɪndɐtə]
sexual harassment die sexuelle Belästigung [di sɛksuˈɛlə bəˈlɛstɪgʊŋ]
shade der Schatten [dɐ ʃatn]; *(colour)* der Ton [dɐ to:n]
shadow der Schatten [dɐ ʃatn]
shampoo das Schampoo [das ˈʃampo/ˈʃampu]
shape die Form [di fɔɐm]
shaver der Rasierapparat [dɐ ʀaˈziɐˀapaˌʀa:t]
shaving brush der Rasierpinsel [dɐ ʀaˈziɐpɪnzl]
shaving foam der Rasierschaum [dɐ ʀaˈziɐʃaʊm]
she sie [zi:]
shin das Schienbein [das ˈʃi:nbaɪn]
shirt das Hemd [das hɛmt]
shoe der Schuh [dɐ ʃu:]
shoe brush die Schuhbürste [di ˈʃu:bʏɐstə]
shoe cream die Schuhcreme [di ˈʃu:kʀɛ:m]
shoe shop das Schuhgeschäft [das ˈʃu:gəʃɛft]
shoemaker's der Schuhmacher [dɐ ˈʃu:maxɐ]
shop das Geschäft [das gəˈʃɛft], der Laden [dɐ ˈla:dn]; **shop window** das Schaufenster [das ˈʃaʊfɛnstɐ]; **go shopping** einkaufen [ˈʔaɪnkaʊfn]
shore das Ufer [das ˈʔu:fɐ]
short kurz [kʊɐts]; **at short notice** kurzfristig [ˈkʊɐtsfʀɪstɪç]
short film der Kurzfilm [dɐ kʊɐtsfɪlm]
short-circuit der Kurzschluss [dɐ ˈkʊɐtʃlʊs]
short-cut die Abkürzung [di ˈʔapkʏɐtsʊŋ]
shorts die kurze Hose [di ˈkʊɐtsə ˈho:zə]
shoulder die Schulter [di ˈʃʊltɐ]
shoulder bag die Umhängetasche [di ˈʔʊmhɛŋəˌtaʃə]
shout *(vb)* schreien [ˈʃʀaɪn]
show *(vb)* zeigen [ˈtsaɪgŋ], vorzeigen [ˈfoɐtsaɪgŋ]; *(exhibition)* die Ausstellung [di ˈʔaʊʃtɛlʊŋ]; *(entertainment)* die Revue [di ʀeˈvy:], die Show [di ʃo:]
shower die Dusche [di ˈdu:ʃə]; *(rain)* der Regenschauer [dɐ ˈʀe:gŋʃaʊɐ]
shower gel das Duschgel [das ˈdu:ʃge:l]
shower seat der Duschsitz [dɐ ˈdu:ʃzɪts]
shrimps die Krabben *f pl* [di kʀabm]
shut *(adj)* zu [zu(:)]; *(vb)* schließen [ʃli:sn], zumachen [ˈtsu:maxn]
shutter *(camera)* der Auslöser [dɐ ˈʔaʊsl :zɐ]
shuttlecock der Federball [dɐ ˈfe:dɐbal]
shy schüchtern [ˈʃʏçtɐn]
sick krank [kʀaŋk]
side die Seite [di ˈzaɪtə]
sidelights das Standlicht [das ˈʃtantlɪçt]
sieve das Küchensieb [das ˈkʏçnzi:p]
sights die Sehenswürdigkeiten *f pl* [di ˈze:nsvʏɐdɪçkaɪtn]
sightseeing tour of the town/city die Stadtrundfahrt [di ˈʃtatʀʊntfa:t]
sign das Schild [das ʃɪlt], das Zeichen [das ˈtsaɪçn]; *(directions)* der Wegweiser [dɐ ˈve:kvaɪzɐ]; *(vb)* unterschreiben [ˀʊntɐˈʃʀaɪbm]
sign language die Zeichensprache [di ˈtsaɪçnʃpʀa:xə]
signature die Unterschrift [di ˈʔʊntɐʃʀɪft]
silence *(quiet)* die Ruhe [di ˈʀuə], *(personal)* das Schweigen [das ʃvaɪgŋ]
silent ruhig [ʀʊɪç]
silk die Seide [di ˈzaɪdə]
silk painting die Seidenmalerei [di ˈzaɪdnma:ləˌʀaɪ]
silly blöd(e) [bl :t/ˈbl :də]
silver das Silber [das ˈzɪlbɐ]
similar ähnlich [ˈʔɛ:nlɪç]

simple einfach ['ˀaɪnfax]
simultaneously gleichzeitig ['glaɪçtsaɪtɪç]
since *(time)* seit [zaɪt]; *(as)* da [da:], weil [vaɪl]
sincere herzlich ['hɛɐtslɪç]
sing singen [zɪŋŋ]
singer der Sänger/die Sängerin [dɐ 'zɛŋɐ/di 'zɛŋəʀɪn]
single ledig ['le:dɪç]
singles das Einzel [das 'ˀaɪntsəl]
sink das Geschirrspülbecken [das gə'ʃɪɐspy:lbɛkŋ]
sinusitis die Stirnhöhlenentzündung [di 'ʃtɪɐnh :lnˀɛnˌtsʏndʊŋ]
sister die Schwester [di 'ʃvɛstɐ]
sister-in-law die Schwägerin [di 'ʃvɛ:gəʀɪn]
sit sitzen [zɪtsn]
situation die Lage [di 'la:gə]
size die Größe [di 'gʀ :sə]; *(paper)* das Format [das fɔ'ma:t]
skateboard das Skateboard [das 'skɛɪtbɔɐt]; *(vb)* Skateboard fahren ['skɛɪtbɔɐt 'fa:ʀən]
ski der Ski [dɐ ʃi:]; *(vb)* Ski fahren ['ʃi: 'fa:(ʀə)n]
ski bindings die Skibindungen *f pl* [di 'ʃi:bɪndʊŋŋ]
ski boots die Skistiefel *m pl* [di 'ʃi:ʃti:fl]
ski goggles die Skibrille [di 'ʃi:bʀɪlə]
ski instructor der Skilehrer/ die Skilehrerin [dɐ 'ʃi:le:ʀɐ/ di 'ʃi:le:ʀəʀɪn]
ski poles die Skistöcke *m pl* [di 'ʃi:'ʃtœkə]
skiing das Skifahren [das 'ʃi:fa:(ʀə)n]
skiing course der Skikurs [dɐ 'ʃi:kʊɐs]
skin die Haut [di haʊt]
skirt der Rock [dɐ ʀɔk]
sky der Himmel [dɐ hɪml]
sledge der Schlitten [dɐ ʃlɪtn]
sleep der Schlaf [dɐ ʃla:f]; *(vb)* schlafen [ʃla:fn]
sleeping pills die Schlaftabletten *f pl* [di 'ʃla:ftaˌblɛtn]
sleeplessness die Schlaflosigkeit [di 'ʃla:flozɪçkaɪt]
sleeve der Ärmel [dɐ ˀɛɐml]
slender schlank [ʃlaŋk], dünn [dʏn]
slice die Scheibe [di 'ʃaɪbə]
slide das Dia [das 'dia]
slight leicht [laɪçt]
slim dünn [dʏn], schmal [ʃma:l], schlank [ʃlaŋk]; *(vb)* abnehmen ['ˀapne:mm]
slow(ly) langsam ['laŋza:m]
small klein [klaɪn]
small packet das Päckchen [das pɛkçn]
smell der Geruch [dɐ gə'ʀu(:)x]; *(vb)* riechen [ʀi:çn]
smoke der Rauch [dɐ ʀaʊx]; *(vb)* rauchen [ʀaʊxn]
smoked geräuchert [gə'ʀɔɪçɐt]
smoked ham roher Schinken [ʀo:ɐ ʃɪŋkŋ]
smoker der Raucher/die Raucherin [dɐ 'ʀaʊxɐ/di 'ʀaʊxəʀɪn]
smoking compartment das Raucherabteil [das 'ʀaʊxɐˀapˌtaɪl]
smuggle schmuggeln [ʃmʊgln]
snack der Imbiss [dɐ 'ˀɪmbɪs]
snake die Schlange [di 'ʃlaŋə]
snapshot der Schnappschuss [dɐ 'ʃnapʃʊs]
snore schnarchen [ʃna:çn]
snorkel der Schnorchel [dɐ ʃnɔɐçl]; **go snorkelling** schnorcheln [ʃnɔɐçln]
snow der Schnee [dɐ ʃne:]
so *(adv)* so [zo:]; *(conj)* also ['ˀalzo:]
soaked nass [nas]
soap die Seife [di 'zaɪfə]
sober nüchtern ['nʏçtɐn]
socket die Steckdose [di 'ʃtɛkdo:zə]
socks die Socken *f pl* [di 'zɔkŋ]
soft weich [vaɪç]
solarium das Solarium [das zo'la:ʀiʊm]
sole die Sohle [di 'zo:lə]; *(fish)* die Seezunge [di 'ze:tsʊŋə]
solid fest [fɛst], hart [ha:t]
soloist der Solist/die Solistin [dɐ zo'lɪst/di zo'lɪstɪn]
some einige ['ˀaɪnɪgə]
somebody jemand ['je:mant]
something etwas ['ˀɛtvas]
sometimes manchmal ['mançma:l]
son der Sohn [dɐ zo:n]
song das Lied [das li:t]
soon bald [balt]
sore throat die Halsschmerzen *m pl* [di 'halʃmɛɐtsn]
sort die Sorte [di 'zɔɐtə], die Art [di ˀa:t]
sound der Klang [dɐ klaŋ], der Ton [dɐ to:n]
soup die Suppe [di 'zʊpə]
soup plate der Suppenteller [dɐ 'zʊpmtɛlɐ]
sour sauer ['zaʊɐ]
sour cream die saure Sahne [di zaʊʀə 'za:nə]
source die Quelle [di 'kvɛlə]
south der Süden [dɐ zy:dn]; **south of** südlich von ['zy:tlɪç fɔn]
souvenir das Souvenir [das zʊvə'niɐ]
souvenir shop der Souvenirladen [dɐ zʊvə'niɐla:dn]
space der Raum [dɐ ʀaʊm]

spare tyre der Ersatzreifen [dɐ ˀɐˈzatsʀaɪfn]
spark plug die Zündkerze [di ˈtsʏntkɛɐtsə]
speak sprechen [ʃpʀɛçn]
speaker der Lautsprecher [dɐ ˈlaʊtʃpʀɛçɐ]
special speziell [ʃpɛˈtsjɛl], Sonder- [ˈzɔndɐ-]
special (of the day) das Tagesmenü [das ˈta:gəsme̦ny:]
special issue stamp die Sondermarke [di ˈzɔndɐma:kə]
specialist der Facharzt/die Fachärztin [dɐ ˈfaxa:tst/di ˈfaxˀɛɐtstɪn]
speciality die Spezialität [di ʃpetsjaliˈtɛ:t]
spectator der Zuschauer/die Zuschauerin [dɐ ˈtsu:ʃaʊɐ/di ˈtsu:ʃaʊəʀɪn]
speed die Geschwindigkeit [di gəˈʃvɪndɪçkaɪt]
speedometer der Tacho(meter) [dɐ ˌtaxo(ˈme:tɐ)]
spell buchstabieren [buxʃtaˈbi:ʀən/-ˈbiɐn]
spend ausgeben [ˈˀaʊsge:bm]; *(time)* verbringen [fɐˈbʀɪŋŋ]; spend the night übernachten [ˀybɐˈnaxtn]
spice das Gewürz [das gəˈvʏɐts]
spinach der Spinat [dɐ ʃpɪˈna:t]
spine die Wirbelsäule [di ˈvɪɐblzɔɪlə]
splendid herrlich [ˈhɛɐlɪç]; *(fig)* glänzend [glɛntsnt]
splint die Schiene [di ˈʃi:nə]
spoiled verdorben [fɐˈdɔɐbm]
spoon der Löffel [dɐ lœfl]
sport der Sport [dɐ ʃpɔɐt]
sports ground der Sportplatz [dɐ ˈʃpɔɐtplats]
sports shop das Sportgeschäft [das ˈʃpɔɐtgəʃɛft]
spot die Stelle [di ˈʃtɛlə]
sprained verstaucht [fɐˈʃtaʊxt]
spring der Frühling [dɐ ˈfʀy:lɪŋ]
squid der Tintenfisch [dɐ ˈtɪntnfɪʃ]
stadium das Stadion [das ˈʃta:djon]
stain der Fleck [dɐ flɛk]
staircase die Treppe [di ˈtʀɛpə]
stairs die Treppen *f pl* [di tʀɛpm]
stalls das Parkett [das paˈkɛt]
stamp der Stempel [dɐ ʃtɛmpl]; *(postage)* die (Brief)Marke [di (ˈbʀi:f-)ˌma:kə]
stamp machine der Briefmarkenautomat [dɐ ˈbʀi:fma:kŋˀautoˌma:t]
stand stehen [ʃte:n]; *(bear)* ertragen [ˀɐˈtʀa:gŋ]
star der Stern [dɐ ʃtɛɐn]
start der Anfang; *(vb)* anfangen
start (from) abfahren (von) [ˈˀapfa:n (fɔn)]
starter *(engine part)* der Anlasser [dɐ ˈˀanlasɐ]; *(food)* die Vorspeise [di ˈfoɐʃpaɪzə]
startle erschrecken [ˀɐˈʃʀɛkŋ]
state *(country)* der Staat [dɐ ʃta:t]; *(condition)* der Zustand [dɐ ˈtsu:ʃtant]; *(vb)* feststellen [ˈfɛ(st)ʃtɛln], aussagen [ˈˀaʊsza:gŋ]
statement die Aussage [di ˈˀaʊsza:gə]
station der Bahnhof [dɐ ˈba:nho:f]
stationer's das Schreibwarengeschäft [das ˈʃʀaɪpva:ʀəngəˌʃɛft]
statue die Statue [di ˈʃta:tuə]
stay der Aufenthalt [dɐ ˈˀaʊfntalt]; *(vb)* sich aufhalten [zɪç ˈˀaʊfhaltn], wohnen [vo:nn], bleiben [blaɪbm], übernachten [ˀybɐˈnaxtn]
steal stehlen [ʃte:ln]
steamed gedämpft [gəˈdɛmpft], gedünstet [gəˈdʏnstət]
steep steil [ʃtaɪl]
steeple der Kirchturm [dɐ ˈkɪɐçtʊɐm]
step die Stufe [di ˈʃtu:fə]
steps die Treppe [di ˈtʀɛpə]
steward/stewardess der Steward/die Stewardess [dɐ ˈstjua:t/di: ˈstjuadɛs]
stick der Stock [dɐ ʃtɔk]
still *(quiet)* still [ʃtɪl]; *(mineral water)* ohne Kohlensäure [ˈˀo:nə ˈko:l(ə)nzɔɪʀə]; *(adv)* noch [nɔx]
still life das Stillleben [das ˈʃtɪle:bm]
sting der Stich [dɐ ʃtɪç]; *(vb)* stechen [ʃtɛçn]; brennen [bʀɛnn]
stink stinken [ʃtɪŋkŋ]
stir spoon der Rührlöffel [dɐ ˈʀyɐlœfl]
stitch (up) nähen [nɛ:n]
stock der Vorrat [dɐ ˈfo:ʀa:t]
stockings die Strümpfe *m pl* [di ˈʃtʀʏmpfə]
stomach der Bauch [dɐ baʊx], der Magen [dɐ ma:gŋ]
stomach-ache die Magenschmerzen *m pl* [di ˈma:gŋʃmɛɐtsn]
stone der Stein [dɐ ʃtaɪn]
stony steinig [ˈʃtaɪnɪç]
stop *(train)* der Aufenthalt [dɐ ˈˀaʊfntalt]; *(bus)* die Haltestelle [di ˈhaltəʃtɛlə]; *(vb, stop doing sth.)* aufhören [ˈˀaʊfh ɐn]; *(car)* anhalten [ˈˀanhaltn], *(person)* stehen bleiben [ˈʃte:nblaɪbm], *(break off)* abbrechen [ˈˀapbʀɛçn], *(bus, train)* halten [haltn]; stop! halt! [halt]
stopover die Zwischenlandung [di ˈtsvɪʃnˌlandʊŋ]

store *(shop)* das Geschäft [das gə'ʃɛft], der Laden [dɐ 'la:dn]; *(supply)* der Vorrat [dɐ 'fo:ʀa:t]
storm der Sturm [dɐ ʃtʊɐm]
story die Geschichte [di gə'ʃɪçtə]
stove der Herd [dɐ heɐt]
straight gerade [g(ə)'ʀa:də]; **straight across/through** quer durch [kveɐ dʊɐç]
straight on/straight ahead geradeaus [gʀa:də'ʔaʊs]
strange eigen ['ʔaɪgŋ], fremd [fʀɛmt]
stranger der/die Fremde [dɐ/ di 'fʀɛmdə]
straw der Strohhalm [dɐ 'ʃtʀo:halm]
strawberries die Erdbeeren *f pl* [di 'ʔeɐtbe:ʀən]
street die Straße [di 'ʃtʀa:sə]
streetcar die Straßenbahn [di 'ʃtʀa:snba:n]
strenuous anstrengend ['ʔanʃtʀɛŋnt]
stroke der Schlaganfall [dɐ 'ʃla:kanfal]
stroll der Bummel [dɐ bʊml], der Spaziergang [dɐ ʃpa'tsiɐgaŋ]; *(vb)* spazieren gehen [ʃpa'tsi:ʀənge:n/-'tsiɐn-]
strong stark [ʃta:k], kräftig ['kʀɛftɪç]
studio couch die Schlafcouch [di 'ʃla:fkaʊtʃ]
study *(vb)* studieren [ʃtʊ'di:ʀən/ -'diɐn]
stuffed gefüllt [gə'fʏlt]
stupid dumm [dʊm], blöd(e) [bl :t/'bl :də]
style der Stil [dɐ sti:l (ʃti:l)]
subtitles der Untertitel [dɐ 'ʔʊntɐtɪtl]
suburb die Vorstadt [di 'foɐʃtat], der Vorort [dɐ 'foɐʔɔɐt]
subway die Unterführung [di ʔʊntɐ'fy:ʀʊŋ]; *(US)* die U-Bahn [di 'ʔu:ba:n]
success der Erfolg [dɐ ʔɐ'fɔlk]
suddenly plötzlich ['pl̩tslɪç]
sufficient genug [gə'nu:k]
sugar der Zucker [dɐ 'tsʊkɐ]
suggestion der Vorschlag [dɐ 'foɐʃla:k]
suit *(for men)* der Anzug [dɐ 'ʔantsu:k]; *(for women)* das Kostüm [das kɔs'ty:m]; *(vb)* passen [pasn]
suitable for the disabled behindertengerecht [bə'hɪndɐtngəˌʀɛçt]
suitcase der Koffer [dɐ 'kɔfɐ]
sum die Summe [di 'zʊmə]
summer der Sommer [dɐ 'zɔmɐ]
summit station die Bergstation [di 'bɛɐkʃtaˌtsjo:n]
sun die Sonne [di 'zɔnə]
sun cream die Sonnencreme [di 'zɔnnkʀɛ:m]
sun hat der Sonnenhut [dɐ 'zɔnnhu:t]
sunbathing area die Liegewiese [di 'li:gəvi:zə]
sunburn der Sonnenbrand [dɐ 'zɔnnbʀant]
Sunday Sonntag ['zɔnta:k]
sunny sonnig ['zɔnɪç]
sunroof das Schiebedach [das 'ʃi:bədax]
sunstroke der Sonnenstich [dɐ 'zɔnnʃtɪç]
suntan lotion die Sonnenmilch [di 'zɔnnmɪlç]
suntan oil das Sonnenöl [das 'zɔnnʔ :l]
supermarket der Supermarkt [dɐ 'zu:pɐma:kt]
suppository das Zäpfchen [das 'tsɛpfçn]
sure sicher ['zɪçɐ]
surf *(vb)* surfen ['sœɐfn]
surfboard das Surfbrett [das 'sœɐfbʀɛt]
surgeon der Chirurg/die Chirurgin [dɐ çɪ'ʀʊɐk/di çɪ'ʀʊɐgɪn]
surgery *(hours)* die Sprechstunde [di 'ʃpʀɛçʃtʊndə]; *(operation)* die Operation [di ʔɔpəʀa'tsjo:n]
surprised, be ~ (at) sich wundern (über) [zɪç 'vʊndɐn ˌʔy(:)bɐ]
surroundings die Umgebung [di ʔʊm'ge:bʊŋ]
sweat *(vb)* schwitzen ['ʃvɪtsn]
sweater der Pullover [dɐ pʊ'lo:vɐ]
sweet der Nachtisch [dɐ 'na:xtɪʃ]; *(adj)* süß [zy:s]
sweet shop das Süßwarengeschäft [das 'zy:sva:ʀəngəˌʃɛft]
sweetener der Süßstoff [dɐ 'zy:ʃtɔf]
sweets die Süßigkeiten *f pl* [di 'zy:sɪçkaɪtn]
swelling die Schwellung [di 'ʃvɛlʊŋ]
swim *(vb)* baden [ba:dn], schwimmen [ʃvɪmm]
swimmer der Schwimmer/ die Schwimmerin [dɐ 'ʃvɪmɐ/ di 'ʃvɪməʀɪn]
swimming lessons der Schwimmkurs [dɐ 'ʃvɪmkʊɐs]
swimming pool *(public)* das Schwimmbad [das 'ʃvɪmba:t]; *(private)* der Swimmingpool [dɐ 'svɪmɪŋpu:l]
swimming trunks die Badehose [di 'ba:dəho:zə]
swimsuit der Badeanzug [dɐ 'ba:dəˌʔantsu:k]
swindle der Betrug [dɐ bə'tʀu:k]
Swiss (man/woman) der Schweizer/ die Schweizerin [dɐ 'ʃvaɪtsɐ/di 'ʃvaɪtsəʀɪn]
Swiss francs Schweizer Franken *m pl* [ˌʃvaɪtsɐ 'fʀaŋkŋ]

switch der Schalter [dɐ 'ʃaltɐ]
Switzerland die Schweiz [di ʃvaɪts]
swollen geschwollen [gə'ʃvɔln]
swordfish der Schwertfisch [dɐ 'ʃveɐtfɪʃ]
symbol das Wahrzeichen [das 'va:tsaɪçn]
symphony concert das Sinfoniekonzert [das zɪmfo'ni:kɔn,tsɛɐt]

T

table der Tisch [dɐ tɪʃ]
table tennis das Tischtennis [das 'tiʃtɛnɪs]
tablecloth das Tischtuch [das 'tɪʃtu:x]
tablet die Tablette [di ta'blɛtə]
tail light das Rücklicht [das 'ʀʏklɪçt]
tailor der Schneider/die Schneiderin [dɐ 'ʃnaɪdɐ/di 'ʃnaɪdəʀɪn]
take nehmen [ne:mm]; *(time)* brauchen [bʀaʊxn]; **take part (in)** teilnehmen (an) ['taɪlne:mm (ˀan)]; **take place** stattfinden ['ʃtatfɪndn]
taken *(seat)* besetzt [bə'zɛtst]
take-off der Abflug [dɐ 'ˀapflu:k]
talk das Gespräch [das gə'ʃpʀɛ:ç]; *(vb)* reden [ʀe:dn], sich unterhalten [zɪç ˀʊntɐ'haltn]
tall groß [gʀo:s]
tampons die Tampons *m pl* [di 'tampɔŋs]
tap der Wasserhahn [dɐ 'vasɐha:n]
taste der Geschmack [dɐ gə'ʃmak]; *(try food)* versuchen [fɐ'zu:xn]
tasty lecker ['lɛkɐ]
taxi driver der Taxifahrer/ die Taxifahrerin [dɐ 'taksifa:ʀɐ/ di 'taksifa:ʀəʀɪn]
taxi rank/stand der Taxistand [dɐ 'taksi'ʃtant]
tea der Tee [dɐ te:]
tea bag der Teebeutel [dɐ 'te:bɔɪtl]
tea towel das Geschirrtuch [das gə'ʃɪʀtu:x]
teach unterrichten [ˀʊntɐ'ʀɪçtn], lehren ['le:ʀən/leɐn]
team die Mannschaft [di 'manʃaft]
teaspoon der Teelöffel [dɐ 'te:lœfl]
teat der Sauger [dɐ 'zaʊgɐ]
telegraphic transfer die telegrafische Überweisung [di telə'gʀa:fɪʃə ˀy:bɐ'vaɪzʊŋ]
telephone das Telefon [das 'te:ləfo:n]
telephone directory das Telefonbuch [das telə'fo:nbu:x]
telephoto lens das Teleobjektiv [das 'te:ləˀɔbjɛk,ti:f]
television lounge der Fernsehraum [dɐ 'fɛɐnze:,ʀaʊm]
telex das Telex [das 'te:lɛks]
tell erzählen [ˀɐ'tsɛ:ln], ausrichten ['ˀaʊsʀɪçtn], sagen [za:gŋ]
temperature die Temperatur [di ,tɛmpəʀa'tuɐ]; *(fever)* das Fieber [das 'fi:bɐ]
temple der Tempel [dɐ tɛmpl]
temporary vorläufig ['foɐlɔɪfɪç], vorübergehend [fo'ʀy:bɐge:nt], provisorisch [pʀovɪ'zo:ʀɪʃ]
tender zärtlich ['tsɛɐtlɪç]; *(soft)* zart [tsa:t]
tennis das Tennis [das 'tɛnɪs]
tennis racquet der Tennisschläger [dɐ 'tɛnɪʃlɛ:gɐ]
tent das Zelt [das tsɛlt]
terminal das Terminal [das 'tə:mɪnəl]
terminus die Endstation [di 'ˀɛntʃtatsjo:n]
terrace die Terrasse [di te'ʀasə]
terracotta die Terrakotta [di tɛʀa'kɔta]
terrible fürchterlich ['fʏʀçtɐlɪç], schrecklich ['ʃʀɛklɪç]
tetanus der Tetanus [dɐ 'tɛtanʊs]
than als [ˀals]
thank danken ['daŋkŋ], **thank you** danke schön ['daŋkə ʃ :n]
that diese(r, s) ['di:zə/'di:zɐ/'di:zəs]; jene(r, s) ['je:nə/'je:nɐ/je:nəs]; *(conj)* dass [das]
theatre das Theater [das te'ˀa:tɐ]
theft der Diebstahl [dɐ 'di:pʃta:l]
then dann [dan], *(in the past)* damals ['da:ma(:)ls]
therapeutic bath das Heilbad [das 'haɪlba:t]
therapy die Therapie [di teʀa'pi:]
there da [da:], dort [dɔɐt], dorthin ['dɔɐthɪn]
therefore daher ['da:heɐ], deshalb ['dɛshalp]
thermal baths das Thermalbad [das tɛɐ'ma:lba:t]
thermometer das Fieberthermometer [das 'fi:bɐtɛɐmo,me:tɐ]
these diese ['di:zə]
they sie [zi:]
thick dick [dɪk]; *(crowd, fog etc.)* dicht [dɪçt]
thief der Dieb/die Diebin [dɐ di:p/di 'di:bɪn]
thin dünn [dʏn]; mager ['ma:gɐ], schmal [ʃma:l]; *(sparse)* spärlich ['ʃpɛ:ɐlɪç], dürftig ['dʏɐftɪç]
thing das Ding [das dɪŋ], die Sache [di 'zaxə]
think denken ['dɛŋkŋ, meinen [maɪnn]; **think (of)** denken (an) ['dɛŋkŋ ˀan]
third dritte(r, s) ['dʀɪtə (-tɐ, -təs)]
this diese(r, s) ['di:zə/'di:zɐ/'di:zəs]

this morning/this evening heute Morgen/heute Abend [hɔɪtə ˈmɔɐgŋ/hɔɪtə ˈʔa:bmt]
those diese [ˈdi:zə]; jene [ˈje:nə]
thread der Faden [dɐ fa:dn]
thriller der Kriminalroman [dɐ kʀɪmiˈna:lʀoma:n], der Thriller [dɐ ˈθʀɪlɐ]
throat der Hals [dɐ hals]; die Kehle [di ke:lə]
throat lozenges die Halstabletten *f pl* [di ˈhalsta͵blɛtn]
through durch [dʊɐç]
Thursday Donnerstag [ˈdɔnɐsta:k]
thus so [zo:], also [ˈʔalzo:]
thyme der Thymian [dɐ ˈty:mia:n]
tick die Zecke [di ˈtsɛkə]
ticket die Karte [di ˈka:tə]
ticket machine der Fahrkartenautomat [dɐ ˈfa:ka:tnʔauto͵ma:t]
ticket office die Kasse [di ˈkasə]; *(transport)* der Fahrkartenschalter [dɐ ˈfa:ka:tn͵ʃaltɐ]
tie die Krawatte [di kʀaˈvatə]
tight *(clothes)* eng [ˈʔɛŋ]
tights die Strumpfhose [di ˈʃtʀʊmpfho:zə]
till bis [bɪs]
time die Zeit [di tsaɪt]; *(occasion)* das Mal [das ma:l]; **in time** *(adv)* rechtzeitig [ˈʀɛçtsaɪtɪç]; **on time** pünktlich [ˈpʏŋktlɪç]
time of arrival die Ankunftszeit [di ʔankʊnf͵tsaɪt]
timetable der Fahrplan [dɐ ˈfa:pla:n]
tin die Büchse [di ˈbʏksə], die Dose [di ˈdo:zə]
tin foil die Alufolie [di ˈʔalufo:ljə]
tin opener der Dosenöffner [dɐ ˈdo:znʔœfnɐ]
tincture of iodine die Jodtinktur [di ˈjo:tɪŋktuɐ]
tint *(vb)* tönen [t :nn]
tip *(information)* der Tipp [dɐ tɪp]; *(gratuity)* das Trinkgeld [das ˈtʀɪŋkgɛlt]
tire der Reifen [dɐ ˈʀaɪfn]
tired müde [ˈmy:də]
to zu [zu(:)], nach [nax]; *(time)* bis [bɪs]
toast der Toast [dɐ to:st]
toaster der Toaster [dɐ ˈto:stɐ]
tobacco der Tabak [dɐ ˈtabak]
tobacconist's/tobacco shop der Tabakladen [dɐ ˈtabakla:dn]
toboggan der Schlitten [dɐ ʃlɪtn]
today heute [ˈhɔɪtə]
toe die Zehe [di ˈtseə]
together zusammen [tsʊˈzamm]; gemeinsam [gəˈmaɪnza(:)m]
toilet die Toilette [di toˈlɛtə]
toilet for the disabled die Behindertentoilette [di bəˈhɪndɐtnto͵lɛtə]
toilet paper das Toilettenpapier [das toˈlɛtnpa͵piɐ]
tomatoes die Tomaten *f pl* [di toˈma:tn]
tomb das Grab [das gʀa:p]
tomorrow morgen [ˈmɔɐgŋ]; **tomorrow morning/tomorrow evening** morgen früh/morgen Abend [mɔɐgŋ ˈfʀy:/mɔɐgŋ ˈʔa:bmt]; **the day after tomorrow** übermorgen [ˈʔy:bɐmɔɐgŋ]
tone der Ton [dɐ to:n]
tongue die Zunge [ˈtsʊŋə]
tonight heute Nacht [hɔɪt(ə) ˈnaxt]
tonsilitis die Mandelentzündung [di ˈmandlʔɛn͵tsʏndʊŋ]
tonsils die Mandeln *f pl* [di ˈmandln]
too auch [ˈaʊx]; *(with adj)* zu [zu(:)]; **too much** zu viel [tsʊˈfi:l]; zu sehr [tsʊ zeɐ]
tools das Werkzeug [das ˈvɛɐktsɔɪk]
tooth der Zahn [dɐ tsa:n]
toothache die Zahnschmerzen *m pl* [di ˈtsa:nʃmɛɐtsn]
toothbrush die Zahnbürste [di ˈtsa:nbʏɐstə]
toothpaste die Zahnpasta [di ˈtsa:npasta]
toothpick das Zahnstocher [dɐ ˈtsa:nʃtɔxɐ]
top station die Bergstation [di ˈbɛɐkʃta͵tsjo:n]
torn ligament der Bänderriss [dɐ ˈbɛndɐʀɪs]
touch *(vb)* berühren [bəˈʀy:ʀən/-ˈʀyɐn]
tough *(not tender)* zäh [tsɛ:]
tour die Tour [di tuɐ], die Rundfahrt [di ˈʀʊntfa:t]; *(of museum, palace)* die Besichtigung [di bəˈzɪçtɪgʊŋ]
tourist der Tourist/die Touristin [dɐ tuˈʀɪst/di tuˈʀɪstɪn]; der/die Reisende [dɐ/di ˈʀaɪzndə]; **tourist information office** das Verkehrsbüro [das fɐˈkeɐsby͵ʀo:]
tow (away) abschleppen [ˈʔapʃlɛpm]
towel das Handtuch [das ˈhan(t)tu:x]
tower der Turm [dɐ tʊɐm]
town die Stadt [di ʃtat]
town centre die Innenstadt [di ˈʔɪnnʃtat]
town hall das Rathaus [das ˈʀa:thaʊs]
town walls die Stadtmauern *f pl* [di ˈʃtatmaʊɐn]
towrope das Abschleppseil [das ˈʔapʃlɛpzaɪl]
toy shop das Spielwarengeschäft [das ˈʃpi:lva:ʀəngəˈʃɛft]
toys die Spielsachen *f pl* [di ˈʃpi:l za:xn]

traffic der Verkehr [dɐ fɐˈkeɐ]
traffic jam der Stau [dɐ ʃtaʊ]
traffic light die Ampel [di ˀampl]
tragedy die Tragödie [di tʀaˈg :diə]
train der Zug [dɐ tsu:k]
training die Ausbildung [di ˈˀaʊsbɪldʊŋ]
tram die Straßenbahn [di ˈʃtʀa:snba:n]
tranquilliser das Beruhigungsmittel [das bəˈʀʊɪgʊŋsmɪtl]
transfer die Überweisung [di ˀybɐˈvaɪzʊŋ]
translate übersetzen [ˀybɐˈzɛtsn]
transmission *(engine)* das Getriebe [das gəˈtʀi:bə]
travel reisen [ʀaɪzn]
travel agency das Reisebüro [das ˈʀaɪzəbyˌʀo:]
traveller's cheque der Reisescheck [dɐ ˈʀaɪzəʃɛk]
travelling bag die Reisetasche [di ˈʀaɪzətaʃə]
treat *(injury)* behandeln [bəˈhandln]
treatment die Behandlung [di bəˈhandlʊŋ]
tree der Baum [dɐ baʊm]
trekking bike das Trekkingrad [das ˈtʀɛkɪŋʀa:t]
trial *(court)* die (Straf) Verhandlung [di (ˈʃtʀa:f)fɐˌhandlʊŋ]
trip die Tour [di tuɐ], die Fahrt [di fa:t], die Reise [di ˈʀaɪzə], der Ausflug [dɐ ˈˀaʊsflu:k]
tripod das Stativ [das ʃtaˈti:f]
trousers die Hose [di ˈho:zə]
true wahr [va:]
trunk *(case)* der Schrankkoffer [dɐ ˈʃʀaŋkˌkɔfɐ]; *(US)* der Kofferraum [dɐ ˈkɔfɐʀaʊm]
try *(vb)* versuchen [fɐˈzu:xn]; **try hard** sich bemühen [zɪç bəˈmy:n]
Tuesday Dienstag [ˈdi:nsta:k]
tumbler das Wasserglas [das ˈvasɐgla:s]
tumour die Geschwulst [di gəˈʃvʊlst]
tuna der Thunfisch [dɐ ˈtu:nfɪʃ]
tunnel der Tunnel [dɐ tʊnl]
turn back umkehren [ˈˀʊmke:ʀən/-keɐn]
turquoise türkisfarben [tʏɐˈki:sfa:bm]
twice zweimal [ˈtsvaɪma:l]; doppelt [dɔplt]
typhoid der Typhus [dɐ ˈty:fʊs]
typical typisch [ˈty:pɪʃ]
tyre der Reifen [dɐ ˈʀaɪfn]

U

ugly hässlich [ˈhɛslɪç]
ulcer das Geschwür [das gəˈʃvyɐ]
umbrella der Schirm [dɐ ʃɪɐm]
unbearable unerträglich [ˈˀʊnɐˌtʀɛ:klɪç]
unconscious bewusstlos [bəˈvʊstlo:s]
under unter [ˈˀʊntɐ]
underground die U-Bahn [di ˈˀu:ba:n]
understand verstehen [fɐˈʃte:n]
underwater camera die Unterwasserkamera [di ˀʊntɐˈvasɐˌkaməʁa]
underwear die Unterwäsche [di ˈˀʊntɐvɛʃə]
unemployed arbeitslos [ˈˀa:baɪtslo:s]
unfit ungeeignet [ˈˀʊngəˀaɪknət]
unfortunately leider [ˈlaɪdɐ], unglücklicherweise [ˌˀʊnglʏklɪçɐˈvaɪzə]
unimportant unwichtig [ˈˀʊnvɪçtɪç]
university die Universität [di ˀunivɛɐziˈtɛ:t]
unpleasant unangenehm [ˈˀʊnangəne:m], *(news)* unerfreulich [ˈˀʊnɐfʀɔɪlɪç]
unsuited ungeeignet [ˈˀʊngəˀaɪknət]
until bis [bɪs]
unusual ungewöhnlich [ˈˀʊngəvø:nlɪç]
up aufwärts [ˈˀaʊfvɛɐts], nach oben [nax ˈˀo:bm], oben [ˀo:bm]
urgent dringend [dʀɪŋŋt], eilig [ˈˀaɪlɪç]
urine der Urin [dɐ ˀuˈʀi:n]
us uns [ˀʊns]
use die Verwendung [di fɐˈvɛndʊŋ], der Gebrauch [dɐ gəˈbʀaʊx], die Anwendung [di ˈˀanvɛndʊŋ]; *(vb)* anwenden [ˈˀanvɛndn], verwenden [fɐˈvɛndn], gebrauchen [gəˈbʀaʊx], benutzen [bəˈnʊtsn]; **be used to s. th.** etwas gewöhnt sein [ˌˀɛtvas gəˈvø:nt zaɪn]
usual gewohnt [gəˈvo:nt], gewöhnlich [gəˈvø:nlɪç], üblich [ˈˀy:plɪç]
usually normalerweise [nɔˈma:lɐvaɪzə]

V

vacation die Ferien [di ˈfe:ʀiən (ˈfeɐjən)], der Urlaub [dɐ ˈˀuɐlaʊp]
vaccination die Impfung [di ˈˀɪmpfʊŋ]
vaccination card der Impfpass [dɐ ˈˀɪm(p)fpas]
vacuum cleaner der Staubsauger [dɐ ˈʃtaʊpzaʊgɐ]
valid gültig [ˈgʏltɪç]
valley das Tal [das ta:l]
valuables die Wertsachen [di ˈveɐtzaxn]
vantage point der Aussichtspunkt [dɐ ˈˀaʊsɪçtspʊŋt]
variety theatre das Varietee [das vaʀiəˈte:]
vase die Vase [di ˈva:zə]
vault(s) das Gewölbe [das gəˈvœlbə]
veal das Kalbfleisch [ˈkalpflaɪʃ]
vegetables das Gemüse [das gəˈmy:zə]

vegetarian der Vegetarier/ die Vegetarierin [dɐ vegəˈtaːʀiɐ/ di vegəˈtaːʀiəʀɪn]; *(adj)* vegetarisch [vegəˈtaːʀɪʃ]
vending machine der Automat [dɐ ˀaʊtoˈmaːt]
very sehr [zeɐ]
vest das Unterhemd [das ˈʊntɐhɛmt]; *(US)* die Weste [di ˈvɛstə]
video camera die Videokamera [di ˈviːdeoˌkaməʀa]
video cassette die Videokassette [di ˈviːdeokaˌsɛtə]
video film der Videofilm [dɐ ˈviːdeofɪlm]
video recorder der Videorekorder [dɐ ˈviːdeoʀeˌkɔɐdɐ]
view die Sicht [di zɪçt], die Aussicht [di ˈˀaʊszɪçt], der Blick [dɐ blɪk]; *(opinion)* die Ansicht [di ˈˀanzɪçt], die Meinung [di ˈmaɪnʊŋ]
viewer der(Fernseh)Zuschauer/ die (Fernseh)Zuschauerin [dɐ (ˈfɛɐnze)ˌtsuːʃaʊɐ/ di (ˈfɛɐnze)ˌtsuːʃaʊəʀɪn]
viewfinder der Sucher [dɐ ˈzuːxɐ]
village das Dorf [das dɔɐf]
vinegar der Essig [dɐ ˈˀɛsɪç]
vineyard der Weinberg [dɐ ˈvaɪnbɛɐk]
virus das Virus [das ˈviːʀʊs]
visa das Visum [das ˈviːzʊm]
visit der Besuch [dɐ bəˈzuːx]; *(vb)* besuchen [bəˈzuːxn], *(sights)* besichtigen [bəˈzɪçtɪgŋ]
visiting hours die Besuchszeit [di bəˈzuːxstsaɪt]
visitor's tax die Kurtaxe [di ˈkuɐtaksə]
volleyball der Volleyball [dɐ ˈvɔlɪbal]
voltage die Stromspannung [di ˈʃtʀoːmˌʃpanʊŋ]
vote die Stimme [di ˈʃtɪmə]; *(vb)* wählen [ˈvɛːln]
voucher der Gutschein [dɐ ˈguːtʃaɪn]
voyage die Seereise [di ˈzeːʀaɪzə], die Seefahrt [di ˈzeːfaːt]
vulgar ordinär [ˀɔdiˈnɛːɐ]

W

waistcoat die Weste [di ˈvɛstə]
wait (for) warten (auf) [vaːtn (ˀaʊf)], erwarten [ˀɐˈvaːtn]
waiter/waitress der Kellner/die Kellnerin [dɐ ˈkɛlnɐ/di ˈkɛlnəʀɪn]
waiting room das Wartezimmer [das ˈvaːtətsɪmɐ], der Wartesaal [dɐ ˈvaːtəzaːl]
wake wecken [vɛkŋ]; **wake up** aufwachen [ˈˀaʊfvaxn]
Wales Wales [wɛɪls (vɛɪls)]
walk der Spaziergang [dɐ ʃpaˈtsiɐgaŋ]; *(vb)* gehen [geːn], laufen [laʊfn]; **go for a walk** spazieren gehen [ʃpaˈtsiːʀən geːn], einen Spaziergang machen [(ˀaɪn)n ʃpaˈtsiɐgaŋ maxn]
wall *(external)* die Mauer [di ˈmaʊɐ]; *(internal)* die Wand [di vant]
wallet die Brieftasche [di ˈbʀiːftaʃə]
want wollen [vɔln]
ward die Station [di ʃtaˈtsjoːn]
warm warm [vaːm]; *(regards)* herzlich [ˈhɛɐtslɪç]; *(vb)* wärmen [vɛɐmm]
warning triangle das Warndreieck [das ˈvaːndʀaɪɛk]
wash *(vb)* waschen [vaʃn]
washbasin das Waschbecken [das ˈvaʃbɛkŋ]
washing-up brush die Spülbürste [di ˈʃpyːlbʏɐstə]
washroom der Waschraum [dɐ ˈvaʃʀaʊm]
wasp die Wespe [di ˈvɛspə]
watch die (Armband)Uhr [di (ˈˀaːmbant)ˀuɐ]; *(vb)* zuschauen [ˈtsuːʃaʊn], *(observe)* beobachten [bəˈˀoːbaxtn]
watchmaker's der Uhrmacher [dɐ ˈˀuɐmaxɐ]
water das Wasser [das ˈvasɐ]
water canister der Wasserkanister [dɐ ˈvasɐkanˌɪstɐ]
water-colour (picture) das Aquarell [das ˀakvaˈʀɛl]
water consumption der Wasserverbrauch [dɐ ˈvasɐfɐbʀaʊx]
waterfall der Wasserfall [dɐ ˈvasɐfal]
waterproof wasserdicht [ˈvasɐdɪçt]
water ski der Wasserski [dɐ ˈvasɐʃiː]; go water skiing Wasserski fahren [ˈvasɐʃiː ˈfaːʀən]
water wings die Schwimmflügel *m pl* [di ˈʃvɪmflyːgl]
wave pool das Wellenbad [das ˈvɛlnbaːt]
way *(manner)* die Weise [di ˈvaɪzə]; *(path)* der Weg [dɐ veːk]
way in der Eingang [dɐ ˈˀaɪngaŋ]; **way out** der Ausgang [dɐ ˈˀaʊsgaŋ]
we wir [viɐ/vɐ]
weak schwach [ʃvax]
wear tragen [tʀaːgŋ]
weather forecast die Wettervorhersage [di ˈvɛtɐfoˌhɐɐzaːgə]
wedding die Hochzeit [di ˈhɔxtsaɪt]
Wednesday Mittwoch [ˈmɪtvɔx]
week die Woche [di ˈvɔxə]; **weekly** wöchentlich [ˈvœçntlɪç]
on weekdays wochentags [ˈvɔxntaːks], werktags [ˈvɛɐktaːks];

at the weekend am Wochenende [ˀam ˈvɔxnˀɛndə]
weekend rate die Wochenendpauschale [di ˈvɔxnˀɛntpaʊʃaːlə]
weight das Gewicht [das gəˈvɪçt]
weight training das Krafttraining [das ˈkʀaftʀɛːnɪŋ]
welcome *(adj, interj)* willkommen [vɪlˈkɔmm]; *(vb)* empfangen [ˀɛmpˈfaŋŋ], begrüßen [bəˈgʀyːsn]
well der Brunnen [dɐ bʀʊnn], *(oil)* die (Öl)Quelle [di (ˈˀøːl)ˈkvɛlə]; *(healthy)* gesund [gəˈzʊnt], wohl [voːl]; *(adv)* gut [guːt]
well-done durchgebraten [ˈdʊɐçgəbʀaːtn]
well-known bekannt [bəˈkant]
wellingtons die Gummistiefel *m pl* [di ˈgʊmiʃtiːfl]
Welsh walisisch [vaˈliːzɪʃ]
Welshman/Welshwoman der Waliser/die Waliserin [dɐ vaˈliːzɐ/di vaˈliːzəʀɪn]
west der Westen [dɐ vɛstn]
western der Western [dɐ ˈvɛstɐn]
wet nass [nas]
wetsuit der Neoprenanzug [dɐ neoˈpʀeːnˌˀantsuːk]
what was [vas]
wheel das Rad [das ʀaːt]
wheelchair der Rollstuhl [dɐ ˈʀɔlʃtuːl]
wheelchair cabin die Rollstuhlkabine [di ˈʀɔlʃtuːlkaˌbiːnə]
wheelchair user der Rollstuhlfahrer/die Rollstuhlfahrerin [dɐ ˈʀɔlʃtuːlˌfaːʀɐ/di ˈʀɔlʃtuːlˌfaːʀəʀɪn]
whether ob [ˀɔp]
while *(conj)* während [ˈvɛːʀənt (veɐnt)]
whipping cream die Schlagsahne [ˈʃlaːkzaːnə]
whisk der Schneebesen [dɐ ˈʃneːbeːzn]
white weiß [vaɪs]
white bread das Weißbrot [das ˈvaɪsbʀoːt]
white wine Weißwein [ˈvaɪsvaɪn]
whole ganz [gants]
wholemeal bread das Vollkornbrot [das ˈfɔlkɔɐnbʀoːt]
whooping-cough der Keuchhusten [dɐ ˈkɔɪçhuːstn]
wide breit [bʀaɪt]; weit [vaɪt]
widow/widower der Witwer [dɐ ˈvɪtvɐ]/die Witwe [di ˈvɪtvə]
width die Breite [di ˈbʀaɪtə]
wife die Ehefrau [di ˈˀeːəfʀaʊ]
wild(ly) wild [vɪlt]
win *(vb)* gewinnen [gəˈvɪnn]
wind der Wind [dɐ vɪnt]; *(med.)* die Blähungen *f pl* [di ˈblɛːʊŋŋ]
wind-force die Windstärke [di ˈvɪntʃtɛɐkə]
window das Fenster [das ˈfɛnstɐ]
window seat der Fensterplatz [dɐ ˈfɛnstɐplats]
windscreen/windshield die Windschutzscheibe [di ˈvɪntʃʊtʃaɪbə]
windscreen wiper der Scheibenwischer [dɐ ˈʃaɪbmvɪʃɐ]
windsurfing das Windsurfen [das ˈvɪntsœɐfn]
wine der Wein [dɐ vaɪn]
wine merchant's die Weinhandlung [di ˈvaɪnhantlʊŋ]
wineglass das Weinglas [das ˈvaɪnglaːs]
wing der Flügel [dɐ flyːgl]
winter der Winter [dɐ ˈvɪntɐ]
winter tyre der Winterreifen [dɐ ˈvɪntɐʀaɪfn]
wisdom tooth der Weisheitszahn [dɐ ˈvaɪshaɪtsaːn]
wish for wünschen [vʏnʃn]
with mit [mɪt]
without ohne [ˈˀoːnə]
woman die Frau [di fʀaʊ]
wonderful wunderbar [ˈvʊndɐbaː], toll [tɔl]
wood das Holz [das hɔlts]
wood-carving die Schnitzerei [di ʃnɪtsəˈʀaɪ]
woodcut der Holzschnitt [dɐ ˈhɔltʃnɪt]
woods der Wald [dɐ valt]
wool die Wolle [di ˈvɔlə]
word das Wort [das vɔɐt]
work die Arbeit [di ˈˀaːbaɪt]; *(vb)* arbeiten [ˈˀaːbaɪtn], *(function)* funktionieren [fʊŋktsjoˈniːʀən/-ˈniɐn]
world die Welt [di vɛlt]
worm der Wurm [dɐ vʊɐm]
worry die Sorge [di ˈzɔɐgə]; *(vb)* sich beunruhigen [zɪç bəˈˀʊnʀʊɪgŋ]; **be worried about** sich sorgen um [zɪç ˈzɔɐgŋ ˀʊm]
worthless wertlos [ˈveɐtloːs]
wound die Wunde [di ˈvʊndə]
wrap einpacken [ˈˀaɪnpakŋ], verpacken [fɐˈpakŋ]
wrapping die Verpackung [di fɐˈpakʊŋ]
wristwatch die Armbanduhr [di ˈˀaːmbantˌˀuɐ]
write schreiben [ʃʀaɪbm]; **write down** aufschreiben [ˈˀaʊfʃʀaɪbm]
in writing schriftlich [ˈʃʀɪftlɪç]
writing pad der Block [dɐ blɔk]
writing paper das Briefpapier [das ˈbʀiːfpapiɐ]

wrong falsch [falʃ]; **be wrong** sich täuschen [zɪç ˈtɔɪʃn], Unrecht haben [ˈʔʊnʀɛçt ha:bm]

X

X-ray die Röntgenaufnahme [di ˈʀœnçnˀaʊfna:mə]; *(vb)* röntgen [ˈʀœnçn]

Y

yard der Hof [dɐ ho:f]; *(US)* der Garten [dɐ ga:tn]
year das Jahr [das ja:]
yellow gelb [gɛlp]
yesterday gestern [ˈgɛstɐn]; **the day before yesterday** vorgestern [ˈfɔagɛstɐn]
yet *(adv)* noch [nɔx]; *(conj)* doch [dɔx]
yoga das Yoga [das ˈjo:ga]
yoghurt der Joghurt [dɐ ˈjo:gʊɐt]
you du [du:], dich [dɪç], dir [diɐ]; ihr [ˀiɐ], euch [ˀɔɪç]; Sie [zi:], Ihnen [ˀi:nn]
young jung [jʊŋ]
your dein [daɪn], euer [ˈʔɔɪɐ], Ihr [ˀiɐ]

Z

zoo der Zoo [dɐ tso:]
zucchini *(US)* die Zucchini [di tsʊˈki:ni]